Mano Dura

Mano Dura

The Politics of Gang Control in El Salvador

SONJA WOLF

University of Texas Press ◄► *Austin*

Requests for permission to reproduce material from this work should be sent to:
Permissions
University of Texas Press
P.O. Box 7819
Austin, TX 78713-7819
http://utpress.utexas.edu/index.php/rp-form

Material from chapter 3 was published as "Creating Folk Devils: Street Gang
Representations in El Salvador's Print Media" in *Journal of Human Security*
8.2 (2012): 36–63 and is used with permission. Material from chapters 4 to 6
was published as "Ethnographic encounters: civil society campaigns against
El Salvador's Mano Dura" in *Más allá de las pandillas: violencias, juventudes y
resistencias en el mundo globalizado*, vol. 2, ed. Mauro Cerbino (Quito: FLASCO,
2011): 61–96 and is used with permission. Material from chapter 5 was published
as "El Salvador's *Pandilleros Calmados*: The Challenges of Contesting Mano Dura
through Peer Rehabilitation and Empowerment" in *Bulletin of Latin American
Research* 31, no. 2 (2012): 190–205, which is also used with permission.

⊗ The paper used in this book meets the minimum requirements of
ANSI/NISO Z39.48-1992 (R1997) (Permanence of Paper).

Library of Congress Cataloging-in-Publication Data

Names: Wolf, Sonja, author.
Title: Mano Dura : the politics of gang control in El Salvador / Sonja Wolf.
Description: First edition. Austin : University of Texas Press, 2017. Includes
    bibliographical references and index.
Identifiers: LCCN 2016023731 (print) | LCCN 2016024709 (ebook)
    ISBN 9781477311219 (cloth : alk. paper)
    ISBN 9781477311660 (pbk. : alk. paper)
    ISBN 9781477311226 (library e-book)
    ISBN 9781477311233 (non-library e-book)
Subjects: LCSH: Gang prevention—El Salvador. | Gang prevention—
    Government policy—El Salvador. El Salvador—Politics and government.
    El Salvador—Social conditions. Non-governmental organizations—
    El Salvador—Social policy.
Classification: LCC HV6439.S2 W65 2017 (print) LCC HV6439.S2 (ebook)
DDC 364.106/6097284—dc23
LC record available at https://lccn.loc.gov/2016023731

doi:10.7560/311219

Contents

Acronyms

AEIPES Asociación de Ex Internos Penitenciarios de El Salvador (Association of Ex-Prisoners of El Salvador)

ANESAL Agencia Nacional de Seguridad Salvadoreña (Salvadoran National Security Agency)

ANSP Academia Nacional de Seguridad Pública (National Academy of Public Security)

APES Asociación de Periodistas de El Salvador (Association of Journalists of El Salvador)

ARENA Alianza Republicana Nacionalista (Nationalist Republican Alliance)

ARPAS Asociación de Radios y Programas Participativos (Association of Participatory Radios and Programs)

CAFE Central American Fingerprint Exploitation Initiative

CAFTA Central America Free Trade Agreement

CARSI Central America Regional Security Initiative

CAT Centro Antipandillas Transnacional (Transnational Anti-Gang Center)

CCPVJ Coalición Centroamericana para la Prevención de la Violencia Juvenil (Central American Coalition for the Prevention of Youth Violence)

CECDH Centro de Estudios Constitucionales y Derechos Humanos (Center for Constitutional Studies and Human Rights)

CEDFI Centro de Desarrollo y Fortalecimiento Institucional (Center for Development and Institutional Strengthening)

CEPES Centro de Estudios Penales de El Salvador (Center for Criminal Studies of El Salvador)

CIDAI Centro de Información, Documentación y Apoyo a la Investigación (Center of Information, Documentation and Research Support)

CNSCC Consejo Nacional de Seguridad Ciudadana y Convivencia (National Council of Citizen Security and Coexistence)

CNSP Consejo Nacional de Seguridad Pública (National Council of Public Security)

COAV Children in Organized Armed Violence

CONJUVE Consejo Nacional de la Juventud (National Youth Council)

CONNA Consejo Nacional de la Niñez y de la Adolescencia (National Council for Children and Adolescents)

CORDAID Catholic Organization for Relief and Development Aid

CRC Convention on the Rights of the Child

CRISPAZ Cristianos por la Paz (Christians for Peace)

CSJ Corte Suprema de Justicia (Supreme Court of Justice)

CRS Congressional Research Service

DHS Department of Homeland Security

DIGESTYC Dirección General de Estadística y Censos

DOS Department of State

ECA *Estudios Centroamericanos*

EDH *El Diario de Hoy*

EDYTRA Fundación Salvadoreña Educación y Trabajo (Salvadoran Foundation for Education and Work)

ERIC Equipo de Reflexión, Investigación y Comunicación (Reflection, Research and Communications Team)

EU European Union

FAES Fuerzas Armadas de El Salvador (Armed Forces of El Salvador)

FARC Fuerzas Armadas Revolucionarias de Colombia (Revolutionary Armed Forces of Colombia)

FBI Federal Bureau of Investigation

FESPAD Fundación de Estudios para la Aplicación del Derecho (Foundation for Applied Legal Studies)

FGR Fiscalía General de la República (Office of the Attorney General of the Republic)

FLACSO Facultad Latinoamericana de Ciencias Sociales (Latin American Faculty of Social Sciences)

FLETC Federal Law Enforcement Training Centers

FMLN Frente Farabundo Martí para la Liberación Nacional (Farabundo Martí National Liberation Front)

FPL Fuerzas Populares de Liberación (Popular Liberation Forces)

FUNSALPRODESE Fundación Salvadoreña para la Promoción Social y el Desarrollo Económico (Salvadoran Foundation for Social Promotion and Economic Development)

FUSADES   Fundación Salvadoreña para el Desarrollo Económico y Social (Salvadoran Foundation for Economic and Social Development)

GANA   Gran Alianza por la Unidad Nacional (Great Alliance for National Unity)

GN   Guardia Nacional (National Guard)

GOES   Gobierno de El Salvador (Government of El Salvador)

GTA   Grupo de Tarea Antipandillas (Anti-Gang Task Force)

GTZ   Gesellschaft für technische Zusammenarbeit (German Development Agency)

HU   Homies Unidos (Homies United)

IACHR   Inter-American Commission on Human Rights

IDB   Inter-American Development Bank

IDESO   Instituto de Encuestas y Sondeos de Opinión (Survey and Polling Institute)

IDHES   Informe sobre Desarrollo Humano El Salvador (Human Development Report El Salvador)

IDHUCA   Instituto de Derechos Humanos de la Universidad Centroamericana (Human Rights Institute of the Central American University)

IDIES   Instituto de Investigaciones Económicas y Sociales (Institute of Economic and Social Research)

IIRIRA   Illegal Immigration Reform and Immigrant Responsibility Act

ILEA   International Law Enforcement Academy

IML   Instituto de Medicina Legal (Institute of Legal Medicine)

INJUVE   Instituto Nacional de la Juventud (National Youth Institute)

INL   Bureau of International Narcotics and Law Enforcement Affairs

IPDL   Instituto Pro Libertad y Derecho (Institute for Liberty and Law)

ISNA   Instituto Salvadoreño para el Desarrollo Integral de la Niñez y la Adolescencia (Salvadoran Institute for the Comprehensive Development of Children and Adolescents)

ITOE   Instituto Técnico Obrero-Empresarial (Technical Institute for Entrepreneurial Workers)

IUDOP   Instituto Universitario de Opinión Pública (University Institute of Public Opinion)

LAM   Ley Anti Maras (Anti-Gang Act)

LAPD   Los Angeles Police Department

LAPOP   Latin American Public Opinion Project

LPG   *La Prensa Gráfica*

MINEC-DIGESTYC Ministerio de Economía-Dirección General de Estadística y Censos

MINGOB Ministerio de Gobernación (Ministry of the Interior)

MJSP Ministerio de Justicia y Seguridad Pública (Ministry of Justice and Public Security)

MOJE Movimiento de Jóvenes Encuentristas (Movement of Young Discoverers)

MPI Migration Policy Institute

MS Mara Salvatrucha

NACLA North American Congress on Latin America

NGO non-governmental organization

NGTF National Gang Task Force

OAJJ Oficina de Apoyo a la Justicia Juvenil (Juvenile Justice Support Office, now UJJ)

ORDEN Organización Democrática Nacionalista (National Democratic Organization)

PCN Partido de Conciliación Nacional (National Conciliation Party)

PDC Partido Demócrata Cristiano (Christian Democratic Party)

PDDH Procuraduría para la Defensa de los Derechos Humanos (Office of the Human Rights Ombudsperson)

PESS Plan El Salvador Seguro (Plan for a Safe El Salvador)

PH Policía de Hacienda (Treasury Police)

PIDB Polígono Industrial Don Bosco (Don Bosco Industrial Park, or Polígono)

PN Policía Nacional (National Police)

PNC Policía Nacional Civil (National Civilian Police)

PNUD Programa de las Naciones Unidas para el Desarrollo (United Nations Development Program)

RIA Red para la Infancia y la Adolescencia (Network for Childhood and Adolescence)

RICO Racketeer Influenced and Corrupt Organizations Act

SC Save the Children

SIU Special Investigative Unit

SJ Secretaría de la Juventud (Youth Secretariat)

STPP Secretaría Técnica y de Planificación de la Presidencia de la República

TAG Transnational Anti-Gang Center

TCS Telecorporación Salvadoreña (Salvadoran Telecorporation)

UCA Universidad Centroamericana (Central American University)

UEA Unidad Ejecutiva Antinarcotráfico (Executive Antinarcotics Unit)

UES   Universidad de El Salvador (University of El Salvador)
UJJ   Unidad de Justicia Juvenil (Juvenile Justice Unit)
UN   United Nations
UNCRC   United Nations Committee on the Rights of the Child
UNDP   United Nations Development Program
UNICEF   United Nations Children's Fund
UNODC   United Nations Office on Drugs and Crime
US   United States
USAID   United States Agency for International Development
YSUCA   UCA-based radio station

Acknowledgments

This book was finalized at the Mexico-based Centro de Investigación y Docencia Económicas (CIDE), my institutional home since 2014. The CIDE has provided me not only with excellent research conditions, but also with important financial support for some of the final field research on gang violence in El Salvador.

The research for this book, however, began to take shape many years ago at Aberystwyth University. For probing questions, perspicacious comments, and words of encouragement during this early phase of my intellectual journey, I thank Lucy Taylor, Hidemi Suganami, Mike Foley, and Doug Stokes.

This study would have been impossible without the generous funding I received during different and critical stages of the research process. Aberystwyth University offered me an indispensable Postgraduate Research Studentship, and the British Federation of Women Graduates made substantial funds available through the Mary Bradburn Scholarship. The Society for Latin American Studies and the Latin American Studies Association awarded me invaluable fieldwork and conference grants. Critical financial support during the writing of the first draft of this manuscript came from the Gilchrist Educational Trust, the Sir Richard Stapley Educational Trust, and the British International Studies Association.

Over the years, many individuals, particularly in El Salvador, have provided personal and professional support without which this book would not have become what it is. In the beginning of this project, Cath Collins and Mo Hume shared vital insights on the dos and don'ts on field research in El Salvador. I am particularly indebted to the NGOs in this Central American country that opened their doors to an aspiring ethnographer. At FESPAD, Abraham Ábrego, Saul Baños, María Silvia Guillén, Ricardo Montoya, and Juan Carlos Sánchez proved to be more patient and responsive than I could have hoped. Thanks also go to Luis Romero at Homies Unidos, as well as to Magdaleno Rose-Ávila and Julienne Gage for sharing with me their own experiences in this organization. At the Polígono Industrial Don Bosco, my express gratitude goes to Father José Moratalla and Raúl Ramírez.

In El Salvador's state and academic institutions, the following individuals were tremendously accommodating to some of my specific research needs. Sidney Blanco Reyes, Aída Luz Santos de Escobar, Celia Bolaños, and Roberto Ramírez Campos helped me understand particular judicial cases, as well as the country's rehabilitation and reinsertion of juvenile offenders. Armando Echeverría and Milton Vega, at the now-extinct Consejo Nacional de Seguridad Pública, showed me El Salvador's early experiments with gang rehabilitation.

In El Salvador and elsewhere, Luis Enrique Amaya, Lucía Dammert, and Ellen Moodie facilitated my access to essential reading material. Throughout the years, Edgardo Amaya Cóbar and Jeanne Rikkers have patiently answered my questions and addressed my doubts about public security, gangs, and criminal justice in El Salvador.

My special gratitude goes to all research participants, some of whom must remain anonymous, who have shared with me their reflections on the past and present of El Salvador and the difficult road of change ahead.

The manuscript benefited from many helpful suggestions by Thomas Bruneau and José Miguel Cruz. At the University of Texas Press, I owe a great many thanks to Theresa May, who first took an interest in a book-length study on gangs, Mano Dura, and civil society in El Salvador, and to Kerry Webb, who saw the manuscript through to publication.

As this book goes to press, El Salvador finds itself in a much more daunting situation—socially, politically, and security-wise—than many probably anticipated with the democratic openings of the early 1990s. The Peace Accords, now largely confined to history books, were meant to be a transformative moment for the country. In the time since, however, most Salvadorans have been struggling to survive—physically, economically, and emotionally—in taxing circumstances. For some, this has entailed a search for opportunities and safety abroad; for others, it has involved hard-fought attempts to create and maintain spaces of shelter and laughter for themselves and their children. The persistence, strength, and courage that these struggles require are hard to over-estimate, but easy to overlook. It is my hope that this book can in some small way help all of us understand why and how El Salvador has developed into the country it is today, and how we might contribute to making it the better, safer, and more inclusive place that its people dream of.

Introduction

After decades of authoritarianism and a twelve-year civil war that ended with a negotiated peace agreement in 1992, El Salvador appears in many ways a country transformed. Over most of Salvadoran history, a small oligarchy had concentrated wealth and political power and sponsored security forces to violently repress popular resistance. These conditions prompted the guerrilla forces of the Frente Farabundo Martí para la Liberación Nacional (Farabundo Martí National Liberation Front, or FMLN) to launch an armed struggle in 1980.

Determined to hold on to their privileges, members of the elite turned to funding extrajudicial death squads and founded their own party, the Alianza Republicana Nacionalista (Nationalist Republican Alliance, or ARENA). Presidential elections in 1989 brought ARENA into power, and the party ruled uninterruptedly for the next twenty years. Spurred by a war-shattered economy and a military stalemate, its leaders embarked on peace negotiations and oversaw the subsequent transition to electoral democracy. Some of the most notable changes the country has witnessed since that time include the conversion of the FMLN into a political party, a more open press, judicial reforms, demilitarization, the abolition of the old security forces (which had been implicated in the death squads), and the creation of a new Policía Nacional Civil (National Civilian Police, or PNC). Civil society has enjoyed greater freedom of expression, and reduced poverty rates point to apparently greater prosperity.

Notwithstanding these advances, El Salvador's democracy remains fragile. The media, traditionally the mouthpiece of the elite, have reversed some of their postwar openness and again provide only limited space for dissenting voices. The neoliberal policies followed by successive ARENA administrations have preserved economic inequalities. Any reductions in poverty are due to large-scale out-migration and the consequent inflow of remittances from Salvadorans abroad, rather than to government policies. Millions of citizens continue to live in dire economic conditions. The judicial system remains marred by both a lack of independence from political influence and general ineffectiveness. Weaknesses in investigative policing contribute to high levels of criminal impunity, and members of the PNC have been implicated in criminal activities, human rights abuses, torture of detainees, and death squad activities. Violent crime has emerged as one of the key problems in postwar El Salvador. The per capita homicide rate has fluctuated over the years, but it is once again increasing and is now among the highest in Latin America.

Street gangs contribute to public insecurity throughout the country. Locally known as "*pandillas*" or "*maras*," the gangs have existed for decades in many marginal communities, which they consider their territory and defend against rival groups.[1] According to a 1993 survey, 47 percent of the population had already identified a gang presence in their communities.[2] It was only in the early postwar period, however, when Salvadoran-born youths deported from the United States brought the US street gang culture with them and infused it into domestic groups, that the gang problem began to attract greater attention. Gang members, who typically identify themselves with distinct tattoos and graffiti, spend their time hanging out, partying, taking drugs, and fighting their opponents. They extort small and medium-sized businesses, and within their own communities, they intimidate residents who do not obey the code of silence ("*ver, oir, y callar*"/"see, listen, and be silent") with threats of retaliation.[3] Their ready use of violence creates both a threatening atmosphere that pervades these neighborhoods and a sense of insecurity in society at large. Gang members' territorial control has increased to the extent that it has restricted residents' movements and spaces of sociability.[4]

Although in recent years many have abandoned the more obvious outward signs of gang membership to avoid detection by law enforcement, there is no indication that the complexity and severity of the problem has lessened. If anything, gang violence has intensified and become more lethal.[5] Nor has incarceration prevented gang members from engaging in criminal activities: the shortcomings of the prison system have permitted them to maintain ties with the outside world, intimidate witnesses, manage extortions, and order killings.[6] Indeed, extortion has developed into the gangs' main source of illicit income, affecting particularly the collective transport sector. Targeted violence by gang members has been mounting to the point that for some Salvadorans, particularly those who have opposed them in some way, seeking asylum abroad is often the only way to escape gang-related persecution.[7] Over time, due to the gang policies that were implemented, the gangs have become more sophisticated, more criminally involved, and more brutal in their violence.

Although the street gangs are not a recent phenomenon in El Salvador, apart from a series of law enforcement activities against them, no coherent gang policy had ever existed.[8] In July 2003, just eight months before presidential elections, the government of Francisco Flores (1999–2004) launched with great fanfare the Mano Dura ("iron fist") gang policy. With it came a proposal for anti-gang legislation, the Ley Anti Maras (LAM), which, once enacted by the Legislative Assembly, would permit the arrest and criminal prosecution of suspected gang members on the basis of their physical appearance alone. At the time, officials claimed that the gangs were responsible for the majority of homicides in the country, the implication being that tough measures against them would lead to a reduction in the murder rate.

This would ultimately not be the case, but given the very real concerns about public insecurity, the highly visible joint army/police patrols and PNC sweeps of gang areas were widely applauded. The popularity of Mano Dura helped ensure ARENA another victory at the ballot box, and incoming President Antonio Saca (2004–2009) continued his predecessor's initiative with a plan titled "Súper Mano Dura." This new measure entailed two additional components—ostensibly for gang prevention and rehabilitation—in response to criticism of Mano Dura's narrow gang suppression approach. Ever since Mano Dura had been introduced, opposition politicians, judges, academics, and human rights defenders had been relentless in their condemnation of both the abuses it sanctioned and the absence of prevention and rehabilitation programs that would address the social roots of the gang problem.

This book examines the advocacy strategies of three Salvadoran nongovernmental organizations (NGOs), all of which sought to achieve a comprehensive and rights-respecting gang policy. Using ethnographic methods, the book considers the ways in which the socio-political context and the inner workings of NGOs shape their advocacy strategies and, ultimately, their political outcomes.[9] It describes how these organizations sought to promote alternative ways to control gangs and why their efforts remained largely ineffective. Mano Dura was a punitive, populist move designed to enhance the electoral appeal of ARENA rather than to mitigate the gang problem. When the measure came under criticism, the government responded by remodeling the initiative, but without abandoning its preference for gang suppression or embarking on serious prevention and rehabilitation programs.

Reductions in gang violence and crime will come only by ending the social marginalization that leads youths into gangs, and this in turn demands a restructuring of Salvadoran society, including its power relations and socio-economic inequalities. Elite resistance to such changes made alternative approaches to gang control difficult, and since the ruling party defended elite interests, it had no incentive to embark on genuine gang control. Mano Dura remained the preferred official response because it allowed the government to appear concerned with public security without having to address structural causes. The country's leading media aided this endeavor by fanning a moral panic over gangs, legitimizing Mano Dura over other policy options, and giving little space to dissenting voices. The NGOs were largely ineffective in advancing alternative gang control because their strategies failed to take account of these tactics and mobilize sufficient political pressure for policy change.

Why Study NGOs?

At the heart of this discussion lies a concern with our understanding of NGO practices and their effectiveness in achieving goals. Nongovernmental organizations have proliferated throughout the world in recent decades, some operating domestically, others conducting activities across borders or even maintaining chapters in more than one country. They differ in size, issue area, and identity—such as humanitarian relief, development, or advocacy—and some are membership organizations.

The sheer diversity among these organizations has made it difficult for writers to agree on a definition of "NGO."[10] This study uses the term "non-governmental organization" as it is defined in Article 71 of the UN Charter, which describes an NGO as a private, formally structured, self-governing, not-for-profit organization that promotes a public cause. NGOs are thus unaffiliated with government, although they may collaborate with it and/or receive some state funding. Further, NGOs maintain at least a minimal organizational structure, such as offices, permanent staff, and financial resources; are autonomously managed and usually, but not necessarily, have legal personality; do not seek profit; and pursue goals that benefit people outside the organization.

The Current State of NGO Studies

A body of literature on NGO operations and effectiveness has grown out of development studies research, much of it stimulated by the concerns of development practitioners. Their findings merit a brief discussion for the insights they can offer into the NGOs that are the subject of this book. One set of studies scrutinizes NGO/state interactions, including instances in which governments act as donors, and raises questions about the extent to which publicly funded NGOs resist government cooptation.[11] These discussions tend to concentrate on issues of project implementation and cost-effectiveness; few writers consider the place of NGOs in evolving state/civil society relations. For example, scholars show how some NGOs in post-authoritarian Latin America adapted to the new environment by abandoning the confrontational stance they had adopted under military regimes, while those critical of the government remained under-resourced and politically marginalized.[12] These findings suggest that NGO studies could usefully explore how and why NGO/environment relations change over time and how these transformations shape the organizations' impact.

The broader theme of NGO/donor relations has prompted scholars to ask whether greater competition for funding might increase NGOs' dependence on donors and erode their autonomy in following their mission and values.[13] The difficulty of balancing organizational sustainability with independence may determine which activities NGOs are able to pursue and what results they can achieve. Scholars tend to approach this problem by offering technical solutions, such as a greater reliance on local fund-raising,[14] which is quite a task in countries like El Salvador, where many people are poor and potential philanthropists view NGO work with suspicion or even hostility. Advocacy organizations and development agencies with a political dimension may face additional hurdles, but existing scholarship glosses over both the constraints imposed by the environment in which the organization operates and the internal struggles NGOs may experience over these issues. Similarly, writers have been reluctant to take a look inside the organizations to explore NGO workers' attitudes toward the sustainability/autonomy dilemma. We might ask, for instance, what staff "get out" of the NGO. Do they see it perhaps as a way to make a living and therefore prize organizational survival over the cause they publicly espouse? Particularly in small NGOs, staff may discard the official mission and values rather willingly if expediency requires it.

Finally, the development literature has addressed specific issues that concern NGO activities—that is, performance, accountability, and legitimacy. NGOs long enjoyed an unquestioned public image as the infallible agents of development, but as evidence of poor practice and a lack of professionalism began to emerge, academics and practitioners alike turned to criticizing NGO capacities and competencies.[15] Much of this criticism takes a functional approach, such as proposing the professionalization of NGO staff and improvements in managerial leadership as ways to enhance organizational effectiveness.[16] These accounts seem to assume not only that more skills will inevitably enhance NGO performance, but also that NGOs are striving to improve their operational effectiveness in the first place. The puzzle, though, remains why some organizations continue to display low levels of competence and professionalism, notwithstanding repeated training efforts. Existing studies tend not to scrutinize the inner workings of NGOs, yet by doing so, they could explore how staff view performance-related issues and what they think the organization should be doing. Thus, one might find that those who run the NGO feel it accomplishes its purposes, even if its outward appearance is one of amateurism.

Questions also arise about whether NGOs are properly accountable for their activities. There is widespread agreement that agencies need to be transparent if they wish to maintain their legitimacy.[17] Some of this criticism is driven by a search for ways to strengthen NGO accountability, but since some writers equate this with ensuring that donors are satisfied, the focus rests on measures such as monitoring and evaluation.[18] Others argue that NGOs are accountable to a number of very different constituencies and may struggle to reconcile these demands.[19] However, Sarah Lister finds that NGOs choose to be answerable to those actors whose opinions and resources are seen as more significant for the organizations' goals.[20] The broader point to consider here is that NGO behavior is better understood when it is examined in light of the politics within specific agencies.

The concept of legitimacy has itself been widely discussed. Much of the literature addresses the elements on which legitimacy is seen to rest, such as accountability, representativeness, and performance.[21] Assuming that organizational characteristics are what determine how legitimacy is gained and maintained, these writers tend to adopt a technical approach to the problem and suggest that adherence to proper conduct and procedures is all that is required. Lister, however, argues that NGO legitimacy depends very much on external actors' perceptions of an organization.[22] Her work confirms that those who study NGOs need to be sensitive to the interaction between organizations and their environment. This still neglects the point, however, that outsiders' view of an NGO's makeup, such as the social background of the staff, may itself constitute an obstacle to public acceptance.

The social science literature also comprises works on NGO advocacy practices, notably strategic choices and policy influence. Few of the writings concern street gangs or related policy issues, such as drugs. Studies on gangs are more common than studies on responses to gangs, and the few that address the work of NGOs are often more concerned with program implementation than policy advocacy. In the case of civil society groups that work to reduce gang violence (through prevention, truces, or rehabilitation) or to shape gang policy, researchers and practitioners have reflected on the challenges of such work. In Guatemala and Honduras, some find that the social and political context may create almost insurmountable barriers to gang intervention and advocacy.[23] Other analysts conclude that a combination of contextual characteristics and strategic decisions play a great role in NGOs' preference for some gang programs over others and in how effective these can be.[24] Researchers focused on organizations' internal dynamics observe that they need to be understood as a space of work and socialization that can help youths develop alternative identities and recognition to those obtained in a gang.[25]

More generally, scholars have examined the factors that lead NGOs to select some strategies over others, even though these might not be very effective in shaping policy processes and outcomes. For example, civil society groups may prefer institutional, nonpublic advocacy over public, citizen-oriented advocacy (or insider strategies over outsider strategies) because of a drive toward NGO professionalization and bureaucratization or because of their dependency on state-provided funding.[26] Organizations' imperatives to survive and grow feed into the choice of strategies as much as, or perhaps more than, their principled agendas.[27]

Scholars concerned with the policy influence of NGOs acknowledge in some instances that such effectiveness is difficult to define and determine or that influence can occur during the policy process without necessarily deciding its outcome.[28] More often, however, the objective is to understand why organizations are sometimes more, sometimes less effective, and how they might intensify their impact. The factors that help explain the varying levels of effectiveness are generally believed to be internal (e.g., organizational structure or limited expertise, resources, and networking), rather than external (e.g., the political regime) or related to the characteristics and timing of the policy itself.[29] It is thought that policy advocacy is more effective when it combines multiple strategies, including the formation of strategic alliances.[30]

Methodologically, studies on NGO policy advocacy tend to rely on interviews and secondary sources and, at times, on surveys and primary sources. Rarely, however, do scholars conduct participant observation or ethnographic research in order to better understand the groups that seek policy influence and thus their relative effectiveness in shaping policy making. Victoria Bernal and Inderpal Grewal, however, highlight the relevance not only of specific historical and political contexts but also of NGOs as spaces for socializing, pursuing careers, and experiencing democracy, and even as sites of gendered struggles over power and resources.[31]

In sum, the existing scholarship on NGOs addresses specific kinds of relations and specific aspects of NGO activities. Recently, writers have acknowledged that while organizational characteristics remain important for our understanding of NGOs, these agencies must be situated more firmly within the structural context in which they operate.[32] To date, however, there is little research that takes a composite approach to the study of NGOs, analyzing both their inner workings and their socio-political environment. Interest in NGO ethnographies has grown in recent years, and this book falls into this category.[33] By examining how context, organizational origins and identity, and daily life within three Salvadoran NGOs have shaped their advocacy of an alternative gang policy, this study contributes to the NGO literature and the study of activism in postwar El Salvador.

The Street Gangs of El Salvador

The history of the Salvadoran street gang—that is, "any durable, street-oriented youth group whose involvement in illegal activity is part of its group identity"[34]—dates back to the 1970s. For two decades, a number of territorial or neighborhood-based entities existed under names such as Gallo, Chancleta, Piojo, Nosedice, Mao Mao, AC/DC, Morazán, or

Fosa. They offered socially marginalized youths the means not only to hang out, party, and fight their rivals but also to engage in a range of illicit pursuits. Recruited by the FMLN during its 1989 offensive against government forces, some of these groups acted as guides for the guerrillas and subsequently joined the combatants' demobilization and reinsertion process.[35] Other gangs dissolved, and those remaining would be largely absorbed by the two gangs, Mara Salvatrucha (MS-13) and Calle Dieciocho (18th Street), that took root in El Salvador through US deportation policies. Their story begins in Los Angeles, California.

Mara Salvatrucha and Calle Dieciocho

The United States has a long legacy of street gangs dating back to the early 1800s.[36] Historically, these groups have emerged primarily in low-income ethnic minority communities, where residents face poor living conditions and discrimination that bars them from opportunities for social advancement through good education or well-paid employment.[37] The continuous immigration of Mexicans into Southern California after 1920 and their chronic marginalization from mainstream society played a significant role in gang growth. These immigrants brought with them a tradition known as *"palomilla,"* or "boy gangs," which metamorphosed into street gangs following the 1943 Zoot Suit Riots.[38] Over the next decades, continued social neglect and ostracism ensured that the street gang subculture would remain an enduring feature of Latino community life in Los Angeles. It was in the city's densely populated and impoverished Pico-Union area that Calle Dieciocho formed in the 1960s.[39]

Most Salvadorans who travelled north in the 1980s were undocumented refugees fleeing the violence of their home country. Under US asylum policy during Ronald Reagan's presidency, Nicaraguans could generally obtain legal status and therefore the possibility to better themselves, but Salvadorans were routinely denied refugee status and had to live clandestinely.[40] Trapped in a Los Angeles neighborhood devoid of recreational facilities and rife with crime and gang activity, these families not only struggled to overcome the trauma of the war back home, but also faced culture shock, language barriers, discrimination, crowded living conditions, and underpaid jobs. Combined with the constant specter of arrest and deportation, these strains often led to conflict, child neglect, and domestic abuse.[41] In response to difficult personal circumstances and gang harassment, some Salvadoran youths joined existing street gangs, notably Dieciocho, and eventually created their own gang, Mara Salvatrucha.[42] Over the years, both expanded their membership, and today they constitute the dominant gangs in the Central American immigrant communities in the United States.[43]

The little that is known about the origins of the hostility between Mara Salvatrucha and the Dieciocho stems largely from anecdotes gang members have supplied to researchers and journalists. Some writers have suggested that the hostility is largely ethnic based or that disputes over control of the drug trade in Pico-Union heightened the antagonism.[44] Others report that a shooting at a party sparked the extreme enmity that characterizes these gangs today.[45]

Whatever the cause, US deportation policy helped spread gang culture, lifestyle, and rivalry abroad. Once the Salvadoran civil war had drawn to a close, US authorities began targeting offending non-citizens more aggressively for repatriation, and changes in the immigration laws in 1996 further facilitated this process.[46] Deported youths, separated from their families and with few memories of their countries of origin, often felt disoriented and alienated by the humble surroundings they encountered.[47] Although many expected to make a fresh start, disaffection and continued marginalization prompted some to continue the gang lifestyle they knew best.[48] The gang members' comparatively smarter dress, money, and romanticized descriptions of gang life held a fascination that local adolescents found hard to resist.[49]

Today Mara Salvatrucha and the Dieciocho maintain a presence in large parts of the United States as well as in Mexico and the Northern Triangle of Central America (Guatemala, Honduras, and El Salvador). For reasons connected with migration patterns, US asylum and deportation practices, and a less suppressive police approach, youth gangs in Nicaragua are numerous, but smaller and less violent than their counterparts elsewhere in the region. Moreover, MS-13 and the Dieciocho have not taken hold there.[50] In southern Mexico, meanwhile, members of the *maras* became known especially for assaulting and robbing undocumented migrants.[51] Given their geographical reach and criminal activities, the *maras* are sometimes portrayed as cross-border crime networks involved in drug and human trafficking.[52] However, although some individual gang members and cliques appear to sustain transnational links and ties to drug trafficking, there is insufficient evidence to suggest that either of these dimensions applies to the street gangs in general. Nevertheless, given the evolution of the gangs since the implementation of the Mano Dura policies, such transnational ties and involvement in organized crime require further research.

Mara Salvatrucha and the Dieciocho remain El Salvador's main street gangs, although other groups, such as La Máquina, Mao Mao, and Mirada Locos, are known to exist. More than three hundred *clicas* (cliques or subgroups) are scattered about the country's fourteen departments (administrative districts).[53] The gangs have long been concentrated in marginal urban communities, particularly those of Greater San Salvador, but have spread into rural areas to hide from law enforcement.

Estimates of gang membership are in constant flux and vary by institutional source. The PNC, for example, initially put the number of gang members at ten thousand, later at thirty thousand, and, in 2012, raised it to almost one hundred thousand.[54] However, difficulties in defining and counting gang members compound attempts to arrive at a global figure. Their actual numbers may exceed official estimates because these reflect only those individuals who came into contact with law enforcement.

Socio-demographic data have consistently revealed gang members to be predominantly adolescents and young men from low-income backgrounds.[55] Those joining gangs continue to be of an adolescent, sometimes preadolescent age.[56] Given the difficulty of "maturing out" of the gangs, however, many of their members are older, often exceeding thirty or even forty years of age. Although they are no longer permitted to join Mara Salvatrucha and the Dieciocho, females, including girlfriends and sisters of male gang members, fulfill important functions for the gang, such as collecting extortion monies, performing domestic chores, or dropping off food and other items at the prisons.[57]

Life in the Gang

Potential gang members hang out with a clique before deciding whether to join, and they are often previously groomed as *postes* or *antenas* (lookouts).[58] Entry into a gang (*el brinco*) occurs through an initiation rite in which recruits are tested for their toughness and commitment to the group. Generally, this involves a beating (*el chequeo*) at the hands of other gang members; females could opt to have sex with one or several of the males (*el trencito*), but those who do often are less respected within the group.[59] It is thought that in some cases the *brinco* may have come to include a "mission" (a murder), but gang-internal information of this kind is not shared with outsiders and thus difficult to confirm.[60]

New members are then socialized into the street gang culture, its values and norms. Loyalty to the gang and its territory is paramount and supersedes even family bonds, an allegiance that is encapsulated in the phrase, *"Por mi madre vivo, por mi barrio muero"* ("For my mother I live, for my gang I die").[61] "Status-setting fights"[62] between rival gangs to defend their name and honor are associated with this lifestyle and, like its symbolic features (e.g., graffiti), have long been a visible reminder of the gangs' presence. Since the implementation of Mano Dura, however, both descriptive traits and gang activity have gone through some notable changes.

Gang identity had been expressed by distinct clothes, hand signs, slang, tattoos, and graffiti, but the PNC's suppressive measures apparently prompted gang members to modify some of these behaviors. While government-sponsored "cleansing" campaigns eliminated many of the gangs' territorial markers (as did some cliques during a 2012 truce), gang members themselves turned to adopting less visible tattoos, more conventional clothing and hairstyles, and less conspicuous forms of communication, all in an attempt to avoid notice.[63]

Conversely, recent years have seen gang members commit more serious violence and crimes. The earlier image of youths hanging out in the streets and *destroyers* (gang hangouts) and fighting their rivals with stones and machetes, or sometimes pistols and hand grenades, now seems obsolete. Gang members these days are often linked to homicides (including of civilians), extortion, car theft, rapes, drug sales, and possession of automatic firearms. Overall, they have acquired a greater logistical capacity to execute illicit activities and, through access to heavy weaponry, are capable of more lethal violence.[64] There is evidence that gang members acquire their weapons not only in exchange for drugs, through theft from private security firms, or in purchases from private sources but also from police and military sources.[65] Nevertheless, it must be stressed that gang members are not equally involved in crime, nor do crime and violence occupy all their time. Rather, their undertakings are perhaps more appropriately described as *el vacil* (the lifestyle), the whole range of licit and illicit pursuits that promise fun and excitement in a gang.[66]

For gang members, there may come a time when the novelty of gang life has worn off or its intensity becomes overwhelming. Motivations for withdrawing from the gang commonly include the stresses and danger of violence and incarceration, the desire to preserve stable partnerships or find meaningful employment, and, for some, religious conversion.[67] Yet, given the proximity to violence and death that gang membership entails, what makes young people want to join a street gang in the first place?

Research has shown that street gangs attract individuals who live in socially disorganized communities and face social exclusion, family problems, and a lack of dignified education and job opportunities.[68] While only a minority of youths in these conditions enters a gang, it is these conditions that encourage gang membership. Moreover, as the risk factors accumulate, the chances that an adolescent will join a gang increase.[69] Thus, a juvenile who resides in a marginal community but has a supportive and caring family may withstand the lure of gang membership, while another youth who lives in the same area but suffers parental neglect or domestic violence may prove less resilient.

To outsiders, street gangs may well appear to be a mob of marauding youths, but, above all, they constitute a space in which young people seek to fulfill their personal needs, some shared, some conflicting. Crime and violence, which allow gang members to obtain respect and status within the group, must be seen as by-products of, rather than as reasons for, gang membership.[70] Economic necessity and access to drugs are among the motivations for joining, but the more common reasons include fun, status, identity, a sense of belonging, friendship, and understanding.[71] These stimuli have not fundamentally changed, despite the trend toward greater criminality.[72] Given the mostly non-material needs that youths seek to satisfy, it is useful to highlight the link between social marginalization and the street gang culture.

In addition to the obvious socio-economic disadvantage, a life of poverty and joblessness creates a whole set of psychological problems. In the words of one researcher, this neglect "is not just a matter of abandoned buildings; it also means abandoned lives and abandoned categories of people."[73] People who live in a state of "multiple marginality,"[74] the manifold exclusion from mainstream society, have few resources to better their lives. The realization that others enjoy comparatively greater affluence, while one's own aspirations are beyond reach, can cause alienation and resentment, especially among the young. Without opportunities to better their lives, youths may seek a place where they are not marginalized and ignored. In this sense, street gangs offer not only excitement, friendship, and emotional support, but also a way of acquiring the respect and status that are otherwise unobtainable.

The use of violence is central in gaining and maintaining this social status. A gang member who robs a local resident or attacks a rival gang member may have the immediate goal of getting money or inflicting harm, but these actions are also means to a higher end. Each gang relies on violence and intimidation to establish a reputation for being daring and superior to other gangs. Individual members simultaneously build a personal reputation for being willing and able to fight and thus achieve status and respect among their peers.[75] The youths interviewed for one study affirmed that they gained respect, friendship, power, protection, confidence, money, and freedom within the gang.[76] Despite the fact that gang membership exposes young people to greater physical risk and ostracism by society, the desire to be recognized and valued is such that many feel a reputation for aggressive behavior and the risk of violent death are preferable to being nobody.[77]

Gang control therefore requires an integrated approach based on prevention, law enforcement, and rehabilitation and reinsertion. Law enforcement, which might comprise intelligence-led policing and community policing instead of single-minded gang suppression, is aimed at the arrest and criminal prosecution of offending gang members. Prevention and rehabilitation/reinsertion both seek to address the socioeconomic disadvantages associated with gang formation and criminal behavior. This would entail measures such as the overhaul of a defective, underfunded education system; the creation of decent jobs with living wages; and generally, the alleviation of social marginalization in the communities that spawn gangs. Clearly, a comprehensive gang policy calls for resources, but ultimately also for the political will to change the structure of society, its institutions, values, and power relations, the imbalance of which has permitted the gang culture to take hold. The struggle over these responses, and the role some NGOs have played in it, is the subject of this book.

NGO Gang Policy Advocacy in El Salvador

This book examines three Salvadoran NGOs and the advocacy strategies they pursued to reshape the government's Mano Dura gang policy. The research, focused on the 2003–2006 period, takes an ethnographic approach in order to delve into facets of the NGO world that would otherwise remain hidden. Rather than merely analyzing how and under what conditions specific NGOs sought to promote an alternative gang policy, the volume explores the everyday activities and social processes that occur in each organization's setting. What motivates the NGO workers? What stories do they tell, and what interests, values, beliefs, and experiences do they bring to their job? The ethnographic method permits a richer understanding of an institution's inner workings and helps both analyze and account for NGO policy influence.

Any explanation of NGO efforts to change gang policy also requires an understanding of the ways in which the social and political environments of the organizations, as well as their characteristics and strategies, inhibited or facilitated their advocacy work. One objective of this study is to show how domestic circumstances in El Salvador affected the advancement of alternative gang policy options. The transition to electoral democracy has improved the general conditions for the expression of civil dissent, but has also preserved the fundamental political and social dynamics that neutralize efforts at social change.

Three factors in particular were salient to the success or failure of NGO advocacy: the persistence of elite influence, the nature of the ruling party, and the concentration of media ownership in elite hands. The Salvadoran oligarchy has traditionally played a central role in the nation's economic and political affairs. Although its composition has altered over the years, the oligarchy has retained its dominant position in society and, unsurprisingly, remains staunchly opposed to measures that would undermine its interests and privileges. From its inception in 1981, ARENA, the party that oversaw the transition to democracy and governed the country uninterruptedly until 2009, was diligent in guarding conservative interests and maintaining a political agenda that supported the status quo against popular encroachment. The media are concentrated in the hands of oligarchic families, and the reporting of the principal news organs is routinely biased in favor of the right-wing political class and the economic elite. The absence of pluralistic media makes it more difficult for dissenting groups to express their views and mobilize political pressure. If the context imposes facilitating and inhibiting conditions for NGO advocacy, organizational characteristics and strategies have a crucial effect on policy formulation and implementation.

NGOs' capacity for activism and the strategies they choose depend on internal dynamics, rooted in how the organizations were formed and are maintained, and are critical for understanding why some are politically influential while others are not. These kinds of organizations often arise because an individual (or a small group) identifies a problem, decides that it should be addressed, and seeks to mobilize people and resources to achieve that purpose.[78] These "organizational entrepreneurs" commit time and energy (and sometimes funds) to establish an NGO, define its mission, and steer it through its initial phase of development.

Once established, the organization must acquire the capacity to carry out its mission while at the same time ensuring its sustainability, a long-term project that demands not only commitment, but also human and material resources. The difficulty of securing and preserving the needed flow of revenue is influenced by the generally limited availability of funding, particularly where international support may have dwindled and local donations are scarce. Since a steady flow of income is essential for an NGO's survival, NGO staff need to develop their fund-raising ability accordingly. At the same time, organizations must marshal the required skills and knowledge to advance their agenda. This involves, for example, the ability of leadership to set clear and attainable objectives and foster collaboration with others.[79] NGOs may undertake media outreach to put the issue of concern on the political agenda, educate the public, and mobilize public opinion. Importantly, they must attract personnel who possess the know-how to promote their cause. The question is not only how much expertise NGOs have, but also what kinds of expert skills they can offer. Staff may have "lived" the problem being tackled, but this firsthand experience does not necessarily equip them with the professional skills to advance their advocacy and propose realistic solutions.

Advocacy strategies vary depending on the objectives that are being pursued. The strategic choices NGOs make, though circumscribed by their organizational capacity, hinge on two endogenous factors: their status and their ideology. Groups that have gained a positive public reputation, often won through demonstrated competence, can draw on their credibility to gain access to the political system and the media more easily. Recognized as serious, reliable, and respectable, these agencies are more likely to be consulted and able to participate in the policy process. Organizations that lack this standing will require different tactics to make their impact felt. Their ideological positions, however, also inform their strategies. NGOs differ widely both in how they view an advocacy issue and in how they seek to effect policy change. These stances have direct consequences for the political outcomes they seek. The gang problem elicits divergent reactions not only between NGOs and the state, but also among the organizations themselves. While there is agreement among NGOs that gang prevention and rehabilitation require a greater allocation of public resources, the fault line runs between those who regard the gangs as inherently destructive groups that need to be dissolved and those who argue that only some aspects of the gangs (violence and drugs) are harmful, and youths should therefore be encouraged to abandon these negative behaviors without necessarily abandoning their gang.

NGOs may support policy changes, but what transformations they can induce will depend on the nature of their involvement in the policy process and the level of their intent to participate. Their ideological position shapes the broader tactical style, which in turn determines substantive priorities and the degree of antagonism with which they approach authorities. The organizations in this study implemented different advocacy strategies, which gave preference to either direct policy influence or change "on the ground." Although the immediate targeting of decision makers may seem the more obvious approach, NGO advocacy can aim to bring about an alternative policy by other means. This may entail empowering weaker social groups to design their own solutions to their problems or creating innovative programs that demonstrate to the government a better way of addressing a problem. While these efforts do not constitute direct interventions in the policy process, they can alter the policy context and, especially when combined with other actions, such as participation in discussion forums or some form of media work, put pressure on the administration to adopt a different set of guidelines. On the downside, however, model programs may unwittingly relieve the government of certain responsibilities, such as providing services to neglected areas, by assuming some of its functions.

Organizational ideology also underlies the perceived role of an NGO within the domestic political system. Some NGOs see themselves as being in cooperation with the state, while others maintain a more antagonistic relationship. The establishment of democracy in El Salvador has meant that the country's general concept of what constitutes legitimate political behavior has shifted from highly adversarial toward a more collaborative attitude. This is not to say that the need for documenting and criticizing state performance has become superfluous or that NGOs have renounced their familiar critical activities; indeed, for many, these tasks remain an important part of their work. Yet, as NGOs are trying to reinvent themselves, many have come to believe that a democratic environment requires them to propose alternative initiatives on a given issue, rather than (merely) exposing the state's inability to address the problem. However NGOs try to straddle the line between confrontation and collaboration, each develops a preferred tactical style. When it helps secure funding, or resource and skills shortages impede the adoption of a different approach, the strategy that characterizes the organization (e.g., partner or gadfly) may prevail even if it is ineffective for changing government policy. Whatever the reasons for adhering to a particular strategy, this choice has consequences for an NGO's ability to influence policy.

It is important to add a note on the meaning of effectiveness. The NGOs in this research did not attempt, nor can they be expected, to resolve the complex social problem of street gangs. They did, however, seek to persuade the government to replace Mano Dura with more comprehensive and rights-based gang control policies, and this book examines both how the NGOs promoted policy change and why their efforts met with only limited success. To assess the organizations' influence, it compares their policy positions with their achievements at three levels: government discourse, policy change, and state behavior.[80] The Saca administration (2004–2009) pledged to commence prevention and rehabilitation programs, but these rhetorical commitments may be interpreted as either a victory for the NGOs or an attempt to stifle further criticism. More important is whether a shift occurred in both policy and behavior: the adoption of a new set of guidelines may seem to denote success, but the existence of policy documents and institutions is meaningless in the absence of implementation. Indeed, the final outcome of the advocacy efforts, notably the persistence of the Mano Dura approach, points to weaknesses in NGO strategies.

The NGOs in this study are a legal advocacy organization, the Fundación de Estudios para la Aplicación del Derecho (Foundation for Applied Legal Studies, or FESPAD); a peer rehabilitation group, Homies Unidos (Homies United, or HU); and a Catholic development NGO, the Polígono Industrial Don Bosco (Don Bosco Industrial Park, or Polígono/PIDB). Each developed from different circumstances and concerns, and while they all advocated the creation of an alternative gang policy, they did so with different strategies and priorities. FESPAD, established by a group of lawyers to promote human rights and the rule of law in El Salvador, was selected for its high profile in the defense of gang members' human rights. Staff applied their juridical expertise in legal and policy research, which they used to publicly criticize Mano Dura and propose one alternative local gang program. Unlike their counterparts in the other two agencies, they also made a concerted effort to express their position in the media. Homies Unidos was chosen for its distinctive nature as El Salvador's only NGO that both was founded by and worked with gang members. Mobilized to design solutions to their own problems, staff worked to empower their peers to imagine a life free of violence and drugs, though not without their gang. Building on their firsthand experience of gang life, they delivered testimonial stories to deter at-risk youths from joining gangs, implemented rehabilitation projects in gang-affected communities, and alerted human rights defenders to police abuse against gang members. The Polígono, conceived by a Spanish priest, provides education and microenterprise training to low-income youths. Located in a gang-affected community in eastern San Salvador, the organization is widely respected for its perceived success in modeling a gang prevention and rehabilitation program. The project incorporates at-risk youth and—when this research began—ex–gang members and juvenile offenders. Through this program, the Polígono team has sought to demonstrate an innovative way of tackling the gang problem that might be replicated by the authorities.

Organization of the Book

Chapter 1 examines the historical and contemporary context of El Salvador and traces the continuity of traditional patterns of elite rule, authoritarianism, and exclusion. It shows that the process of democratic consolidation has experienced certain setbacks and highlights the circumstances in which Mano Dura emerged. Chapter 2 argues that Mano Dura constituted a populist penal policy designed to enhance ARENA's electoral appeal rather than to address the gang problem. It considers how the Saca administration adapted its own Súper Mano Dura to criticism of the previous initiative and demonstrates that the administration maintained its preference for suppression without seriously addressing the need for prevention and rehabilitation. Chapter 3 focuses on the role of the media in fanning a moral panic over the street gangs and depicting suppression as the most appropriate response to these groups. It examines the contemporary media system and presents the findings of a content analysis of gang-related coverage by El Salvador's leading newspapers, *La Prensa Gráfica* and *El Diario de Hoy*. The chapter demonstrates that the reporting by these conservative broadsheets exhibited a consistent pro-government bias and swayed public opinion toward support for Mano Dura.

The subsequent three chapters turn to the NGOs and their strategies for advocating an alternative gang policy. These efforts were largely ineffective because the organizations, for reasons of internal characteristics and tactical choices, put insufficient pressure on the government. Chapter 4 considers FESPAD's methods to contest Mano Dura and the ways in which its political inexperience left it unable to deal with institutional unresponsiveness and lack of access to the media. Chapter 5 surveys the work of Homies Unidos with at-risk youth and gang members, discusses the consequences of the staff's overidentification with gang members, and notes the difficulties it encountered in sustaining itself. Chapter 6 examines the Polígono gang prevention and rehabilitation program and suggests that a showcase project, unless combined with greater direct lobbying, is unlikely to affect government policy. The conclusion compares NGO strategies, reflects on the implications of this study, and offers some policy recommendations for gang control in El Salvador.

CHAPTER 1

Power, Politics, and Exclusion

The 1992 Chapultepec Peace Accords ended a twelve-year civil war in El Salvador and paved the way for the democratization of a country that had hitherto experienced decades of uninterrupted authoritarianism. The civic achievements of this postwar period include the demilitarization of society and the construction of a new civilian police force, the political enfranchisement of the left, and regular multiparty elections, as well as improved respect for human rights and greater freedom of expression. The process of democratic consolidation since then has been uneven, however, and has failed to meet popular expectations. Poverty and economic inequality remain high. Combined with high levels of crime and violence, these chronic problems have eroded support for democracy. Most importantly, traditional power structures have survived the political regime change, permitting the economic elite to maintain strong influence over Salvadoran society and politics.

This chapter describes the background to Mano Dura and explains the dynamics that led the ARENA government to prefer gang suppression and that constituted contextual barriers to NGO policy advocacy. The story begins with the emergence of a landowning oligarchy in the first half of the twentieth century. These elites protected their interests and privileges against dissent through direct political control and institutionalized violence. A military coup in 1931 led to a five-decades-long alliance between the military and the oligarchy, during which the army held the reins of government and acted as the guardian of the civilian elite.

When the civil war broke up this "protection racket," the Salvadoran right responded by creating its own political party in a bid to restore the status quo through electoral participation. The ruling class conceded de jure democracy in exchange for an end to the war and the possibility of rebuilding its economic and political influence. With the ARENA party in power for twenty years, the postwar period has been marked by government resistance to democratic consolidation and the failure to build basic democratic institutions, such as a professional police force, or democratic forms of public policy making. Both the authoritarian nature of the police and undue elite influence over the state obstructed NGO efforts to promote a comprehensive and rights-respecting gang policy.

Historical Patterns: Independence to 1931

The characteristics of contemporary El Salvador, and the constraints they pose for NGO advocacy of alternative gang policies, must be understood in light of the country's historical development and past patterns of governance. Spanish colonial rule had seen the development of a mono-crop economy and a related trend toward the privatization of indigenous peoples' communal land. With the expansion of commercial farming, the ownership of land and wealth became increasingly concentrated while the exploitation of laborers sharpened. Landowners began to enjoy greater political influence, and they established economic structures that would endure for many years.[1] The indigenous and *campesino* (peasant) populations, faced with massive deprivation, responded to these perceived injustices with periodic revolts. These uprisings were regularly crushed, a pattern that would remain a feature of the postcolonial period.[2]

In the wake of El Salvador's independence from Spain in 1838, an intra-elite conflict simmered. Conservatives defended authoritarian government and centrally regulated economies, in opposition to liberals, who espoused limited representative democracy and free trade. Ultimately, the conflict was resolved in favor of the latter.[3] Following their rise to political power, liberal elites embarked on a series of reforms that encouraged a major expansion of the agrarian export economy and further exacerbated the marginalization of rural workers. The policies entailed a shift from the cultivation of indigo, the dominant export crop to this point, to coffee production and precipitated important changes in landholding patterns. Although coffee had been grown since the 1840s, the consolidation of this industry required more land. Since the agricultural areas that were most suited to coffee growing had been settled by the indigenous communities, the encroachment on communal lands, which had begun during the colonial era, intensified. In the 1880s, legislation was enacted that turned these communal holdings into private property and forced the dispossessed population to work on the newly created plantations.[4]

The concentration of land ownership led to the emergence of an enormously wealthy and powerful elite. Dubbed "the fourteen families" after the republican family groups that constituted its nucleus, this oligarchy expanded in size and influence with the arrival of immigrants, who provided capital and technical knowledge and married into the existing dynasties. Together, these families largely controlled coffee production, processing, export, and finance.[5] While the rapid growth of the coffee economy permitted both the development of the country's infrastructure and greater prosperity among the upper echelons of society, the vast majority of the populace labored for very little pay and endured appalling poverty and social exclusion.[6] From the very beginning of the republic, inviolability of private property and maintenance of order were its guiding principles. The idea that the state might bear some responsibility for the health, education, and general well-being of all citizens was not part of Salvadoran political culture.[7]

Spurred by both the heightened social injustice and a perceived assault on their identity, indigenous peoples mounted active resistance to the liberal reforms. In response, landowners fielded private armies. Elements of these corps eventually became the National Police, which emerged from the earlier Rural Police, and the National Guard, founded in 1912. A third security force, the Treasury Police, would be formed in 1936. Whereas the national army defended the national territory, these internal security forces upheld public order and soon acquired a reputation for brutality.[8]

By virtue of its vast economic and social power, the elite was able to exercise substantial influence over state institutions and public policymaking. Political control was not won in the electoral arena but merely transferred from one section of the ruling class to another.[9] Between 1911 and 1927, two prominent coffee- and sugar-producing families dominated the presidency. The coffee boom of the 1920s led the subsequent government to allow some political openness, and in January 1931, a progressive landowner, Arturo Araujo, won El Salvador's first free elections on a pledge of social reforms and employment, a program that was popular with the lower strata of society. Amid an economic crisis and growing social disturbances, however, the prospects for reform did not find favor with the elite, and the country's flirtation with democracy proved short-lived.[10]

The Military-Oligarchy Alliance: 1931–1979

In December 1931, a military coup toppled Araujo and installed General Maximiliano Hernández Martínez. A dictator who fostered a cult of personality, Martínez stifled dissent by means of press censorship, army-controlled rural patrols, and an urban network of spies.

The only political party allowed to operate was his own, Pro-Patria (Pro-Fatherland).[11] After 1931, the oligarchy ceded the reins of government to the military, but retained its own dominant economic power and control over economic policy-making. As part of this "protection racket," the army served as the guardian of the oligarchy, suppressing by force any challenge to the status quo.[12] This alliance lasted until 1979 and constituted the longest period of uninterrupted military rule in modern Latin American history.[13] Even when this partnership broke apart, the army retained its political influence until the end of the twelve-year civil war.

The next event to leave an indelible impact on the nation followed shortly after the coup. The Great Depression of 1929 and the accompanying collapse of coffee prices had led to declining profits for the coffee growers, unemployment, falling wages, and hunger for the laborers. Stolen elections in January 1932 exacerbated the escalating social crisis facing the overwhelmingly rural and poor population. The Communist Party, founded during the previous period of political liberalization by Farabundo Martí, won many predominantly indigenous municipalities in western El Salvador, but the Martínez regime annulled the results.[14] Later in that same election month, local Indian communities rose in insurrection. The army responded with unprecedented brutality, swiftly crushing the revolt and, in the space of a few days, executing anyone suspected of participating in the rebellion or aiding the rebels. *La matanza* (the massacre) saw the indiscriminate killing of an estimated ten thousand to thirty thousand *campesinos* and has remained significant in Salvadoran history and politics.[15] *La matanza* preserved oligarchic rule, instilled a "lasting memory of terror" among the lower classes, and neutralized further rebellions for the next four decades.[16] It was only after the 1970s that people would defy state-sponsored violence to seek social and political change.

Another legacy of the 1932 elections and insurrection was the oligarchy's rigid hostility to even the most moderate reforms. Indigenous people, the protagonists of the uprising, had sought to protest deteriorating economic and social conditions. During the insurrection, they took the lives of about one hundred people, but they were poorly armed and posed no threat to the established order.[17] However, the Communist Party had attempted to side with the popular movement, and this association allowed the oligarchy and the army to portray the uprising as communist-inspired and the subsequent repression as a victory over communist subversion.[18] The official discourse on the events of 1932 created a legend of barbaric hordes attacking thousands of upright citizens and a heroic army that could barely stave off the assault.[19] Anticommunism entered elite political culture, and reform efforts were henceforth framed as attempts to undermine the institutions that had brought progress to the country.[20] The defense of elite privileges became the primary political objective, and actual or potential challengers of the status quo were depicted as a threat to society that had to be contained by force. Such political and media "narratives of fear" had been used since the nineteenth century to warn of new menaces that required social control.[21]

Violent responses to indigenous uprisings were followed in the 1980s by a counterinsurgency war against antiregime guerrillas. In similar ways, the Mano Dura narrative of the 2000s would depict the street gangs as a great danger that justified the use of state force against them.

General Martínez governed until 1944, when a civic strike forced his resignation.[22] His relatively progressive successor was overthrown only a few months later, and after four years of instability, military authoritarianism was reinstated.[23] Over the next decades, popular sectors were repressed and political competition was strictly limited: presidential elections were celebrated, but victory was always reserved for the military's own party, inaugurated in 1961 as the Partido de Conciliación Nacional (National Conciliation Party, or PCN). Although the military defended both its own rule and the oligarchic economic model, individual regimes differed in their ideological orientation. Some sought to introduce democratic institutions and moderate social reforms, but were met with opposition by the elite and military hard-liners.[24] Reforms were tolerated only insofar as they allowed economic modernization without structural change.

These tensions heightened in the 1950s, and more so in the 1960s, when the United States sought to forestall further Cuban-style revolutions in Latin America. Through its Alliance for Progress, the Kennedy administration encouraged economic development and channeled monetary and military aid to El Salvador and other countries in the region.[25] Prior to these policies, successive governments had already begun to promote agricultural diversification into cotton and sugar production as well as light manufacturing. The Alliance essentially helped expand the industrial sector through regional integration and new private investment. Economic growth and the implementation of education, health, and housing programs notwithstanding, existing trends of poverty and inequality were only reinforced. The expansion of export agriculture led to further land concentration and increased the number of landless *campesinos* who had to rely on low seasonal wages. Population increases, combined with the forced return of some 130,000 emigrants after the "Soccer War" with Honduras, only intensified rural poverty.[26]

Given the worsening conditions in the countryside, many workers migrated to urban areas in search of jobs. However, industrialization did not generate significant employment opportunities, and many people had to turn to the informal sector, typically street vending.[27] The coffee oligarchy controlled commercial agriculture and extended its reach into the banking sector and the nascent industrial sector. Economic power remained in the hands of a few extended families and allowed them to maintain their influence over state policy. Although the development process saw the emergence of a small middle class, oligarchic control over the economy prevented the rise of a new industrial elite that might have challenged the social and political dominance of the landed oligarchy.[28] Although they resented the few reformist efforts that occurred during that time, the elite tolerated these attempts as long as they did not undermine dominant interests.

In tandem with its economic assistance, the Alliance for Progress also sponsored a counterinsurgency program aimed at containing revolutionary movements. With the help of US advisers, the Salvadoran military developed a nationwide paramilitary network and a centralized intelligence agency to provide early warning signals of "communist" infiltration. The paramilitary organization, Organización Democrática Nacionalista (Nationalist Democratic Organization, or ORDEN), was established by National Guard commander General José Alberto Medrano in the mid-1960s and was tasked with identifying suspected communists among the rural population. ORDEN patrols gathered information and carried out repressive activities when ordered to do so. Most of the victims who were disappeared or killed for being "enemies of the state" were simply poor people who tried to improve conditions for their families and communities.[29] One of the most brutal acts of repression occurred in December 1981 in the northern village of El Mozote, where government forces killed some one thousand unarmed civilians in a bid to eliminate guerrilla sympathizers.

The existence of these security structures, and the political violence they conducted, fostered fear and mistrust among neighbors and eroded local social networks. Such was the level of past insecurity that contemporary social relations remain affected by it.[30] The Agencia Nacional de Seguridad Salvadoreña (Salvadoran National Security Agency, or ANESAL), co-founded by Medrano and National Guard Major Roberto D'Aubuisson, who served as ANESAL's deputy director, processed the intelligence obtained by ORDEN members. The unit, staffed by officers of the various armed services, also participated in death squad activities.[31] In the years prior to and during the civil war, both entities played a key role in targeting real or imagined opponents of the status quo.

A political opening in the 1960s saw the emergence of moderate opposition parties, notably the Partido Demócrata Cristiano (Christian Democratic Party, or PDC). The PDC had made gains in legislative and mayoral elections and challenged the PCN in the 1972 presidential contest. However, amid a mass mobilization, the military handed the victory to its own candidate; arrested and tortured the PDC's contender, José Napoleón Duarte; and brutally suppressed subsequent protests.[32] This blatant electoral fraud convinced many Salvadorans that peaceful change was unattainable and that armed struggle was the only viable route. Revolutionary organizations began to form and throughout the 1970s carried out sporadic bombings and kidnappings.[33] The major opposition during that decade came from a popular movement that brought together students, teachers, and industrial workers. These urban coalitions occupied buildings and held marches and demonstrations to demand an end to economic and political exclusion.[34]

In the capital's marginal zones, but particularly in many rural areas, the Catholic Church played a key role in organizing the poor into Christian Base Communities. Inspired by liberation theology, which encouraged the church to abandon its previous message of passivity and submission and become an advocate for the poor, Catholic clergy and lay workers formed bible study groups in which *campesinos* discussed teachings on social justice.[35] Emboldened by an increasing sense of dignity and understanding of human rights, the rural population began to demand economic reforms. The church, for its part, criticized the government and the elite for their indifference to the suffering of the lower classes. The Salvadoran right labeled these activities subversive and responded to this political mobilization with violence. *Campesinos* were murdered or disappeared, and several priests were tortured or killed by death squads during the 1970s.[36] One of El Salvador's most powerful voices for peace and social justice, Monseñor Óscar Romero, was assassinated in March 1980. His killing and the killings of other prominent religious figures demonstrated how much the oligarchy and the military resented calls for profound social and political change.

By the time of elections in 1977, the military had resorted to greater levels of intimidation and fraud to deter the opposition. In the face of persistent popular action, the new government instituted full press censorship, banned public meetings, and outlawed strikes. The torture, disappearances, and murders of political dissidents, priests, students, and trade unionists continued. State violence further radicalized the left, which intensified its guerrilla activities.[37] In October 1979, concerned by the revolutionary threat and the Sandinista victory in Nicaragua a few months earlier, a progressive faction of the Salvadoran army staged a coup. The officers installed a military-civilian junta and promised to end the repression, to create a democratic political system, and to initiate a series of pro-poor policies, including agrarian reform. These measures would have nationalized the elite-controlled banking system and affected many of the oligarchy's coffee estates, but the Salvadoran right ultimately deterred these changes.[38] In the short term, conservative army officers blocked the junta's reforms, and its civilian members resigned within three months.[39] The civil war would soon begin in earnest, and, significantly, the long-standing military-oligarchy alliance had broken.

Civil War: 1980–1992

The revolutionary organizations, now unified under the FMLN, launched their military operations in January 1981, targeting power lines, bridges, and export crops. This economic sabotage hurt many ordinary Salvadorans and would become increasingly unpopular with time, but the war also produced economic transformations that were to have important political implications. The fighting brought a rapid decline in national output and massive capital flight. By the end of the decade, the profitability of the agro-export sector decreased sharply while the commercial and service sectors surged, prompting a macrolevel shift in elite economic interests.[40]

The military, inefficient and corrupt, had limited capabilities to fight an insurgency.[41] After the 1979 coup, however, the Ronald Reagan administration (1981–1989) made it a US foreign policy objective to prevent the left from seizing power and began to supply substantial military aid.[42] With US assistance, the army was able to halt, if not defeat, the revolution, but it did so at an enormous human cost. In an attempt to eliminate sources of support for the guerrillas, the army deliberately targeted the civilian population in the countryside, who were assumed to belong to, or collaborate with, the guerrillas. Throughout the war, *campesinos* risked being the target of indiscriminate violence, such as occurred at El Mozote in 1981.[43]

In the wake of the 1979 coup, the elite could no longer rely on the army to safeguard their interests. They first sought to regain control of the government through two unsuccessful coup attempts and by creating their own death squads, which were either embedded within the security forces or otherwise tolerated by the state.[44] Roberto D'Aubuisson left the National Guard, taking ANESAL intelligence files with him, and began building clandestine security structures with the financial support of wealthy businessmen, like the founder of one of El Salvador's main national newspapers, *El Diario de Hoy*, Napoleón Viera Altamirano.[45] In regular television appearances, D'Aubuisson identified "subversives," who were assassinated shortly afterward. Other victims were intimidated through threats published in the national press.[46] The government was shielded from accountability by the covert nature of death squad activities, which in turn ensured impunity for the perpetrators.[47] People in civilian clothes shot or abducted their victims in broad daylight, often torturing and killing them and leaving their mutilated corpses along roadsides or in "body dumps."[48]

The brunt of the violence in the 1980s was borne by union activists, clergy, students, teachers, human rights defenders, and journalists. Critical press organs were driven out of existence. Arrests, murders, the disappearances of its leaders, and the fears of the survivors decimated the nascent social movement. In the worst years of the war, between 1980 and 1983, more than thirty thousand civilians fell victim to the army, the security forces, and the death squads.[49]

Second, the oligarchy created its own political party in an effort to maintain its power. Founded in 1981, ARENA espoused an ideology anchored in anticommunism, capitalism, and nationalism. The formation of this openly partisan political vehicle signaled a major transformation of the way in which, henceforth, the elite would exercise its power. Under the leadership of Roberto D'Aubuisson, the party prepared to compete in elections held as part of a US-sponsored political liberalization process. While Washington continued to help fight the guerrillas militarily, it also sought to undermine the revolutionary movement by promoting democratization and a centrist government, beginning with the 1982 elections for a Constituent Assembly, which also selected a provisional president. The ARENA campaign favored the complete annihilation of the FMLN and proved hugely successful with the right. The left, fearful its candidates would be killed, was essentially unable to participate.[50] In coalition with the PCN, ARENA gained control of the Assembly and swiftly proceeded to stop recently initiated agrarian reforms.

Concerned that D'Aubuisson's involvement with death squads might prompt the US Congress to cut military aid, the Reagan administration blocked his nomination as provisional president and had an alternative candidate installed.[51] When D'Aubuisson ran for president in the 1984 elections, the United States channeled covert funding to the PDC to ensure Duarte's victory, in the hope of fostering reforms.[52] Once voted in, Duarte's centrist government was hamstrung as the rightist-controlled Assembly blocked any initiatives the elite disapproved of.[53]

In 1984, Duarte attempted to hold peace talks with the FMLN. Although hugely popular in the country, these efforts were opposed by the army and the United States, still committed to a military defeat of the left, and eventually broke down. The signing of the 1987 Esquipulas II regional peace treaty initially provided a fresh impetus for a negotiated solution to the conflict, but it was boycotted by the military and then suspended completely.[54]

The elections of the 1980s nevertheless ushered in two significant developments. The first was the opening of some political space and, with it, the reemergence of organized civil society. Labor unions demanded better wages and working conditions, community organizations asserted the basic needs of their members, and NGOs monitored the human rights situation, provided development services, and assisted refugees.[55] In 1988, social and religious organizations, through their participation in an attempted reconciliation process known as the National Debate, called for peace. This, together with opinion polls showing public support for dialogue, built a popular consensus in favor of negotiations that could not be ignored.[56]

The second development, and the one with greater long-term consequences, was the metamorphosis of ARENA into a seemingly more moderate party. After two electoral defeats in the mid-1980s, the party began to soften its image in an attempt to expand its constituency and gain power. Untainted personally by death squad ties, Alfredo Cristiani, a US-educated entrepreneur from a wealthy coffee-growing family, replaced D'Aubuisson. Although ARENA did not shed its militant anti-communism, it integrated a broader range of less hard-line businesspeople and relative moderates.

Aided by generous donations and logistical, technical, and communications skills that other parties lacked, ARENA vastly improved its vote-getting ability.[57] The party also benefited from the Duarte government's corruption and its inability to deal with the economic crisis or to end the violence. ARENA made significant gains in the 1988 municipal and legislative elections, culminating with victory in the 1989 presidential contest. Ten years after the coup that had challenged its political and economic dominance, the oligarchy returned to power. The right was now in a position not only to influence the negotiation and implementation of peace accords, but also to shape the postwar context in which civil society, including NGO advocacy, would develop.

Once in office, Cristiani restarted negotiations with the FMLN, but both the government and the army still hoped the left could be defeated militarily.[58] ARENA's acceptance of democracy reflected a purely pragmatic decision aimed at restoring the elite's dominant position in the country, rather than a commitment to a more inclusive regime as such.

An FMLN retaliatory offensive within the capital in November 1989, however, dispelled illusions of an army victory.[59] The right's options further diminished when, that same month, government troops assassinated six Jesuit priests and two employees at the Central American University, prompting widespread condemnation and a cut in US military aid.[60] Both the offensive and the murders were watershed events that spurred UN-mediated talks, which resulted in the Chapultepec Peace Accords, signed on 16 January 1992.[61]

The Postwar Period: From 1992

After twelve years of fighting and a death toll reaching seventy-five thousand, the 1992 Peace Accords ended one of the most intense internal conflicts in Latin America and left implementation of the peace in the hands of Cristiani's ARENA government. The Chapultepec Agreement was intended to end the war, promote democratization, guarantee unrestricted respect for human rights, and reunite society. In pursuit of these objectives, it mandated demilitarization, the elimination of the security forces, and the establishment of a new national civilian police force. On the other side, the guerrilla army was dissolved, the FMLN became a legal political party, and electoral and judicial reforms and socio-economic measures were instituted to address grievances. The Ad Hoc Commission reviewed the human rights records of senior army officers to purge the military, and the Truth Commission was created to investigate major human rights violations committed on both sides during the conflict.[62] The implementation of the Accords was verified by a UN peace-building operation and benefited from significant amounts of international financial aid. Both the monitoring activities and the resources were critical for applying pressure on the government to comply with the peace terms.[63] Since ARENA and the groups it represented had more to gain from the preservation of the status quo than from these looming socio-economic and political changes, resistance to the transition process was expected.

Among their accomplishments, the Accords finalized the end of hostilities, removed the military from political life, and politically integrated the left. In other respects, the outcome was more mixed. The right created continual delays and obstructions to slow the adoption of the human rights and socio-economic reforms that a democratic El Salvador would require.

The Chapultepec Accords outlined a series of measures designed to alleviate poverty and foster egalitarian development, but these remained the most neglected part of the agreement. A key component, the Social and Economic Forum, was initially boycotted by the private sector and disintegrated when it failed to produce agreements on basic economic and labor issues.[64] By creating the Ad Hoc and Truth Commissions and replacing the security forces with the new National Civilian Police (PNC), the Accords also intended to depoliticize the military structures and guarantee respect for human rights. The right resisted all these reforms. Although the army was reduced in size and constitutionally limited to national defense, the government delayed removing the officers responsible for the worst abuses, and members of the High Command were retired with full honors.[65] Despite the new constitution, a postwar crime wave saw army patrols assisting the police in enforcing public security.[66]

The Truth Commission attributed 85 percent of wartime killings to state agents and 10 percent to paramilitary groups and death squads.[67] It established that ARENA founder Roberto D'Aubuisson had personally planned and directed death squad activities, including the infamous assassination of Archbishop Óscar Romero.[68] The Commission report urged an investigation into the death squads to prevent their reactivation and recommended that named perpetrators be removed from their current positions and banned from public office for at least ten years.[69]

The right-wing press attempted to discredit the document, and both the military and the Cristiani government rejected the Truth Commission findings.[70] Five days after the publication of the report, on the initiative of President Cristiani, the ARENA-dominated Legislative Assembly passed a blanket amnesty.[71] The law contains a number of unconstitutional provisions, but the Supreme Court of Justice has upheld it.[72] (In 2013, the Court admitted a constitutional challenge of the Amnesty Law, which by the end of 2015 had yet to be ruled on.) The state thus not only failed to maintain that the violence of the past was unacceptable, but also gave those who had enforced and tolerated repression a free pass. These same individuals would subsequently seek to undermine the Accords' democratic and human rights successes.

In the months prior to El Salvador's first postwar elections, in 1994, several FMLN leaders were attacked or killed in ostensibly politically motivated circumstances.[73] The authorities' inability or unwillingness to discover the perpetrators led the United Nations to form the Joint Group for the Investigation of Politically Motivated Illegal Armed Groups. Following its investigations into the murders, the Joint Group confirmed that the old death squads had metamorphosed into highly organized criminal organizations that carried out both illicit activities and acts of political violence.[74] They aimed to destabilize the transition process by preventing the PNC from becoming an effective institution, created conditions that favored the continued militarization of society, and sparked fear among citizens to inhibit popular political organizing.[75] The Joint Group called on the government to eradicate all illegal armed groups and recommended strengthening the PNC's investigative capacity to deal with political violence and organized crime.[76]

Resistance to Police Reforms

The National Civilian Police is a key actor in the execution of present-day gang policy. Its inability to tackle El Salvador's gang situation, and violent crime more generally, reflects serious and entrenched institutional weaknesses. Many of the PNC's current problems—notably its poor investigative capacity and abusive tendencies—can be traced back to the government's deliberate efforts to prevent and subvert the formation of an independent professional police force.

The PNC was intended to replace the militarized police forces, which had lacked specialized investigative skills, maintained order through intimidation, and relied on torture to extract confessions.[77] Besides manning right-wing death squads, the police had been complicit in a range of criminal activities, including arms and drug trafficking.[78] During the civil war, a US-funded judicial reform effort created the Special Investigative Unit (SIU) and an antinarcotics unit (UEA) to improve investigative policing. However, the project emphasized training and resource provision, while neglecting the need for political commitment and leadership reform, and failed to achieve its objectives. Despite having enhanced technical capabilities, SIU officers remained ineffective and repeatedly covered up human rights abuses.[79]

The Peace Accords stipulated that the Treasury Police and the National Guard be dissolved immediately, while the National Police would be phased out during a two-year transition period. In its place emerged the PNC, whose mandate stressed the civilian, apolitical, and professional nature of the corps. A new police academy (Academia Nacional de Seguridad Pública, or ANSP) would train new recruits and instill a respect for human rights. An independent inspector-general would oversee disciplinary units tasked with monitoring police services and probing misconduct.[80] Crucially, an entry quota system dictated that during the transition phase, the new force would recruit 60 percent of its personnel at all levels from among civilians who had no direct participation in the war and, following a vetting and retraining process, 20 percent each from former National Police members and ex-FMLN combatants.

The entry quota system had been adopted in lieu of the left's earlier proposal to merge government and guerrilla armies, but it remained a controversial step. During the peace negotiations, some had warned of potentially damaging power struggles within this hybrid PNC and the danger that holdovers from the old forces would perpetuate the institutional culture of crime, violence, and corruption so central to their previous career and poison efforts to construct a professional and law-abiding police.[81] Integrating them successfully into the PNC required transforming deep-rooted attitudes and practices, something that would not be achieved merely through new training curricula and a change of uniform. The entry quota system therefore made the responsible implementation of the police reforms all the more important.[82]

From the very beginning, the right sabotaged the restructuring of the public security apparatus. The government, concerned about losing its influence over a key instrument of political and social control, agreed to the restructuring only as a way to achieve the disarmament of the FMLN, without any real commitment to its objectives.[83] Thousands of former Guardsmen and Treasury Police were folded in to the National Police, which delayed its demobilization. Further, the authorities' reluctance to provide both the ANSP and the PNC with the necessary resources for the transition hindered the training and deployment of the new force.[84]

The transition to a new security model occurred amid a postwar "crime wave" that the PNC seemed unable to deal with. The population began to lose trust in the force, and the government, rather than accelerate the deployment of a professional police, exploited public anxieties to foster nostalgia for authoritarian responses and justify the deployment of soldiers to assist with public security operations.[85]

Most significantly, the government did everything possible to ensure the dominance of authoritarian elements within the PNC. Many on the right feared that a PNC that included FMLN members and civilians would be an unreliable guarantor of order.[86] Various efforts were therefore made to retain the influence of old security forces personnel, notably by circumventing the regulations concerning their admission and promotion. For example, some ex-National Guard members and Treasury Police who may have engaged in human rights abuses entered the ANSP as civilians or joined the new force via the National Police quota.[87] In contravention of the Peace Agreements, the government also transferred the SIU and UEA—both staffed exclusively by military personnel who were associated with serious human rights and criminal violations—into the PNC without prior vetting and retraining.[88] The UEA chief, Major Óscar Peña Durán, previously identified by the Ad Hoc Commission as a drug trafficker, was inappropriately appointed deputy director of operations in 1993 and immediately imposed an authoritarian style on the PNC. Peña Durán was quickly pressured into resigning and went on to start his own private security company, yet his harmful influence over the PNC remained.[89]

A strong civilian presence in the police leadership might have prevented authoritarian attitudes from hardening within the PNC, but the government deliberately placed a disproportionate number of former military in the senior posts.[90] Their hard-line influence has remained undiminished over the years and is probably the chief reason the PNC has not only failed to become an effective and rights-respecting institution but also continued to slide back into old patterns of abuse.[91]

Issues in El Salvador's Unconsolidated Democracy

NGO advocacy was shaped in critical ways by the contemporary political and socio-economic environment. The transition to democracy was a significant achievement, and even critical observers concede that El Salvador is qualitatively very different today from how it was before the civil war. Large-scale political violence has ended; citizens participate in regular, free, and competitive elections; freedom of expression is considerably greater; and poverty rates have somewhat declined. Despite these appreciable advances, however, El Salvador remains polarized and its democracy fragile.[92]

It is important to understand the ARENA government's preference for Mano Dura and those obstacles to democracy building that limit NGO advocacy. The underlying fault line is the unwillingness of ARENA and its backers to create a society that serves the needs and interests of all its members. The party's posture, combining a commitment to protecting elite privilege with indifference to the country's long-standing problems, helps explain the government's reluctance to adopt and implement an alternative gang policy. Another set of actor-related challenges involves the police, which remains politicized, abusive, and corrupt; the economic elite, who continue to exert a strong influence over government policy in favor of the status quo; and civil society. The relative weakness of civil society shaped the degree to which NGOs could exert political weight and persuade the authorities to adopt and implement alternative gang policies.

Lingering Political-Institutional Problems

Following the signing of the Peace Accords, El Salvador made important strides in the area of civil and political rights, yet conspicuous problems persist in virtually every other sphere.[93] ARENA held the presidency from 1989 to 2009 and remains a dominant political power in the country. General dissatisfaction with the party's policy initiatives and a slumping economy enabled the FMLN to win the presidency in

2009 (and again in 2014) and make gains at the municipal and legislative levels, but political competition has occurred in very unequal conditions. Significant and unregulated campaign financing permits ARENA to outspend other parties. Further, the country's leading media outlets remain biased in favor of the political and economic elites, while routinely discrediting the left.[94] Partisan electoral authorities have long prevented the correction of chronic technical problems and irregularities in the voting process,[95] although electoral reforms of recent years have achieved important improvements. Until 2009, the right's political and economic control of the state made democracy another instrument for the preservation of elite power and privileges.

The conservative sector's lukewarm commitment to democracy contributed to weak institutions and poor regime performance. The justice system remains corrupt, politicized, and incapable of dealing with crime and violence. Impunity and continued death squad activity have progressively eroded the rule of law.[96] The Procuraduría para la Defensa de los Derechos Humanos (Office of the Human Rights Ombudsperson, or PDDH), created by the Peace Accords to safeguard human rights, is hampered by severe budgetary limitations.[97] Its recommendations are routinely ignored by other parts of the state, and its staff have received death threats.[98]

The policies of successive ARENA governments failed to resolve the population's most pressing concerns, notably socio-economic welfare and public security, which are also relevant to gang control. For most Salvadorans, the signing of the Peace Accords not only brought an end to the war but also provided an opportunity to address the structural factors that had sparked the conflict.[99] In subsequent years, public opinion consistently has identified economic issues and crime as the country's main problems. A general perception that little has been done to tackle them has led to widespread disillusionment with democracy itself.[100] This has been reflected in a persistently low voter turnout—with the exception of 2004—and, more importantly, a gradual rejection of democracy as the preferred political system.

Salvadorans continue to express support for democracy as a form of government, but since the late 1990s, a growing number say they would willingly discard their recently won political freedoms in exchange for greater socio-economic justice and security.[101] The continued high levels of crime and violence serve to perpetuate an authoritarian political culture and play into the hands of those who do not favor the construction of a democratic, more egalitarian society. Salvadorans' acute desire for greater physical safety is easily exploitable for political ends and ex-plains both the popularity of Mano Dura and the uphill task faced by NGOs advocating a more rights-respecting gang policy.

Social and Economic Exclusion

Gangs develop, at least in part, from the conditions of poverty and so-cial exclusion that mark many urban communities. Salvadoran youths have continued to join these groups despite apparent government ef-forts to address the underlying structural factors. Following its 1989 as-cent to power, ARENA initiated a series of economic reforms centering on privatization, trade liberalization, deregulation, and monetary mea-sures that culminated in the adoption of the US dollar as the national currency. The policies stimulated Central American economic integra-tion and transformed the Salvadoran economy into one based on non-traditional exports (including the products of maquila industries), ser-vices, tourism, commerce, and remittances.[102] Until 1996, the country experienced high economic growth, which benefited the financial sec-tor and permitted the elite to expand its wealth.[103] Economic growth has been low for many years, and the Central America Free Trade Agree-ment that entered into force in 2006 deepened existing wealth dispar-ities. Ordinary Salvadorans were hit disproportionately hard by the reforms and have seen no substantial improvement in their living condi-tions since then.

In 2003, the year Mano Dura was launched, 36.1 percent of the pop-ulation remained in poverty, and the proportion of those in absolute or extreme poverty reached 14.4 percent.[104] According to the household survey of 2014, 31.8 percent of Salvadorans lived in poverty, including 7.6 percent in extreme poverty. Despite an increase in social spending, many still lack access to basic social services. Figures for 2014 show that 13.9 percent of homes had no source for potable water, 6.3 percent had no sanitary services, 48.7 percent had no access to rubbish collection, and 16 percent lacked electricity. An alarming 76.2 percent of Salvador-ans had no medical insurance, and 65.1 percent had no social security.[105]

One of the country's challenges is to create better educational and economic opportunities, particularly for its youth. El Salvador is a pre-dominantly young nation, with 55.5 percent below the age of thirty.[106] Their social mobility is impeded by a poor education system and the in-capacity of the labor market to absorb the growing workforce. Young

people, especially males, have been disproportionately affected by unemployment, and the absence of sufficient and decent jobs has confined
an increasing number of individuals to a situation of underemployment.

After a slight decline in the early 1990s, income inequality rose
again: between 1992 and 2002, the top quintile increased its share of national wealth from 54.5 percent to 58.3 percent while that of the lowest quintile declined from 3.2 percent to 2.4 percent. In 2002, the richest 20 percent of society received twenty-four times the income of the
poorest 20 percent.[107] In 2012, the richest 20 percent of society received
48.4 percent of the national income, while the poorest 20 percent of society received only 4.9 percent.[108] If the country is to achieve greater human development and equality, it must have a fairer tax structure and
crack down on tax evasion. While the private sector is not opposed to
better social welfare policies, it remains unwilling to pay for them.[109]

Poverty appears to have diminished in the postwar period, but, according to a government study on multidimensional poverty published
in 2015, the number of indicators used to measure poverty needs to be
expanded in order to measure quality of life, not just income. If calcula-
tions are adjusted, the national rate of multidimensional poverty stands
at 35.2 percent.[110]

Since 1996, the lack of decent job opportunities has prompted an increasing number of Salvadorans to leave the country and seek employment abroad, often as undocumented migrants.[111] Today an estimated
2 million Salvadorans live and work in the United States and send
home a portion of their earnings.[112] By 2000, the inflow of remittances
reached US $1.750 billion, or 13.2 percent of the El Salvador GDP, and
in 2004, 22 percent of Salvadoran homes received remittances totaling
US $2.548 billion, or 16 percent of the GDP.[113] In 2013, the remittances
totaled US $3,910.9 billion, or 16.4 percent of the GDP.[114] These pay-
ments are not only a key support of the domestic economy, but also a
principal source of income for poor families.

Both migration and the remittances, by absorbing excess labor and
ameliorating the conditions of those who stayed behind, respectively,
have done more than public policies to raise El Salvador's human development and poverty standards.[115] Successive governments have not
made serious efforts to improve basic services or develop meaningful
employment. The lack of political will to undertake substantial social
transformation aggravated the gang problem and lay behind the resistance of ARENA administrations to comprehensive gang control.

Crime and Violence

Crime and violence, along with social exclusion, rank as El Salvador's most serious problems. Although the country has historically had a high murder rate, it has risen to alarming levels during the postwar period. The numbers are fluctuating, and due to different institutional measurements, reliable figures are hard to come by. According to the Fiscalía General de la República (Office of the Attorney General of the Republic, or FGR), the number of murders reached 138 per 100,000 inhabitants between 1994 and 1995.[116] Thereafter, the rate declined, only to escalate again during the Mano Dura period (2003–2006), the pre-gang truce years (2009–2011), and the post-gang truce years (2014–2015). In 2009, with a murder rate of 71 per 100,000 inhabitants, El Salvador ranked as one of the most violent countries in the world, and in 2015, it topped this indicator, with a murder rate of 103 per 100,000 inhabitants.[117]

The World Health Organization considers homicide rates over 10 per 100,000 inhabitants as an epidemic, and there is understandable alarm concerning the enormous economic and social costs such levels of violence inflict on society. The United Nations Development Program (UNDP), for example, has calculated that in 2003 alone, El Salvador spent some US $1.717 billion, or 11.5 percent of the GDP, for health, administration of justice, private security, and loss of investment and property related to social violence.[118] In 2007, the estimated economic cost of violence reached US $2.225 billion, or 10.9 percent of the GDP.[119]

Interestingly, the geographical distribution of homicides provides a clue as to why the nation continues to squander scarce human, physical, and material resources rather than going after the causes of endemic violence. Although crime and violence cause citizens to feel insecure, the urban poor are disproportionately affected. They are separated both spatially and socially from the middle-class city of public services and general security.[120] In San Salvador, a city with one of the highest murder rates in the country, marginal neighborhoods have long seen much greater levels of violence than more affluent areas.[121] Social exclusion may be one factor, but a culture of violence, an ineffective justice system (on which more below), and the availability of firearms are also factors.[122] An estimated 450,000 weapons are in civilian hands, and their ubiquity makes violence much more lethal: in 2003, they were used in 71 percent of homicides.[123] To this day, firearms are used in at least seven out of ten murders.[124]

The public's perception of street gang violence is that it has increased in recent years. Yet, establishing what percentage of homicides can accurately be blamed on gang violence has been a rather difficult task. Figures vary widely, depending on the source. In 2004, for example, the PNC attributed up to 80 percent of murders to the gangs, while the Instituto de Medicina Legal (Institute of Legal Medicine, or IML) suggested that it might be a mere 10 percent.[125] In 2015, by contrast, the PNC attributed some 30 percent of homicides to the gangs, whereas the presidency claimed the figure stood at 60 percent.[126] Only sound investigation can shed light on the perpetrators and the motives for the thousands of homicides that annually occur in El Salvador, but the investigative capacity of both police and prosecutors has remained extremely deficient.[127] This fundamental weakness has precluded better crime control over the years and prompted the punitive anti-gang legislation enacted in 2003.

According to one survey, more than 75 percent of citizens thought human rights favored criminals and prevented the state from dealing with them.[128] Many better-off Salvadorans, frustrated by insecurity and police ineffectiveness, have turned to private, at times illegal, means, such as security guards, personal firearms, and even *sicariato* (contract killings), to ensure their safety.[129] Aided by incendiary media reporting, conservative politicians have exploited public anxiety about crime to justify tougher laws and militarized policing.[130] Mano Dura merely followed an established preference for punitive measures that offer political credit and no commitment to changing the status quo.

Actions that could have had a real impact on the levels of crime and violence, such as developing a comprehensive crime strategy and greater precision in the recording of homicides, have been neglected. So far, the three institutions (PNC, IML, and FGR) that collect the relevant statistics typically publish different figures, and attempts since 2005 to harmonize data-collection methods have produced mixed results.[131] The failure even to ensure reliable data for policy making highlights the leadership's utter disinterest in dealing with one of the country's most serious problems.

Another problem is the prevalence of firearms among civilians. The authorities have done little to tackle the black market or sufficiently tighten the laws on gun possession. Although the firearms legislation has undergone a series of reforms since its adoption in 1999, it entails no restriction on the number of weapons a citizen may own and even permits civilians to use assault rifles.[132] Since 2007, the government has been creating gun-free zones in municipalities with critical levels of crime and violence.[133] In some cases, officials' conflicts of interest, such as owning gun shops or providing private security, may preclude them, in the absence of legal constraints, from acting in the public interest.[134]

Actors

Of all homicides committed in 2005, only 3.8 percent were investigated and resulted in a conviction.[135] Between 2011 and 2013, convictions were obtained in only 5 percent of homicides.[136] The chronically poor investigative capacity of both police and prosecutors confers impunity and promotes crime, while the lack of reliable data also prevents lawmakers from having a clear understanding of the problem's causes. This means there is little reason to believe the official justification for Mano Dura: that gangs are responsible for the majority of homicides. While giving more resources to the relevant institutions makes sense, there is no reason to assume that their leadership is committed to resolving more cases. One recent study indicates that police tend to dismiss homicides in which the victims are poor and/or suspected gang members as gang-related killings that do not merit investigation.[137]

The National Civilian Police

The politicization of the police, notably in the selection of its most senior personnel, continues. Under ARENA rule, the PNC director-general's post was staffed by either a civilian who identified more or less explicitly with that party (Mauricio Sandoval and Rodrigo Ávila) or a member of the old security forces (Ricardo Menesses).[138] Ex-military officers have often dominated the command structure and, with the approval of their superiors, reconverted the post–Peace Accords police back into a vertical and authoritarian force.[139] In late 2000, revelations about police involvement in illicit activities resulted in a massive purge of the institution. While the cleanup eliminated some criminal elements, it also was a useful excuse to expel "inconvenient" individuals, among them a disproportionate number of officers whose origins had been with the FMLN.[140] The removal of individuals who might have opposed corrupt influences within the organization, especially from the higher ranks, made it easier for abusive practices to flourish.

PNC professionalism has been undermined in a variety of ways. The institution's budget has been progressively reduced over the years, limiting necessary equipment upgrades and pay and training for personnel.[141] While this affects the force's ability to carry out its roles, it also prevents the hiring of high-quality personnel and leads to graft and poor discipline. Corruption, a persistent problem within the PNC, has been actively encouraged by some of its directors while being tolerated at the highest levels of government. For example, during Sandoval's tenure, the *partida secreta* (a discretionary presidential spending account, declared unconstitutional in 2010) supplied monthly kickbacks to individuals within the FGR and the PNC, including the inspector-general, the police leadership, and elite units.[142] Commissioner Menesses, a professed evangelical Christian, founded a sizeable religious movement within the PNC that is linked to the Tabernáculo Bíblico Bautista Amigos de Israel, one of the fastest-growing evangelical churches in El Salvador. (Menesses has been under investigation for collusion with a known drug trafficker and in 2010 was expelled from the PNC.) Promotions and preferential access to off-duty work came to depend on membership in this church or other bonds of loyalty to the police leadership.[143] Partial police reforms, as well as ineffective oversight, have meant that corruption and collusion with organized crime have persisted in the PNC.[144]

Another serious problem is the pervasive tolerance of human rights violations, compounded by the absence of effective control mechanisms. Although the police academy provides new recruits with the necessary training, the absence of a human rights culture within the PNC makes it difficult to promote respect for citizens' rights among the lower ranks.[145] Internal disciplinary systems should play a key role in preventing police abuse and are generally evaluated as an important indicator of authorities' commitment to professional conduct and the rule of law.[146] An outside inspector-general initially oversaw the PNC disciplinary units, but in 2001, a new organic law brought this post under the authority of the director-general and, in doing so, seriously undermined the existing system of checks and balances.[147] With insufficient resources and no organizational independence, the inspector-general could not exercise appropriate control over police abuse and ultimately favored the impunity of perpetrators.[148] In 2014, the body was placed under the command of the Ministry of Justice and Public Security, but in practice this has not meant greater accountability. The current inspector-general, for example, has defended officers who kill in supposed self-defense and has declared reports of extrajudicial executions an urban legend.[149]

The PDDH has repeatedly condemned the excessive use of force, beatings of detainees, and torture to extract confessions, sometimes done in the presence of police chiefs.[150] Reforms were ignored, and the frequency of the abuses intensified during the 2000s.[151] Between 2004 and 2006, the number of cases rose in which police-run social cleansing groups beat or tortured and subsequently killed individuals, including gang members, virtually unchecked by investigations or prosecutions.[152] Police brutality against suspects has remained a pervasive and unchecked problem.[153]

Although the government rejected allegations that extermination groups were operating anywhere within the state,[154] an interviewee confirmed that a death squad structure had indeed developed within the PNC.[155] Managed by ex-military personnel, Grupo Omega maintained intelligence units within some of the ministries and received information and logistical support from senior PNC officials, including Commissioner Douglas Omar García Funes and Commissioner José Luis Tobar Prieto.[156] At one time, three extermination groups were embedded in the police elite units. There is an urgent need to conduct inquiries into the composition, operation, and financing of these structures and to investigate those involved in them. The failure of the postwar governments to eradicate the death squads of earlier periods is precisely what permits the persistence of these destructive practices. The lack of investigations suggests that the authorities condone death squad activity and police abuse. Given the reluctance of the government and the PNC hierarchy to enforce professionalism and respect for rights in the police corps, it is difficult to see how NGOs could successfully promote a form of gang control that eschews brute force.

The Economic Elite

To understand the limits of NGO activism, it is crucial to grasp the influence that El Salvador's affluent minority exerts over the state and public policy making. Studies have documented how the elite consolidated its power over the decades through the further strengthening of kinship ties and business alliances among the dominant family groups.[157] The economic diversification that began in earlier periods and intensified with the reforms of the 1990s reconfigured the elite to some extent. Factors such as the war and the structural shift from an agro-export model to a new growth pattern based on nontraditional exports, services, and commerce also prompted some businesses to expand their activities within Central America.[158] Since 1990, both the elite globalized economic class that emerged from this process and the transnational corporations that were drawn to the isthmus by trade liberalization and privatization have pushed for even stronger regional economic integration. Competition between these two powerful constituencies, however, intensified polarization within the private sector, with serious consequences for Salvadoran society as a whole.[159]

After a renewed process of transformation, the elite can nowadays be categorized as follows: transnational groups, more powerful than the others and with investment elsewhere in Central America; national elites, with investment chiefly in El Salvador and thus politically very influential; and new elites, including the representatives of transnational corporations and members of the FMLN who amass fortunes through Alba Petróleos and exercise great influence over the Sánchez Cerén government (2014–2019).[160]

Besides their ability to influence policy making through institutions, including the media, one of the more direct ways El Salvador's elite can shape government policies and programs is through their control of ARENA. Many businessmen have held important posts in past administrations, and the economic agendas of right-wing governments have tended, unsurprisingly, to coincide with the agenda of the country's wealthy.[161]

Of greatest concern is the elite's reliance on informal lobbying mechanisms and their ability to obtain privileged access to the highest authorities.[162] Many Salvadorans believe that these big businesses determined economic policy and were the only ones to have benefited from the policies of ARENA governments, while leaving the rest of Salvadoran society marginalized.[163]

Civil Society

NGO advocacy is part of the changing dynamics of civil society activism in El Salvador. Once at the forefront of calls for peace and democratization, the social movement lost its unity and sense of purpose when these objectives were achieved. Since then, it has remained weak and fragmented, lacking the analytical capacity, creativity, and strategic skills necessary to increase its political influence as the need for social reform has deepened.[164] Movement struggles are now oriented toward sectorial demands, such as health, the environment, women's rights, consumer protection, and human rights; this very diversity has prevented activists from developing a common agenda. Broad mobilizations, like the famous *marchas blancas* (white marches) against the privatization of the public health system between 1999 and 2003, are rare, and the overall atmosphere is marked by widespread apathy.[165] Analysts have attributed the absence of a strong and coherent social movement to the leadership vacuum that developed when middle-class activists gravitated to the newly legalized FMLN.[166] This trend may have been compounded, however, by the growth of the NGO sector.

Salvadoran NGOs formed in the course of the armed conflict, but it was in the postwar period when they really began to flourish. New funding requirements have encouraged many civil society groups to adopt NGO status. El Salvador has experienced a veritable NGO boom since 1979. A mere twenty-two of these organizations were registered in that year; the number grew to seventy-four during the war, and it now exceeds five thousand.[167] This sector attracted many middle-class professionals away from El Salvador's social and civil rights movements, sapping their intellectual strength. The main consequence of these developments, however, has been the fragmentation of civil society into small and competing NGOs.[168] They risk duplicating activities, and, thanks in part to the funding structures of international donor organizations, their work tends to focus on a series of isolated projects rather than on the creation of conditions for long-term social and political change.[169]

In recent years, Salvadoran NGOs have shown little capacity to propose alternatives to existing policies or influence public opinion.[170] They are limited by internal weaknesses and exogenous constraints, both of which must be overcome if NGOs hope to make a greater political impact. On the one hand, the organizations lack adequate human and financial resources, a common agenda, and strategic alliances.[171] On the other hand, they operate in a new political environment that frowns on the confrontational behavior of the past and is biased toward the search for consensual solutions. NGOs have been largely supportive of democratic forms of action, such as lobbying of public officials, but unequal access to decisionmakers and the press leaves them struggling for fair representation.[172] Moreover, partisan divisions within civil society—as well as polarization between civil society and the state—hamper alliances, sharpen policy debates, and complicate the adoption of technical, not political, responses to policy issues.

The challenge for NGOs is to create more space for pluralistic participation and expression. They must strengthen their capacity to effect change and give greater priority to networking, advocacy, and community empowerment, with support for the broader social movement toward economic and political fairness.[173] Above all, they must acquire a better understanding of how El Salvador's existing power structures operate and how these might be influenced.

Conclusion

Historically, El Salvador's political and economic affairs have revolved around the country's elite. Throughout republican times, this powerful minority used its influence over the state to protect its privileges while the rest of the population was marginalized. Reform efforts met with strenuous resistance, and real or potential challengers to the status quo were depicted as a threat to society to be contained by force. For five decades, the oligarchy relied on the military to protect elite interests, but when this alliance broke down, the landowning and business elite sought to reassert itself through state-sponsored violence and the creation of ARENA. The Mano Dura discourse of the 2000s, following this familiar pattern, painted Salvadoran street gangs as a new menace that required authoritarian social control. Public demand that the government do something to improve security made it likely that Mano Dura would be greeted with applause, regardless of its suppressive nature or level of effectiveness.

ARENA offered a political project that the elite could rally around. It achieved a major electoral triumph in the 1989 presidential contest and took steps to negotiate an end to the civil war. While many factors facilitated a political settlement of the armed conflict, one key reason was the shift in elite economic interests toward globalization and the associated need to manage a transition to democracy. A moderate faction decided that the introduction of a pluralistic political system was an acceptable concession in return for an end to the fighting, but de jure democratization was not accompanied by needed changes in elite political culture or any commitment to democratic consolidation. Predictably marred by obstructionism, the transition process advanced largely due to international financing and monitoring. In recent years, many of those initial gains have been halted or reversed. El Salvador's democracy remains weak, with many of its institutions maintaining authoritarian practices.

The country continues to lack a democratic political culture and well-resourced, responsive institutions, including unaligned, independent media. Successive ARENA governments have made no serious effort to reduce social exclusion or to provide all citizens with adequate public security. Instead, economic policy has exacerbated existing inequalities, while public anxiety about crime is exploited to foster nostalgia for authoritarian responses, justify tougher laws, and militarize policing.

At the time Mano Dura was launched, El Salvador remained highly polarized, complicating rational policy debates, and had developed two characteristics that made NGO advocacy of alternative gang control difficult. First, the police had been turned into an authoritarian and abusive force that lacked a culture of human rights or an investigative capacity to tackle gang crime and violence. Second, elite influence over the state precluded the rest of society from participating in the decision-making process. The ARENA mandate to protect elite interests drove government resistance to the implementation of a comprehensive and rights-respecting gang policy. The complexity of these contextual constraints in turn would require NGOs to contest Mano Dura in creative ways, as well as to overcome internal weaknesses and unequal access to decisionmakers and the press.

CHAPTER 2

Mano Dura

El Salvador has had a long-standing gang problem, which assumed greater visibility after the civil war ended in 1992 and Salvadoran youths deported from the United States brought with them the violent US street gang culture. Despite mounting public concern about the impact of gang activity on public safety, the authorities failed to tackle the problem in a coherent manner for years. In 2003, the outgoing Francisco Flores government launched a gang policy in the form of its widely publicized Mano Dura plan. The measure proved immensely popular and was continued by the succeeding Antonio Saca administration, though with certain modifications.

This chapter analyzes why gang control suddenly became a national priority and what changes the gang policy underwent once it became the target of judicial and civil society criticism. The evidence suggests that Mano Dura was a cynical populist move to win votes rather than a genuine effort to institute effective gang control, and the measure was quietly buried once it became a political liability. Even the prevention and rehabilitation initiatives that the Saca administration adopted were meant to deflect further criticism rather than represent a serious effort to reduce gang crime and violence. Suppression remained the preferred approach for a government reluctant to allocate more resources to investigative policing or do anything substantive to lessen the social marginalization that many Salvadorans endure.

The Flores Administration: Mano Dura

On 23 July 2003, President Francisco Flores launched Mano Dura from one of the capital's gang-controlled neighborhoods. Positioned in front of a wall covered with oversized graffiti, he informed the assembled journalists that gang members would be systematically arrested and order thus re-established in the affected communities.[1] Since the police had publicly attributed the majority of homicides to these groups, the implication was that the plan would not only dismantle the gangs, but also lower the country's high levels of violent crime.[2] In the following months, amid considerable media publicity, the authorities embarked on graffiti removal; joint police/military anti-gang squads (Grupos de Tarea Antipandilla, or GTA) could be seen patrolling the streets; and police carried out massive area sweeps to detain suspected gang members. The young men and women seized in these operations were often publicly exhibited to the press, which played a critical role in framing Mano Dura as an effective policy by supplying abundant coverage of these spectacular crackdowns.

A temporary anti-gang law (Ley Anti Maras) was meant to facilitate the criminal prosecution of arrested gang members. The bill, intended to expire after six months, made gang membership itself a crime, punishable by two to six years in prison, and targeted anyone above the age of twelve. These provisions violated a number of constitutional guarantees and international human rights norms, such as lowering the age of legal responsibility to thirteen and requiring no evidence of any offense. By this law, the police could detain anyone they thought might be a gang member, based on superficial features like tattoos, language, or clothing. The proposed law brought immediate resistance from human rights defenders, judges, and opposition politicians. Those who objected insisted that there was no need for this kind of special legislation and called for greater emphasis on prevention and rehabilitation to mitigate the gang problem.[3] The government was faced with an unexpected dilemma when judges released most of the recently detained gang members for lack of evidence.

However, under relentless pressure from President Flores and other officials, ARENA and PCN lawmakers ratified the decree in October 2003.[4] The PDDH quickly submitted a constitutional challenge to the new measure, and many judges opted not to apply a law they considered to be in violation of human rights.[5] The Supreme Court of Justice eventually ruled the legislation to be unconstitutional, but the ruling came only days before the Ley Anti Maras was due to expire. With presidential elections approaching, the decision helped the ruling party save face.[6] Furthermore, on the day the verdict was delivered, the Legislative Assembly passed another three-month anti-gang act that closely resembled the previous measure.[7] In June 2004, domestic critics of the law were encouraged when the United Nations Committee on the Rights of the Child (UNCRC) requested that the law be vacated. At the same time, President Saca entered office and prepared to announce his own gang policy.[8]

Meanwhile, government and law enforcement officials defended their approach to gang control, insisting that Mano Dura served to take dangerous gang members off the streets, lower the homicide rate, and restore tranquility in the communities.[9] The judges, who continued to release gang members if no evidence of an offense was presented, were publicly accused of siding with criminals and interfering with the authorities' efforts to provide public security.[10] The crackdown enabled the police to gather data on many of El Salvador's gang members, but it also squandered scarce resources and was utterly ineffective in securing convictions or controlling crime. Between 23 July 2003 and 30 August 2004, when the launch of Súper Mano Dura signaled the beginning of a new phase in gang control, police made a total of 19,275 gang-related arrests (including repeat arrests), but more than 95 percent of these cases were dismissed in court.[11] More importantly, IML data showed that the homicide rate rose from 2,388 murders in 2003 to 2,933 in 2004.[12] Press coverage glossed over these problems and helped sustain public support for the measure, despite its discriminatory nature, disregard for basic rights, and failure to curb crime and violence.

Mano Dura's Populism and Popularity

As noted, prior to 2003, the authorities had not developed a consistent approach to El Salvador's street gangs. Critics might argue that even Mano Dura did not amount to a full-fledged strategy or policy but was merely a codification of the police's suppression tactics. Nonetheless, the measure constituted the first explicit national attempt to address the gang problem. Since there had been no recent spike in gang violence and homicide figures had actually declined in the years prior to Mano Dura's enactment, what explains the sudden need for gang control? The cynical explanation is that Mano Dura was a penal populist attempt to improve ARENA's electoral advantage in the run-up to the 2004 presidential elections. ("Penal populism" describes criminality as the result of willful antisocial behavior, rather than a symptom of social exclusion, and promotes imprisonment as a principal crime reduction strategy.[13]) Mano Dura exploited public anxiety about crime by depicting gangs as the main source of citizens' insecurity and offered harsh punitive measures as the best response. Although fundamentally weak, the plan focused on a highly visible target, paving the way for some striking police operations. These actions, in the short term at least, boosted ARENA's image while circumventing messy criminal investigations and expensive, time-consuming prevention and rehabilitation programs.

At the time Mano Dura was launched, El Salvador was barely eight months away from the 2004 presidential elections. Although ARENA had held the presidency since 1989 and dominated the Legislative Assembly in coalition with other right-wing parties, it was beginning to suffer increasing losses at the municipal and legislative levels. Growing disenchantment with the country's weakening economy benefited the FMLN, which steadily augmented its share of seats in the Legislative Assembly and municipalities. The first significant swing occurred when the left regained control of the San Salvador mayor's office in 1997. The trend deepened with the elections of 2000 and 2003, in which the FMLN overtook its main adversary, ARENA, in the Legislative Assembly.[14] Although victory would again go to the right in 2004, in the months preceding the election, many felt that the FMLN's recent gains had strengthened its prospects for winning power.[15] The ruling class was alarmed at the possible erosion of its privileges, and ARENA would rapidly have to bolster its own electoral appeal if it was to retain its influence over the state.

Surveys have shown that Salvadorans favor the FMLN if they are concerned with economic issues at the time of an election and ARENA if they are preoccupied with crime.[16] For much of 2003, public opinion identified the economy as the overriding problem facing the nation, an assessment that eroded ARENA's levels of support.[17] In an October 2003 poll, however, almost half the population indicated that crime and public insecurity were their most important concerns, rather than the economy, and for the first time, as many as 21 percent of respondents singled out street gangs as the key problem.[18] The same survey revealed that 88 percent of interviewees were in favor of Mano Dura, and a majority believed the plan would help lower crime.[19] In the space of a few months, ARENA displaced the FMLN in polls of voters' intentions.[20]

One factor behind this shift was the popularity of ARENA's presidential candidate, but another was the introduction and promotion of Mano Dura.[21] The ruling party's good showing might have been an unintended effect of the plan rather than its purpose, but both the timing and the inconsistent nature of the gang policy imply that the strategy's primary aim was not to reduce gang violence, but to win votes. This interpretation was confirmed by a leaked memo from ARENA's executive council, which acknowledged that Mano Dura's popularity gave ARENA an immediate opportunity to associate itself with a winning theme and present itself as the party toughest on crime.[22]

Mano Dura and the accompanying media campaign allowed the government to deflect attention from its poor economic performance and define the gangs as the most pressing national problem, for which it offered the appropriate solution. The measure instantly appealed to a population that lived in constant fear of victimization. Once it was clear that gang control gave ARENA substantial political benefits, it became a central campaign theme and was one of the reasons for the right's presidential victory.[23] Difficulties such as widespread criticism of suppressive crackdowns, the judges' lack of cooperation, and the expiration of the Ley Anti Maras required newly inaugurated President Antonio Saca to adopt a revised gang policy.

The Saca Administration: Súper Mano Dura

The new government's strategic plan recognized that crime and violence remained one of the country's main challenges. The plan affirmed that a special effort would be made to address the gang problem through prevention, law enforcement, and the rehabilitation of gang members.[24] Prior to the launch of Súper Mano Dura, each of its components went through a consultation process with a wide range of experts and stakeholders. In mid-2004, the Foro Antipandillas (Anti-Gang Forum) brought together government and police officials, judges, NGOs, and international donor agencies in what was billed as a consensus approach to gang control. The proposals that emerged during the two-week event were meant to constitute the basis of President Saca's gang policy, but the intent of the administration's organization of the roundtable was to secure new punitive anti-gang legislation. Some prevention and rehabilitation initiatives were debated and subsequently adopted to placate critics of Mano Dura, but these were trivial and did not amount to a fundamental policy change.

The forum was structured around three thematic roundtables: criminal and criminal procedural laws, juvenile penal legislation, and prevention and rehabilitation. The majority of participants rejected the creation of special anti-gang legislation. Instead, they agreed on an amendment of Article 345 of the Penal Code, which sanctions membership in an "illicit association," that is, a group or organization whose purpose is the perpetration of crimes.[25] Prevention would require better education and job opportunities for young people and improvements in the community environment. Similarly, rehabilitation of gang members would entail psychosocial assistance, economic opportunities, and intervention in the family and community.[26]

The legal reforms were instantly sent to the Legislative Assembly and enacted in early August 2004. At the end of that month, President Saca formally initiated Súper Mano Dura and deployed more anti-gang task forces in gang-affected areas. Continuing its raids, the PNC sought to dismantle the gangs through the targeted arrest of their leaders.[27] At the same time, the police largely persisted with their established method of detaining individuals merely for suspected gang membership. They claimed that the street gangs were criminal organizations and anyone who displayed gang-specific tattoos could be prosecuted. Judges, however, remained unconvinced and continued to release gang members if there was insufficient evidence of a crime.[28]

While the authorities kept gang suppression a priority, the new prevention and rehabilitation programs were introduced only after a considerable delay. Mano Amiga was aimed at preventing at-risk youths from joining gangs, while Mano Extendida sought to help gang members reintegrate into society. The institutions tasked with the implementation of these initiatives were the Secretaría de la Juventud (Youth Secretariat, or SJ) and the Consejo Nacional de Seguridad Pública (National Council of Public Security, or CNSP).

The Secretaría de la Juventud

The Secretaría de la Juventud, an office within the Presidency of the Republic, was established in 2004 to execute the presidential program JóvenES and promote the development of young people.[29] (The Mauricio Funes administration closed the Youth Secretariat in 2011.) In pursuit of this objective, the SJ carried out a nationwide survey of youths' needs and subsequently developed the National Youth Plan 2005–2015. The survey, in its published version, revealed little useful data about the difficulties facing young Salvadorans and constituted a weak foundation on which to build public policy.[30] The plan made no reference to the ideas proposed during the Anti-Gang Forum and offered no coherent strategy to improve the quality of life of gang members or at-risk youth.[31] One of its proposals concerned "Vulnerable Groups" and proposed Mano Amiga and Mano Extendida.

Although Mano Amiga was publicized as a gang prevention program, it was outlined in the plan as a much broader form of early intervention, designed to assist vulnerable youths to avoid crime, gangs, drug addiction, and teenage pregnancies. Similarly, Mano Extendida was described as an initiative to rehabilitate and reintegrate into society gang members, juvenile offenders, drug addicts, and street children between the ages of fifteen and twenty-four years. Its programs ostensibly taught values; offered spiritual assistance, education, and job training; provided health services, including tattoo removal; offered cultural and sports activities; and facilitated the search for employment. The plan's approach of *"focalización"* (focusing) meant a targeting of the twenty communities most affected by crime and violence.[32] Programs were carried out by a multi-agency system, which was coordinated and managed by the Youth Secretariat.[33] The SJ oversaw the participation of other institutions with youth-related functions—such as ministries and local governments, the police, the CNSP, NGOs, churches, and the private sector—and produced a number of brochures that described its mission and activities. However, meetings with officials at the Youth Secretariat's headquarters offered little concrete information.[34] The meetings confirmed the perception that the Youth Secretariat and its programs had critical problems.

At the institutional level, the Youth Secretariat's broad mandate to foster the development of all youths put it in direct competition for scarce resources with the Instituto Salvadoreño para el Desarrollo Integral de la Niñez y la Adolescencia (Salvadoran Institute for the Comprehensive Development of Children and Adolescents, or ISNA), the country's child protection agency. The ISNA is best known for administering the country's juvenile detention centers, but has a wide range of functions aimed at ensuring the well-being of all individuals below the age of eighteen years.

Chronically under-resourced, the ISNA has struggled for years to meet its responsibilities.[35] Rather than further inflating the state bureaucracy and its budget with a new agency, it would have made more sense to restructure existing institutions and mandate the Youth Secretariat to coordinate national gang policy, which was sorely needed in El Salvador. The SJ seemed intended to showcase President Saca's commitment to prevention and rehabilitation by spending vast amounts of public money on such things as promotion, instead of producing tangible, sustained results.[36] The administration had shown little, if any, interest in developing a strong and effective institution. The secretary's post was held by three different individuals in as many years, while most technical staff lacked the necessary expertise to deal with the complex issues of gang control. Many were young ARENA members who received generous salaries while being groomed as future party cadres.[37]

The community-level gang work carried out by the institution also suffered from a series of inconsistencies. *Focalización* was meant to concentrate gang mitigation efforts in the most crime-ridden zones. Local programs to alleviate the community factors that spawn gangs, however, must be combined with a comprehensive national gang strategy that addresses broader systemic issues, such as gun control, economic development, development of urban infrastructure, improved educational opportunities, and access to jobs and vocational training.[38] In reality, these are precisely the areas that no ARENA government wanted to tackle. Gang scholars stress that a gang policy needs to correctly target individuals, groups, and communities to be effective.[39] In the absence of publicly available information, it was impossible to assess the criteria the SJ used to select program participants. The fact that communities were chosen for their homicide rates rather than because of their gang problems suggests that there was either no awareness of the need for gang-specific targeting or no clear definition of the policy's goals. Either case points to a lack of explicit capacities and intentions to undertake gang control.

There was a further degree of arbitrariness in the choice of the communities. Some gang-affected places were ignored entirely because their homicide indicators were not considered serious enough to warrant inclusion in the program.[40] Other areas were disregarded because their gang problem was so severe that they were considered to be beyond all hope, meriting only suppression.[41] What is worse, those within the SJ technical staff with no ties to ARENA were pressured to give preference to municipalities governed by that party.[42] Where the Youth Secretariat did maintain a presence, it helped create youth committees. However, their leaders reportedly acted as *orejas* (government informants) and were said to inform party affiliates if local residents planned to hold demonstrations or meetings with the FMLN mayor.[43]

The coordinating function of the SJ was no more coherent than its community-related activities. Although the institution was tasked with synchronizing, monitoring, and evaluating existing initiatives and disseminating their results, it made only feeble attempts to fulfill this part of its mandate. One NGO working with at-risk youths and imprisoned gang members professed never to have been contacted.[44] Another affirmed that not only had it not been offered assistance, but the government had accused it of covering up gang crime and threatened to withdraw its legal status if its gang prevention program continued.[45]

For most of those who collaborated with the SJ, the encounter was disappointing. One NGO, offered some funding in return for sharing its experience, faced repeated delays and was still waiting to be reimbursed a year later.[46] The Youth Secretariat seemed to associate itself with other actors' efforts merely for political capital. On repeated occasions, the SJ offered groups financial contributions and then requested that the money be spent on its own promotional agenda. Then either the secretary or the President of the Republic would appear in the inauguration ceremony. Media publicity ensured that these officials reaped the credit for activities that others had organized.[47]

Such incidents kindled resentment among those who were interested in working for Salvadoran youths, harmed the government's credibility with the organizations, and suggest that the authorities' primary goal was image management rather than gang control. This perception is reinforced by the fact that nothing was done to balance suppression with prevention and rehabilitation efforts.

Several interviewees expressed concern that their rehabilitation work in the communities was hindered by police harassment and the arrests of gang members who were clearly identified as program participants. In one case, the project organizer asked the PNC's director-general for an explanation and was informed that gang members merely joined rehabilitation initiatives to obtain a safe-conduct.[48] The possibility that some gang youths manipulate those who seek to help them start a new life cannot be ruled out and did reportedly occur.[49] If this is the dominant assumption, however, then nonrepressive gang control approaches are thwarted from the beginning. If the SJ had taken its coordinating function seriously, it would have sought to ensure that the police did not interfere with these rehabilitative activities.

It is unclear what the Youth Secretariat's achievements were. No evaluations of either its output or the programs it monitored are publicly available.[50] The SJ appeared to be a fundamentally weak and politicized institution that operated with little transparency and displayed neither a vision of comprehensive gang control nor a real interest in it. The fact that one of the institutions expressly created to promote prevention and rehabilitation failed in its most basic responsibilities casts doubt on the Saca government's commitment to reducing gang violence.

The Consejo Nacional de Seguridad Pública

Unlike the SJ, the Consejo Nacional de Seguridad Pública was actively engaged in gang prevention and rehabilitation. The United Nations had originally proposed the creation of this body to advise the President of the Republic in public security matters. In 1996, the administration of President Armando Calderón Sol (1994–1999) agreed to establish the CNSP, more in response to international pressure than out of conviction that it was necessary.[51] In its early years, the institution produced a series of important studies, but its recommendations were rarely implemented.[52] The Flores government then changed the Council's profile, assigning it a role in crime prevention. Subsequently, its mandate was extended to cover gang rehabilitation. Like the Youth Secretariat, the CNSP was also closed by President Funes in 2011 in order to create the Consejo Nacional de la Juventud (National Youth Council, or CONJUVE) and in 2012, the Instituto Nacional de la Juventud (National Youth Institute, or INJUVE).

VIOLENCE PREVENTION

Through its Program for the Social Prevention of Violence and Crime, the CNSP had been helping with community organizing, education and vocational training, sports and arts, and improvement of social infrastructure. Geographically, like the SJ, the Council's activities were limited to the municipalities with the highest homicide rates in the departments of San Salvador, La Libertad, and Sonsonate. The selection of communities by homicide indicators rather than by their gang problem, however, suggests that the program was not sufficiently gang-specific. It assumed that broader efforts to increase citizen organizing and opportunities would also help reduce gang violence. In both its prevention and rehabilitation efforts (examined below), the CNSP relied on *focalización*, the concept that also guided the SJ's work. The Council directed its focus to specific areas (the most insecure communities) and beneficiaries (at-risk youths, juvenile offenders, and gang members), arguing that gang and gang-prone youths live in marginalized zones.[53]

The program received an important financial boost in 2003 when the European Union (EU) began supporting the CNSP with ProJóvenes, a five-year project for violence prevention, co-funded by the EU and the government of El Salvador. ProJóvenes comprised four components: institutional development, community development, vocational training, and recovery of public space. Similar to the CNSP's long-term program, it was aimed at youths from ten to twenty-five years of age. ProJóvenes operated in the fourteen municipalities within Greater San Salvador, although different communities were selected each year. In the main, both initiatives sought to create a violence prevention model based on local actors, such as community leaders and municipal governments.[54]

Although this view recognized the role of community factors in the emergence of gangs, the overriding problem was that El Salvador had not developed a national gang strategy. Local initiatives could therefore have only a limited effect. Another uncertainty was the selection of participants. Targeting them appropriately was important, but the paucity of available information about the process makes it difficult to establish what selection criteria the Council adhered to.

By the same token, the CNSP's decision not to operate in certain communities raises concerns. Factors such as weak or nonexistent organizing, domestic violence, demographic density, low educational levels, extortion, and gang activity itself were perceived as barriers to successful intervention.[55] However, among the excluded communities were several that were notorious for gang activity and therefore should have been prioritized for gang-control efforts.[56] The Council's preference for areas seen as amenable to its programs allowed it to demonstrate its commitment to helping troublesome youths, but it was not the way to handle a complex and growing social problem.

Since its inception, ProJóvenes had experienced a number of setbacks in technical assistance and personnel disagreements and had achieved little.[57] By mid-2006, only 27 percent of its budget had been disbursed,[58] and the little money that was paid out was not well spent. For example, in fiscal year 2005, 78 percent of the budget went to overhead and only 4 percent to project activities.[59] The Council, to balance the earlier underspending, substantially increased its expenditure for sports and social infrastructure development.[60] There is nothing intrinsically wrong with the construction of football pitches and the like in communities that require more positive recreational space, but their contribution to gang control is minimal if that is all that is done. The final evaluation of ProJóvenes indicated that the project had lacked a qualified technical team and objectively verifiable indicators, as well as an efficient monitoring system and interinstitutional coordination. Furthermore, prevention activities in the communities were decoupled from the government's law enforcement response. Its main achievement having been the creation of social infrastructure, the project served mostly as a laboratory for the prevention of urban violence, but its overall effectiveness was low.[61]

ProJóvenes was scheduled to terminate in 2008, but the CNSP sought to make the project sustainable beyond that date. If it had continued the program alone, the Council would have required considerably more public funds. The institution relied on a small annual budget of close to US $1 million (most of it spent on salaries and operating costs) and stayed afloat largely through EU funding.[62] The government had shown little interest in supporting the Council's work and seemed unlikely to do so in the future.

Back in 2006, the CNSP hoped to strengthen community participation and local government-led initiatives for violence prevention.[63] The most important challenge for the Council became to restore trust and build a working relationship with the mayors. The public security approach of successive ARENA administrations, however, led to widespread cynicism, and FMLN-governed municipalities initially showed strong resistance to the CNSP's attempts at collaboration.[64] As difficult as the development of a gang policy is, the political nature of this undertaking often seemed to be the greater obstacle.

ProJóvenes II (2009–2014) was implemented—again in fourteen municipalities—while the CNSP was shut down and the INJUVE was being created. The project built or remodeled social infrastructure and provided job training to youths and single mothers, but the final evaluation suggests that their incorporation into the labor market was limited. Furthermore, gang rivalries required the operators (themselves local youths) to negotiate with gang members and to speak about coexistence, not prevention, in order to be able to carry out their work. The fact that fourteen volunteers were killed during ProJóvenes I suggests that prevention in gang-affected communities remained a challenge.[65] The creation of a full-fledged monitoring and evaluation system, as well as a municipal-level capacity for prevention, is a pending task.[66]

Tasked with implementing the National Youth Policy, the INJUVE is meant to take over the prevention work of the CNSP. However, it is unclear whether the institution has the necessary technical capacity.[67] There are also signs that, like the Youth Secretariat, it is a political entity that may accomplish little more than demonstrate the government's commitment to the social prevention of violence.[68]

GANG REHABILITATION

The Council began gang rehabilitation in 2004 following the appointment of its president, Óscar Bonilla, who completed his tenure at CNSP in 2009 and in 2010 died of a terminal illness.[69] Bonilla reapportioned scarce resources in an attempt to provide a more comprehensive response to the gang problem.[70] Activities included territorial work aimed at the collection of local data on gangs, the training of community leaders, self-help workshops, and job creation; prison-based vocational training; and a tattoo removal program. In 2006, only three individuals—the director and two rehabilitation officers—staffed the CNSP's rehabilitation unit. This serious lack of human resources constrained these efforts, and the CNSP's community-based work entailed mostly self-help and job training workshops in selected communities.[71]

The program centerpiece was the *granja-escuela* (farm-school), a rehabilitation center located in Izalco, Sonsonate, which opened in 2005. Each year the *granja* housed one group of former Mara Salvatrucha and Dieciocho members, aged sixteen to twenty-five, alternating between male and female groups. During a period of six months, the youths were offered spiritual and psychological assistance, health services, tattoo removal, sports, education, and vocational training. Initially, a group of twenty males learned to grow roses and breed chickens, then fourteen females were given classes in chicken farming, baking, and cosmetics. In an effort to offset the lack of domestic job opportunities, the center supplemented practical skills with a short course in business administration to facilitate self-employment.

The CNSP declared the first experience to be satisfactory because participants were able to complete the program and did not kill each other.[72] The Council avoided major conflicts between the internees—largely because its target population was restricted to individuals who retained no ideological commitment to their gangs. Even so, supervision of the first group was sufficiently lax as to allow the youths to smuggle in drugs and weapons, and two were injured.[73]

One of the key challenges for the project concerned the creation of viable jobs. The Salvadoran private sector largely refuses to hire former gang members, a stance that severely limited the Council's options.[74] The best alternative was thought to be self-employment, but the training was in areas in which competition was likely to be strong.

The agricultural sector holds no appeal to most Salvadoran youths, who prefer work in urban zones to backbreaking, underpaid rural labor.[75] So the CNSP's choice of training options became even more questionable. More problematic was its ambition to prepare youths with little formal education for the labor market within a few months. Some of the females in the 2006 contingent were illiterate and could not realistically be expected to acquire the level of competence required for self-employment.[76]

The Council's rehabilitation program had mixed success: in 2005, only fifteen participants completed the process, while the 2006 group was reduced to eleven after one desertion and two deaths. Four of the males were placed in the Catholic development NGO, Polígono Industrial Don Bosco, for further education and training. This gave the Council's project an appearance of success, although it had delegated its responsibility to another institution.[77]

The most critical test facing the CNSP was the need to transform the *granja* into a true rehabilitation initiative and to make it sustainable over the long term. Some staff members privately acknowledged that gang rehabilitation required more than a six-month commitment.[78] Part of the problem was that the project originally was conceived as a temporary halfway house to assist ex-convicts with their social adaptation, but it evolved into a gang rehabilitation center.[79] Council personnel lacked expertise in gang control, however, and struggled to locate a model. They hoped eventually to convert the *granja* into a more consistent, sustained project.[80] To achieve this goal, it was essential to gather reliable gang data and hire staff who demonstrated technical competence and principled behavior. The director for rehabilitation, for example, had to be denied access to the *granja* after he solicited sexual favors from some of the females.[81]

Financial limitations undermined the institution's ability to develop a larger and more sophisticated rehabilitation initiative and jeopardized even this modest effort. Regardless of how serious El Salvador's gang problem may have been, the *granja* was too small to have a significant impact. Rehabilitation is not cheap: a six-month program cost some US $70,000 and to kick-start it, the first participants helped renovate the building used for their housing.[82] Council staff believed that gang rehabilitation was the state's responsibility, but the government failed to supply adequate funding.[83] To increase the viability of the *granja*, CNSP members opted to sell some of the produce grown there and to seek more international donor support. In 2008, the project entered its fourth year, suggesting that their efforts had borne fruit. However, a program that was so underfunded that its beneficiaries needed to work to ensure its sustainability testifies to the dire state of gang rehabilitation in El Salvador. The Saca administration had yet to make comprehensive gang control a greater priority, and the CNSP might have furthered that goal if it had sought to exercise greater political influence over key actors in this field, notably the government and the private sector.

In 2009, the *granja-escuela* encountered funding constraints and was converted into a center providing job training and other services to ex-gang members and other youths. Following the closure of the CNSP in 2011, this center was converted into a *granja-penal*, operated by El Salvador's directorate-general of the prison system. No systematic evaluations of the *granja-escuela* were ever made. The available information indicates that rehabilitation efforts were more successful in the case of female gang members, whereas many of the men returned to gangs and crime.[84]

THE POLITICAL WEIGHT OF THE CNSP

The Council was established for the purpose of designing and proposing solutions to public security problems. Although it had many ex-FMLN members among its senior officials and had been more supportive of prevention and rehabilitation than others in the government, its impact remained negligible.[85]

Salvador Samayoa, Council president between 2004 and 2009 and a former member, like his successor Óscar Bonilla, of the FPL guerrilla organization, had introduced the idea of the social prevention of violence, but received no support for it. Changes to the CNSP mandate then transformed the advisory body into an implementing agency and, in doing so, only further reduced its influence.[86] When Mano Dura and the Ley Anti Maras were introduced, Samayoa spoke out against the measures and requested that more money be spent on prevention, but to no avail.[87] Similarly, Bonilla called for a restructuring of the gang policy and a reallocation of resources, but the government was unreceptive to his pleas.

Not surprisingly, given the twin constraints of limited resources and lack of political will, the Council failed either to enhance its existing programs or to help persuade the government to implement a national gang policy. The CNSP concern with reducing gang violence led to at least some work in this area, but clearly much more was required. To alleviate the gang situation, the government must be committed to comprehensive gang control. Additionally, the private sector must help reduce socio-economic inequality and create more and better jobs. For the

CNSP, however, this may have been as difficult to accomplish as it was for the NGOs. Unless its leadership had exploited its status as a governmental agency more forcefully and had been more vocal about the need to connect its work to a broader gang control policy, Council achievements would have remained limited.

Overall, the CNSP output appears superior to that of the Youth Secretariat, yet the Council remained marginalized and its work underappreciated by the government. The Saca administration, despite its change in rhetoric, made no concerted effort to combine law enforcement with prevention and rehabilitation.

The "Re-launch" of Súper Mano Dura

In the months following the 2004 launch of Súper Mano Dura, government and police officials repeatedly declared the plan a success. Much like the Flores government, the Saca administration relied on ambiguous indicators, such as the amount of graffiti removed, the number of gang-related arrests, the restoration of tranquility in gang-affected communities, and a dubious decrease in the murder rate. Gang arrest figures were certainly impressive, totaling 14,601 between September 2004 and August 2005 alone (including repeat arrests).[88] IML data showed, however, that homicide figures maintained a sharp upward trend, from 2,933 in 2004 to 3,812 in 2005, and eventually to 3,928 in 2006 (a rate of 56 per 100,000 inhabitants).[89]

These statistics are the best evidence that the gang control initiative was a resounding failure when it came to reducing crime. The authorities sought to downplay the deteriorating crime levels by suggesting that Súper Mano Dura was effective, but that the gangs deliberately committed more homicides to defy the state. The situation, they insisted, would be worse without the plan (see chapter 3), but in the face of escalating crime, claims for the measure's efficacy began to lose credibility. Although Súper Mano Dura remained hugely popular, according to the IUDOP's 2005 end-of-year survey, as many as 45.4 percent of Salvadorans believed it had helped little or not at all.[90]

The country was to hold municipal and legislative elections in March 2006, which meant that public opinion could not be ignored. Publicly, President Saca remained adamant that his plan was workable. He declared that it needed to be adjusted and re-launched because the gangs had evolved into organized crime groups.[91] A subsequent organizational reshuffle saw the return of Rodrigo Ávila as police chief (a position he had held between 1994 and 1999) and the creation of a new elite unit aimed at reducing gang extortion.[92] Beyond cosmetic changes, however, gang control saw no major reorientation until mid-2006 and the introduction of a new plan, Maestro de Seguridad. This latest suppression effort maintained patrols, but shifted the focus from area sweeps and mass detentions to the investigation of individual gang leaders and of gangs as organized criminal structures.[93] The Mano Dura policies were quietly withdrawn once they threatened to become a political liability and had outlived their original purpose of enhancing ARENA's electoral image.

The new plan was not a credible attempt to articulate a comprehensive gang policy. Instead, the authorities continued to pursue prevention, suppression, and rehabilitation activities in a disconnected fashion and to prioritize suppression. Central to this preference was a shift toward rhetoric that emphasized the gangs' ostensible mutation into organized crime groups and a newfound interest in transnational cooperation on gangs.

THE "MUTATION" OF THE STREET GANGS

Since the launch of Mano Dura, government and police officials associated the street gangs with terrorism and organized crime, depicting them to the public as having a transnational structure.[94] These portrayals intensified under the Saca administration and were used to justify officials' choices of certain gang control efforts over others.

The connection between street gangs and terrorism was construed in two ways. One was to liken gang violence to "acts of terrorism" or to declare that the gangs were "sowing terror" in local communities.[95] The second involved a rumored link with Al-Qaeda.[96] Both claims lacked credibility and can be dismissed as politically motivated fearmongering. It is true that gang members' ready use of violence and brutality creates a threatening atmosphere. "Terrorism," however, refers specifically to the systematic use of violence, or the threat thereof, in pursuit of political aims.[97] The gangs pursued no such objectives, nor were most of their targets innocent civilians. (An exception to this was the June 2010 bus massacre in Mejicanos, committed by Dieciocho members in an apparent extortion dispute. The gang members, however, were later sanctioned for the act.[98]) Applying the terrorist label to these groups only distorts the nature of the problem and stymies the search for appropriate policy options.

As for supposed gang ties to Al-Qaeda, US authorities repeatedly denied the existence of such links, although they did not rule out the possibility that gang members might one day accept payment to smuggle terrorists into the country.[99] Nonetheless, Salvadoran politicians and police periodically revived this fictive connection, fed at least in part by the US government's post-9/11 focus on counterterrorism and its willingness to provide funding for this purpose.

The purported association between street gangs and organized crime had even greater resonance within the government and became a cornerstone of gang control efforts. Salvadoran authorities insisted that street gangs form to commit crimes, maintain a structure that resembles criminal enterprises, and are involved in organized crime and drug trafficking.[100]

These claims misrepresent the nature of gangs and exaggerate their criminal component. Youths join these groups to fulfill a variety of individual social needs, not specifically to engage in criminal and violent acts. Antisocial behavior is a by-product of gang affiliation, rather than its goal, and, as such, requires different responses.[101] Street gangs are generally incapable of operating like organized crime groups, which require mature, professional members with organizational skills, well-defined leadership, and specialist group roles. Neither are they like drug gangs, which demand a clear and hierarchical leadership, strong group cohesiveness, a code of loyalty, a narrow focus on drug sales, and an avoidance of non-sales-related criminal involvement. Street gangs, by contrast, tend to have shifting leadership and intermediate levels of cohesiveness. Members frequently break codes of honor and commit crimes independent of the group.[102] The available research on Central America suggests that individual gang members may act as foot soldiers for organized criminal groups, but there is no evidence that street gangs control drug sales or engage in other organized criminal activities.[103] Although there are signs that individual gang members and cliques have become involved in drug trafficking, the gangs as such remain qualitatively different from organized crime in El Salvador.[104]

As noted above, officials also described the street gangs, notably Mara Salvatrucha and the Dieciocho, as transnational entities. This derived from their presence in the United States, Mexico, and northern Central America; their cross-border contacts via cell phones and the Internet; and gang movements within the region.[105] Some Salvadoran gang members are deportees, so transnational connections are unsurprising. The fact that youths in different countries claim affiliation with the same gang, however, does not necessarily point to the proliferation of a regional network that answers to a single chain of command. One multicountry study confirmed sporadic links between Salvadoran gang members and their counterparts elsewhere in North and Central America, but it found that no structured cross-border relations or regional gang network exists between the gangs.[106] The ties between gang members in the United States and El Salvador are real, however, and their nature and extent require further research.[107] Nevertheless, the existence of transnational street gangs was the conventional wisdom among US and Salvadoran government and police officials and underpinned cooperation in this area.

The organizational characteristics that the authorities ascribed to the gangs have significant implications for gang control. Depicting the gangs as criminally motivated and transnational in nature legitimized suppression rather than prevention/rehabilitation and shifted responsibility for the solution away from the domestic sphere and the sociopolitical inequalities of Salvadoran society.

The Saca government, which paradoxically had promised to undertake gang prevention and rehabilitation, intensified the mischaracterization and undermined the rationale for any alternative strategies. The administration's focus on suppression became more evident with gang-related law enforcement cooperation, a trend that began halfway through the implementation of Súper Mano Dura and deepened even when the policy was officially withdrawn.

TRANSNATIONAL COOPERATION ON GANGS

El Salvador has shown a keen interest in a regional approach to the gang problem and has repeatedly encouraged neighboring countries to join in policing and intelligence activities.[108] The United States also has become a key partner in transnational gang control efforts.

Four major regional initiatives have come to light, but a comprehensive review is impossible because little public information is available.[109] These measures require further research to determine their impact on national and regional gang policies. Since the creation of the Central America Regional Security Initiative (CARSI) in 2008 to tackle gangs and organized crime, there has been a greater move toward gang prevention.[110] Suppression, however, remains the dominant strategy, and the lack of transparency makes monitoring and evaluation more difficult for NGOs and other actors concerned with gang violence reduction.

One of these initiatives was an annual gang conference organized by the PNC beginning in 2005. Law enforcement officials from the United States, Mexico, and Central America shared information and best practices and established strategies to counter the regional expansion of the street gangs and their putative transnational networks.[111] Both the

CNSP and the Polígono were invited to present their prevention and rehabilitation programs at these conferences, but the final agreements regularly focused on the importance of intelligence sharing and other policing activities.[112] At the 2007 forum, for example, it was decided to establish the Transnational Anti-Gang Center and a fingerprint database to better identify and apprehend gang members.[113] Apart from the notable absence of attempts to develop a comprehensive gang strategy, the heavy emphasis on law enforcement networking and intelligence sharing may prove less effective than expected because it serves to reinforce the official mischaracterization of street gangs as organized criminal groups. The conference was last held in 2009, and it is unclear why the event was discontinued.[114]

FBI-directed anti-gang enforcement, both in the United States and in El Salvador, represents a second initiative. In December 2004, the Bureau created the MS-13 National Gang Task Force (NGTF) to respond to a perceived expansion of Mara Salvatrucha and gruesome MS-related violence in the Washington, DC, area.[115] (In November 2012, the US Department of the Treasury designated Mara Salvatrucha a significant transnational criminal organization.[116]) The goal was to coordinate investigations and cooperate against the largest and arguably most dangerous street gang.[117] In 2007, the FBI added the Dieciocho to the mandate of the MS-13 National Gang Task Force.[118]

The FBI believes that gangs form specifically to commit offenses and views them as organized criminal syndicates. Based on this assumption, the Bureau has applied methods previously used to dismantle the Mafia to its street gang operations, targeting gang leaders for arrest to induce the dissolution of the entire group.[119] In 2006, the use of the Racketeer Influenced and Corrupt Organizations (RICO) Act, originally created to prosecute drug traffickers and organized crime syndicates, permitted US federal authorities to secure the conviction of two MS members.[120] The PNC has long applied the individual leadership stereotype to the gangs and, after the demise of Mano Dura, modeled its gang control strategy on the FBI approach.[121] In 2007, El Salvador adopted RICO-style antiracketeering laws to apply to gang members.[122] The FBI had opened a liaison office in San Salvador in April 2005, to expedite data sharing and to coordinate regional gang control with local police forces. The rationale for establishing the office was Mara Salvatrucha's overwhelmingly Salvadoran membership, but the primary reason was Washington's interest in curbing gang migration.[123] The United States routinely deports offending gang members who are not US citizens in an attempt to lessen its own gang problem. Many of them have been in the

United States since early childhood, so the policy creates a revolving-door effect as many deportees seek to return to the country they know best. The FBI's presence in El Salvador is meant to help deter the return to the United States of deported gang members and thus also deter an expected rise in gang activity.[124]

It is important to stress that El Salvador's strategy to reproduce the US approach is unlikely to lead to a substantial reduction in gang violence. Although many gang members break the law, the police view that gang activity in general constitutes a type of conspiracy to commit crimes is misconceived. Law enforcement officers come into contact primarily with suspected offenders and deduce from these experiences that crime and violence constitute the core of gang life. This perspective, however, glosses over street gangs' structural roots and overstates their criminal activity. The assumption that organized crime and street gangs are similar, when they are in fact quite different, only leads to inappropriate forms of gang control.

Similarly, the idea that targeting gang leaders will result in the group's dissolution is mistaken because street gang leadership is typically more flexible and diffuse than police officials portray.[125] Contrary to conventional wisdom, the stereotypical gang leader is an individual with a reputation for criminal activity or a willingness to engage in violence, who tends to have little actual influence over other gang members. Rather, leadership is dispersed and shifts over time.[126]

The key personality image serves a simplistic law enforcement perspective that attributes gang members' crime to the influence of a single leader. This view implies that the removal of one person will suffice to curtail illicit activities. In reality, since gang leadership does not reside in one individual, the arrest of individual "leaders" will not have an effect on the group itself. The PNC's adoption of gang control methods advocated by the FBI may give its efforts greater political legitimacy, but the tactics are unlikely to mitigate the domestic gang problem.

A third initiative that deserves mention is the US-sponsored International Law Enforcement Academy (ILEA), which opened in San Salvador in mid-2005. Overseen by a US-directed policy board and funded by the US State Department's Bureau for International Narcotics and Law Enforcement Affairs, the ILEA supports criminal justice institution-building and works to strengthen regional law enforcement cooperation. Its programs train Latin American police, judges, and public prosecutors to deal with transnational crime, particularly drug trafficking, human smuggling, terrorism, and money laundering.[127]

The parts of the curriculum relevant to this discussion are its human rights classes and an anti-gang training program. Gang modules cover subjects such as gang hand signs, forensics, and witness and judicial security. The instructors reportedly are gang experts affiliated with the FBI, the Department of Homeland Security, and other US federal agencies, and they address the street gangs from an organized crime perspective.[128]

Due to the paucity of publicly available information, it is difficult to assess either the teaching content at the ILEA-San Salvador or its impact on gang control. The academy operates with little transparency and, despite repeated information requests by both domestic and international activists, has not disclosed the course materials.[129] Nonetheless, two observations can be made.

First, in hoping to improve law enforcement abroad, the ILEA seeks to strengthen local policing capabilities as much as to advance US security interests in the region.[130] Drug trafficking and the street gangs are considered the principal sources of instability in Central America and hence threats to US security.[131] In this sense, the ILEA is a mechanism that permits the United States to kill two birds with one stone: to export its own criminal justice priorities and enable Latin American police forces to help address shared security concerns.[132]

Second, the ILEA's presence in El Salvador may serve to confer greater legitimacy to El Salvador's own gang control efforts. But it is uncertain whether it can help make these more effective if it hardens existing views of gangs and gang control and does not make its students aware that gang control is not only a policing matter.

Further, it is unclear how the academy can help make gang control more rights-respecting merely by adding human rights courses to the curriculum. The ANSP already provides such training, yet PNC agents are regularly implicated in abuses. Through other channels—perhaps as part of the CARSI—the United States could work to strengthen the PNC in other ways, notably by promoting the creation of a human rights culture, fostering a more effective implementation of use-of-force protocols, and strengthening accountability mechanisms. In the absence of an institutionalized commitment to human rights, ILEA activities are unlikely to leave a positive imprint on gang control in El Salvador.

The fourth and final initiative concerns the Centro Antipandillas Transnacional (Transnational Anti-Gang Center, or CAT/TAG) and the associated Central American Fingerprint Exploitation Initiative (CAFE). Like parts of the ILEA, the two measures are funded under the CARSI. The CAT, established in October 2007 in San Salvador, is composed of FBI agents and Salvadoran police. It strives to counter transnational gang activity in the United States, Mexico, and Central America through information sharing, investigations of gangs as criminal enterprises, and anti-gang operations.[133] The CAFE program, for its part, was initiated by the FBI's MS-13 NGTF and entails the creation of a regional fingerprint database to facilitate the identification, tracking, and apprehension of gang members.[134] Also included is the FBI-developed Officer Exchange Program, which oversees the temporary assignment of CAT-embedded PNC officers to the Los Angeles Police Department (LAPD) and the Los Angeles Sheriff's Office to participate in gang-related training and observation activities.[135] The CAT has begun to investigate cases of homicide and extortion committed by Salvadoran gang members in the United States, or in El Salvador under the orders of their US counterparts.[136] The center's impact on gang control is unclear, and it has been implicated in the torture of imprisoned gang members in El Salvador.[137]

There is a risk that, as these initiatives are implemented, ex–gang members may be misidentified and experience continued police harassment.[138] The utility of the database will strongly depend on the definition of a gang member and is complicated by the fact that turnover in gangs is high.

Serious questions must be asked about the training efforts and their value for gang control in El Salvador. Not only do FBI and LA-based gang experts reinforce the prevalent, misconceived view of street gangs in El Salvador, but also the LAPD's "war mentality" and preference for suppression are changing slowly.[139] It is unclear how gang policing in El Salvador might improve if officers learn from such counterparts.

Despite the failure of Mano Dura, a senior PNC official stated that El Salvador was chosen as the CAT base for its high level of professionalism in dealing with its gang problem.[140] The CARSI does provide limited funds for prevention projects.[141] However, the Salvadoran government remained reliant on foreign donors to finance action in these areas and did not even develop a comprehensive and long-term strategy. While NGO advocacy helped push for some limited policy change, this pressure was insufficient to achieve a transformation of state behavior.

Conclusion: The Legacy of Mano Dura

Some commentators have claimed that the street gangs undermine Central American democracies.[142] In El Salvador, at least, the state's response to this social problem may well be the greater threat, given that single-minded gang suppression has effectively promoted social profiling and discrimination, greater insecurity, and nostalgia for authoritarian measures.

The earlier focus on tattoos and other descriptive traits for the identification of suspected gang members has outlived Mano Dura, with detrimental results for certain sectors of Salvadoran society. Individuals with tattoos, even if artistic in nature, have been denied admission to schools and are routinely rejected by prospective employers.[143] Regrettably, police continue the pattern of social profiling and arbitrary arrests based on people's age, social background, or appearance. Young, poor males, regardless of gang affiliation, are subject to frequent stop-and-search practices and may be wrongfully accused of being gang members. Arbitrary stops and arrests are often accompanied by police abuse, including beatings, on the street or in police holding cells.[144]

Street gangs constitute oppositional cultures, and central for understanding their reaction to control efforts is the concept of cohesiveness. Although gangs are not tightly structured, they can become more close-knit, delinquent, and resistant to further interventions in reaction to police suppression, which tends to strengthen gang members' ties to one another and their gang.[145] Mano Dura, with its area sweeps and mass detentions, thus counterintuitively served to spread insecurity by reinforcing gang identity and cohesiveness, as well as gangs' criminal sophistication. Adverse changes have been twofold, involving more clandestine conduct and a consolidation of gang power, particularly within the prisons. First, gang affiliates have adopted a number of strategies aimed at hiding their membership and evading capture, including an end to compulsory tattooing, the use of graffiti, and the public display of hand signs, and the adoption of a more conventional dress code and hairstyles.[146] Second, gang members have made prisons a base from where they direct their criminal activities. A poorly thought-out decision in 2004 to segregate each gang into separate penitentiaries to prevent violent clashes between the inmates is as responsible for this development as the absence of serious reinsertion programs.[147] Shared prison time has allowed gang members to forge closer bonds and, via intermediaries and cell phones, manage extortions and give orders to kill.

As a result of Mano Dura, people continue to be stigmatized and mistreated simply for living in particular zones. Police brutality and disrespect for basic rights contribute to the erosion of El Salvador's already fragile democracy, while the ARENA governments remained indifferent to the need for an alternative gang policy and more effective policing. Mano Dura complicated the gang problem and made life for many Salvadorans more perilous as a result.

Finally, Mano Dura fostered authoritarian attitudes and nostalgia for undemocratic measures. The plans used a "politics of fear" whereby the discursive construction of the gang threat legitimized the continuation of authoritarian crime-fighting strategies.[148] It must be emphasized that the media's demonization of gang members and its obsession with suppressive actions have also served to stimulate popular preferences for such responses over more promising alternatives.

The perceived lawlessness that resulted from the inflated gang threat encouraged extrajudicial killings of gang members, even as President Saca denied that anti-gang extermination squads were operating from within the state.[149] There is information suggesting, however, that certain people were prepared to mete out justice on their own. For example, in November 2005, the Mano Blanca group made a radio broadcast announcing its intention to cleanse the eastern town of San Miguel of all gang members, their reason being that Mano Dura had proved ineffective.[150] In August 2006, another death squad, the Comando Central XGN Maximiliano Hernández Martínez, killed a gang member in San Miguel. Flyers distributed by the self-styled Sombra Negra group warned of the impending death of gang members and other suspects unless the authorities enforced order.[151] In 2005, people who had lost relatives to gang violence lynched three gang members, justifying their act by claiming that Súper Mano Dura "did not work." Some observers subsequently expressed their belief that more such cases existed but simply remained undisclosed.[152] Such incidents, no matter how rare they may be, are a serious challenge to El Salvador's democracy. They signal state acquiescence to extrajudicial violence against gangs. Notwithstanding these consequences and persistent calls for an alternative gang policy, the Saca government remained wedded to suppression. The continued resistance to more sophisticated policing alongside prevention and rehabilitation programs confirms that the authorities lacked the necessary political will to bring about effective change.

CHAPTER 3

Creating Folk Devils

News media play a central role in public agenda-setting and policy debates. As a space for the articulation of different interests and perspectives, the media constituted an important strategic resource in the ideological struggle over Mano Dura. The government relied on the media to sell the policy to the population, and the NGOs used the media to put forward an alternative view of the gang problem. The extent to which these actors met with success depended on their respective resources and their ability to use news production to their advantage. Selecting information that influenced the public perception of street gangs ostensibly gave the media power to promote or marginalize competing voices and policies.

This chapter analyzes El Salvador's contemporary media system to reveal the extent to which political openings translated into a democratized press and to identify the principal obstacles facing Salvadoran journalism today. This profile serves to highlight media barriers to the NGO advocacy examined in subsequent chapters and to ground the content analysis of gang-related news coverage of the Mano Dura and Súper Mano Dura plans (2003–2006). The current climate may be more conducive to journalistic pluralism and freedom of expression than that of the past. However, the persistence of oligopolistic ownership structures and the political use of advertising soften media content, encouraging a journalism that is passive and self-censored. In this politicized environment, the press exaggerated the gang problem and influenced the public to support ineffective Mano Dura policies. Gang violence has become more serious and complex, largely as a result of Mano Dura, and the media coverage is assessed here for the ways it depicted the gangs before this transformation occurred.

The News Media and Public Perceptions of Crime

The media, to varying degrees of effectiveness, perform a number of important political functions: they can monitor the conduct of public officials and facilitate accountability, constitute a forum for public debate, and provide information from multiple perspectives. Given their communicative role, the media have the power to shape citizens' views of political and social issues by deciding which items to include in the news agenda and how to portray them. They also offer a finite set of causes and remedies for the problems they frame.[1]

Communication researchers agree that although media messages do not determine our understanding of the world, they influence it and make some interpretations more likely than others.[2] Studies show that representations of crime news affect both the public's perception of the seriousness of a crime problem and its beliefs about the required solution.[3] Political and media discourses can frame crime in different ways—for instance, as a consequence of individual pathological tendencies and moral failings or of broader socio-economic injustices. Each perspective has distinct policy implications. If crime is the personal fault of the perpetrator, punitive policies are likely to seem the appropriate answer. If it is explained in terms of the social exclusion prevailing in certain residential neighborhoods, strategies that emphasize prevention and rehabilitation will appear as the most sensible response.

This chapter seeks to provide not an exhaustive examination of the process of gang news production, content, and reception, but rather an analysis of gang news coverage, itself located within the production context. It draws on existing surveys to evaluate media effects on public opinion of gangs. Journalists and the establishments that employ them operate within an environment that constrains and shapes news production.[4] The research presented here explores the extent to which reporters enjoy autonomy in particular newsrooms and how El Salvador's media system affects journalistic work.

"Media system" refers to the structure of the national media industries and their relations—shaped by a range of social, economic, political, and legal factors—with the government and the business elite. Overall, the analysis is guided by the assumption that the media are themselves political institutions "whose functioning cannot be understood separated from larger political dynamics."[5]

Political Openings and the "Transformation" of El Salvador's Media

The civil war and the subsequent transition to electoral democracy seemed to prompt significant changes in the Salvadoran media.[6] The political openings of the early 1990s, ending decades of state censorship and repression, gave birth to novel experiments and permitted unprecedented openings in the traditionally dominant press. The overall climate warmed to journalistic pluralism and greater freedom of expression, which allowed a number of promising newspapers to launch.[7]

The monthly news magazine *Tendencias*, published since 1990, maintained a pluralistic editorial line and addressed primarily opinion leaders. However, it proved unable to become self-supporting once crucial international funding ceased, and the magazine folded after seven years.[8] Foreign journalists who had descended on El Salvador to cover the armed conflict created *Primera Plana*. This weekly newspaper, which offered critical coverage of current events, began circulating in 1994, again with much-needed international assistance. Insufficient advertising revenue forced its closure after only nine months, but the paper is credited with introducing investigative journalism in the country.[9]

State-sanctioned violence against reporters and open censorship ceased with the end of the civil war, and by and large, the media have enjoyed greater independence from the state.[10] Reprisals, although serious, have become sporadic rather than systematic. In interviews, journalists and NGO media staff conceded that El Salvador had made important strides in its respect for freedom of expression.[11] However, all respondents noted concern about continued limitations in this area. The overall picture was eloquently summarized by Mauricio Funes, at the time a news anchor:

> Some sectors, particularly the government, maintain that freedom of expression is unlimited here, but the number of media is not synonymous with freedom of expression. We need to consider the room for maneuver in which the media operate, but above all the population's level of participation. In El Salvador there exists more freedom of the press and freedom of expression than in the past. Compared to the situation during the war, there is much more tolerance toward dissenting thoughts and opinions, but there continue to be serious restrictions of both journalistic work and freedom of expression when the opinions that one seeks to express, or when the information that one seeks to disseminate through the existing media, challenge the status quo and challenge the power groups in this country.[12]

Critical reporting is hampered in a number of ways. Under El Salvador's penal code, for example, individuals found guilty of defamation once risked a prison sentence; in 2011, the prison sentence was replaced by a fine. The existence of such provisions, even if they are rarely enforced, may prod journalists into silence and stifle the articulation of critical ideas. Journalists interviewed for this research, however, feel that the threat of sanctions is unnecessary because El Salvador's journalism remains docile.[13] Limited access to public information also affects investigative journalism and inhibits its performance of public oversight. Transparency of public records is a right enshrined in the Salvadoran constitution, but officials were not required to grant access to records and data, a loophole that effectively rendered transparency moot.[14]

The Access to Public Information Law was adopted only in 2011. However, in an attempt to evade criticism and maintain a positive public image, state institutions have since developed practices to avoid disclosing public information, including declarations of a time embargo, contempt of compliance orders, and declarations of inexistence.[15] Limited access to public information remains an important obstacle to effective Salvadoran journalism.[16] Reporters confirm this finding, noting that many domestic journalists have developed an apathetic attitude toward newsgathering. Rather than investigate independently, they prefer to transcribe official speeches and press releases.[17]

The political and economic interests of individual media outlets also foster apathy. Journalists tend to favor a routine that relies on a small number of institutional news sources and prescheduled official events.[18] Official sources, by virtue of their status, enjoy privileged access to the media.[19] Government representatives and law enforcement agents exercise considerable influence on the news-making process, defining which issues are newsworthy and how they are presented. As a result, news coverage reflects establishment interests and reaffirms the basic social order.[20] These practices put alternative voices at a disadvantage. Resource-poor groups cannot compete with the spending power, news management skills, and public cachet of official actors. Thus, the Salvadoran government's priorities directly affected gang-related news and manipulated public responses to it.

The Trend toward Greater Professionalism

The presence of foreign war correspondents in El Salvador is widely believed to have helped raise professional standards among younger journalists of the time.[21] US and European correspondents' inquisitive approach to reporting left an indelible impression on a new generation of Salvadoran media personnel. Over time, the latter would replace the *empíricos*, established reporters who had learned their trade on the streets and notoriously accepted bribes to slant their coverage.[22]

Several local universities started offering journalism degree programs, and it is estimated that 95 percent or more of the country's reporters have undergone academic training.[23] However, most receive their degree in communications, not journalism, and their analytical capacity is often limited.[24] Furthermore, academic training has in practice limited consequences since the editorial policies of larger media companies heavily influence news content and the media are not very diversified. In the newsrooms, these individuals demanded autonomy and showed commitment to the development of investigative journalism.[25] Continued constraints on newsroom autonomy, modest monetary compensation, and weak ethical norms, however, eroded many of the gains from professionalization. Since most reporters' salaries are low, and the journalistic job market is crowded, it is likely job security that prompts them to abandon ethical principles and critical reporting.[26] The tension between professionalization and structural constraints underlies the problems facing Salvadoran journalism today and is perhaps most striking in the transformation pursued by the leading press.

The emergence of a more pluralistic environment after the civil war prompted the existing pro-regime news institutions to undergo an extensive makeover, although this process was uneven. The most striking innovations occurred in *El Diario de Hoy* and *La Prensa Gráfica*, once considered two of the most backward Latin American newspapers in their technical presentation and their viewpoints.[27] Modernization could be discerned in two key areas: their printing and graphic design processes and their content. The latter was revised to soften their ideological slant, the pages were opened to previously excluded actors and ideas, and investigative supplements (*Vértice* and *Enfoques*, respectively) were added.[28] In each case, improvements advanced at different paces and for different reasons.

The most conspicuous of these innovations was the introduction of investigative journalism. Historically, the country's mainstream press had been tied to the political and economic elite and therefore shunned critical reporting. However, as a younger generation took over management, some of them recognized that the country's vast political changes demanded changes in their news operations. In the case of *El*

Diario de Hoy and *Vértice*, these efforts were strongly supported by the newly hired editor-in-chief, Costa Rican journalist Lafitte Fernández. (Fernández left *El Diario de Hoy* in 2012 and is director-general of the digital newspaper *Diario1*.) Despite clashes between the reporters and the paper's owners over content, the former successfully defended their project for several years.[29] Meanwhile, the company paid for its permissiveness with the loss of prized advertising revenue when patrons felt offended by the public airing of corruption and scandal.[30] Over the years, *Vértice* experienced a qualitative decline until it quietly folded in 2006.

La Prensa Gráfica—nowadays more moderate than its chief competitor—initially resisted the need for change. In 1998, however, production came to a standstill when the entire newsroom commenced a walkout to demand greater editorial freedom.[31] The Dutriz family, which owns the paper, responded by appointing former Education Minister Cecilia Gallardo as editor-in-chief. Under her stewardship, *La Prensa Gráfica* finally achieved greater journalistic innovation. It even turned to criticizing the ruling party, which had earlier denied her the presidential candidacy.[32] After the demise of *Vértice*, critical reporting remained largely confined to *Enfoques*, but there, too, boundaries were drawn. Issues such as the privatization of the banks, postwar death squad activities, and organized crime were not probed.[33] (*Enfoques* folded in 2008 with the launch of the Sunday magazine *Séptimo Sentido*, which includes in-depth journalism.)

By and large, the postwar period has shown some qualitative improvement of news content and greater space for critical voices. Patterns of the past, however, when the press helped preserve elite control, never vanished. The advances that did occur need to be understood in the light of the very restricted freedom of expression that existed during authoritarian times, when dissent was synonymous with a death sentence.[34] A "journalistic spring" has never occurred in El Salvador.[35]

Anatomy of the Contemporary Media Landscape

El Salvador appears to be blessed with an extensive range of print and electronic media. The country has seven national print newspapers, some 180 radio stations, and about a dozen TV channels (excluding cable).[36] This picture of diversity is nevertheless deceptive. Each market niche is dominated by a handful of advertising-rich, audience-strong outlets that fail to offer a critique of the dominant political and socio-economic order. The alternative media that exist are poorly funded, reach a very small number of viewers and listeners,[37] and are unable to mount a challenge to mainstream journalism or improve the variety and quality of news. Perhaps the exception is the digital newspaper *El Faro*, El Salvador's only solid source of investigative journalism. Founded in 1998, *El Faro* has covered issues such as organized crime and public corruption, but limited Internet access among the population means the newspaper reaches a limited audience, mainly among the urban middle class.

Among the news media available in El Salvador, radio and television enjoy greater popularity than newspapers. Radio, however, is largely a source of entertainment, while the political content offered by television and newspapers tends to shape popular perceptions of the country's main problems.[38] Despite the fact that circulation is limited to urban centers, print media exercise a significant influence on public opinion, largely because the issues they consider newsworthy tend to be taken up by television.[39]

Among the print media, *La Prensa Gráfica* and *El Diario de Hoy* are still considered the leading publications, although daily circulation figures are not independently verifiable. It is thought that with the growth of online content, the newspapers now sell fewer copies. The remaining newspapers match neither the reach nor the political influence of their main competitors. *Más*, owned by the Altamirano family, and *Mi Chero*, owned by the Dutriz family, are sensationalist in nature and contain little political information. *El Gráfico*, also owned by the Dutriz family, focuses on sports. *Diario El Mundo*, founded by the affluent Borja family as a centrist afternoon paper, switched to a morning format and became increasingly conservative. When faced with mounting debt, the *Diario Co-Latino*, El Salvador's oldest daily, was purchased by a staff cooperative that has been running the paper ever since.[40] Originally intended to build a social movement in support of the FMLN, it continues to represent left-wing ideology. Digital newspapers, such as *El Faro*, *Raíces* (closed in 2008), and the more recent additions *La Página*, *El Blog*, *Diario1*, *Revista Factum*, and *ContraPunto*, play a corrective role. However, as of 2015, only 29.7 percent of the Salvadoran population had Internet access through computers, cell phones, or other devices, so that the impact of digital media is limited.[41]

Greater competition exists on the airwaves, but here too space for critical news coverage is limited; few broadcasters with an alternative vision supplement the vast number of commercial stations. Former rebel stations became more traditional enterprises, and social justice issues were largely confined to two networks: YSUCA, the Universidad Centroamericana radio station, and the close to twenty-five community radio stations affiliated with the Asociación de Radios y Programas Participativos (Association of Participating Radios and Programs, or ARPAS).[42]

The television market presents a similarly discouraging picture. State-owned Channel 10, a wartime propaganda instrument for the government and the Armed Forces, airs mainly cultural programming and does not counterbalance the news coverage offered by the Telecorporación Salvadoreña (Salvadoran Telecorporation, or TCS).[43] Owned by a media mogul and long-standing supporter of El Salvador's conservative causes, Boris Eserski, the TCS is the country's dominant and most established broadcast medium. Its stations 2, 4, and 6 cater to the agenda of ARENA and bring in some 90 percent of the nation's viewing audience.[44] Channel 33/Tecnovisión and stations 15, 19, and 21 (all part of Megavisión) offer diverse information, but remain marginal players. Gentevé, launched in 2013, maintains an editorial line that has reflected the news interests of FMLN governments.

The only station that sought to breach the TCS monopoly was Channel 12. Launched in 1984, it was known for high-quality news coverage and a pioneering early-morning news interview format until it was sold to Mexico's TV Azteca in 1997.[45] Today the station's journalism is *oficialista*—passive in political newsgathering and self-censored.[46] In 2005, Mauricio Funes—a journalist at the time and later the president of El Salvador—was dismissed from his well-respected morning interview program after years of internal disputes. With the closure of this important space, the broadcasting has become even more homogeneous.

Media power remains in the hands of three family businesses with a commitment to the political and economic interests of ARENA and the private sector. TCS owner Boris Eserski wields extraordinary advertising power. His media empire comprises the three-channel group, cable TV franchises, radio stations, and the country's leading advertising agencies and public relations firms.[47] While the government no longer openly restricts media content, the failure of the state to regulate the airwaves has permitted the consolidation of an oligopolistic media system.

Like their owners, media outlets tend to embrace one or another political perspective, and problems arise when these biases distort news production. For example, the two leading newspapers and a radio station affiliated with Samix, former President Saca's company, refused to publicize the views of opposition parties and civil society groups.[48] At *La Prensa Gráfica*, the newsroom enjoys relative independence until the owners feel their social and economic status may be threatened. In contrast, *El Diario de Hoy* exercises internal censorship from the start, and the elderly owner, Enrique Altamirano, pens the editorials.[49] Under the Funes government (2009–2014), the director of Channel 10 was fired when a video dealing with the 2012 gang truce was broadcast.[50]

All this suggests that media independence remains an unfulfilled promise in El Salvador. Although competing interests shape all news organizations, proximity to the country's economic and political elites makes its leading press unlikely to act as watchdogs or challenge the status quo.[51] The Salvadoran media's oligopolistic ownership structures ultimately undermine the consolidation of the country's democracy.

Advertising Power

Advertising is a critical source of income for most media organizations and thus exerts an indirect but significant influence on content. In order to maximize their advertiser base, profit-driven media outlets target affluent and middle-class audiences, the main consumers of commercial products and services. News that appeals to these groups rarely includes stories about the poor, except when they commit crimes or violate basic social norms.[52] As a result, the public is not as fully informed as it needs to be about the broader society.

The Salvadoran advertising market is very small. The primary patrons are to be found among the economic elite, but the state maintains the largest media budget. When ARENA first came to power, official advertising was allocated to the media according to their editorial line, rewarding news organizations that offered favorable coverage and punishing those that did not. Successive administrations coaxed private sponsors to pull out of programs or outlets when their content was deemed inconvenient.[53] These practices have continued under FMLN governments, which, it is thought, have been sending subtle messages that pliant coverage is expected in return for official advertising.[54] Among the print media, *La Prensa Gráfica* and *El Diario de Hoy* control an estimated 90 percent of the advertising market.[55] The TCS, meanwhile, benefits from the ties to Boris Eserski's advertising agencies and absorbs an estimated 70–85 percent of the television advertising market.[56]

The inevitable result of this concentration of power in the media sector is reportorial self-censorship. Journalists adhere to a tacit agreement on what must stay out-of-bounds, skewing their work and omitting information, possibly entire stories, to avoid sanctions or to avoid jeopardizing their careers.[57] Occasionally, however, sensitive investigations make it through editorial filters. One example was a 2014 story in *La Prensa Gráfica* on *sicariato* (contract killings) in the Armed Forces. The current generation of Salvadoran journalists appears to discard critical reporting in favor of job security.[58] Like media owners' interference in editorial decisions, these practices can tilt reporting in favor of the status quo.

Media Representations of Street Gangs and Mano Dura

To establish the degree to which elite control of media content influenced public opinion about gangs and crime, this section offers a qualitative content analysis of all gang-related news items published in *La Prensa Gráfica* and *El Diario de Hoy* over a period of three years, beginning with the launch of Mano Dura in 2003.[59] It provides a brief, but revealing, snapshot of the media's role in molding a biased public image of the gangs and reiterating pro–Mano Dura arguments, while delegitimizing alternative gang control policies.

Three elements emerged to characterize the publicity campaign in favor of Mano Dura. First, gang members were depicted as deviant outsiders and a danger to society. Second, media defined the gang problem as stemming from individual character deficiencies rather than from social conditions. This latter argument served to eliminate any discussion of structural factors from causal explanations of the gang phenomenon. The third part of the strategy endorsed Mano Dura, highlighted its success, disparaged criticism, and glossed over its failures.

Two additional observations are warranted. The first concerns the notion of bias in journalistic constructions of reality, while the second relates specifically to the treatment of violence in *La Prensa Gráfica*. Newspapers acknowledge certain biases openly and explicitly—for example, in editorials and opinion columns. Yet bias also lurks in what appears to be objective news, often as a result of news routines and the propaganda efforts of news sources. Once it has been decided which of the day's happenings are newsworthy, reporters must glean sufficient information about them and still meet their deadlines. Faced with these constraints, journalists need to routinize the newsgathering process, so they rely heavily on official sources and prescheduled events.[60] This reliance orients news coverage toward the views of elite institutions, which are organized and funded to provide a steady stream of information, but are relatively devoid of alternative voices. Objectivity suffers in proportion to the paucity of sources, as politicians and government and law enforcement officials become de facto gatekeepers of reality. Reporters, for their part, will offer competing facts as if they were equal, without questioning or challenging the veracity of various accounts.[61]

In May 2005, following the murder of one of its employees, the newsroom at *La Prensa Gráfica* launched a campaign aimed at promoting reflection and debate about violence in El Salvador.[62] At the same time, *La Prensa Gráfica* improved the quality of its reportage and began to critically monitor public and private initiatives designed to build a more peaceful society.[63] The campaign, known as *Todos contra la violencia*, produced a special issue on violence, published entirely in black and white, and drafted the *Manual for the News Treatment of Violence*, which included recommendations for reporters to apply in their daily work.[64]

These recommendations will sound obvious to anyone from a country with a functioning free press, but for El Salvador they were fairly revolutionary. For instance, reporters should avoid oversimplification of causes and put events into a meaningful context for readers. They should consult multiple sources and verify and contrast different versions of events, while taking into consideration the potential biases and agendas of their sources. Reporters were warned to avoid stereotyping and stigmatizing suspects or specific social sectors or eulogizing perpetrators and their crimes. When it came to reporting on gangs, they should omit individual monikers and group names, as well as images of tattoos and signs, to avoid both stigma and publicity for gang members. Finally, criminal justice coverage must respect the principle of presumed innocence to avoid harming innocent citizens. The findings of the three-year content analysis that follows illustrate the extent to which these recommendations for responsible journalism were implemented.

Analysis of Gang-Related Media Coverage

For Mano Dura's punitive response to appear preferable to other gang control programs, officials needed to spread a correspondingly disparaging depiction of the street gangs through the press.[65] The Salvadoran press acted as willing amplifiers of a moral panic driven by the government and law enforcement. In Stanley Cohen's classic definition of "moral panic":

Societies appear to be subject, every now and then, to periods of moral panic. A condition, episode, person or group of persons emerges to become defined as a threat to societal values and interests; its nature is presented in a stylized and stereotypical fashion by the mass media; the moral barricades are manned by editors, bishops, politicians and other right-thinking people; socially accredited experts pronounce their diagnoses and solutions; ways of coping are evolved or (more often) resorted to; the condition then disappears, submerges or deteriorates and becomes more visible. . . . Sometimes the panic . . . has more serious and long-lasting repercussions and might produce such changes as those in legal and social policy or even in the way society conceives itself.[66]

This section explains how gang members were portrayed and discusses the endorsement or rejection of causal explanations of the problem and their policy equivalents and options for gang control. The government's approach to gang control can be divided into three phases. Phase one covers the period between President Flores's launch of Mano Dura (2003) and President Saca's introduction of Súper Mano Dura (2004). Phase two covers the first year of Súper Mano Dura, while phase three covers the period when this second initiative came under increasing doubt and was "re-launched" before being quietly discarded.

Representations of gang members in the media, together with opinions about the factors that lead gangs to form and then flourish, shape policy interventions. By their descriptions of gang members, journalists establish definitions. Much of the information they gather for news stories about the gangs is controlled by official sources,[67] particularly the PNC, Gobernación, and the Presidency of the Republic, which set the parameters for the coverage of street gangs.[68] The analysis discerned five techniques for discussing gangs in the media: categorization, criminalization, dichotomization, the use of metaphors, and the extolling of violence against gang members. These techniques served both to shape public perceptions of gang members as "other" and to support suppressive policies against them.

CATEGORIZATION

Through categorization, individuals are assigned to a group, which in turn is presented as homogenous ("gang," "gang member"). A collective identity is created, and the characteristics associated with the group can be attributed to all its members. If the category becomes linked with negative traits and activities, these unfavorable inferences will then be seen to apply to everyone in the group.[69] Categorization can be observed in these newspaper excerpts from headlines and subtitles: "Mara 18 Attacks Guard in Soyapango" (EDH, 2 August 2003) and "Gang Members Assassinate More Women" (LPG, 31 December 2003).

Categorization has serious repercussions insofar as it entails stereotyping—that is, a simplified and reductive image is applied to an entire group. Media stereotypes provide partial and therefore misleading impressions and invite readers to form erroneous opinions of the members of a group. When the behaviors or characteristics of the group are portrayed negatively, society will marginalize and reject all individuals associated with this category, whether they personally engage in the stereotypical behaviors or not.

In the case of the street gangs, the inferences that could be drawn from the above excerpts were that (a) gang members constituted an undifferentiated group that was regularly linked to crime or violence, and (b) everyone defined as a gang member was criminal and violent. The Salvadoran press reproduced stereotypes about gang members on both the textual and pictorial levels. Coverage tended to highlight descriptive traits, such as dramatic nicknames or tattoos, and involvement in drugs, crime, and violence. Attention-grabbing but sometimes misleading headlines might often be all that readers absorbed. For example, headlines beginning with "*Maras* Assassinate" declared with certainty that gang members had killed someone, yet the corresponding articles suggested that this "fact" was merely the unverified statement of a police officer. Reporting of this kind encouraged negative stereotypes about gang members as universally violent. The recurrent publication of photos showing tattooed alleged gang members in the hands of law enforcement agents falsely implied that gang members were persistently involved in criminal activities.

CRIMINALIZATION

Categorization invoked a crude image of gang members as criminal and relentlessly violent individuals. Media coverage reinforced this association by explicitly criminalizing gang members in a variety of ways, including singling out emblematic gang members, blaming unattributed criminal activities on gang members, constructing the idea of "gang bosses," and quantifying the "gang threat" with circumstantial information. Collectively, these descriptive elements painted a picture of gang members as irrational, perverse, and motivated by a desire to terrorize the population. The reports further manipulated the qualitative nature of this ostensible menace with selectively deployed statistics.

The figure of the emblematic gang member, an individual singled out by the media through profiling and repeated references, served to symbolize the world of criminal, violent, and threatening gangs. These individuals attracted media attention for their striking nicknames, tattoos, and dress as much as for their arrest and criminal records and their attempts to evade justice. For example, a young man known as "el Crazy" acquired notoriety for his jailbreaks and alleged involvement in the decapitation of a woman. Articles about "el Dark" reflected fascination with the large "18" tattooed across his face, his repeated detentions, and his outburst of anger at being apprehended for a triple homicide (for which he was later convicted). Stories about "el Diablito," one of the first to be captured under Mano Dura, exploited his penchant for skull and horn tattoos, his defiant look, and twenty-three arrests.

Carlos Mojica—known as "el Viejo Lin"—was the figure most often in the media spotlight. News items generally charted his recurring arrests, court hearings, and suspensions of criminal proceedings. Police alleged that he was the national leader of the Dieciocho and linked him to the dismemberment of a young girl, despite the tenuous nature of both assertions. News reports depicted Carlos Mojica as a dangerous individual who could be expected to commit more crimes. The population, particularly the residents in his former community, was told to fear the worst, and as long as his conviction remained elusive, more policing was the only response. It was asserted that his rank within his gang made the need for his incarceration all the more urgent, and he (and others like him) should remain in prison.

The officials' assertions were conveyed as factually correct, and the journalists disowned any responsibility for what was said by failing to question its premises. The idea of a clear, hierarchical leadership structure within the gang appeared to be endorsed by the reporters. In short, the image of a sociopathic gang leader, who commanded a group of similarly criminal and violent individuals, was established and disseminated without mitigating information. Thus, the media not only denigrated Mojica, but also misled the public about gang structures and the crime associated with gangs.

PORTRAYALS OF GANG CRIME AND VIOLENCE   The media advanced a number of chilling but distorted claims about gang crime patterns. While the link between street gangs and crime is real, it was mischaracterized and overstated in press reports. The media-reinforced image of highly structured, organized, and extremely violent criminal groups had two significant implications. First, by misinforming the population about the reality of the gangs, it stoked fear and fostered greater public support for punitive measures. Second, by painting gang members as increasingly vicious and destructive, apparently motivated by pathology rather than by social and economic disadvantage, media coverage allowed the authorities to justify a punitive response and to give preference to it.

A variety of techniques were used to depict the gangs as purposefully criminal entities. For instance, the media repeatedly quoted government and police officials who made claims to that effect, thus constructing—rather than objectively reporting—knowledge about the gangs. President Flores referred to them as "criminal gangs . . . with truly savage rites" (LPG, 15 January 2004) and as "organized groups of murderers" (EDH, 9 February 2004). Note his choice of frightening imagery, and his assumption that all gang members are the same. Emotional language was also used by police officers, as in this comment by Police Commissioner Pedro González: "I have never seen an MS gang carrying out social works. . . . They gather to commit crimes" (EDH, 27 July 2003).

Neither newspaper limited itself to simply reporting official declarations, but endorsed various definitions of the "criminal street gang" in its coverage. One item that purported to offer a profile of the typical gang member explicitly warned readers: "The exception of not committing crimes does not exist" (EDH, 23 September 2003).

El Diario de Hoy chose to attribute criminality to gang members based on their group affiliation and certain descriptive traits. The following article reported the arrest of three gang members for a multiple homicide before describing the reporter's encounter with the detainees:

> During the interviews the three seemed calm. Their short and softly spoken answers made you think that they were well behaved and incapable of committing crimes. However, when they admitted to be active Dieciocho members and showed their tattooed backs and legs, they demonstrated the opposite to be the case. (EDH, 22 June 2006)

This excerpt determines the suspects' alleged culpability from nothing more than personal characteristics (tattoos) and association with a lifestyle (gang membership). It is misleading with regard to the facts of who these men are, offering one more example of how the media propagated stereotypes about gang members.

It is not a dominant behavior, such as violence or particular crime patterns, that marks a street gang, but rather crime versatility.[70] It is inaccurate to see gang crime as more than a by-product of the group context. Street gangs come into existence not for criminal reasons but because they serve to fulfill the social needs of their members.[71] While individual gang members certainly do commit crimes, the assumption that all gang members do so to the same extent as the worst among them is unfounded. Media accounts such as the above not only are factually incorrect but also invite misguided gang control policies.

The likelihood that the public will support punitive measures is heightened when news items incorporate stereotypically alarming photos that emphasize the "otherness" of the gang members. During the period of analysis, the pages of both *La Prensa Gráfica* and *El Diario de Hoy* abounded with such pictures. Gang members were usually shown in one of several positions that suggested they were in permanent conflict with the law. For example, after a police operation, gang members were photographed either on the ground and restrained, while police officers in military-style outfits pointed high-caliber weapons at them, or standing and in handcuffs. They also appeared locked up in a cell. Males were mostly shown without shirts to reveal their tattooed torsos, casting defiant looks and flashing gang hand signs.

Invariably taken from the point of view of the police, the images reinforced the idea that those being arrested had broken the law. Furthermore, the ways in which the images were framed had the effect of making the subjects appear alien and menacing. Both newspapers sometimes published such photos even if they were unrelated to the content of the article. Photographs are the most eye-catching elements of a news story, and these images served to perpetuate gang stereotypes.

Another method of exaggerating the criminal nature of the gangs was to repeat official sources that portrayed their alleged acts of violence as senseless, the result of individual pathologies. For example, *La Prensa Gráfica* quoted Police Chief Ricardo Menesses, who described gang activity as an "irrational fight" (LPG, 11 June 2004). In an interview, reported without comment, Police Chief Menesses replied to one question with the following opinion: "Gang members have a mental illness called murder" (LPG, 24 October 2004). From *El Diario de Hoy*: "Various gang members killed a youth for no apparent reason" (EDH, 24 July 2003). Sure to prejudice a strongly religious population, this opinion piece described gang activity as rooted in evil: "It suffices to investigate some of the most notorious cases of the *maras* who, according to the PNC, participate in satanic rites. This is why body parts appear in various parts of the country" (EDH, 28 June 2006).

Media accounts highlighted the supposed character deficiencies of gang members, such as irrationality and a disregard for human life. Stereotyping individuals in this way dissociated them from normal society by categorizing them as "other" than the reader and, together with certain causal explanations of the gang phenomenon, paved the way for suppression.

The media coverage of gangs tended to emphasize serious and violent criminal acts, including *sicariato* and extrajudicial executions ostensibly carried out to spark collective fear. Extrajudicial executions include multiple homicides and cases of extreme brutality, such as the mutilation, torture, and decapitation of victims, often committed for no apparent reason.[72] Predictably, claims of gang involvement in these crimes were made by official sources and repeated by the press. For example, *La Prensa Gráfica* drew on an unnamed PNC study to describe gang behavior: "According to the police, gang members commit the majority of homicides, rapes, robberies, thefts and injuries" (LPG, 25 July 2003).

Media accounts that concentrated on serious offenses failed to recognize that criminal acts were only a minor part of gang members' activities and that gang members were not equally involved in crime.[73] Furthermore, it is misleading for law enforcement to count every crime committed by a gang member as "gang crime" (gang member designation), rather than counting only those crimes known to be directly related to gang membership (motive designation).[74] Using such a broadbrush practice, as the PNC appeared to do, ensured that the resulting picture would be a caricature of the gangs.

Gang members have been linked officially and in the press to the majority of homicides in El Salvador and, for a number of years, to the grisly decapitations of girls and women, despite no proof of a connection in most cases.[75] Depictions of gang members as ever more violent and barbaric would logically undermine the rationale for prevention and rehabilitation programs. Not only did both newspapers paint Dante-esque scenes of violent gang crime, they also failed to question the official interpretation of events and endorsed it to their readers.

Although violence serves an important symbolic function in street gangs, their members do not specialize in violent crimes. In the words of one leading gang researcher, their offending is "cafeteria-style," spanning a wide range of violent and nonviolent transgressions.[76] Furthermore, gang homicides, compared to non-gang homicides, are more likely to occur on the street in broad daylight and to involve firearms, male participants, and victims who are identifiable gang members.[77] The clandestine mutilation and dismemberment of victims, particularly females, did not bear the hallmarks of gang violence. Indeed, a 2006 study of extrajudicial executions found that most of these crimes did not display the characteristics of gang violence, but rather looked like death squad–style killings, which accords with the historic pattern of human rights abuses in the country.[78]

Violent crime makes for dramatic news stories that capture readers' attention but may come at the expense of accuracy. The media reluctance to probe official statements disseminated a narrow view of street gang behavior. Press overemphasis of violent gangs encouraged public misperception of these groups and promoted the parochial interests of the authorities.

The two newspapers further portrayed the street gangs as a collective criminal threat by evoking the specter of transnational gangs and associating them with organized crime and international terrorism. News reporting on the purported transnational links included numerous stories on events in the United States. There, Mara Salvatrucha became a priority of federal law enforcement when it was linked to several high-profile incidents in the Washington, DC, area. In the Salvadoran media, MS-13 symbolized the transnational street gang: organized, criminal, and violent. The press located "authoritative" sources who agreed with this characterization, such as Central American police chiefs or, as in the following excerpt, the US ambassador to El Salvador: "The US ambassador to this country, Douglas Barclay, . . . also maintained that the gangs are not simple criminal groups. 'The *maras* rape, kill, and that is a great threat to the whole region. . . . They are part of organized crime with international ties,' warned Barclay."

Existing research suggests that while some gang members maintain links abroad, there is insufficient evidence to support the idea of institutionalized cross-border contacts at the group level.[79] Mara Salvatrucha and the Dieciocho have a presence in the United States, parts of Mexico, and across Central America, but they do not form a transnational criminal network. Rather, they must be seen as localized groups that identify with the name of an umbrella organization.

Rhetoric that perpetuates the perception of all gangs as transnational criminal networks, and goes unchallenged by the Salvadoran press, has two implications. First, it insinuates that if these gangs pose a threat to a country as powerful and well resourced as the United States, then surely the danger is even greater to a country as small and resource-starved as El Salvador. Second, the image of transnational criminal gangs deflects attention from the conditions of social and economic disadvantage that fester in local communities and must be addressed by the government of each of the countries concerned.

The purported links among street gangs, organized crime, and international terrorism received significant attention by the press. Editorial pages uncritically echoed the concerns voiced by President Saca, Gobernación and PNC officials, Honduran and US authorities (such as the Department of Homeland Security and the State Department), and Central American police chiefs and military officials. Police Chief Menesses was quoted without comment after one anti-gang operation: "For us, they are terrorists. They are the new terrorists of El Salvador" (LPG, 4 March 2004).

Although *La Prensa Gráfica* made an effort to balance the statements of official actors with alternative voices, champions of prevention and rehabilitation appeared to be selectively quoted to play down the social nature of the gang phenomenon. For example, when the then-president of the CNSP, Óscar Bonilla, was asked about a link between gangs and organized crime, he stated that the gangs, once related to marginalization and poverty, needed to be re-characterized. The gangs, he said, no longer competed for territory, but for drug and weapons markets (LPG, 3 November 2005). With this statement, the representative of the state agency that had done the most to promote gang prevention and rehabilitation in El Salvador was supporting the opposing view.

The media seemed determined to keep the alleged links alive despite conflicting information from officials. In its editorials, *La Prensa Gráfica* accepted the purported alliance between street gangs and organized crime, while *El Diario de Hoy* placed these two in the same category as terrorist groups. Each newspaper featured only one critical opinion piece each, rejecting the notion that street gangs and terrorist groups behave alike. These items, however, were buried among the editorials and op-eds that took the opposite view.

This has important consequences for gang control, so it is necessary to dispel two of the myths that the media were spreading. Most street gangs lack mature, professional members with organizational skills; well-defined leadership and specialized group roles; codes of conduct with clearly understood sanctions; and locations for profits to be used for group purposes. Typically, organized crime groups develop relationships with legitimate businesses, as well as with political and legal institutions.[80] Illegal activity forms part of street gang identity, but this is insufficient to classify them as organized criminal groups. A note of caution also applies to alleged gang involvement in drug trafficking. Some gang members or cliques may provide logistical or security support, but street gangs, whose members tend to be very young, are unlikely to possess the skills required for the drug trafficking business.[81]

As for street gangs resembling terrorist groups, suffice it to make two points. First, violent crime, whether or not it is gang-related, raises fear within the population, but the gangs did not pursue political objectives, and most of their targets were other gang members, not innocent civilians. Second, officials were frequently cited speculating about a future link between the street gangs and terrorist groups. However, it seems unlikely that Al-Qaeda or other terrorist networks would require the services of street gangs. Invoking a terrorist threat in a post-9/11 environment helps to secure financial aid to confront the danger, but it is of little use in the control of street gangs. Regrettably, the Salvadoran media lent themselves to such demagogy.

THE "GANG BOSS"   Gang members were also criminalized by the construction of the "gang boss." Press coverage included repeated references to *líder* (leader), *cabecilla* (ringleader), *jefe de las pandillas* (gang boss), or *jefe de clica* (clique boss), inspired in part by the authorities stereotyping gang leadership to suit their law enforcement strategies.

Two comments must be made about gang leadership. First, the word *cabecilla*, with its connotation of the professional criminal world, reinforced the idea that illegal activities constituted the primary motivation of street gangs. Second, researchers have found gang leadership to be functional, shifting, and shared among many gang members. It often depends less on physical strength or criminal involvement than on verbal skills, social capacities, and age.[82] Interviews with former gang members affirmed that the gangs had no leaders as such. At most, some individuals enjoyed influence within a clique because they had gained respect. This makes gang leadership quite unlike the hierarchical and command-oriented concept implied by the Salvadoran media.

THE "GANG THREAT" IN NUMBERS   Finally, media coverage quantified the gang threat through both estimates of membership and the number of gang homicides, but used these statistics in misleading ways to support erroneous conceptions about patterns in gang-related crime. The exact number of gang members in any country is notoriously difficult to establish and is not important to this analysis. The point here is to show how the newspapers used their own statistics to produce a particular image of the gang problem.

During the period of analysis, gang membership figures cited in news reports differed significantly and suggested that *El Diario de Hoy* in particular intended to mislead its readers. In one example, both papers quote President Flores at the launch of Mano Dura, but the EDH article manipulated the statistics, probably to buttress his assertion that gang members vastly outnumbered the police and military. "'There are more *mareros* than police and soldiers combined; so they are already a threat to all Salvadorans,' he said" (LPG, 24 July 2003). The EDH article stated that "according to Saldec, there are an estimated 17,000 gang members in the country, but other sources believe that there could be more than 30,000. 'There are more armed gang members than police and soldiers combined,' affirmed the President. According to official sources, the police have 18,000 officers and the army some 12,000 men" (EDH, 24 July 2003).

During the Mano Dura period, official figures oscillated, citing between 9,000 and 10,500 identified and recorded gang members. Police estimates are limited to those gang members with whom the police have had contact, but no evidence confirms that the actual figures might have reached "more than 30,000." *El Diario de Hoy* may have used such an inflated figure to substantiate the president's assertion that gang members outnumber (and "outgun," as the paper hinted) the security and military forces. Subsequently, *La Prensa Gráfica* continued to publish the lower PNC figures, while *El Diario de Hoy* most often referred to "government estimates" of either 17,000 or 33,000 gang members, thus amplifying the "gang threat" by combining questionable statistics with reporting that suggested that all gang members were armed criminals. The paper failed to ask why, if this was indeed the case, government and police had not stepped in earlier to prevent gang growth. It also implied that the state lacked the capacity to confront the problem. This was a disconcerting claim that might prompt citizens to take justice into their own hands, especially given the country's history of vigilantism. With these facts in mind, it is important to understand gang members' actual contribution to the country's homicide rate.

Over the years, the IML attributed between 8 and 10 percent of annual homicides to gang members.[83] A UN study suggested that a 60 percent share in the country's murder rate, which was the figure most commonly attributed to gang members by Salvadoran authorities, would have been highly atypical for street gangs.[84] Since most of those who died by gang violence were other gang members, this rate meant that the numbers of gang members should have gone down dramatically because most of them would have already died!

El Diario de Hoy and *La Prensa Gráfica* uncritically reported whatever percentage the police provided, which was anywhere between 40 and 80 percent of all homicides. By doing so, the papers were complicit in giving the public conflicting messages, since the figures at times referred to gang involvement in crimes (not all of which are homicides) or to gang homicides that involved gang members as *either* perpetrators *or* as victims. The manipulative use of statistics made it difficult for readers to put the public security consequences of the street gangs into perspective and appeared to legitimize the escalation of punitive measures against these groups.

DICHOTOMIZATION

The press accentuated the popular perception of gang members as a homogeneous class of criminals by fostering a number of binary concepts. The main theme running through the media coverage was that of good versus evil. In the first category were the "honest citizens," the majority of Salvadorans, who were law-abiding and hard-working and deserved to have their rights protected. On the fringes of humanity and society, by contrast, were the gang members: criminal, irresponsible, "infected" with drugs and violence, dominated by evil, and unworthy of human rights defense. Based on perceived physical and behavioral traits, gang members were depicted as an atypical minority and compared with idealized images of the rest of society. These polarized representations typecast gang members as "folk devils" who deserved the public's hostility and the aggression of "the people."[85]

Both newspapers adopted these black-and-white representations in their reporting and in their editorial pages. *El Diario de Hoy* featured a number of paid advertisements that reinforced these images and were designed to lobby for anti-gang legislation. Emphasizing the "innocent victims" of evil gangs supported the perception of opposing sides in a fight. Reports portrayed non–gang members, particularly children and adolescents, who died as a result of gang violence with emotional wording that highlighted laudable personal attributes and achievements, such as dedication to study and work, religious values, and the pursuit of "healthy" recreational activities. The media encouraged audiences to identify with those on the white side (the public) and to reject those on the black side (gang members).

The newspapers explicitly described the gangs as satanic movements and cast gang control as a fight of good against evil, requiring strong institutions and harsh measures to defeat the threat. *La Prensa Gráfica* even reiterated the supposedly malevolent nature of gang members by depicting them as bloodthirsty vampires: "[T]he tense calm that prevails there during the day changes when night falls. The neighbors know that the gang members have adopted the habits of the vampires in the movies: they dress well during the day and at night occupy the streets and take control of the area" (LPG, 14 June 2004).

By invoking the image of parasitic beings that feed on mortals, and who in folklore were the embodiment of satanic activity, the paper linked gang members with an evil that must be warded off to avoid further danger.[86]

METAPHORS

The vocabulary used to describe gang members included metaphors evocative of natural disasters, the animal world, disease, rubbish, and war. The first of these inflates the gang problem to the proportion of a national menace, thus justifying the elaboration of extreme measures. The other four types of metaphor, however, dehumanize gang members. By repudiating their humanity and depicting them as enemies to society, such metaphors insinuate that gang members may be eliminated by whatever means necessary. The use of metaphors was pervasive in accounts of both gang activity and gang control options.

Likening gang activity and US deportations of gang members to natural disasters, *El Diario de Hoy* told readers the gangs "unleashed a wave of violence" (EDH, 21 February 2004). The newspaper compared deportations of gang members from the United States to a "tsunami" (EDH, 18 January 2005) or an "avalanche" (EDH, 18 October 2005), while *La Prensa Gráfica* warned of "a seaquake provoked by the repatriation of all these criminals" (LPG, 17 November 2003). Thus, in each case, the image was of a sudden, unstoppable event that brings great destruction to life and property. These warnings of catastrophe also suggested that the gang problem was of such magnitude that it threatened to overwhelm state institutions. The measures that come to mind to mitigate these disasters are barriers that, when used against people, foster segregation and exclusion. If the disaster is not stopped and becomes more destructive, however, the population may lose its confidence in the state's ability to provide public security and maintain the rule of law and may turn to vigilantism.

The papers also used metaphors to liken gang members to animals, implicitly inferior to humans. The implication, articulated in some accounts, is that gang members ought to be chased and killed in the same way that animals are stalked and attacked. The gangs were equated in another instance with an octopus: "The minister pointed out that the gang phenomenon has spread its tentacles over 30,000 students" (EDH, 19 August 2003). Articles, editorials, headlines, and photo captions told of real or imaginary animals that pursue and attack their quarry: "According to the police, the characters were lying in wait for potential victims, wolves prepared to attack the lambs" (editorial, EDH, 24 May 2006). The dwellings of gang members were similarly couched in metaphorical language: "The PNC asks the population to report the dens and hideouts of the *maras* in the neighborhoods" (EDH, 22 August 2003). Additionally, *El Diario de Hoy* often compared the police and soldiers, who jointly patrolled the streets, to hunters dispatched to chase the animals, as in this headline: "Deployment of the Gang Hunters" (EDH, 16 September 2004).

The above descriptions depicted gang members as inferior to the rest of the population, creating a psychological distance between different social groups. Disease, rubbish, and war metaphors reinforced this antagonistic relationship and invited aggression toward those who were perceived as abnormal and lesser beings. For example, a community with a local gang was described as being "infected with gangs" (LPG, 7 February 2005), suggesting that the gangs were a source of infection rather than a symptom of a deeper societal illness. On other occasions, the gangs were likened to a malignant tumor or a virulent and deadly epidemic: "The *maras* have spread like the plague" (EDH, 24 July 2003). Once the disease has been diagnosed, a treatment must be developed: "The *maras* and their by-products are a very serious social illness that requires a strong curative treatment and at the same time effective preventive measures" (editorial, LPG, 19 December 2005).

President Flores articulated the need for stronger treatments: "For Flores, the changes to the laws are 'aspirin . . . for a problem that requires surgery'" (EDH, 13 September 2003). Media coverage demanded that the source of the illness (gang members) be removed by any means necessary to avoid the contagion spreading within the social body. Associating gang members with rubbish meant the gang problem might be "cleaned up" by eliminating gang members. Both newspapers publicized President Flores's visit to a neighborhood in the city of San Miguel for another inauguration of Mano Dura. This area had gained notoriety in the 1990s for the emergence of the Sombra Negra death squad. Media accounts of the event clearly saw the significance of presenting gang control measures in a zone known for the execution of "undesirables." These reports stated unequivocally that gangs were rubbish or filth and that police and military cleanup operations were decontaminating the streets: "The party is over. The National Civilian Police and the military will sweep the gang members from El Salvador's neighborhoods and communities . . ." (EDH, 24 July 2003).

War, however, was the dominant metaphor to describe gang activity and the state's response to it. Presidents Flores and Saca, as well as PNC and other government officials, often voiced belligerent rhetoric. The media not only uncritically reproduced these statements, but also constructed their own "combat stories," perpetuating images of "warring gangs" and of a "war against the gangs." They depicted these groups as military forces with a clear chain of command and specialized units. These paramilitaries were, according to news accounts, engaged in urban guerrilla warfare, turning besieged communities into battle zones, harming civilians, and collecting "war taxes": "*Maras* Still Besiege 15 Municipalities in the Country" (EDH, 25 September 2003); "The *Maras* Collect a War Tax" (LPG, 4 May 2005).

Calling gang rivalry an armed conflict made the gangs appear much more goal-oriented and threatening than they were. Worse, it portrayed gang violence as the problem while diverting attention from the structural context that gives rise to gangs. Thanks to this kind of media coverage, gang members became the new public enemy, who could be targeted with malicious force and extreme violence.

Since the introduction of Mano Dura, the media have been complicit in the waging of "war" against the gangs. Newspapers legitimized this confrontational approach and did not question the appropriateness of framing gang control in this way. Photos of soldiers on armored vehicles or anti-gang squads conducting raids bolstered the message that El Salvador had declared war against street gangs to defend the nation, defeat and disarm the enemy, and liberate occupied areas. The newspapers uncritically portrayed the military deployments as necessary to support the police in their fight against an overwhelming opponent. A headline that declared "Total War against the *Maras*" was followed by the announcement that "[l]ast night President Flores announced a plan to liberate neighborhoods and communities from the gangs, with the support of the military and the PNC" (EDH, 24 July 2003).

The war metaphor assigned the gangs and their mitigation to the security realm, irresponsibly suggesting that the solution was retaliation against or elimination of the other side. A vocabulary of force elides the structural factors that shape the gang problem and detracts from the importance of social policies that will specifically address the needs of marginalized young people. The press might argue that their coverage only mirrored social reality and described government-sanctioned suppression efforts, but by merely echoing official terminology in their news reporting and failing to question the overall approach, the newspapers chose to take one side in the debate. This choice meant they would not fully inform citizens of the issues or present more useful alternatives.

EXTOLLING VIOLENCE AGAINST GANG MEMBERS

The newspapers covered vigilantism against gang members by suggesting that in return for security, such illegal actions might be permissible. Accounts of this kind appeared more frequently in *El Diario de Hoy*, which appeared to condone incidents of lynching in Honduras and Guatemala by publishing uncritical reports on the grisly incidents: "Tired of the crime wave, the inhabitants of Palín took the law into their hands and tried to burn two gang members alive" (EDH, 27 April 2006). A *La Prensa Gráfica* article quoted a vigilante: "'Súper Mano Dura does not work, that is why we had to take justice into our own hands. Seven months ago they killed one of our brothers. Yesterday they killed the second. That was the last thing they did, these people from that *mara*'" (LPG, 10 July 2005). Disregard for the law and human rights was treated as justifiable by the press and made to seem understandable rather than horrifying.

Factors for Gang Development

The next step in the research explored how the newspapers addressed the reasons why young people joined gangs, as well as why gangs emerged in the first place and then persisted. The factors associated with gang development fell into one or more of six areas: the individual, the family, the community, the society, a communist conspiracy, and US deportation policy.

La Prensa Gráfica and *El Diario de Hoy* leaned toward episodic (event-oriented or case history–focused) rather than thematic framing, which puts events and issues into context and fosters a more analytic comprehension.[87] The need to meet tight news production schedules, along with journalistic attempts to make news more entertaining, helps explain the prevalence of episodic coverage. The result is that structural processes and circumstances are not given the treatment that would allow the public to understand complex social problems such as street gangs. Episodic news framing leads audiences to assign blame to the individual rather than to the larger societal causes of misbehavior.[88] This episodic format is likely to increase public support for Mano Dura, rather than for social policies. Ultimately, it reflects a choice not to publish content that jeopardizes the status quo.

El Diario de Hoy maintained a more consistently conservative editorial line, vigorously rejecting the idea that social and economic disadvantages influence gang development. Although it embraces a more pluralistic editorial line, *La Prensa Gráfica* also shied away from taking a position that could prove controversial with powerful actors in the country. Showing a predilection for personal stories and interviews, the paper would attribute references to structural factors to other sources.

INDIVIDUAL-LEVEL FACTORS

To join a gang is an individual choice, typically made in a context of social marginalization and motivated by a desire to fulfill certain needs that gang affiliation may partly satisfy. Anyone attempting to understand why youths might want to be in a street gang should consider the interaction of psychological and structural variables and acknowledge that while there are some predominant reasons for participation, none applies across the board.

La Prensa Gráfica rarely considered young people's motivations, or it referred to them in only the most general terms. *El Diario de Hoy* mostly portrayed gang joining as a private decision taken by incomprehensibly dangerous and immoral individuals who chose criminality over work and personal responsibility. In "Radiografía del fenómeno: Las maras," a three-part feature that inquired into the causes of gangs, the paper told its readers that a street gang is "a group of youths who gather to have fun and commit crimes."

The prospect of fun—and, to a lesser extent, illegal activity—is indeed one reason young people join a gang, but not the primary one. If the systemic influences on young people's lives were acknowledged, social policies would seem to be logical measures. Instead, biased reporting invites moral condemnation and simplistically punitive responses.

FAMILY- AND COMMUNITY-LEVEL FACTORS

Family breakdown and the presumed inevitable loss of moral values was one of the causal themes that dominated gang-related media coverage, particularly that of *El Diario de Hoy*. Editorials blamed parental neglect and moral lapse for gang growth, with a cursory reference to dysfunctional families, yet remained apparently oblivious to these families' social and economic circumstances. Judging from the number of features and editorials, *La Prensa Gráfica* assigned greater importance to this explanation than did *El Diario de Hoy*. LPG coverage was striking for the stream of editorials that broached family breakdown, though mostly with obscure references—for example, a "fractured family structure"— that left readers guessing what the actual problem might be.

These rationalizations were misguided for several reasons. First, many gang members in El Salvador were raised in single-parent households or by relatives, but many others were not. The dominant risk factors are dysfunctional families, parental neglect, and domestic violence, not family structure.[89] Second, low-income families do not inevitably produce gang members, but parental abandonment can be caused as much by economic need as indifference. Adults who work long hours to make ends meet will find it harder to monitor their children and socialize them adequately.

The two major newspapers rarely mentioned the importance of the community context in gang growth and gang control. In "Radiografía," *El Diario de Hoy* noted that gangs emerge in the poorest areas of the country, but reduced the connection between gangs and their environment to one of inappropriate living conditions. *La Prensa Gráfica* was equally remiss: a handful of articles offered only that gang youths were from poor barrios or that such places were overcrowded and had "precarious" public services. Press coverage implied that street gangs were one more product of environments that "infect" their inhabitants with moral pollution.

SOCIETY-LEVEL FACTORS

To explain the broad societal factors influencing gangs, the media referred to the criminal justice system, a culture of violence, and social exclusion. Advocates of Mano Dura argued that gang growth was a consequence of the impunity generated by permissive legislation and liberal judges, and press coverage echoed this position to varying degrees. Although *La Prensa Gráfica* rarely connected gang proliferation to the perceived lenience of the criminal justice system, *El Diario de Hoy*, in contrast, made the justice system a recurrent theme. A series of articles and paid advertisements—the latter supporting the enactment of the Ley Anti Maras—criticized "guaranteeist" penal laws that provided "excessive" protection for criminals. The sentiment was most conspicuous in editorials alleging that the low number of convictions must indicate judicial complicity with gang members, which, when viewed alongside the work of human rights groups, sent a message of impunity. They derided "laws for the Swiss," which seemed to favor the rights of criminals over those of the honest population. *El Diario de Hoy* used the accusation of impunity in its calls for stricter laws and for the arrest and punishment of anyone involved in a gang. One editorial specifically urged the authorities to act firmly and suggested that this might entail shoot-to-kill orders for the police.

The history of El Salvador is inextricably intertwined with the use of violence, much of it once perpetrated by agents of the state. Generations of young people have been raised and socialized in an environment where cultural norms and attitudes favor aggressive behavior, both in interpersonal relations and as a means of conflict resolution. Studies have suggested that this context has much to do with the violence committed by gang members.[90] The armed conflict served as a classroom for the use and legitimization of force. The war spread weapons throughout society and precipitated the emigration of traumatized refugees. Subsequent deportations of Salvadoran youths helped spread US gang culture in their native, but often alien and unremembered, land. The civil war created some of the conditions that would influence the local character of the street gangs, but the culture of violence has greater explanatory weight in the gangs.

Media coverage, however, avoided reference to this factor and maintained that the war had directly triggered the gangs. *El Diario de Hoy* editorialized that these groups were the consequence of the hate, rebellion, and incitement to crime preached during the "years of madness." The unspoken assumption was that the gangs were an expression of the class resentment fostered by the FMLN's war against "the Salvadoran people."

One of the factors that stimulate gang growth is social exclusion, which translates into the socio-economic deprivation experienced by households and the social neglect of communities. Families that struggle to survive and can offer few educational opportunities for their children are those that may produce gang members.[91]

Street gangs emerge in marginal communities: places with inadequate housing conditions, lack of recreational space, deficient basic services, substandard roads, often no street lighting, and derelict public buildings.[92] Although the media covered this issue extensively, it was addressed in very different ways, perhaps due to its policy implications. The editorial line of *La Prensa Gráfica*, for example, was ambivalent. The sizeable number of editorials that addressed structural factors in the emergence of gangs did not reject the association between poverty and gang membership. Indeed, the paper appeared to argue that deep-seated socio-economic disadvantages accounted in large measure for gang development and needed to be alleviated. Systemic causes nevertheless were consistently phrased in very vague terms, such as "social imbalances" or "the basic arrangements of society and the living conditions of large parts of the population," suggesting that the paper did not wish to alienate certain powerful audiences.

By contrast, *El Diario de Hoy* was at pains to deny the impact of structural factors on gang development. Most revealing were the editorials and "Radiografía," which sought to dispel the idea that poverty was important to gang emergence. The former pointed to the examples of Nicaragua (a very poor nation with low levels of gang violence) or "prosperous" US cities that gave birth to violent gangs to counter the "poverty myth," or else it simply rejected the claim as a perverse "leftist" or "communist" analysis.

"Radiografía" admitted that street gangs emerge in poor communities, but contended that it was young people's domestic living conditions, not their situation of poverty, that encouraged gang membership. This argument was supported with reference to volume two of the study *Maras y pandillas en Centroamérica*, but the research found that street gangs develop not in the *most* deprived communities, but in those that boast relative economic equality among residents. The reality remains that communities with a gang presence are always those that experience need and state neglect.[93]

A COMMUNIST CONSPIRACY

Some of the coverage by the two newspapers suggested that the gangs were part of a left-wing conspiracy. This resembles the idea that the gangs are the consequence of the "FMLN's war against the Salvadoran people," but it ascribes a greater degree of intentionality to what was then the main opposition party. According to this line of reasoning, the political left was trying to destabilize the country in a bid for power, and the street gangs were the means to do so. Gang crime and violence, combined with demonstrations against the conservative government by the FMLN's "front groups," were intended to create despair among the population. This apparently would drive people to believe that the "communists" were in a better position to solve El Salvador's problems than ARENA.

La Prensa Gráfica somewhat distanced itself from these assertions, confining them to opinion columns and an interview with President Saca. *El Diario de Hoy*, in contrast, adopted this position as its editorial line. The allegations seemed intended to vilify the FMLN and surfaced more often in the run-up to elections. Gang members may well have participated in social protests whose goals they supported or if they were hired to march by either side of the political spectrum. The conspiracy theory, however, does not account for gangs in El Salvador. Rather, it is an explanation concocted by those who prefer to scapegoat the FMLN for the country's social ills rather than to acknowledge that street gangs exist because of the social marginalization of large parts of Salvadoran society.

US DEPORTATION POLICY

Finally, the press insinuated that a primary cause of El Salvador's gangs was the US policy of returning non-citizen gang members who were convicted of crimes to their country of origin. There are two dimensions to this claim, which was encountered in both EDH editorial pages and news coverage that reported or endorsed official statements. The first one argues that since El Salvador's two main street gangs, Mara Salvatrucha and the Dieciocho, originated in Los Angeles, they were an imported problem, not a domestic creation. Street gangs, however, have existed in El Salvador since the 1970s, while the numbers of deportations were relatively insignificant before the late 1980s. What deported gang members brought with them was a distinct US street gang culture and particular gang identities, which then spread among the local groups.

The second dimension to the "imported gangs" theory holds that deportations exacerbated the gang problem in El Salvador. Upon arrival in their native country, it was said, repatriated individuals reunited with their gang and went on to commit crimes, driving up the crime rate.

Both newspapers endorsed this claim in editorial pages and news reports, regurgitating the views of government and police officials.

Returned gang members who remained involved in gang life or broke the law may have included committed gang members. However, there were also those who found themselves in what was for them an alien country, where they may have been unable to speak the language, were offered no social insertion opportunities, and lacked any family or support network other than the street gang. Continued gang membership says as much about the Salvadoran government's neglect of rehabilitation programs as it does about individuals' gang loyalty.

Statistical analyses of the impact of repatriated gang members on the receiving society are unavailable. Without data, sweeping claims that deported gang members amplify El Salvador's crime rate appear exaggerated. The street gangs are a homegrown problem that emerges from socially marginalized communities and comprises largely local youth. Media coverage that pointed to external causes and inflated the impact of deported gang members implied that the Salvadoran authorities had no responsibility other than to arrest and prosecute offenders. Further, this coverage excused the government's failure to develop a coherent public security strategy. The third and final section of the content analysis examines how the press treated the gang control strategies pursued by the governments of Francisco Flores and Antonio Saca.

Gang Control: Mano Dura, Prevention, and Rehabilitation

Media coverage of both gang activity and the factors that led gangs to emerge and young people to join them tended to favor a punitive approach. This part describes how critically the newspapers viewed suppression, prevention, and rehabilitation. The reporting encompassed three one-year-long phases: Mano Dura (2003–2004), Súper Mano Dura (2004–2005), and the plan's eventual "re-launch" (2005–2006).

PHASE I: MANO DURA

The timing and suppressive tactics of Mano Dura suggested to skeptical observers that the plan was electorally driven and would likely prove ineffective. Bias in favor of suppression pervaded the coverage of the two major newspapers, but to what extent was there space for criticism of Mano Dura, and how was it conveyed?

El Diario de Hoy staunchly defended Mano Dura and proffered little, if any, criticism of the initiative. The commentaries in this phase char-

acterized the plan as entirely appropriate, faulted its opponents for being oblivious to the common good, and dismissed the need for social
policies, since these had failed in the past. Consistent with EDH hostility toward structural factors, the editorials unfailingly backed Mano
Dura. The plan was appropriate not only because of its immediate effects, but also because punishment was the best deterrent for crime.

For human rights advocates and opposition politicians, newspaper
articles provided the only space in this first phase to voice disapproval
of Mano Dura and call for prevention, rehabilitation, and a coherent
crime policy. Selective editing and a tendency to bury criticism in the final lines of items on punitive aspects of gang control, however, often diminished their influence. Juxtaposing criticism with official statements
stressing the alleged benefits of the plan accomplished the same end.

Unlike its competitor, *La Prensa Gráfica* did not explicitly support
Mano Dura. While it displayed greater tolerance for dissent in its pages,
its own stance was one of muted disagreement, if not exactly neutral-
ity. Government policy was assailed most vigorously in opinion columns
and paid advertisements, the latter purchased mostly by FESPAD and
other NGOs. The main thrust of these pieces was that Mano Dura was
a superficial initiative, neglected non-gang crime, and, by mass detentions alone, purported to resolve a problem rooted in social exclusion.

For these observers, the solution to the country's public insecurity
must be a three-pronged gang policy—prevention, law enforcement,
and rehabilitation—that included the criminal prosecution of all offenders. LPG editorials took a similar line, but generally strove to present
both sides of the argument without passing judgment. The criticism focused on the years of official indifference to the gangs that permitted
their unrestrained growth. Also, the sudden interest in and timing of a
gang policy raised questions about its relation to electoral politics and
the government's deeper commitment to finding a solution.

From late 2003 onward, when the increasing murder rate began
to evince the plan's failure, *La Prensa Gráfica* shifted to a reliance on
"safe facts." Official statistics indicated that only 5 percent of arrested
gang members had been imprisoned, and annual homicide figures had
climbed under Mano Dura. Journalists used this information to "ob-
jectify" their value judgments and to observe that the policy had not
demonstrated its efficacy. Over time, persistent allusion to the escalating homicide rate became the paper's preferred method of questioning the government's approach to gang control and public security. *La
Prensa Gráfica* became less likely to be attacked for picking a fight with

the authorities, but as a news provider it did nothing more than state the obvious.

THE SPECTACLE OF MANO DURA   To convince the public that the authorities were acting decisively against the gangs, the persecution of these groups had to be publicized. The media played an important role in selling the supposed effectiveness of Mano Dura. This included the spectacle of Mano Dura: the dramatization of police operations and public exhibitions of arrested gang members.

The dramatic suppressive operations attracted the attention of journalists more than other gang control strategies did. Anti-gang sweeps, often with preplanned press coverage, satisfied both governmental public relations concerns and the media's interest in exciting news. Both papers, but particularly *La Prensa Gráfica*, offered gripping accounts of nighttime raids conducted by hundreds of heavily armed uniformed officers, describing with relish how police battered down doors and raided homes to arrest suspects. An abundance of photos documented and bolstered this display of state power, resolve, and authority.

After the operations, detainees were rounded up and presented to the media without regard to guilt or innocence. These ritualistic exhibitions completed gang members' transition to folk devil status. As "ceremonies of public degradation," the displays marked them as deviants that could be controlled only by the security apparatus of the state.[94] News coverage identified suspects with their full names (unless juveniles) and referred to them as "suspected killers," "suspected murderers," or even "criminals" in an explicit imputation of guilt. Pictures showed handcuffed individuals, half-naked or at least bare-chested to reveal their tattoos, guarded by heavily armed police and sometimes displayed with confiscated weapons.

When the media provided a platform for these exhibitions and a priori convictions of alleged offenders, they violated the legal presumption of innocence and helped create a public atmosphere in which gang members were regarded as having no rights. The papers published individual arrests, but nothing about the release of gang members who had not committed crimes. Thus, in the public mind the acquitted or wrongfully accused remained associated with crime. The damage to their reputation was irrevocable and was in no way mitigated by journalistic use of the term "suspected." Unlike many countries, including Spain, the United States, and Uruguay, where restrictions exist on the publication of photos and names of persons under arrest or investigation, El Salvador imposes no such constraints on its reporters.[95] Practices that undermine constitutional rights are perpetuated by a weak and corrupt criminal justice system. Journalists who fail to question them do so as members of a society that has an underdeveloped notion of individual rights.

MEASURING THE SUCCESS OF MANO DURA   The press relied on four kinds of benchmarks to gauge the alleged impact and effectiveness of Mano Dura: the apparent success of public security operations, tranquility in the communities, public opinion, and homicide figures.

Mano Dura advocated suppression as the only viable gang deterrence method, and the accomplishments of law enforcement served to project an image of success. In both newspapers, a series of PNC-sponsored paid ads—"Mano Dura in Action"—highlighted the dedication and self-sacrifice of police and soldiers and furnished weekly summaries of the "war on gangs." Against a background of dramatic imagery, these pieces recounted how these "very effective" anti-gang activities resulted in arrests, the removal of graffiti, and the recovery of *destroyers* (gang hangouts); decreased or prevented homicides; and generally made residential areas much safer and quieter. Publicity in support of Mano Dura was most evident in these stories and permeated news reports that depended on police data.

The bulk of this coverage focused on graffiti removal and arrests. Journalists described how walls in community after community were repainted. They quoted officials affirming that the elimination of gang symbols indicated that these places were now gang-free. The papers never questioned government priorities or the deeper significance of the elimination of these emblems. Should time and resources be expended for graffiti removal while gang activity persisted? Might the special attention and publicity actually enhance the gangs' self-image and status? Could the absence of gang symbols reflect an acceptance of this countermove rather than any cessation of gang activity (which is what actually occurred)? In short, the press merely spotlighted the authorities' promotional efforts and failed to ask whether these steps might have been premature, or possibly counterproductive.

A similar lack of deliberation extended to detentions. The newspapers provided arrest statistics, and bold headlines proclaimed more gang members had been taken off the streets. Buried in the articles or dismissed by the police chief was the fact that most were later released. Arrest figures were touted as a sign of police effectiveness and a validation of Mano Dura. The media published no deeper investigations and raised no doubts about the possible waste of resources or the evidentiary quality of the cases taken to court.

One of the more dubious claims about the positive impact of Mano Dura cited greater calm in the communities. Both newspapers repeated police assurances that the use of force was bringing peace and security to Salvadoran families. Reporters were dispatched to some of the gang-affected areas to talk to locals, who concurred that PNC operations had restored serenity in the streets. (How many people were interviewed was left unclear.) Close to the anniversary of Mano Dura, journalists returned from their field trips to report that in reality the tranquility reflected gang members' adaptation to the police's regular patrols and sweeps. It was only these later accounts that suggested that "tranquility" did not equal security and that the apparent respite in gang activity offered no positive conclusions about the government's program.

The government's gang policy could also garner legitimacy by citing popular support through the publication of citizens' views and media-commissioned polls. On several occasions, *La Prensa Gráfica* published a collection of reader comments on Mano Dura. The paper printed a mix of favorable and critical opinions, but misled its audiences with sweeping headlines exclaiming that "the people" backed the measure. Officials invoked these reports of popular sentiment to dismiss any criticism and contend that Mano Dura was successful.

El Diario de Hoy and *La Prensa Gráfica* regularly commissioned surveys on issues such as the economy, crime, government performance, and voter preferences. This analysis of the two newspapers focuses on polls that asked respondents about their views on gangs and gang control measures. *La Prensa Gráfica* featured only one gang-related poll in this phase, while *El Diario de Hoy* conducted five, an indication perhaps of the paper's strong desire to invest Mano Dura with popular legitimacy. The EDH reports withheld survey questions, were inconsistent with the figures they provided, manipulated statistics, and drew unwarranted conclusions. Only the third of these survey reports actually divulged the approval rate of Mano Dura (70 percent), while the remainder found that the plan was considered only the second main achievement of the Flores government or was the most-remembered news story. This led the paper to deduce that the policy had been well received by the population. Yet, people may have simply recalled the initiative because of the striking images or the quantity of stories, rather than because they endorsed it.

This third EDH poll was remarkable for two additional reasons. First, it solicited interviewees' opinions on the causes of crime and gangs (assuming one was synonymous with the other). While the report highlighted those opinions that favored punitive responses, it glossed over the lack of job opportunities. Second, although it neglected prevention, the poll asked whether interviewees thought gang members could be rehabilitated and whether rehabilitation should be offered. In both respects, the answers were mostly affirmative (46 percent and 58 percent, respectively) rather than entirely negative (12 percent and 6 percent). The article appeared to highlight support for Mano Dura, noting that 18 percent of Salvadorans believed there was little possibility for rehabilitation. Not only was this conclusion inaccurate based on the data, it obscured the significant level of support for alternative gang programs. The poll suggested that at the same time that people endorsed gang suppression, they thought it should be complemented by rehabilitative measures.

The single LPG poll report was published early in this phase (August 2003) and included the survey questions. It revealed that the majority of respondents requested the immediate enactment of the Ley Anti Maras and felt the government genuinely sought to address the gang problem. Nonetheless, 40 percent of Salvadorans believed the policy was pandering to the electorate.

Surveys appear to reflect public opinion, yet they can also serve to legitimate partisan beliefs and add an element of influence to media coverage. Survey design can manipulate and shape the answers that respondents give. In El Salvador's case, different questions could have painted a different picture of the views of Salvadorans. But the poll results selected for publication, in the absence of more accurate data, retained their legitimacy in readers' minds as yardsticks of public opinion. Therefore, the surveys could construct favorable views of Mano Dura and influence the public's perception of the gang problem and the available remedies. Rather than merely measuring public opinion, the polls could mold it, which could be significant in a pre-election year.

Finally, consider how the media covered the authorities' use of homicide figures to declare the gang policy a success. Officials made two kinds of claims: Mano Dura was effective because first, it saved lives, and second, it lowered the homicide rate. The first assertion is specious on its face, given that no one can know who would have been killed in the absence of detentions, yet the newspapers did not challenge it.

Police often contended that Mano Dura had lowered the country's murder rate. Any attempt to compare the published data ends in confusion, however, as the figures offered by the two papers were at odds with each other. For example, after the policy had been in place for two months, *La Prensa Gráfica* spoke of a 40 percent reduction in homicides while *El Diario de Hoy* mentioned only 20 percent. To add to the ambiguity, journalists did not always clarify whether the decline was nationwide or limited to specific areas, such as Greater San Salvador. In Mano Dura's first few months, the press failed to challenge the information they were given and even endorsed it in headlines, though it appeared the PNC was manipulating the statistics. For instance, officers would argue that the homicide rate had diminished by 22.5 percent in the first one hundred days of Mano Dura, contrasted with the same period prior to the plan. By making selective comparisons, police could bolster their argument, but they failed to mention that the homicide rate had begun to rise in 2003.

It was only later that year, when police publicly acknowledged that the annual murder rate exceeded that of 2002, that *La Prensa Gráfica* began to question official rhetoric and Mano Dura. At that point, officials offered various justifications for the policy's emergent failure. For example, police insisted that the increase in homicides had occurred in the first half of 2003 and the upward trend had been halted because of Mano Dura. Justifications of this kind recurred in phases two and three: the introduction and decline of Súper Mano Dura.

PHASES 2 AND 3: SÚPER MANO DURA AND ITS "RE-LAUNCH"

Although Súper Mano Dura was meant to be more comprehensive than its precursor, it still focused on suppression, and press coverage reflected the dominance of this theme. This review of President Saca's gang policy examines three points: media references to gang control strategies and programs, assessments of the policy's impact, and explanations offered to justify the failure of Súper Mano Dura.

GANG CONTROL STRATEGIES AND PROGRAMS   Some support for the punitive strategies continued in both phases, but was mainly confined to the editorial pages in *El Diario de Hoy*. The paper, though gradually less vocal in its praise of suppression, was loath to acknowledge the need to revise law enforcement efforts and prioritize alternative approaches to gang control. The little criticism that the paper permitted was largely restricted to opinion columns and mostly decried the government's strategy as a publicity campaign that focused on crackdowns to the detriment of comprehensive crime and social policies. *La Prensa Gráfica* commentators echoed these concerns, but the paper also published some criticism in its news pages. These were carefully attributed to sources and juxtaposed with officials' insistence that the plan was delivering good results. Notably, a series of LPG editorials gently insisted on the adoption of prevention and rehabilitation programs, but stopped short of declaring Súper Mano Dura a failure.

Throughout, neither newspaper demonstrated much interest in covering prevention and rehabilitation. Both featured some stories of private initiatives, such as a tattoo removal clinic or a handicrafts microenterprise program. *La Prensa Gráfica* included an occasional account of CNSP-sponsored recreational activities and sports infrastructure projects. They limited themselves to noting the launch of Mano Amiga, a gang prevention program, and Mano Extendida, a gang rehabilitation program, and the inauguration of the CNSP's *granja-escuela*, or the "graduation" ceremony of ex-gang members. The *granja-escuela* attracted most of the attention, but journalists merely enumerated the activities on offer or the number of gang members in rehabilitation. The government never followed up on its claim that it would open two, possibly ten, more *granjas*, and reporters failed to evaluate whether the government's alternative programs were in any way successful.

ASSESSING THE IMPACT OF SÚPER MANO DURA   Media accounts continued to reveal a fascination for large-scale police operations and public exhibitions of suspects. Moreover, news reporting persisted in legitimizing violations of detainees' rights. Police security operations and apparent tranquility in the communities, once indicators of policy success, now received little or no attention from the media. Instead, the papers focused on public opinion and homicide figures. LPG journalists occasionally drove to gang-affected communities, but their reports stopped when residents repeatedly affirmed that the gang problem showed no signs of abating.

Both newspapers still published regular surveys, but surprisingly, it was *El Diario de Hoy* that documented the steep decline in effectiveness ratings. In each poll, the number of Salvadorans who thought Súper Mano Dura had helped reduce violence and crime decreased. *La Prensa Gráfica* only traced this fall in the first year of the new policy. The final gang-related surveys in the period of analysis appeared at the start of President Saca's third year in office, and, perhaps as a face-saver, both newspapers asked what the government should do to address the gang problem. LPG respondents showed little support for job training and job creation, more often requesting greater police presence and stricter laws. Even more conventionally, EDH interviewees expressed huge support for military deployment, harsher punishment, the death sentence, and more police. In sum, while the existing gang policy was widely considered ineffective, people wanted more of the same, and the government was vindicated in its approach.

Government and police officials offered a series of arguments to explain why, despite the deteriorating security situation, Súper Mano Dura remained an effective gang control plan. Most explanations began with the assumption that gang members were responsible for the majority of homicides. Officials changed course briefly and declared that when most murders were gang-related, Súper Mano Dura had succeeded in lowering their number. Now, they explained, individuals not related to gangs were committing more killings, keeping the overall homicide rate high. Generally, it was implied that gang members still were the main culprits.

Officials argued that homicides were on the rise for one or more of the following reasons: tolerant judges failed to convict gang members; gang rivalries over leadership and control of drug sales had intensified; gang members deported from the United States fueled violent crime; gangs were eliminating those members who sought to join the government's rehabilitation program, and this upsurge in murders had been anticipated; and gang members turned to planned killings, which the police were powerless to prevent. Additionally, two conspiracy theories were circulated: gang members deliberately committed more homicides to defy government policy, and the gangs escalated their homicides as part of an FMLN-led destabilization process (a popular premise prior to the 2006 elections).

Again, the principal problem with the media coverage was journalists' preference for reporting these claims without close examination. Not once did either paper suggest that the government's approach to gang control, let alone its failure to develop a comprehensive crime policy, exacerbated the situation. Indeed, when President Saca announced that Súper Mano Dura required adjustment because the gangs had evolved into organized crime groups, the papers not only failed to question his assertion, but also remained reluctant to write of the policy's failure. Instead, they allowed coverage of the plan to fade slowly. Eventually, *El Diario de Hoy* remarked that Súper Mano Dura had become extinct, and *La Prensa Gráfica* concluded that the 2006 gang policing plan, Maestro de Seguridad, had substituted for the former. As the authorities quietly buried President Saca's plan, the media seemed willing to let the matter rest, and in July 2006, they ceased their coverage of Mano Dura.

Discussion and Conclusion

This last section pulls together the central points of the content analysis before addressing two questions: What factors might explain media bias toward the official interpretation of the gang problem and its solution? What effects did the coverage have on its audiences? To answer the first of these questions, the discussion revisits some of the issues pertaining to El Salvador's media system. For the second question, it will draw on a number of polls conducted by the IUDOP between 2003 and 2006.

The content analysis of gang-related news coverage sought to ascertain how El Salvador's two leading dailies represented gang members, discussed the factors stimulating gang membership and gang emergence, and depicted gang control strategies. The research revealed subtle differences between the papers, but these variations were overshadowed by the similarities in newsgathering practices and an informational bias toward the government's agenda. Journalists took a passive, noncritical approach to reporting that focused on official sources and events and relied on the transcription of speeches and press releases without further investigation. Both papers kept areas of controversy off-limits, confined criticism to opinion columns, balanced competing viewpoints without questioning their veracity, and preferred to frame events episodically rather than thematically.

La Prensa Gráfica is a submissive and docile paper, with a conservative though more tolerant editorial line than its main competitor. Its reporting is characteristically neutral, keeps debates within the bounds of acceptable premises, and produces bland and conformist coverage. *El Diario de Hoy* is striking for its sharp language, highly conservative outlook, and disapproval of dissent. Criticism was regularly dismissed as communist rhetoric, particularly in the often offensively phrased editorials, and news treatment displayed an ideological stance that was more explicitly and deliberately supportive of Mano Dura and the interests of the country's privileged groups.

Both papers typecast gang members as "folk devils," a minority of criminal and violent individuals responsible for the majority of homicides. Visual imagery "documented" the danger these tattooed and defiant young men posed, while metaphoric language further dehumanized them and rendered their extermination permissible. Reports linked gang affiliation with lifestyle decisions or family breakdown and decoupled gangs from the broader societal context. The papers blamed gang emergence on the civil war and US deportation policy, while the EDH editorial line also equated the gang problem with a communist conspiracy and a lenient criminal justice system. Whereas *La Prensa Gráfica* at least alluded to socio-economic disadvantage, *El Diario de Hoy* strongly rejected this factor. Neither questioned Salvadoran society's structural inequities. Coverage of police operations and public exhibitions of gang members sought to entertain audiences at the cost of tolerating human rights violations. While *El Diario de Hoy* resolutely defended Mano Dura, *La Prensa Gráfica* insisted on the need for a three-pronged gang policy, but avoided criticizing suppression. Instead, the paper pointed to the escalating homicide rate to cast doubt on the government's approach to gang control.

Both newspapers fanned a gang panic, amplified the official interpretation of the gang problem, and encouraged public support for Mano Dura through episodic framing. Their content did not include a consistent and coherent range of critical voices, but was saturated by the pro–Mano Dura theme. Because alternative readings of the gang problem were scarce, this bias diminished the possibility that a comprehensive gang policy would develop and find popular support. In the case of *La Prensa Gráfica*, irresponsible and unethical journalism persisted even after the introduction of its 2005 *Manual for the News Treatment of Violence*, which had encouraged reporters to contextualize events, provide truthful news stories, avoid stereotyping suspects, and respect the presumption of innocence. Some of the *Manual* guidelines, such as omitting the names of the gangs, had proved controversial, and it lost its relevance for journalism that genuinely tried to explain the violence in El Salvador.[96]

Media sector characteristics and reportorial practices affected gang-related news coverage. This chapter showed that El Salvador's postwar political openings had increased freedom of expression, raised academic standards among journalists, and heralded the modernization of the traditional media. Journalistic freedom of expression encountered limits, however, when reporting targeted the status quo or the country's power groups. Defamation legislation and restricted access to information discouraged critical reporting, while journalistic professionalism remained curbed by limited newsroom autonomy, modest salaries, and weak ethical norms. Salvadoran journalism encounters its principal obstacles in oligopolistic ownership structures, the political use of advertising, and journalistic self-censorship. Media owners' political and commercial interests, as well as reportorial practices, help explain why news coverage framed the gang problem and its solutions in ways that promoted penal populism.

El Diario de Hoy and *La Prensa Gráfica* are both family businesses with ties to the elite and a commitment to the political and economic agenda of ARENA and the private sector. Their owners appear willing to use news production to advance shared interests in protecting private property and maintaining the status quo. The ideological stance and editorial influence of Enrique Altamirano are leaving a mark on the highly partisan *El Diario de Hoy*, while the Dutriz family apparently considers *La Prensa Gráfica* a for-profit enterprise rather than a journalistic venture.[97] Minor differences aside, both companies are in the business of selling news and compete for audiences and advertisers. Their owners are uninterested in controversial journalism that might jeopardize their commercial interests. Both papers tolerate criticism that remains within certain boundaries, but appear to cultivate an image of openness, rather than deliver substantive coverage of alternative views and information. The newspapers' commercial logic encourages their journalists to routinize the newsgathering process and rely on official sources for much of their reporting. This elite orientation makes it difficult for resource-poor outsider groups to garner coverage and bring their ideas to the public's attention.

The relative absence of alternative viewpoints in the Salvadoran mainstream press also derives from journalists' tendency to self-censor. Reporters working for the country's two principal newspapers are all too aware of their employers' interests. They may be committed to critical journalism, but correspondents' fear of dismissal in the face of limited job opportunities pushes many to censor their writings. Interviews with journalists confirmed the practice at *El Diario de Hoy* and *La Prensa Gráfica*. The dilemma between professional demands and job security is what led LPG reporters, instead of criticizing Mano Dura directly, to adopt a surreptitious form of criticism by highlighting the mounting homicide rate.

Although media depictions do not determine public opinion, they may shape it and make one interpretation of social reality more likely than another. Indeed, scholars have suggested that while the effect of a single media item may be minimal, repetitious messages could have a very significant cumulative effect.[98] Salvadoran television and newspapers convey political information and have been found to influence the citizenry's view of the country's paramount problems. Through their agenda-setting function, the newspapers exercise an important influence on public opinion.

To establish whether the media had influenced Salvadorans' perception of the gang problem, this research drew on a series of IUDOP-conducted polls that revealed public opinion on the seriousness of the gang problem, support for Mano Dura policies, and perceptions of policy effectiveness. While respondents' views were colored by their personal experiences and entrenched attitudes, the survey findings revealed the media's effects.

A 2004 survey of security perceptions raised the gravity of the gang problem. When asked which crime issue needed to be tackled most urgently, almost half the interviewees (48.4 percent) pointed to the gangs.[99] This answer is puzzling, since 68.6 percent of the respondents acknowledged that these groups were a small or non-existent problem in their own communities.[100] When people were specifically asked whether they considered the gangs a problem in their communities, only 20.8 percent affirmed gangs were a great problem, while 10.6 percent felt they were somewhat of a problem. Only 10.6 percent stated they had ever been directly affected by gang activity in their communities.

An astounding 91 percent of respondents believed the gangs constituted a significant national problem, while 6.5 percent thought this was somewhat the case. Those who had been gang victims were more likely to see these groups as a problem, locally and nationally. Yet, the poll also disclosed the impact of media messages: the greater the exposure to news, the greater the view that the gangs affected local communities.

Although the survey did not probe media effects among those who considered the gangs a national problem, it is safe to assume that the findings would have been similar. It is likely that media coverage contributed to the perception that gangs were a national nuisance since the vast majority of respondents reported no gang presence in their area.

Public support for Mano Dura remained steadfast, criticism and the ineffectiveness of both plans notwithstanding. According to a 2003 IUDOP survey, a remarkable 79.7 percent of respondents thought Mano Dura and the Ley Anti Maras deserved backing despite the law's unconstitutional character, while 3.7 percent felt the law did not contravene the constitution and should be endorsed.[101] Clearly, the warnings of Mano Dura critics had not reached many Salvadorans. Furthermore, although public support for Mano Dura dropped eventually, it remained surprisingly high even when respondents acknowledged that Súper Mano Dura had also failed to decrease crime. For example, the 2005 and 2006 IUDOP end-of-year surveys showed that 82.9 percent and 67 percent, respectively, favored the plan, although respondents believed that it had shown little or no effectiveness in lowering crime (45.4 percent and 63.5 percent).[102]

The media messages that were at play here also influenced perceptions of policy effectiveness. Homicide figures had steadily risen since 2003, but until mid-2005 successive surveys showed that at least 45 percent of interviewees thought crime had in fact decreased.[103] More than half of the Salvadorans who were consulted felt that the government's plan had succeeded in alleviating the gang problem.[104] One of these polls revealed that 88.1 percent of respondents had learned of the government's performance through the media. It appears, therefore, that the media coverage worked to the advantage of the authorities. It was only months after the termination of the gang policy that it finally received a largely negative evaluation, although the police continued to be seen as effective in their "fight" against crime.[105]

The survey research suggests that media content influenced both Salvadorans' perception of the gang problem as being more serious than it was and their support for Mano Dura policies despite their actual ineffectiveness. The implication is that a different media framing of the gangs could have better explained the complex nature of the gangs and the need for comprehensive gang control.

CHAPTER 4

Contesting Mano Dura

The promotion of comprehensive and rights-respecting gang control has been highly political in El Salvador. Efforts to alleviate social marginalization and protect human rights have traditionally met with resistance from society's most powerful elements. Therefore, when NGOs protested the application of Mano Dura and advocated an alternative form of gang control based on prevention and rehabilitation, combined with more effective law enforcement, these efforts typically met with opposition. Three societal conditions had a direct effect on NGO advocacy: the persistence of elite influence over the state and policy making; the nature of ARENA as the guardian of conservative interests; and the absence of a pluralistic media, which makes it difficult for dissenting actors to express their views and mobilize political pressure. Given these exogenous constraints on gang-related advocacy, NGO strategies played a key role in contesting Mano Dura.

This chapter focuses on the Fundación de Estudios para la Aplicación del Derecho (Foundation for Applied Legal Studies, or FESPAD) and its criminal law center, the Centro de Estudios Penales de El Salvador (Center for Criminal Studies of El Salvador, or CEPES). Established in 1988 by a group of Salvadoran lawyers, notably Francisco Díaz with the Instituto de Derechos Humanos de la Universidad Centroamericana (Human Rights Institute of the Central American University, or IDHUCA), and friends from the arts and sciences, FESPAD is dedicated to the defense of human rights and the rule of law. Given the human rights violations associated with Mano Dura, reform of gang policy necessarily entered the NGO's advocacy agenda. Via the CEPES, FESPAD pursued legal and policy research, a strategy that aimed for the adoption of alternative gang control through direct influence on policy making. As argued throughout this book, the NGOs' origins shaped their strategic choices, which, combined with organizational characteristics, shaped their ability to affect policy.

The CEPES attempted to contest Mano Dura through a variety of advocacy tools, which included research and limited media work, a legal aid clinic, and a proposal for the local prevention of gang violence. FESPAD's relatively unsuccessful advocacy efforts offer some insights into the lawyers' assumptions about the political process, its power dynamics, and the ways in which this thinking informed their strategic choices. The organization's media strategy and its steps toward alliance building as a mechanism for amplifying its political voice and influence also deserve reflection.

FESPAD helped publicize the abuses and flaws associated with Mano Dura. It therefore contributed to the rhetorical and policy changes that occurred under the Saca administration. In the end, however, its advocacy tools were not powerful enough to compel a change in state behavior, notably as regards policing practices and the implementation of full-fledged prevention and rehabilitation programs. While exogenous factors hindered the promotion of an alternative gang policy, strategic limitations also prevented FESPAD from advancing its advocacy agenda more successfully. Importantly, the NGO perceived gang control as a technical issue that could be resolved through the documentation of human rights violations and the formulation of new policy ideas. As a result, the advocacy tools it chose did not put sufficient political pressure on a government that was ideologically opposed to comprehensive gang control. Nor did FESPAD target other key actors, such as the economic elite.

The Institutional History of FESPAD

FESPAD emerged during the final years of the armed conflict. In the hope that postwar El Salvador could be erected on the pillars of democracy, human rights, and the rule of law, a group of Salvadoran lawyers set out to translate these aspirations into reality. When the NGO was established in 1988, the objective was to put the law to a use that was novel for that place and time and to do so from the sphere of civil society.[1] From the perspective of decades later, the promotion of the rule of law may seem nothing out of the ordinary, but in a society where the legal system had traditionally impeded social change, FESPAD ventured into new territory.

In the broadest sense, the founders aspired to craft a more democratic and just society built on constitutional principles and human rights. Since the legal order would become a tool for democracy building only if both the rulers and the ruled submitted to it, FESPAD considered public institutions and the existing judicial structure, despite their limitations, to be the best instruments to achieve its mission. Its strategic planners regarded formal engagement at the policy and legislative levels indispensable while the organization was advocating proposals for long-term change. This strict adherence to democratic channels has characterized FESPAD throughout its existence and posed certain difficulties for its gang-related advocacy.

Equally, the founders of FESPAD believed that the law should apply to the entire citizenry. In a country where the poor had historically been denied their constitutional guarantees, many people did not see themselves as holders of human dignity and rights. There was thus a need not only to raise popular awareness of the notion of human rights, but also to foster a greater understanding of the law and its use in the defense of basic entitlements. As lawyers, the founders of FESPAD were trained to use legal mechanisms for the resolution of juridical problems. However, they intended to launch what was in essence a political project: to place the law at the service of the most vulnerable people of society and accompany them in their individual and collective struggles.

This philosophy has characterized FESPAD throughout the years and allowed it to play an important role in El Salvador's transition from war to peace. From the very beginning, the organization combined academic work with popular legal education. In the marginal zones of Greater San Salvador, FESPAD trained community and union leaders and promoted community access to justice, particularly in the area of economic and social rights. When the peace negotiations precipitated the need for constitutional reform, FESPAD presented its own proposal and embarked on an extensive civic education project. The book that derived from this work, *La Constitución Explicada*, has since sold more than eighty thousand copies in El Salvador.[2]

These endeavors helped the NGO to both raise its public profile and establish itself as a point of reference in the areas of human rights and the administration of justice. When FESPAD sought to promote an alternative gang policy, its reputation as a respectable and professional organization was important for gaining access to decisionmakers.

FESPAD quickly expanded its contribution to the restructuring of the Salvadoran judicial system and began to monitor the implementation of criminal justice reforms. Given the authorities' traditionally suppressive approach to crime, the lawyers sought to inject a prorights culture into the country's criminal law and policy.[3] Since 1993, this objective has been pursued by the CEPES, one of four centers that formed FESPAD's structure until an organizational restructuring in 2008. The CEPES, which advocated an alternative gang policy, emerged from the efforts of Argentine penologist Alberto Binder, an authority in his field and an advocate of legal reforms across Latin America. Binder helped create a critically minded legal team determined to see the country's judicial reforms succeed.[4] Members were drawn from a student movement at the University of El Salvador (UES) Law Faculty, whose graduates include key figures of the Salvadoran left, such as Farabundo Martí and Schafik Handal. Well-versed in Salvadoran political history, these students began meeting on FESPAD's premises to study with Binder, one of the region's most distinguished legal scholars, and eventually joined the organization. Within FESPAD, they pledged to apply their knowledge in two ways. One was to convey their own expertise to future generations of law students, mostly in the form of a seminar that provided space for reflection as well as academic training. The other, equally important, was to infuse their thinking in the center's advocacy work.[5] Over time, FESPAD remained faithful to its political vision, although the strategies to accomplish it varied between its two thematic centers (public security and criminal justice and socio-economic rights).

A Repertoire of Strategies

The office-based part of FESPAD's legal and policy work takes place in a middle-class neighborhood near the University of El Salvador. Past the FESPAD bookshop is the two-story institute itself, which on any given weekday teems with clients and visitors. Posters of Archbishop Romero adorn the wall, and an internal notice board, known as the "mural newspaper," displays memos and newspaper articles concerning FESPAD activities. The atmosphere is one of quiet busyness, interrupted only when one of the suited lawyers emerges from the in-house juridical library or one of the small offices lining the corridors.

Some sixty legal and administrative staff operated in the organization's four centers.[6] Each of the centers enjoyed considerable thematic and strategic independence. Nevertheless, all were required to help implement FESPAD's political vision, which reflected the NGO's analysis of El Salvador's reality and was promoted both internally and externally.[7] FESPAD's leadership sought to build consciousness among its employees by means of a weekly talk that addressed the country's current situation. Equally, though, the directors pledged to foster the dream of justice for all in the institution's investigative and educational output. The staff, particularly in the legal-professional category, tended to be fairly homogeneous in their critical thinking. Yet, differences of emphasis were apparent, notably in the advocacy strategies the two principal thematic centers had adopted.

In the promotion of human rights and the rule of law, FESPAD targets two main entry points for its advocacy: formal political structures and citizen organizing. In its attempts to influence the design and implementation of legislation and public policies, the NGO draws on a variety of tools, including human rights education and legal aid to victims of abuses, investigation and documentation of violations, and evaluation of policies and state behavior, as well as legal-political analyses and proposals. In the public eye, FESPAD is mainly known for its reports, the publication of juridical texts, and public statements on issues within its mandate. While this brief portrait of FESPAD may create the impression that the NGO ably combined different types of advocacy strategies, in practice these were not given equal weight. A preference for either research or action-oriented work, though conditioned by the thematic focus, was readily apparent in the activities of the two main centers, described below. Although only one of them promoted an alternative gang policy, the following overview of both centers will help clarify the limitations of the CEPES gang-related advocacy.

FESPAD's Thematic Centers

The Centro de Estudios Constitucionales y Derechos Humanos (Center for Constitutional Studies and Human Rights, or CECDH) was created in 2000 to continue FESPAD's initial activities concerning constitutional, social, and economic rights. Human rights work in El Salvador inevitably had focused on civil and political rights. As the country began its democratic transition, FESPAD opted for the comprehensive promotion of human rights. The CECDH thus retained the organization's constitutional oversight function, but also began the work of sensitizing poor communities to society's structural problems and means of legal redress. Like their colleagues in the CEPES, the CECDH staff places great importance on directly targeting government to enhance state compliance with human rights standards. Press monitoring and regular reports are among their principal activities, although the lawyers also give human rights classes to public officials.

The CECDH is the center that most readily embraced the idea that the poor must be empowered to claim their rights. Educational programs in rural and urban communities seek to help people organize themselves and channel their concerns into campaigns. This combination of research and community-based work reflects FESPAD's identity as an academic institution that deliberately aims to combine its expertise with activism. According to Abraham Ábrego, then CECDH director and later FESPAD's executive director, blending different strategies is indispensable if human rights and the rule of law are to become a reality in El Salvador:

> The construction of the rule of law requires a diversified strategy because FESPAD on its own cannot achieve it. People need to participate. The strongest part needs to be people's participation. Participation generates changes in the system. That is why we try to do it, because there is no space for participation. This space needs to be created.[8]

FESPAD must strike a difficult balance between social mobilization and research. The CEPES mostly adopted the latter path, engaging decisionmakers in direct ways. Its crowded office, where Che Guevara memorabilia and the occasional sound of revolutionary music provided inspiration, accommodated only a small group of lawyers. Over the years, these individuals carried out various activities in the fields of public security, criminal justice, and juvenile justice. Annual reports offered legal analyses and assessments of policies and institutional developments. To provide constructive criticism, these publications included specific recommendations, often followed by separate and more comprehensive proposals. Since FESPAD aims to stimulate improvements at the policy, legislative, and institutional levels, it also holds public events where these documents are presented to the target audience and disseminated free of charge. It is partly through these reports that FESPAD sought to advocate an alternative gang policy.

Like other members of the FESPAD family, the CEPES also relied on paid ads to publicize its stance on specific issues. Inevitably confrontational, these statements often invited counterattacks by defenders of the status quo, and FESPAD's rejection of Mano Dura was no exception to this pattern. Polemics notwithstanding, the technical expertise of the CEPES was hard to deny, and government officials readily consulted the lawyers on legal affairs or sent police officers to FESPAD's training workshops on community policing. Given both its extensive range of concerns and the persistent difficulties in resolving them, FESPAD enjoys regular participation in the country's political life and, by implication, public visibility. The NGO lacks the resources, however, to make a sustained and consistent commitment to the resolution of long-term problems. Consequently, the organization has mostly limited its involvement to particular junctures where it may exert the most leverage. As discussed below, its gang-related advocacy illustrates the implications of this reactive posture.

Fund-Raising Activities

The availability of sufficient material resources is crucial for any organization's sustainability and operations. For FESPAD, as for other Salvadoran NGOs, securing sufficient funding has been a chronic difficulty and has inevitably constrained attempts to promote alternative gang control. FESPAD is not a human rights organization in the traditional sense—that is, concerned with the systematic collection of testimonies and the documentation of civil and political rights violations. Its activities are nonetheless political in nature.

Unsurprisingly, the organization's position limits its fund-raising options. To begin with, FESPAD has found it difficult to raise domestic private money. The main beneficiaries of the NGO's work are the least well-off citizens, who can provide no financial support. By contrast, those who could afford to make substantial contributions are least likely to share FESPAD's vision for Salvadoran society. The NGO therefore long depended on international donor assistance. Once El Salvador became formally democratic, however, such donors focused their attention elsewhere, and these aid flows severely diminished. After the first decade of its existence, the agency found itself engulfed in its first financial crisis. Staff went elsewhere, encouraged to some extent by the lure of higher salaries outside the non-governmental sector. More financial difficulties followed in 2005, and the FESPAD leadership decided to temporarily discontinue employees' social security payments. Though more staff resigned, the organization at least survived.[9]

The need for financial diversification prompted a quest for greater self-sustainability. This has met with some success, but within FESPAD resentment lingers over foreign donors' perceived abandonment of El Salvador. Staff are alarmed that the relative absence of international scrutiny makes it more difficult to forestall abuses.[10] Unfortunate as this re-prioritization by the international community is, it would seem nevertheless that the onus is on local players to demonstrate the need for continued external support.

Equally problematic, however, has been donors' shift toward funding specific projects, rather than organizations, and their insistence on measurable results. On the one hand, the emphasis on quantitative indicators has posed difficulties for an NGO that considers greater popular human rights awareness an important achievement, but is required to mass-produce workshops and reports that will satisfy donors without necessarily leaving a lasting impact.[11] The shift toward project funding, on the other hand, has had two implications. First, since financial support covers only temporary activities, it has greatly affected FESPAD's ability to address long-term problems, of which the gang situation is but one. Second, donor assistance no longer applies to the administrative and operational costs of the organization, which must be covered in different ways. FESPAD has responded to this problem largely by drawing on its most valuable source: its legal expertise. The Amigos de FESPAD membership program raised some revenue, but became dormant when its director left the NGO in 2009. The institution is sustained essentially by means of four services: the legal editorial service FESPAD Ediciones and its bookshop, legal training courses, consultancies (including for the government and private sector clients), and rental of the NGO's conference rooms.[12] This commercially generated income notwithstanding, individual centers retained responsibility for the writing of funding proposals. Although internal assistance was available throughout the project cycle,[13] some lawyers privately resented having to juggle this time-consuming task with their research. Both the different funding model and the time required for fund-raising activities distracted from substantive work and affected the ability of the CEPES to advocate for an alternative gang policy.

Contesting Mano Dura

Like other critics of Mano Dura, FESPAD objected to the policy for two reasons. First, although it agreed that gang control had to include law enforcement, the NGO insisted that it had to respect constitutional norms and human rights. Second, FESPAD maintained that the street gangs were a social problem and therefore could never be solved solely through legislation and police operations. Rather, the problem required a comprehensive gang strategy that combined law enforcement with prevention and rehabilitation. FESPAD relied on a variety of advocacy tools to criticize Mano Dura and promote alternative forms of gang control, initially protesting the government's existing gang policy, then carrying its advocacy forward through the legal aid clinic and a policy proposal for gang violence prevention.

Media and Research-Based Advocacy

President Flores had barely announced Mano Dura and the Ley Anti Maras (LAM) when various observers began to express concerns about the "war on gangs." Determined to defend the rule of law, FESPAD opted to publicly state its opposition to Mano Dura. In a paid ad published in *La Prensa Gráfica*, FESPAD lawyers condemned the LAM as an authoritarian measure. They cautioned the government that the country's crime problem would not be resolved by targeting only the gangs and that these groups, even if eliminated, would resurface unless associated structural factors were addressed. At the same time, FESPAD faulted the government for not adopting prevention and rehabilitation programs, requested that the Ley Anti Maras be studied in a public forum, and insisted it be declared unconstitutional in the event its enactment could not be prevented. The NGO explicitly stated that it did not side with criminals, but was merely asking for the crime problem to be addressed comprehensively.[14]

Days later, *El Diario de Hoy* published a series of paid ads by the Instituto Pro Libertad y Derecho (Institute for Liberty and Law, or IPLD), a front organization that was associated with lawyer Ivo Priamo Alvarenga, then an adviser to the Interior Ministry and a columnist for *El Diario de Hoy*.[15] These advertisements attacked the supposed *hiper garantismo* (hyperguaranteeism) of rights that FESPAD and other human rights defenders had supposedly expressed in support of gang members.[16] One of these statements specifically vilified FESPAD for its "legal populism" and refusal to support hard-line solutions to what was termed the "gang epidemic."[17] These insinuations that the NGO was coddling criminals, while leaving ordinary Salvadorans unprotected, dented neither FESPAD's reputation nor its conviction. The then executive director, María Silvia Guillén, for example, considered the IPLD's comments insolent, but dismissed them for their failure to recognize that individuals do not relinquish their rights when committing a crime.[18] The IPLD's limited view of rights, however, remains widely accepted in El Salvador. More critically, by neglecting to engage with its opponents in a public discussion of this idea, FESPAD lost the opportunity to gain greater acceptance for its position and to put greater pressure on decisionmakers.

FESPAD was indeed consulted on the Ley Anti Maras in both judicial and legislative forums and submitted to the Legislative Assembly the outline of an alternative gang strategy. The forums received considerable media coverage and briefly appeared to sway the lawmakers against the bill, but ultimately they did not prevent the enactment of the Ley Anti Maras. Following this development, and the adoption of similar gang suppression strategies in neighboring countries, FESPAD sought to take its advocacy to the next level. Like-minded civil society groups were invited to a regional seminar, but this meeting also led to little more than a jointly issued paid advertisement that called for comprehensive gang control, and the coalition that formed on that occasion became inactive soon afterward.[19] Thus another important opportunity was lost to build a civil society alliance that might have acted as a counterweight to regional government and law enforcement cooperation. Paid ads permitted FESPAD to express its view publicly, but, in the absence of more explicit lobbying, were unlikely to persuade the government to reform gang policy.

A critical development, however, concerned judicial opposition to the Ley Anti Maras. Following the announcement of Mano Dura, some judges raised doubts about the constitutionality of the LAM. They ordered the release of gang members if there were no legal grounds for their arrest.[20] When President Flores verbally attacked judges for their refusal to apply the legislation, members of the Foro de Jueces Independientes y Democráticos (Forum of Independent and Democratic Judges) publicly defended their position with reference to their constitutional powers.[21] These pronouncements reflected the judges' own resolve to defend the rule of law in El Salvador. The CEPES had played an important role in enabling the work of the democratic judges through its support for the creation of three such judicial associations within the country.[22]

At the same time, the CEPES issued the first of its annual reports, which evaluated Mano Dura and exposed to public scrutiny the human rights violations associated with it, as well as the myths surrounding its supposed effectiveness. Unfortunately, after their initial presentation, these texts were only made available on FESPAD's website and not reinforced by further lobbying activities. The reports were intended to shame the government into action, but this "shaming methodology" can work only if the media are willing to reveal abuses and the authorities are vulnerable to such publicity.[23] Presumably, the government was aware of the adverse effects of Mano Dura, but lacked the political will to take a different approach. It therefore was imperative for FESPAD to buttress its advocacy tools with greater pressure. The failure to do so was one of the most glaring omissions in the organization's advocacy efforts.

FESPAD took an important step in its attempt to promote an alternative gang policy, however, by resorting to international mechanisms. While Antonio Saca campaigned on the theme of Súper Mano Dura, FESPAD helped alert the United Nations to the policy's human rights record. As a member of the local Red para la Infancia y la Adolescencia (Network for Childhood and Adolescence, or RIA), FESPAD contributed to a shadow report presented to the UN Committee on the Rights of the Child.[24] When this body released its findings in mid-2004, its recommendations echoed the concerns of FESPAD and other domestic human rights defenders.[25] By projecting this information onto the international stage and triggering external demands for state compliance with human rights standards, these actors had initiated a "boomerang pattern" that helped unblock the local policy process.[26] Although a comprehensive gang policy would ultimately not be implemented, these developments sent the message that single-minded suppression and constitutional infringements were unacceptable and forced President Saca to embark on a different approach to gang control.

Participation in the Anti-Gang Forum

The incoming Saca administration convened the Anti-Gang Forum, and FESPAD was among the few civil society organizations invited to share their expertise. The NGO saw the invitation as a welcome break with the Flores government and its unwillingness to heed calls for an end to Mano Dura. The CEPES members therefore decided to cooperate with the authorities to achieve two objectives: to prevent the design of further LAM-like gang legislation and to insist on the adoption of prevention and rehabilitation programs.[27] The two-week forum received considerable media coverage that gave the government positive publicity and suggested that it was serious about gang control.

From FESPAD's perspective, however, the outcome did not entirely meet its policy reform expectations. Although the participants decided against special anti-gang laws and reaffirmed the need for prevention and rehabilitation, the CEPES was unprepared for the way in which the discussions and voting were conducted. The overrepresentation of state agencies, such as the PNC, skewed the voting process and led to the adoption of many technical-procedural changes that were irrelevant for gang control. Furthermore, the government's focus on legal reforms left little time for any in-depth consideration of alternative responses. The recommended prevention and rehabilitation programs were subsequently carried out with much less urgency than the suppressive measures.

Although disillusioned by this experience, the CEPES participants felt encouraged by President Saca's announcement of Mano Amiga and Mano Extendida. These programs initially lacked substance, but at least the government had made the necessary public commitment and could, it was hoped, be persuaded to back up its words with action. FESPAD therefore refocused its tactics on accountability politics,[28] writing in its thematic reports about the continued weakness of alternative gang control strategies as a way of pressuring the government to implement the initiatives it had announced. The organization thus exposed the gap between official discourse and practice, but again, its failure to engage in explicit lobbying activities made it unlikely that the government would heed FESPAD's requests. Indeed, the weakness of the Mano Amiga and Mano Extendida plans suggests that NGO advocacy failed to have an impact.

While this campaign was under way, the CEPES was further debilitated by staff flight. When even its director resigned, the center was engulfed in a crisis that made its work to promote alternative gang control even more difficult.[29] Although the CEPES applied two other advocacy tools, both also appeared to suffer from the center's internal weaknesses and the country's socio-political dynamics. The Saca administration, like its predecessor, continued to safeguard the interests of the upper classes, acknowledging a need for prevention and rehabilitation programs to placate Mano Dura critics. Given these exogenous constraints on NGO advocacy, it was always going to be difficult for FESPAD to reorient gang policy. However, precisely because the government was likely to resist calls for alternative gang control, NGO strategies assumed greater importance.

FESPAD's positive public reputation afforded it access to policymakers, but at the decision-making table, the organization proved less adept at managing the power dynamics involved in gang control. The reasons for these limitations pertain to the nature of the policy space and FESPAD's apparent lack of political sophistication. On the one hand, although the organization had helped to build the pressure that led to the Anti-Gang Forum, the roundtables were convened at the behest of the Saca government, and FESPAD was not permitted to participate on its own terms.[30] On the other hand, the NGO appears to have misjudged the possibilities for consensus and underestimated the need for greater negotiating power. It was only after the forum was over that the CEPES lawyers realized that they had been co-opted for publicity purposes and, consequently, could not translate their access to decision-makers into influence over them.[31] FESPAD possesses considerable legal expertise, but seemed in this case to lack the political experience required to advance its cause with greater strategic skill. This weakness also affected its use of the remaining advocacy tools, which were singularly ineffective in creating additional incentives for comprehensive and rights-respecting gang control.

The CEPES Legal Aid Clinic

While FESPAD expected that the government would fully develop its prevention and rehabilitation programs, an additional opportunity arose to challenge Mano Dura. As part of its legal aid work, the organization sought to build a representative case that would expose and halt police harassment. These efforts, which did not produce the desired results, not only exposed FESPAD's inability to deal with institutional unresponsiveness but also illustrate the limitations of using legal mechanisms in a country with weak and politicized institutions.

In the belief that the justice system must be accessible to all citizens regardless of their social background, the CEPES lawyers had established a legal aid clinic specializing in the defense of low-income juvenile offenders. This advice center aimed to set legal precedents as a means of lobbying for state accountability on certain human rights violations. The lawyers were looking out for potential test cases that included charges of police harassment, police misconduct, and abuses in juvenile detention centers.

When Óscar Díaz, a thirty-year-old ex–gang member, contacted FESPAD in early 2005, the lawyers did not hesitate to assist him. Although his age made him an atypical client, Óscar related experiences that the NGO felt could strengthen its criticism of Mano Dura.[32] His family had fled war-torn El Salvador for Los Angeles, where he ended up joining La Mirada Locos, a local rival of the Dieciocho. In time, he was arrested by the LAPD Rampart Division and sent to prison for possession and sale of drugs. Eight years later, when it emerged that police had planted evidence in cases against some one hundred gang members, many convictions were overturned, including Óscar's. Subsequently, US immigration officials authorized his deportation back to El Salvador.

Long before returning to his home country, Óscar had decided to distance himself from gang activities and start a new life. Once back in El Salvador, however, he endured frequent police harassment. The very day of his arrival, in March 2003, PNC officers detained him, pocketed the money he carried, and held him on charges of illicit association, only to release him a few days later. This incident was the first of five similarly unfounded arrests over the next two years. In February 2005, Óscar finally became weary of the repeated arrests and the beatings he had received from police. When they battered down the door of his home as part of a nightly raid conducted to impress FBI observers with the effectiveness of Mano Dura, he decided to take legal action against the PNC and approached the CEPES for help. The staff began preparing a formal complaint.

Since their client could provide no evidence against any specific police officers, the lawyers had to ask the FGR to investigate the allegations before anyone could be held responsible through the courts. Anticipating that a criminal complaint lodged directly with the FGR might not advance due to institutional inertia, the CEPES intended to request the responsible justice of the peace to order investigations. In April 2005, the CEPES members sought to lodge the Díaz petition with the court, but met with immediate resistance. The court clerk refused to accept the document, and a file was opened only when the lawyers identified themselves as FESPAD staff and insisted on meeting directly with the judge.

Regrettably for Óscar, his case did not advance beyond this point. Lack of evidence was one problem, but another was institutional reluctance to address police misconduct. The public prosecutor assigned to the case considered it "political" and flatly refused to investigate police, who, as he characterized them, merely sought to tackle El Salvador's gang problem. By July 2005, the FGR had closed its file, and FESPAD saw another avenue for reform closed.

At one point in this process, Óscar spotted some of his tormentors in FESPAD's offices, where a group of plainclothes policemen were attending a workshop on community policing. The incident was a cold reminder that in the absence of institutional commitment to human rights and real police reform, and thus to more effective gang enforcement, such limited technical assistance as the CEPES could provide was unlikely to improve policing practices. Once the CEPES lawyers grasped that parts of the criminal justice system were unwilling to curb police abuse, a feeling of powerlessness set in. Their attempts to set a legal precedent against police abuse of gang members and thus challenge Mano Dura failed partly because horizontal accountability within and between institutions continues to be ineffective in El Salvador.

In the case of Óscar Díaz, the criminal justice institutions were unresponsive because the FGR is politicized and does not investigate police abuse.[33] Additionally, however, post–civil war legal reforms had failed to transform the existing judicial culture and, therefore, to improve the responsiveness of the system.[34] The barrier to judicial access in this case may well have been a social one. Institutions are run by individuals who may be inclined by social bias to scapegoat a particular group or class for society's unresolved problems. The public prosecutor assigned to Óscar Díaz's case, for example, was a professed evangelical Christian who believed that gang members deserved to be punished, while the police were merely fulfilling their duties. He therefore chose to shelve the case.[35] The persistence of such arbitrary conduct made it difficult for FESPAD to press ahead with its advocacy agenda. Unfortunately, the organization simply abandoned its campaign rather than seeking to develop more creative strategies. Given the justice sector's inability to protect human rights, FESPAD needed to reconsider the utility of formal legal channels for advocacy purposes.

In 2006, the importance of stopping police abuse against gang members resurfaced with a different incident in La Campanera, a gang-affected community in northern Soyapango.[36] Homies Unidos, working in the area at the time, alerted FESPAD to the case, which concerned police harassment and the subsequent murder of a gang member. The young man's mother had been called on earlier by a policeman, who pointed at his identification number and told her to remember it because he would soon return to kill her son. Although that particular officer did not return, other policemen did, and days later, the youth was shot dead near his house. The mother asked FESPAD for legal assistance, and the lawyers again initiated the necessary legal steps. After suffering repeated intimidation and a raid on her home by masked policemen, who seized all documents pertaining to her deceased son, the terrified mother dropped the complaint. Given their client's wish not to pursue the matter further, the FESPAD staff were resigned to the apparent impossibility of challenging Mano Dura through the legal aid clinic and instead began working on a local project for gang violence prevention.

Walking the Tightrope between *Denuncia* and *Propuesta*

FESPAD has never relied exclusively on the documentation and public condemnation of human rights violations. Since its founding, technical assistance, legal analyses, and the identification of alternative solutions to political-juridical problems have constituted the organization's raison d'être. Given its emphasis on monitoring policies and state behavior, however, the NGO was frequently assailed for exposing failures and abuses without also suggesting improvements. Eventually, FESPAD staff came to think that it might be appropriate to collaborate more closely with the authorities. The idea was not to abandon its critical perspective, but to make it the basis of more proactive advocacy work. FESPAD therefore shifted its strategic emphasis away from *denuncia* (public condemnation) toward that of *propuesta* (proposal-making).

Gang Violence Prevention: The COAV Cities Project

The shift from confrontation to policy making, and the predicaments it invites, are well illustrated by a 2006 CEPES project. The Children in Organized Armed Violence (COAV) Cities Project followed a ten-country study that had investigated the global phenomenon of organized youth violence.[37] El Salvador's street gangs were included both in the research and in the subsequent COAV Cities Project. In the case of El Salvador, the objective was to develop a municipal-level policy proposal for the prevention of gang violence. This section, which is chiefly concerned with the policy process and the implications of FESPAD's turn to proposal-making, covers three points. First, it describes the policy design process to explain the resource limitations of FESPAD's advocacy strategy. Second, it offers a cursory appraisal of the policy itself, which did not advance beyond the drafting stage and ultimately failed to be implemented. Its main aspects nevertheless help highlight the importance of developing a capacity for policy making. Third, FESPAD's collaborative posture illustrates the possible tensions between *denuncia* and *propuesta* in the contemporary Salvadoran setting.

The international study, *Neither War nor Peace*, was coordinated by the Brazilian NGO Viva Rio and inspired by that organization's own work with youths involved in the drug rings of Rio de Janeiro's favelas. Concerned that countries across the world were seeing their young people caught up in armed violence, Viva Rio determined that a comparative, policy-oriented analysis would be a valuable approach to examining groups that, although not homogeneous, were similar in origin and purpose.[38] In its second stage, the COAV Cities Project would convene local actors to develop targeted prevention and rehabilitation programs. Overall, the initiative aimed to help policymakers and practitioners develop a strategic approach to the problem of child violence in their communities.

Both the study and the policy components of the program relied for their execution on in-country research partners. The CEPES had been asked to carry out the initial investigation, but had declined due to staff and time shortages. Although the center's internal problems had not improved as the second stage approached, its support was still considered important, so the CEPES conducted the Cities Project jointly with the Instituto Universitario de Opinión Pública (University Institute of Public Opinion, or IUDOP), which had prepared the research report on El Salvador. These two institutions would establish the parameters of the policy process, drawing on the study's suggested framework for understanding and addressing youth involvement in organized violence.

The study put forward two main points, which would shape the COAV Cities Project. First, based on the similarities brought to light in the country reports, the study offered a common analytical framework that identified a number of risk factors and influences prompting youth involvement in violence. Guided by this framework, a working group in each of the selected municipalities would propose a policy aimed at helping young people resist these dynamics through prevention and rehabilitation. These working groups required the participation of state and civil society actors. Second, the research acknowledged that the alleviation of structural risk factors would be a lengthy and difficult process. As a result, it viewed local-level interventions as more appropriate in the short term, but acknowledged that they would be more effective if combined with macrolevel national programs.

Proceeding from these provisos, the CEPES and IUDOP staff identified a suitable municipality and, over a six-month period, convened twelve workshops. The target site was Zacatecoluca, a town of some 62,000 inhabitants and an hour's drive away from the capital, San Salvador. As of 2004, when the COAV study was undertaken, the city had a murder rate of 91 per 100,000 inhabitants and ranked sixth among the twenty municipalities with the highest homicide rates in the country. It was also known for drug trafficking and the presence of the Dieciocho, 460 members of which the PNC had officially registered by 2006.[39]

Each workshop was structured around one of the risk factors and influences spelled out by the study, such as social exclusion and peer pressure. The working group was not specifically created for this purpose, but had been established two years earlier to work on the wider problem of violence in Zacatecoluca. The project coordinators opted to use this existing mechanism rather than create a new one because it brought together representatives of the state and civil society. In each meeting, participants were expected to discuss the local manifestation of a problem and its causes before identifying possible solutions and the actors responsible for implementing them. The CEPES and IUDOP staff then wrote the recommendations into a policy paper for submission to the city's mayor for future implementation. This individual was expected to be the FMLN incumbent who had previously convened the committee and personally attended the COAV Cities sessions.

The 2006 municipal elections, however, brought in an ARENA government. Medardo Alfaro, a young television journalist who took office as mayor in May, was initially elusive when approached with the policy document, but then warmed to the idea of gang prevention and the possibility it created of positioning Zacatecoluca internationally.[40] Alfaro, however, stood at the beginning of his political career and never committed to implementing the COAV proposal. FESPAD and the IUDOP distanced themselves from the project due to other work priorities, and the recommendations were ultimately not acted on. Alfaro, when asked about this outcome, later claimed that he had never received the document.[41] The COAV Cities Project ended here, and with it, FESPAD lost another advocacy tool.

The lack of a pilot program was perhaps the project's starkest weakness, but ultimately it was only one of many. The selection of Zacatecoluca as the target site was itself not problematic because gang dominance in that city was a recognized concern. If anything, the location was chosen for convenience because the CEPES sought to sidestep the difficulty of mobilizing citizens around a divisive problem and instead relied on the existing committee and the mayor's support for it. The preprogram assessment, the policy design process, and the final policy guidelines were more questionable. The first two highlighted FESPAD's resource constraints, while the latter pointed to the need for expertise, which was itself a vital resource.

An initial assessment of violence and gang crime in Zacatecoluca was meant to guide policy formulation. The final working paper, however, though it listed aggregate homicide figures, provided virtually no specific information on *gang* crime issues, such as violence, the use of firearms, and drug sales.[42] Moreover, no local data was collected to describe the communities and the gangs the program would have targeted. Carefully collected and time-sensitive data, permitting an analysis of trends, is indispensable for gang violence prevention. When the COAV Cities Project was planned, FESPAD was already weakened by staff flight and lacked the financial resources to hire a researcher. An on-the-ground assessment was therefore dispensed with, and the coordinators merely pooled the scarce data available through the PNC and the IML.

Resource constraints and expediency also influenced the policy design process. The need to balance the COAV Cities Project with the many other responsibilities of the CEPES injected an unhealthy sense of urgency into the workshops. The four-hour meetings, for example, allowed participants little time to discuss very complex issues. The contributions that the organizers might have wished for were further limited by the fact that attendance was often low (although the PNC was routinely overrepresented). Some important actors, such as the Ministry of Education, were absent altogether.

More importantly, FESPAD's decision to work through the existing interinstitutional committee may have seemed the easier route at the time, but was not the best fit for the design of a gang program. The state agencies had not sent any senior-level representatives with some decision-making power. Crucially, none of the participants had expertise on gangs or the design of gang control programs. Thus, at an early stage, FESPAD's internal constraints and pragmatism prompted some decisions that interfered with both the program's design and its continuity.

The final policy document merits comment less for the actions it proposed than for what it conveys about FESPAD's approach to the formulation of a gang policy. The paper offered a number of laudable objectives, but it was unclear how, under the existing circumstances, some of the actions proposed to achieve them ("improving the economic model") might be carried out or how they related to gang control ("restricting alcohol sales"). As a gang policy, the proposal seemed poorly thought out, chiefly due to the degree to which it ignored issues of targeting, gang processes and structures, and community contexts.[43]

These weaknesses can be understood, if not excused, by the fact that FESPAD had agreed to a project of policy design, not implementation. Its staff aimed to develop a set of guidelines that the mayor's office was expected to convert into a more detailed plan and subsequently to help execute. This postproject stage would have required the recruitment of gang control experts to design community-specific prevention programs. The fact that FESPAD opted for a limited proposal over none at all was a positive step, and their document provided an advocacy tool that at least sustained the idea of alternative gang control for a little longer.

Over the years, FESPAD had become involved in a great variety of issues, but largely from a legal perspective. For the CEPES, which co-coordinated with the IUDOP, the challenge was to bring to the COAV Cities Project in El Salvador the sociological and criminological expertise that the organization lacked. Although the CEPES staff acknowledged the importance of doing so, they failed to act on this knowledge. Conducting projects for which the CEPES lawyers were ill-prepared was likely to result in broad but empty recommendations, and they ultimately would have had little standing to argue what the state should do.

The final point of criticism relates to FESPAD's shift from *denuncia* to *propuesta*, as illustrated by the COAV Cities Project. First, however, two further aspects of the project deserve comment: the local approach to gang control and the policy's nonimplementation.

The CEPES pursued a local preventive program in compliance with the international study's requirements, but it did so also because the center was interested in working with a municipal government on an issue that received no serious attention from the central government. Community-based programs are vital if a gang control strategy is to achieve results, but the highly centralized nature of the Salvadoran state, with decision-making power and financial resources generally concentrated at the national level, means local initiatives are unlikely to prosper without interinstitutional cooperation at the highest level. What, for example, can a local approach to gang prevention and rehabilitation achieve as long as the police do not reform their approach to gang control? Furthermore, the nature of problems such as social exclusion or the lack of job opportunities may vary among different communities, but they remain structural issues that need to be addressed at the macro level.

In the case of the COAV Cities Project, a broader approach might have ensured the economic and political viability of local programs in two ways. First, with successful lobbying, a comprehensive national gang policy would tackle the structural factors in gang development, which cannot be alleviated at the local level alone. Second, if institutionalized nationally, such a policy would endure a change of government, and state agencies would be required to commit the resources necessary to adopt and sustain the proposed program.

Admittedly, FESPAD turned to a municipality precisely because its advocacy efforts targeting the central government had not delivered the desired results. Yet, by shifting its strategy to a lower level, the organization merely relocated the difficulty of institutionalizing a gang policy and, with it, the risk of drafting a proposal that might not get implemented. The fact that this risk became a reality demonstrates that FESPAD failed to anticipate the possibility of a change of government or that a new mayor might not support the project. The FMLN had governed Zacatecoluca continuously since 1997, and FESPAD was confident that the party would again win in 2006. More importantly, the proposal's nonimplementation reflects the lawyers' lack of the political experience required to successfully carry forward their advocacy. In short, the organization made two mistakes. One was the lawyers' assumption that the gang problem was a technical one that could be resolved by submitting a proposal and requesting its implementation. The other was the CEPES decision to concede defeat when the most immediate lobbying mechanisms were exhausted.

Like previous attempts to contest Mano Dura, the COAV Cities Project was left to peter out at a time when it needed to be reinforced. One possibility might have been to bring other state institutions with more political weight onboard, but given Viva Rio's preference for mayoral participation, this was not attempted. At the time, it was difficult to see how an ARENA-governed municipality might commit to gang prevention when nationally the same party had pursued gang suppression. Viva Rio, for its part, was not surprised by these complications and closed the project. It is impossible to know how different the situation of gangs and violence in Zacatecoluca might be today had the COAV Cities proposal been implemented. Today the municipality is marred by a bloody conflict between the rival Dieciocho factions, citizens have formed self-defense groups to protect their lives and land, and the homicide rate for 2015 was 143 murders per 100,000 inhabitants.[44]

The potential concern about FESPAD's shift to *propuesta* is that the organization has largely maintained the same adversarial relationship with the state that was dominant during the authoritarian period. Yet, the group also reconfigured this relationship to offer proposals and other forms of technical assistance to government agencies. This nonconfrontational mode shows that a different and more collaborative form of engagement is possible. However, as FESPAD's critique of Mano Dura revealed, less conflictive strategies may be inappropriate under a government that permits different viewpoints to be expressed, but is ideologically opposed to more than tactical concessions. This does not mean proposal-making is necessarily a wasted effort, but it may be, if legal and policy changes are considered technical rather than political problems that can be resolved through proposals alone. In the absence of political will, such proposals will not motivate government action unless accompanied by persistent campaigning. FESPAD needed to rethink its advocacy strategies and identify more appropriate targets. One first step in such a reconceptualization would be an accurate analysis of the political landscape.

Mapping the Political Landscape

Advocacy strategies are shaped by assumptions about the political process and the power dynamics driving it. FESPAD's own work has been characterized by two broad tendencies. One entails the belief that the law should serve the struggle of the people for equal rights, yet FESPAD is more often involved in direct advocacy than in popular education and social mobilization. The latter two strategies do receive attention, but not as consistently as the organizational vision implies. More often, FESPAD seeks to effect legal and policy changes by directly targeting decisionmakers. From here, it is a small step to the second tendency, whereby the group uses its legal expertise to prepare analyses and proposals for the government.

To a degree, these predispositions reflect the view that the state is responsible for the enactment of legal and policy change. The preference for formal mechanisms nevertheless reveals something about FESPAD's own understanding of politics and power and its inability to grasp the limitations of its advocacy strategies, weaknesses apparent in FESPAD's attempts to contest Mano Dura. The poor outcome can partly be attributed to the government's ideological preference for suppression over prevention and rehabilitation. Nonetheless, FESPAD apparently failed to base its advocacy goals and strategies on the organizational self-assessments and contextual analyses that were part of its advocacy planning.[45]

As indicated earlier, FESPAD's choice of advocacy issues and strategies is often determined in reaction to particular events, rather than by prioritizing problems based on an analysis of the political context and its own organizational strengths. The promotion of an alternative gang policy is a case in point. For FESPAD staff, the street gangs may have seemed merely another reminder of the government's traditional indifference to social problems. Yet, by dispensing with a macro-analysis of El Salvador's social, economic, political, and cultural structures, the lawyers misjudged the possibilities for, and obstacles to, gang-related advocacy.

For advocacy strategies to be effective, their tactics need to suit the particular characteristics of the political environment.[46] These include the nature of the regime, the political space in which organized civil society operates, and the power dynamics through which some actors are marginalized from the policy process.[47] El Salvador had witnessed important political openings, but elite interests continued to control policy making. NGOs that promoted majority concerns therefore needed to grasp where power was located and how it operated before they could decide which actors to target and how to influence them.

FESPAD's five-year strategic plan, developed by the executive director and the leadership of each center, charted both El Salvador's national reality and the agency's internal situation and constituted the basis for annual action plans.[48] The difficulties with translating this information into action, however, were twofold. First, the national analysis did not scrutinize power in all its forms, an omission that could lead to poor strategic choices.[49] Second, the internal evaluation was carried out at the highest level, but not necessarily within the individual centers. While FESPAD was committed to a combination of advocacy strategies, its constituent centers functioned in essence as separate NGOs that were free to plan and conduct their own campaigns. As a result, they did not necessarily combine their different approaches, or assets, when tackling a particular issue. Nor was their strategic choice based on a prior mapping of the political environment and its power dynamics.

It is important to understand the nexus between power and advocacy and why an appreciation of its complexities is significant for all advocacy work, not only that of FESPAD. Political theorist Steven Lukes argues that power is three-dimensional.[50] Though operating on different levels, these three dimensions—visible, hidden, and invisible power—are interactive and collectively set the parameters of the political process. *Visible power* is associated with observable decision making, including formal rules and institutions. Visible expressions of power can be detected, for example, in laws or policies that favor one social group at the expense of others.

Hidden power is similarly exercised in the public arena, but reflects the ways in which certain individuals and groups manipulate the political agenda so as to exclude other actors and their concerns. Those who wield this kind of power can influence agenda-setting by, for example, preventing certain issues or points of view from being voiced, thus rendering them invisible and potentially skewing policy making to suit the interests of the powerful. Barriers to media access and biased media coverage can further reduce the visibility and apparent legitimacy of those without power.[51] Chapter 3 showed how mainstream news reporting favored the official definition of the gang problem and its solution rather than increasing the diversity of the public debate. Hidden power dynamics also affected FESPAD's own media work.

Finally, *invisible power* operates by shaping people's beliefs, values, and attitudes, keeping issues not only off the political agenda, but also out of popular consciousness. This form of power works through culture and ideology and ensures that institutions such as the state, the education system, and the media promote norms that sustain the status quo. A pertinent example is ARENA's tendency to foster nostalgia for authoritarian measures.

This analysis suggests that if individual advocacy strategies are going to be effective, they must target all three levels of power, not just the more visible forms. The promotion of legal and policy reforms, one of FESPAD's key activities, is an important strategy, but it targets only visible power. It can do little to advance an issue unless accompanied by actions that target the influence of hidden and invisible power.[52] An effective strategy will focus on social organizing (hidden power) and consciousness-raising (invisible power). This strategy is the most critical for making real change, yet also the hardest one to pursue successfully because its fundamental aim is to reshape a society's political culture. Ideology remains a significant barrier to change and was ultimately the battleground on which proponents and critics of Mano Dura confronted each other. Whether or not FESPAD's advocacy could have reoriented

El Salvador's gang policy had the NGO designed a more sophisticated strategy remains a moot point. Experienced activists have argued, however, that change is less likely to occur unless lobbying, citizen mobilization, and popular education form part of a unified approach.[53]

A single organization may not be able to pursue all the required activities simultaneously. Within FESPAD, resource constraints forced staff to make important strategic choices, with very different outcomes. The CECDH, for instance, tried to combine lobbying and popular education, but prioritized the former, while the CEPES focused exclusively on monitoring, research, and lobbying. Resource limitations notwithstanding, or perhaps because of such constraints, a campaign is likely to be more effective when groups build alliances in pursuit of common objectives.[54]

In any case, the NGO's promotion of an alternative gang policy need not have ended as prematurely as it did. The lawyers' inability to press for further changes in policy and state behavior suggests that they did not understand how to conduct a useful structural analysis, identify appropriate targets, or shape a campaign. The choice of target depends partly on how an advocacy issue is framed. If one prioritizes gang violence prevention from among the many issues posed by the broader problem of street gangs, a critical target might be the economic elite whose interests shape public spending and policy making. If one promotes respect for gang members' human rights, certainly one of the more difficult tasks given El Salvador's political culture, one might target the media to change reporting practices and to influence public opinion.

The Media as a Forum for Political Action

FESPAD's efforts to advocate legal and policy change routinely include some form of media work, such as press conferences or the publication of paid ads. Useful though such activities can be, the campaign against Mano Dura raises questions about the effectiveness of that media strategy. The following news story helps shed light on FESPAD's attempts to reach and persuade external audiences.

In early December 2005, *La Prensa Gráfica* featured a three-page illustrated report on a meeting held in the maximum-security prison in Zacatecoluca between what the article characterized as the country's "most dangerous convicts" and a supposedly FMLN-led delegation. Under the headline "*FMLN aboga por reos más peligrosos*" ("FMLN Defends Most Dangerous Criminals"), the paper reported that a prisoners' committee (which included gang members) had invited the FMLN and FESPAD to discuss its concerns about solitary confinement. The article for the most part recounted the FMLN's suggestion that a disputed provision of the Penitentiary Law be repealed, then it summarized the government's reaction as one of indignation.[55] President Saca and other senior officials accused the party of backing gang crime in order to finance its 2006 electoral campaign.[56]

The delegation, however, also included FESPAD and the IDHUCA. Although no journalists had been present at the meeting, a photo showed the guests facing the handcuffed prisoners, who were sitting in front of a row of security guards in bulletproof vests.[57] For the unsuspecting reader, this coverage led to the conclusion that the FMLN and two human rights organizations had unjustifiably "negotiated" with some of the country's worst criminals. In a subsequent press conference, again publicized in *La Prensa Gráfica*, the authorities reiterated their charge that the FMLN and the NGOs were manipulating the prisoners and using the banner of human rights to destabilize El Salvador.[58]

FESPAD's leaders were taken aback by these remarks.[59] A group of prisoners had indeed requested a meeting, but the invitation had also been extended to the justice system authorities. Apart from the sentence enforcement judge, however, none had accepted the offer. The participating FMLN legislator attended not as a party representative but in her role as president of the legislative Committee of Justice and Human Rights. Crucially, the event had been filmed by prison guards.[60] The photo that accompanied the story must therefore have been extracted from that material and leaked to the press in order to spin a story about FMLN and NGO collusion with dangerous criminals. The event, however, was actually a dialogue among prisoners, the state, and human rights defenders about the conditions of confinement.

The reasoning behind the manipulation of the story is better understood if placed in the political context of that time. Weeks earlier, relatives of inmates had marched in downtown San Salvador and occupied the Metropolitan Cathedral as a way of protesting the denial of basic rights inside Zacatecoluca and other prisons.[61] As on previous occasions, the government tried to link this popular expression of grievances to the FMLN, arguing that the party was seeking to destabilize the country prior to the 2006 elections.[62] When journalists asked to be shown evidence of these allegations, Minister of the Interior René Figueroa asserted that proof had to be withheld for security reasons.[63]

The story of the meeting inside Zacatecoluca, then, can be seen as an opportunistic move to turn a lawful endeavor into propaganda. The two human rights organizations, well intentioned but ill prepared for such maneuvering, became caught up in the political crossfire. Their reactions to the report in *La Prensa Gráfica* differed considerably though, and, again, the FESPAD response was revealing on a tactical level. When the director of IDHUCA contacted the interior minister and threatened legal action, an apology followed.[64] FESPAD, in contrast, hoped to publish a paid ad in *La Prensa Gráfica* refuting the story, but the paper rejected the request. The NGO subsequently wrote to both the interior minister and President Saca, but never received a reply. After those two abortive efforts, its leadership let the matter drop.

For FESPAD, the Zacatecoluca incident constituted the first direct attack on it by the government and was therefore considered serious enough to merit a response.[65] Generally, the organization ignores bullying tactics and relies on other avenues to counter the stereotypical images of human rights advocates as defenders of criminals. Legal expertise, reliable research, and a deliberate rejection of ties to the political parties have enabled the organization to maintain its authority and credibility. While outsiders' distorted messages have not besmirched the name of FESPAD, they continue, quite successfully, to raise doubts about the human rights discourse in general. FESPAD's inability to dispel public misgivings about gang members' human rights reflected the persistence of an authoritarian political culture, but the group also failed to design a media strategy that would have turned news about Mano Dura into contested terrain.

FESPAD recognizes the importance of communication in its advocacy work and employs a number of strategies to reach external audiences with its messages. The most common media tools include press releases, news conferences, and paid ads in El Salvador's main newspapers. Additionally, reports and briefings are made available via the organization's website. El Salvador's principal media outlets also regularly consult FESPAD lawyers on juridical matters or request their appearance in televised interviews. The NGO's reputation for veracity and accuracy has allowed it to become a respected source, despite the mass media bias toward insider institutions. FESPAD aims to reach a variety of audiences with these activities, particularly decisionmakers and the general public. It seeks to make issues visible, shape policies and state behavior, inform the population, and change public attitudes. It is valuable to target the leading media, given their influence over public opinion and values, because it permits the organization to reach those who have yet to embrace its agenda.

A number of the obstacles faced by FESPAD's media advocacy are self-made. Some pertain to the audience the organization seeks to reach and the kinds of media it chooses to transmit its messages. Although it is not uncommon for their concerns to be raised on TV or radio programs, FESPAD more often targets El Salvador's print media, particularly the largest national newspapers, *La Prensa Gráfica* and *El Diario de Hoy*. Generally, choices about delivery depend on factors such as a group's resources, its desired audience, and national characteristics.[66] Funding constraints may force FESPAD to make some difficult decisions in a country where people's primary sources of information have traditionally been radio and television. The reliance on the leading newspapers permits the organization to reach a narrower yet powerful segment of society (the political and economic elites), while exercising some influence over the policy agenda. The dominant print media are a critical arena for some of FESPAD's key objectives, such as exposing injustices and proposing policy alternatives, but they do not give challenger perspectives a fair hearing. FESPAD's message, therefore, often came across as distorted with very limited possibilities for raising awareness among the broader population and thus creating political pressure for change.

Independent news media are a vital ingredient of democracy, informing the public and facilitating political debate. As indicated in Chapter 3, however, mainstream news corporations in El Salvador have traditionally been closely aligned with the economic and political elites. Their politics and business interests shape news production and impinge on the media access sought by civil society groups. FESPAD encounters difficulties getting its messages heard because its advocacy goals sometimes conflict with the politics and editorial lines of the media. As the Zacatecoluca incident demonstrated, one of the persistent uncertainties FESPAD faces is whether its messages will be conveyed as planned, distorted to some degree, or suppressed entirely. Although the staff were all too aware of the constraints imposed by the Salvadoran media landscape, FESPAD had not designed a media strategy that might have enabled it to overcome barriers of access and coverage.

The problem of media coverage related to the *kind* of reporting the NGO received rather than to the lack of it. FESPAD found, for example, that the mainstream media generally dispatched journalists to the organization's press conferences, but often did not publish or broadcast the stories.[67] On other occasions, journalists consulted the NGO on a specific issue, but the lawyers' perspective was later fragmented or stripped of context when it was presented as news. Not all space in the media is controlled by dominant individuals and institutions, and FESPAD has been able to gain public attention on certain issues. Nevertheless, it proved less adept at countering the bullying tactics that are used to discredit critical voices. The mass media routinely rely on familiar cultural themes, both to stereotype social and political actors and to promote the dominant interpretation of reality. For example, "human rights defenders coddle criminals" and "the answer to crime is suppression" are two such ideas that retain widespread currency in El Salvador. FESPAD's failure to respond to distortions by the mainstream press was politically costly because it let undemocratic values and attitudes remain unchallenged.

FESPAD's efforts to contest Mano Dura highlight the dangers of their passive approach to news coverage in two important ways. First, given the NGO's involvement in a variety of areas, its media coverage focused on actor visibility rather than on issue visibility. Second, even though FESPAD managed to publicize its perspective on specific questions, its standpoint was diffused by the dominant framing of reality by the media. The Mano Dura campaign clearly demonstrated that the organization's mere presence in the public debate was insufficient to produce policy change. Ultimately, the NGO's inability to advance its standpoint more strongly prevented it from turning the news about Mano Dura into contested terrain.

Staff members seemed to assume that press work is tantamount to a set of practical details that can simply be added to a campaign. Each FESPAD center complied with news protocols, but did not appear to see media work as a central political element of advocacy planning. Communications was a separate department in the organization, and the lawyers seemed not to appreciate the importance of the media as a strategic arena of political contention. The media in El Salvador are not only a tool for influencing public opinion, but also an arm of institutional power that must be targeted if the political space for alternative ideas is to expand. One of the most critical ways for an organization to do so is to join forces with other like-minded groups to challenge media priorities and biases.

It must be remembered that the population strongly supported Mano Dura, despite its cost in human rights violations and extralegal violence and its ineffectiveness in controlling street gangs. Without a strong, sustained media campaign, FESPAD's advocacy could find little resonance in a country where many people continue to believe that lawbreakers lose their rights. The persistent support for the measure confirms that Salvadoran society remained relatively indifferent to the group's attempts to change perceptions. The ability to affect public opinion could have given rights advocates some leverage over the government and persuaded it to implement a comprehensive gang policy.[68]

In light of these past failures, demands that the state adhere to constitutional precepts will likely lack the necessary weight—unless the citizenry accepts that promises of security are not a fair trade for human rights. Consciousness-raising is one step in that direction, but given the magnitude of the undertaking in El Salvador, it is hardly an option that FESPAD could have pursued alone. The group must consider forming alliances with other social organizations to amplify its political voice and influence.

The Disjointedness of Civil Society Action

FESPAD's advocacy in opposition to Mano Dura helped bring about an important, but ultimately limited, shift in the government's gang policy by compelling the Saca administration to commit itself, at least on paper, to comprehensive gang control and to adopt Mano Amiga and Mano Extendida. Although El Salvador's socio-political environment blunted the impact of the NGO's lobbying and policy-making efforts, the group's activities also reflected strategic shortcomings. Resource constraints exacerbated these weaknesses, but the organization could have converted its limitations into a tactical advantage by joining forces with like-minded actors. Since both the street gangs and the structural factors that support their development will endure for many years to come, this possibility remains alive.

Some in FESPAD have acknowledged the importance of civil society partnerships, but the end of the armed conflict engendered a strategic dislocation that remains to be overcome. For social and human rights organizations, the postwar period created not only political openings, but also a number of difficulties. One of these is the social environment, which continues to favor the guardians of the status quo, not its critics. Although opposition organizing is no longer as risky as in the past, those who find fault with public policies and the trampling of human rights have confronted a Janus-faced regime. Successive ARENA governments cultivated a democratic image, but routinely blocked demands for social and economic justice. The Saca administration in particular maintained an aura of openness and dialogue behind which lurked implacability. In the view of FESPAD's executive director and former CECDH director, Abraham Ábrego:

> The context is more unfavorable, because the work of NGOs needs to be more astute. . . . The government of [President] Saca is not more conciliatory than that of [President] Flores. In appearance it is, but in reality it is more authoritarian because the behavior of the government has been harsher on many issues. We need to be more astute in what we do because, for example, the conditions to promote alternative proposals from within civil society do not exist. This limits our work because one can have a proposal but not achieve anything if there is no political will to build a consensus.[69]

FESPAD's leaders recognize that they could have a broader impact if they collaborate with other NGOs and find ways to support the Salvadoran social movement. This has, however, proved more difficult than anticipated for a couple of reasons. First, the movement now lacks the sense of unity and vision that characterized it during the war. There is a feeling that these loosely connected groupings have veered off course and remain in search of a compass to show them the way back to relevance. Juan Carlos Sánchez, coordinator of FESPAD's Transparency Program and former head of the Project Planning Unit, explained:

> In this country, strategic alliances remain a challenge; coordination among actors remains a challenge. Unfortunately, we are not overcoming these challenges, precisely because we have lost our way, we are too fragmented, we have different visions and interests. The social movement is in a crisis of dispersion, and we do not know how to resolve it.[70]

The second problem is that FESPAD is unclear what its supportive role might be as long as the social movement's conceptual ambiguities remain unresolved. In 2007, in response to the arrest of fourteen anti–water privatization protesters on terrorism charges, FESPAD helped form the Concertación por la Paz, la Dignidad y la Justicia Social (Alliance for Peace, Dignity, and Social Justice). This coalition of some thirty organizations aimed to unite activists and induce a shift from protesting human rights violations in the country to making proposals. The group produced a series of studies, including an evaluation of the fulfillment of the Peace Accords, but it became dormant when some of the participating NGO leaders started working for the Funes government.[71]

Some interviewees felt that such alliances tended to be of limited use; they might achieve some visibility and political space, but more often they conveyed an impression of unity that did not in fact exist.[72] More importantly, however, FESPAD apparently found it difficult to bridge the social distance between its lawyers and the social movement. Overall, the lawyers saw themselves as dedicated to fighting for the poor, but for some, this commitment never went beyond their traditional role as legal professionals. Few, for example, were willing to participate in protest marches. The limits of FESPAD members' contact with the reality they seek to transform may affect the credibility and impact of their campaigns.[73] Without this social distance between some of the lawyers and the victims of Mano Dura whom they sought to represent, FESPAD might have pursued its efforts to advocate for human rights with greater urgency and persistency.

FESPAD's campaign against Mano Dura provides two lessons. First, legal rights and policy advocacy are not purely a technical-legal challenge, but also a political one. Above all, strategies need to go beyond a focus on deficient laws and policies and tackle the political processes that exclude entire social strata. Second, one NGO by itself cannot address all the factors associated with a problem as complex as the street gangs, as FESPAD largely tried to do in the case of Mano Dura. A single organization is simply too small and politically insignificant to pose a threat to the government. When the authorities are inaccessible or indifferent to the claims of individual civil society groups, such groups must use "the power of their information, ideas, and strategies" to effect change.[74] Ultimately, such social pressure needs to be applied on the elite, who have nothing to lose from continued gang crime and street violence, but everything to gain from the persistent social marginality that enables gangs to form.

Conclusion

FESPAD explicitly contested Mano Dura through its legal and policy research, seeking to promote gang control policies that combined rights-respecting law enforcement with prevention and rehabilitation. Contextual factors, notably elite influence over policy making, the nature of ARENA as the guardian of conservative interests, and an oligarchic media system, constituted significant barriers to gang-related advocacy. Criticism from FESPAD and other actors, combined with judicial opposition to Mano Dura, compelled the Saca administration to commit to comprehensive gang control and to adopt Mano Amiga and Mano Extendida. As chapter 2 made clear, however, these programs lacked substance, and suppression remained the government's preferred approach.

FESPAD used a variety of advocacy tools to promote its policy agenda, including research reports, paid ads, a legal aid clinic, and a proposal for the local prevention of gang violence. These activities were important in that they permitted the NGO to publicize the abuses and weaknesses of Mano Dura. In this way, FESPAD contributed to the changes in public discourse and policy that were introduced by the Saca administration. Even so, they brought no change in state behavior, particularly in gang-related law enforcement and the implementation of prevention and rehabilitation programs. FESPAD's ability to influence policy was shaped not only by exogenous factors, such as the nature of the state, but also by the group's own strategic and tactical choices, which in turn were shaped by the NGO's identity and its organizational characteristics.

FESPAD emerged from the aspiration of a group of lawyers who sought to defend human rights and the rule of law in El Salvador, a legacy its leadership has endeavored to sustain over the years. FESPAD's nature as a legal NGO that seeks to build democratic institutions underlies its staff's preference for formal channels over more confrontational tactics, a choice that hampered its gang-related advocacy.

Limited resources have also affected FESPAD's ability to propose alternative policy ideas. Sporadic financial difficulties, staff shortages, and the project-funding model of international donor groups, in particular, eroded the NGO's capacity to follow up long-term problems such as the street gangs. Whether from lack of funds or poor planning, or both, the organization developed neither the gang-specific expertise that was vital for the design of a gang prevention initiative nor the capacity for media outreach that would sway public opinion. Although FESPAD as an organization cultivated some media skills and gained public visibility, the lawyers tasked with legal and policy research failed to adequately publicize their position on the gang problem.

The reports FESPAD produced, for example, reminded the government of abuses and policy gaps, but this relatively "silent" presentation of facts was unlikely to effect changes where the necessary political will did not exist. Likewise, the paid newspaper ads, though useful as part of a broader strategy, were simply drowned out by the dominant anti-gang discourse. They were not combined with more extensive media work that might have sought to transform reporting practices and influence public opinion and thus increase the pressure for an alternative gang policy. The staff's professionalism and legal expertise nonetheless are the organization's main assets and have substantially contributed to raising FESPAD's status. Its positive public reputation gave it access to policymakers at a time when the redefinition of gang control was at stake. At the same time, ideology and strategic choices limited the group's influence on policymakers.

The legal aid clinic, for its part, was an interesting but limited method of exposing the abuses associated with Mano Dura. FESPAD displayed no capacity for dealing with institutional reluctance to end police harassment of gang members. Similarly, the proposal for gang violence prevention that was developed for the COAV Cities Project could have bolstered the NGO's advocacy demands, but the lawyers lacked the political experience either to anticipate a change in local government or to reorient their approach once it had proved ineffective.

FESPAD's lawyers apparently shared the prevailing view that the antagonistic state/civil society relations of the civil war period had become inappropriate and that activities such as proposal making and consensus building constituted more legitimate political activity. Yet, this perspective can depoliticize NGO work by limiting its targets to unresponsive institutions and thus considerably weaken its ability to apply pressure for policy change. In the long run, FESPAD failed to undertake more explicit and persistent lobbying activities and neglected to target other relevant actors, notably the economic elite for public spending and job creation and civil society for alliance building.

CHAPTER 5

Peer Rehabilitation and Empowerment

Homies Unidos (Homies United, or HU) was founded in San Salvador in 1996 by longtime US civil rights activist Magdaleno Rose-Ávila. It was the only NGO in El Salvador that was managed by, and worked directly with, gang members, until its closure in 2012.[1] The group's goal was to empower gang youths to cooperate with one another to resolve their problems and envision a life without drugs and violence.

Magdaleno departed El Salvador before the NGO was fully established, however, and left leadership and operations in the hands of individuals who had yet to overcome their identification with gang culture and values. These initial stages in its development remain crucial to understanding Homies Unidos and its advocacy efforts. The group publicly argued for a comprehensive and rights-respecting gang policy, but it held unconventional views of the gang problem and its solution. These views would create hurdles for its future activities. Homies Unidos and other NGOs that called for an end to Mano Dura faced an establishment power structure that caused the Salvadoran government to resist their appeal for an alternative approach to gang control. In addition, the stigma associated with gang members meant that HU staff faced even greater obstacles than other advocacy organizations.

Homies Unidos continued to pursue its empowerment strategy, which did not seek direct policy influence, but could shape the policy context. The organization's approach largely relied on the implementation of gang outreach programs. These programs deserved to be evaluated for their effectiveness in reducing gang violence, a study that is outside the scope of this book. Rather, this chapter chronicles how Homies Unidos sought to bring about a different form of gang control through indirect policy action. Since both internal factors and strategic decisions affected Homies Unidos's ability to influence policy, the account begins by examining the organization's characteristics.

Homies Unidos and its programmatic content emerged from the organizing efforts of a committed activist and a gang study that he had helped conduct. The chapter describes the link between HU identity/ideology and the concept of *pandilleros calmados* (retired or nonactive gang members) and explores its implications for gang-related advocacy. After considering Magdaleno's attempt to set up a functioning NGO, the chapter scrutinizes HU staffing issues, programs, maintenance difficulties, the use of storytelling, and job routines. It examines two of the organization's advocacy tools: information politics and a bakery microenterprise project in a gang-affected community. It concludes with some observations on the arrest and subsequent conviction of one HU director, as well as the collapse of the group's community-based gang work.

It is apparent that the Homies Unidos empowerment strategy was ineffective in promoting alternative gang control because staff were focused mostly on the welfare of their peers, rather than on effecting policy change. They failed to develop additional advocacy tools—such as lobbying activities, media work, and alliance building—to bring more political pressure for different forms of gang control. What is more, the interests and values of Homies Unidos conflicted with those of state authorities, leaving a strained relationship that was too limited to allow the NGO to influence either policy making or policing practices. In the end, faced with a skills and resource deficit, personnel were too preoccupied with organizational survival to give sufficient attention to the work of advocating for changes in gang policy.

The Story of Homies Unidos

The inspiration of Magdaleno Rose-Ávila, Homies Unidos emerged from his organizing efforts.[2] A Mexican-American with a history of teenage gang membership and violence, he also used and dealt drugs until he turned his life around in the 1960s when he joined César Chávez's United Farm Workers Union in Colorado. After his wife, Carolyn Rose-Ávila, was appointed regional director of Save the Children for Latin America, Magdaleno accompanied her to her new posting in El Salvador.

It was at a Save the Children–sponsored workshop with US-deported gang youths that Magdaleno became fascinated by participants' accounts of migration to the United States as civil war refugees and their subsequent gang life. He decided he wanted to learn more about their experiences and began to meet with them in their hangouts. Magdaleno sought to persuade the youths to conduct a gang study and to establish their own NGO. Although not initially warm to the idea, some eventually agreed to collaborate on the research project. Once he had secured financial and research support from Save the Children and the IUDOP, Magdaleno recruited twenty-two active members of Mara Salvatrucha and the Dieciocho, who would play a central role in the design and execution of the study. The description of the characteristics and key recommendations of the research below will help explain the nature of Homies Unidos and its choices of strategy and programmatic content.

The twenty-two gang members Magdaleno hired and helped train were tasked with making contact with the target population and assisting in the design, administration, and analysis of an unprecedented survey. Its main objective was to explore the reasons why young people joined a gang, their perceptions of gang life, and their personal needs. The IUDOP 1998 publication *Solidaridad y violencia en las pandillas del gran San Salvador* reported the results of the survey, which had reached more than one thousand active gang members.

Magdaleno and the IUDOP researchers decided to incorporate gang members into the polling team for two reasons. First, the researchers had difficulty gaining access to and establishing rapport with gang members, who were suspicious of outsiders and reluctant to collaborate. Magdaleno thought the recruits would find it easier to locate potential interviewees and secure their cooperation. Even this team, however, met with considerable mistrust because many respondents feared any information they supplied would be given to the police. Second, the IUDOP academics had no previous gang research experience (let alone gang association), and they saw themselves as only "pseudo-experts." Gang members, with their firsthand experience, could provide a more accurate portrayal of gang life and propose more informed solutions than could outsiders.

Given that access was a problem, the issue of expertise became more controversial than the research directors acknowledged. Active gang members did not merely participate in the research, but injected, inevitably perhaps, their ideology and values into the survey design, analysis, and recommendations. This is not a critique of their viewpoint, but serves to explain what followed. Homies Unidos emerged from this study and based its philosophy and work on the principal research findings, which had implications for HU's advocacy efforts.

The research presented socio-demographic data about gang members. It discussed why youths joined gangs; how they viewed their gang experience, including drugs, violence, and the least or most favored aspects; and how they perceived their social conditions and personal needs. Based on the responses, the data offered two main conclusions. First, structural, community, and individual factors facilitate gang membership. These might include poverty, social exclusion, the lack of educational and job opportunities, and dysfunctional families.[3] Second, respondents were asked if they wanted to adopt the retired gang member status of *pandilleros calmados* rather than to withdraw completely from gang life. Among the interviewees, 85 percent said they would like to abandon drugs and violence, but they would not want to sacrifice the benefits of gang membership, such as friendship, solidarity, and respect.[4] Based on these findings, the study called for programs to help gang members reintegrate into society and suggested that gang programmers accept the *calmado* status instead of promoting gang desistance.

Homies Unidos came to adopt the viewpoint suggested by the research on how to address the gang problem. On the one hand, the HU vision centered on the idea that youth can renounce drugs and violence, yet remain emotionally attached to their gang. Neither the authorities nor some other NGOs, however, would endorse this perspective, and HU never developed the advocacy tools that might have won it allies. On the other hand, Homies Unidos's strategy and programs were proposed and developed by external sources (the initial research study and the founder, Magdaleno), rather than by those within the NGO itself. Once Magdaleno was gone, the group never developed the capacity to build on his original vision and adapt its advocacy tactics to the requirements of Salvadoran politics. Homies Unidos was able to maintain the appearance of a functioning NGO, but never matured enough to effectively advance its agenda.

The idea of an NGO that focused on peer rehabilitation had surfaced prior to the study, but met with little enthusiasm from gang members. After the research project was completed, some of the interviewers continued to reject the idea of working with their rivals. However, Magdaleno persisted and assembled a sizeable group. In homage to all deceased gang members, Homies Unidos–San Salvador was founded in 1996 on 2 November, the traditional Day of the Dead in much of Latin America. The following year, a branch was established in Los Angeles, where most deportations of Salvadoran gang members originated.

The identity and purpose of Homies Unidos are largely reflected in its name. In gang argot, "homie" is used to refer to one's peers. According to director Luis Romero, "'homie' means much more than a friend. A homie is like a relative, but it [the term] entails much more than the love of a relative. It is a much bigger friendship."[5] Homies Unidos sought to empower gang members by bringing together former rivals who could design solutions to the problems facing their peers, while reaching out to gang youth to encourage them to abandon drugs and violence. The objective was to act as a bridge between gang members and the conventional world and provide access to opportunities for those who wanted them.

Homies Unidos rejected the idea that the way to reduce gang violence was by dissolving gangs. The group took this position partly because of the physical risk associated with attempts to break up gangs and partly because of the belief that gangs have positive functions, such as offering friendship, a sense of family, and respect. Additionally, gang members possess talents, such as leadership and organizing skills, that, the thinking went, can be co-opted for prosocial causes. HU staff positions were reserved for gang members because they were thought to identify with, and respond to, their peers more readily than those with no experience of gang life.

Unfortunately, these assumptions entailed two weaknesses, which were built into the organization from the start and later affected HU advocacy. First, despite the perceived benefits of gang affiliation, gang life is destructive and further isolates socially excluded youths from legitimate opportunities. Established gang scholars argue that control efforts should aim at dismantling gangs and persuading their members to adopt conventional lifestyles and values.[6] This was also the view of the Salvadoran authorities and other NGOs working on the gang issue; thus Homies Unidos was likely to encounter difficulties accessing and influencing government officials and cooperating with other civil society actors.

Second, it was expected that HU staff could be more effective in reaching out to gang youths because of their shared experience. Researchers find, however, that ex–gang members often lack the professional skills to carry out this kind of work.[7] Some exceptional cases have successfully channeled their abilities into civil rights organizing, but generally, gang members are inadequately educated or prepared for such purposes. Moreover, some such programs suffered from poor implementation and malfeasance.[8] This is not to suggest that Homies Unidos was bound to follow this path, but this research shows that a leadership and skills deficit hampered its advocacy work.

The experience of Homies Unidos shows that it was founded with high hopes and expectations that the staff struggled to meet. Given his own personal transformation, Magdaleno believed deeply in the NGO and the gang members he brought together, without perhaps recognizing the personal qualities that had made him successful. His activist experience notwithstanding, Magdaleno himself lacked professional gang intervention skills and may have overlooked the pitfalls of an organization run solely by insufficiently trained gang members who continued to identify with gang values.

Pandilleros Calmados

HU staff generally introduced themselves as ex–gang members, a status more complex than might be assumed. Research conducted in other contexts suggests that while gangs foster the idea that leaving the group is nearly impossible in order to ensure the group's survival, youths can and do withdraw from gangs.[9] The withdrawal process can be difficult because it means rejecting friends. Loyalty is central to gang culture and commonly expressed through tattoos.[10] To sever all ties to a gang and to remove tattoos is seen as a form of disrespect or betrayal, punishable with death. To avoid retaliation for leaving the gang, members often choose to withdraw gradually from its activities.[11]

In Salvadoran gang argot, *calmarse* ("to calm down") refers to the process of retiring from the gang, notably from participation in violence and drug use.[12] Adopting the status of *pandillero calmado* allows individuals to assume a more conventional lifestyle and distance themselves from their gang while maintaining due respect toward the group. *Pandilleros calmados*, however, continue to identify with gang culture and to consider themselves gang members. One former MS member described these circumstances as follows:

> You can disengage from the gang, because you are going to start your own family, because you become a Christian and give your life to God, or because you are going to continue your education and want to undergo job training. You have the opportunity to disengage from it [but] I think not to leave it, because a part of you remains in the gang. I am an ex–gang member, but I feel the pain of active gang members who are suffering the consequences of Mano Dura. Something remains in you even though you are not active in the gang; you share the suffering of your former mates.[13]

For society, the difference between *pandilleros calmados* and ex–gang members may be immaterial as long as those who remember their gang past with nostalgia are no longer involved in crime and violence. The problem may be when individuals, like HU staff, continue to identify with gang values while trying to carry out gang mitigation work. Some scholars have suggested that ex–gang members are unsuited for this kind of work precisely because they overidentify with gang values and norms and may harbor the pro-gang/anti-police biases that help make the gangs more cohesive and more delinquent.[14] It can be argued that HU staff identification with gang culture limited their policy influence because it informed their strategic choices and shaped external perceptions of the NGO and thus constrained what should have been important relationships with other actors.

Gang norms, for example, stipulate that members must not enunciate the name (e.g., Dieciocho or Mara Salvatrucha) or number (18 or 13) of the rival gang. This meant that HU staffer Miriam, herself a former Dieciocho member, would not say the name of the opposing group, even in the course of her work. She also spoke of the pain she felt when one of her former peers died, and she cheered at the death of a perceived enemy. Under such circumstances, it is questionable whether Miriam could work effectively on behalf of all gang members, regardless of their group affiliation.

Homies Unidos staff straddled the gang/society divide in other ways. In their gang work, HU staff deliberately exploited their identities as *pandilleros calmados*, leveraging the respect this status afforded them to gain access to the target population.[15] When dealing with other sectors of society, by contrast, HU staff presented themselves as ex–gang members because this concept found greater social acceptance than that of *pandilleros calmados*.[16]

Homies Unidos, like other NGOs, depended for its moral and financial support, and the resulting organizational survival, on exogenous perceptions of the agency. Staff compliance with the prevailing view of what constitutes past gang membership was therefore aimed at promoting a likeable public image and building and maintaining the necessary relationships on the street.[17] HU personnel's identity as *pandilleros calmados* was generally known among officials and NGOs, however, and arguably, this knowledge weakened the status of Homies Unidos and its advocacy relationships with these actors. Despite the fact that HU staff were no longer active gang members, they were still vulnerable to gang-related attacks, while to the Salvadoran authorities they were pigeonholed as delinquents who derided rehabilitation efforts.[18] The mistrust was mutual. HU staff nurtured their pro-gang and anti-police attitudes and therefore constructed only limited relationships with the authorities responsible for implementing gang policy and gang enforcement.

The fact that Homies Unidos was not invited to the 2004 Anti-Gang Forum, for example, suggests that it was not considered to have a legitimate role in the policy process. The opposing values of Homies Unidos and other potential NGO allies, some of which rejected, or doubted, the viability of the *calmado* status, further limited possibilities for alliance building.

Homies Unidos: The Formative Years (1996–1999)

A main theme of this study is that both organizational formation and maintenance are critical for understanding the relative ability of NGOs to influence policy. Homies Unidos took shape because Magdaleno decided to help gang members change their lives. He invested time and resources in the start-up of the NGO.[19] Sustaining an organization over the long run is the more difficult task. Adequate funding and qualified, committed staff are key ingredients, the lack of which ultimately threatened Homies Unidos's organizational survival and neutralized its advocacy efforts.

Once Magdaleno persuaded the initial group of gang members to establish a peer rehabilitation initiative, he used his organizing skills and fund-raising contacts to create a functioning NGO. The office was provisionally located in his house, where staff training sessions commenced. The great majority of HU staff were deportees from the United States and hard-core gang members. Homies Unidos required them to foreswear violence and drugs, but the recruits had limited education and little or no legitimate work histories, nor had many fully adopted conventional norms and values. None had previously worked in an NGO, nor were they acquainted with any of the tasks, such as grant writing and bookkeeping, that they would need to perform.

Magdaleno nevertheless was convinced that gang members possessed many talents and that these could be applied to licit activities. In his view, the only difference between a drug deal and a legal transaction carried out on behalf of an NGO was a receipt.[20] Yet, by the time of this research, nearly a decade after the founding of Homies Unidos, the organization had yet to master these challenges. In retrospect, it seems naïve to assume that gang members can instantly, or even quickly, be turned into professional employees.

While Magdaleno was with Homies Unidos–San Salvador, he kept the emphasis on staff development, the internalization of the HU mission, and press conference training. Programmatic content initially comprised mural painting and outreach activities aimed at spreading the message of nonviolence among gang youth. These included rap performances that highlighted the themes of migration, cultural alienation, parental neglect, and social exclusion. HU representatives met with police chiefs to discuss how gang control might be exercised with greater respect for human rights. Staff were to take a human rights course that would be prepared and taught by Julienne Gage, a US journalist on an Amnesty International grant.

These last activities failed to materialize, however, because Magdaleno and his team were trying to kick-start the organization and deal with the manifold difficulties that arose in the establishment phase.[21] The stigmatization of gang members, for example, meant that HU staff met with suspicion from various quarters. The US embassy reportedly suspected Magdaleno of pooling money for drugs and advised the Salvadoran government to be vigilant toward HU activities. Homies Unidos struggled to raise sufficient funds to sustain its operations. Although Magdaleno invested some US $100,000 of his own money into the organization and helped raise more money, these contributions were quickly absorbed in operating costs.[22]

The nature of gang life also made staff recruitment and retention a greater problem for Homies Unidos than for other NGOs: frequent personnel changes further hampered the group's professionalization and sustainability. An estimated five to six HU members were killed in shootings, and Magdaleno himself received threats from both police and hostile gang members who disagreed with the HU mission and incited others to kill him.[23]

Perhaps most importantly, the HU leadership neglected the need to transform HU members' values and thinking or to monitor whether they actually withdrew from drug use, crime, and violence. A series of incidents suggested that staff members required counseling, yet these were not decisively addressed.[24] For example, sexual harassment was rampant, but largely ignored. During a weekend retreat, when asked to reflect on how they had been respecting human rights, one of the male gang members giggled and said, "Well, at least we didn't rape anyone."

His comment went unremarked. Staff member Sigfredo "Ringo" Rivera Hernández appeared at internal meetings with photos of his toddler son dressed in gang attire and holding a pistol, but no one explained to him that this was no laughing matter.

Human rights volunteer Julienne Gage believed the HU partner organization Save the Children was prepared to use Homies Unidos for publicity purposes, but not to assist the gang members in changing their lives. In Julienne's view, HU staff, initially attracted by the prospects of job training, wanted to draw a line under their gang past but were unable to do so without more help:

> It seemed obvious to me that [they] were interested in changing psychologically and emotionally, they just did not know how to. The organization was supposed to be there to show them the way, and when the organization was weak, the guys went back to doing what they had been doing before. It was the only thing they knew.[25]

When the gang members were sent on errands, they would sometimes disappear to take care of other business. Although there is no solid evidence of criminal activities, it appears that some HU personnel may have been involved in drug sales in the San Antonio Abad neighborhood of San Salvador. In 1999, Sigfredo, by then HU director, was shot in one of the area's bars, where he and other gang members had gathered for drinks. While Sigfredo's friends insisted on his innocence, eyewitnesses affirmed that he started the shooting in which he and a bartender died. The events of that night remained shrouded in mystery, and Homies Unidos refused to concede that one of its staff might be complicit.[26] In an interview, Magdaleno acknowledged that after his departure, the organization deteriorated because some of the new recruits merely sought to find a cover for continued gang activity:

> Some people saw Homies Unidos as a money tree. There were people with strong gang politics coming in, [and] it was difficult to control the situation. . . . Some elements of bad blood came in; some of them went to jail later.[27]

Homies Unidos struggled to establish itself as a professional organization. Without the contribution of Magdaleno, who tried to build the NGO despite enormous physical risks and financial cost, it might never have formed. When he left the project, he put the agency's maintenance and operations in the hands of individuals who had yet to overcome their gang past, much less conduct effective gang-related advocacy.

Homies Unidos Today

A visit to the offices of Homies Unidos provided few clues to the organization's turbulent history. Tucked away in an apartment building near San Salvador's largest shopping center, a nondescript door gave way to a quiet and sparsely furnished flat. The walls were adorned with diplomas, posters, and the HU banner that proclaimed the possibility of gang rehabilitation and of integration between gang members and society. Over the years, the NGO defied the odds and demonstrated its capacity to survive despite recurrent difficulties.

As described above, Homies Unidos aimed to empower gang members by encouraging rivals to cooperate in solving their own problems and persuading them to abandon drugs and violence. During the group's formative years, Magdaleno worked to bring together MS and Dieciocho personnel in equal numbers. Given the long-standing hostilities between the two gangs, however, it was a struggle to maintain a balance. One or the other of the groups tended to dominate the organization at various times.[28] At the beginning of this research, and until Homies Unidos closed its doors, the NGO was staffed exclusively by former Dieciocho members, whose work perhaps predictably focused mostly on their own gang.

There are two salient points to make. First, HU staff primarily sought to improve the welfare of their gang peers rather than to design and execute a coherent advocacy agenda. Second, the staffing bias was known among other NGOs, some of which viewed the organization with skepticism and were unwilling to collaborate with it. This antagonism diminished the possibilities for networking, building alliances, or exerting greater political pressure for the implementation of an alternative gang policy.

The complexity of gang integration can be understood through the social psychology of group identification and intergroup relations. To identify with either the MS or the Dieciocho, gang members divide the world into in-groups ("us") or out-groups ("them"). Most people do this to some degree as a means to specify their place in society and to organize their relations with other groups.[29] In an environment where social identity plays a crucial role, as it does in the gang world, in-group identification elicits feelings of affection for, trust in, and cooperation with in-group members. These feelings are not extended to any member of an out-group.[30] This strong emotional identification means that relations between different gangs tend to become competitive or threatening, even in the absence of any overt threat.[31]

Homies Unidos sought to give members of rival gangs a common in-group identity and to empower them to cooperate toward a shared goal. The expectation was that personnel would shed their previous gang identity, see themselves as constituents of a single new social entity, and develop more positive attitudes toward each other.

Research shows that bringing members of different groups together may lead to friendlier relations between particular individuals, but it is an ineffective way of changing intergroup attitudes or improving intergroup relations.[32] Magdaleno's presence may have permitted temporary collaboration between rival gang members, but his charisma alone was unlikely to ensure their enduring allegiance to the organizational culture he had sought to foster. The fact that Homies Unidos did not maintain the original balance among its personnel indicates that its staff remained opposed to gang integration. Indeed, the killing of Héctor "el Negro" Pineda, Homies Unidos's first director and a former MS member, by Dieciocho HU members shows that some staff intended for their own gang to gain control over the organization.[33]

When asked why the NGO was run exclusively by ex–Dieciocho members and limited its activities to this group, the staff gave evasive answers. They pointed out that Homies Unidos once included MS members and claimed that it would continue to assist them if asked. The HU staffing bias, and its evident contradiction of the group's founding principles, also caused some NGOs to distrust Homies Unidos, raising a further barrier to networking or alliance building that might have strengthened HU advocacy efforts.

Homies Unidos staff also acquired a reputation for being unreliable and presumptuous. Some interviewees spoke of occasions when HU personnel failed to maintain their participation in networks or implied that their past history made them greater authorities on the subject of gangs than anyone else. Following these types of encounters, many NGOs were understandably disinclined toward further collaboration.

PROGRAMS AND INSTITUTIONAL SUSTAINABILITY

Officially Homies Unidos carried out six programs designed to further its empowerment strategy: staff development, prevention or information politics (testimonial stories), education (school placement and access to university scholarships), health education (sexual health education and HIV/AIDS awareness sessions), rehabilitation (access to drug treatment, tattoo removal, job training and development), and human rights efforts (defense of gang members' rights). In addition, the NGO was a reference point for journalists, students, and researchers, largely from abroad, who sought information on or access to El Salvador's street gangs.

To facilitate these efforts, Homies Unidos maintained a newspaper archive on gang-related arrests, deportations, and deaths. Moreover, HU tried to secure interviews with gang members for journalists. The material that was produced over the years was intended to raise both the organization's public profile and awareness of the gang problem and the need for policy alternatives to Mano Dura. Yet the group's media activities presumed that interested parties would come to Homies Unidos because it neither promoted its research and related projects nor initiated media work that might have publicized the gang situation.

Before going into a fuller discussion of HU advocacy, it is important to identify the principal difficulties the organization faced. Three areas are key to any successful NGO operations: funding, job routines, and staff skills. In the case of Homies Unidos, all three constituted critical barriers to more effective work.

NGO management is more demanding than might be assumed. According to those involved in establishing and running Homies Unidos, its staff underestimated the sheer difficulty of this task.[34] The weak financial viability of the organization repeatedly resulted in unpaid bills and salaries. Like other Salvadoran NGOs, Homies Unidos was constrained by the project-driven nature of donor assistance and a hostile domestic funding environment, but HU staff's gang history further complicated its fund-raising situation. The fact that Homies Unidos was for many years able to overcome threats of permanent dissolution was seen as a sign of commitment and hard work.[35] It may also be interpreted as a lack of ability or motivation to hone the group's grant-seeking skills and strengthen organizational sustainability. For example, Homies Unidos obtained its legal personality as a nonprofit association only in late 2010, even though this is a funding requirement and staff had received application guidance.[36] A personal friend of some HU members had helped prepare grant proposals, but all funding had to be channeled through another NGO's bank account. In addition, the HU director pursued a series of stopgap measures to keep the organization afloat, such as soliciting donations by e-mail or from visitors. The point is not the appropriateness or otherwise of such methods, but that they signaled the group's inability to develop the procedures that would have made the NGO financially secure.

The second endogenous limitation to HU work concerns the extent to which staff carried out basic job routines. If Homies Unidos was to function as an organization, its staff had to respect a conventional work ethic and conform to agency standards, but this was rarely the case. For example, rules on computer use and office cleaning were broken as swiftly as they were established, and the weekly staff meeting to plan day-to-day activities was regularly cancelled at short notice. Homies Unidos lacked strong leadership, the commitment from its staff to perform tedious but necessary chores, and the ability to plan and organize its advocacy agenda. These weaknesses resulted from the general lack of skills and professionalization.

Given the nature of the organization, Homies Unidos probably had to cope with a higher staff turnover than other NGOs. Over the years, some of its members managed the transition to a more conventional lifestyle and moved on; others abandoned the agency and the rehabilitation process to return to the street. Still others tried to return to the United States, one ex-director received threats and resigned, and some twelve individuals were killed while on staff.[37] These frequent personnel changes weakened the organization and required that time and resources continually be invested in staff training instead of advocacy efforts. During the research period, four paid staff and one volunteer ran Homies Unidos. For reasons discussed below, this number was subsequently reduced. Volunteering had been introduced during the establishment phase and was intended to ensure that recruits would only enter the salaried workforce once they had demonstrated their commitment to Homies Unidos and its activities. Luis Romero, the director, described repeated occasions when he had been approached by gang members whose interest in HU affiliation, he was sure, was not genuine but only meant to camouflage continued gang activity.

The challenge for Homies Unidos was not only to rigorously screen staff, however, but also to prepare them to work with the organization. Many staff members were trained in various skills—including basic bookkeeping, computing, and health education—and used HU funding to help them finish their secondary or university education. Even so, many did not consistently apply the skills they had acquired and instead preferred to solicit the assistance of outsiders.

Homies Unidos also resisted recruiting non–gang members whose abilities might have strengthened the organization and its advocacy work. Its director, Luis Romero, defended this practice by arguing that gang members were committed to working with their peers even in difficult times, whereas outside professionals would leave if their wages could not be paid.[38] This remained an unproven assumption since Homies Unidos never hired qualified staff. The use of storytelling within the group seemed to be a characteristic of the NGO and served to explain discrepancies between the story of Homies Unidos and the reality encountered.

STORYTELLING

Some individuals may rely on storytelling to make sense of their working lives.[39] These tales can help communicate certain experiences, explain successes or failures, or sustain a particular impression of their organization. The stories told by Homies Unidos staff were of two kinds, rationalizations and image management, and tended to concern the difficulties of maintaining operations and HU activities. What follows are three examples that relate to the staffing, lack of a media strategy, and HU activities.

First, when asked about bringing in more highly trained personnel, Homies Unidos staff dismissed the idea and routinely cited the supposed commitment gap between gang members and external professionals. Given the obvious disadvantage for the organization of such intransigence, this argument justified the exclusion of individuals who might have controlled how HU staff spent their time and limited the freedom and flexibility they enjoyed.

Second, to an outside observer it was apparent that Homies Unidos lacked a media strategy to help strengthen its advocacy efforts. In a staff meeting, when asked to suggest improvements, I raised the need for better media relations. Luis, despite evidence to the contrary, insisted that the NGO had a strategy in this area. On another occasion, staff member Heriberto affirmed that Homies Unidos had ceased all media work because previous coverage was perceived as negative. As a way of raising greater awareness of the nature of the gang problem and the need for alternative responses to it, engagement with the Salvadoran press could have served to publicize the programs of Homies Unidos. Staff preferred to blame unfavorable reporting for their neglect of an important advocacy tool.

The third and most prominent story came to the fore when HU personnel were required to speak about their activities, particularly when visitors stopped by to learn about Homies Unidos and its programs.

Staff had developed the habit of documenting workshops and other events with photos, and these were presented together with "the story of Homies Unidos" to construct a particular account of the organization and its contributions to alternative gang control. The information conveyed little about the organization's contemporary situation, however, and was intended simply to sustain a positive image of Homies Unidos and its work. Below are snapshots of some job routines that demonstrate the NGO's largely reactive approach to gang-related advocacy.

"Hanging Out" and "Cruising" with Homies Unidos

HU staff spent much of their time outside the office, often attending meetings and responding to human rights cases or other situations. On one of these occasions, Luis was concerned about the infatuation of an MS member with a fourteen-year-old girl.

Also known by his street name, "Panza Loca" (Crazy Belly), Luis had been working with Homies Unidos since its founding, and in 2002, he became its director. Prior to his 1992 deportation from the United States, he had been a Dieciocho member in Los Angeles. His family had sent him to the United States to protect him from the Salvadoran civil war and allow him to finish his high school education, but his stay with relatives was short-lived. By his own account, loneliness led him to join the Dieciocho and become involved with drugs, violence, and crime. Asked why he remained emotionally attached to his gang despite the harmful dimensions of gang life, Luis acknowledged that it might be difficult to understand why he felt friendship for individuals who received him with violence and supplied him with drugs. Yet, despite all the negative aspects, the gang was prepared to share everything with him, and it was their support he appreciated. With hindsight, he described the experience as painful but "necessary" and expressed the hope that he could use his gang past to prevent others from making the same mistake.

As we left the office to attend to the teenage girl's case, Luis clutched the photo ID that indicated his affiliation with Homies Unidos and was meant to prevent his arrest for his tattoos. In his dilapidated car, listening to the sound of Luis's favorite crooner songs (a reminder of gang life), we set off to meet the teenager at a restaurant. Over pizza, Luis counseled her to stay away from gang hangouts, and later, we accompanied the girl back to her home in Soyapango, a populous industrial city outside the capital. Luis tensed up because the drive took us through rival gang territory. However, we arrived without incident at our destination, where we walked along a bumpy path that traversed a dusty community of laminate shacks, sporadic electricity services, and no potable water. After a brief stop at the family's home, Luis and I returned to the office. The trip was typical of many that squandered staff time and scarce resources in response to the personal needs of some youths, but were unlikely to further Homies Unidos's advocacy agenda or promote alternative gang policies.

THE HUMAN RIGHTS PROGRAM

The promotion of alternative gang control could have been substantially advanced by Homies Unidos's human rights program. Of all the NGO's work, this was the most consistently and enthusiastically implemented program. It sought to deal with the discrimination, police harassment, arbitrary arrests, and appalling detention conditions facing gang members. However, program activities also suffered from the same aforementioned organizational and strategic weaknesses that undermined the entire organization and achieved little more than to address individual problems in isolation.

The difficulties associated with the human rights program were twofold. First, the authorities took the view that gang members use the human rights discourse to escape justice.[40] Government and law enforcement officials were largely unreceptive to calls to respect the human rights of gang members, and even less receptive if these requests came from former gang members themselves. Homies Unidos therefore found it difficult to promote rights-respecting gang control.

Second, by following media coverage of other actors' critiques of Mano Dura, HU staff learned how to speak the language of human rights and when to deploy it. Yet, they had no organizing strategy that might have permitted them to advocate these principles in practice. The activities Homies Unidos pursued over the years sought to counter gang suppression in various ways, but were of limited reach. In 2003, for example, HU staff joined with the PDDH to submit a constitutional challenge to the Ley Anti Maras. On other occasions, they supported rallies organized by relatives of detained gang members to protest the prison situation. However, Homies Unidos acted as a bystander, expressing solidarity with the cause but not incorporating such events into a broader advocacy strategy.

The NGO had some success in alerting the PDDH to human rights violations by police officers. Reporting served to expose abusive policing practices in some instances, but it too did not develop into a more sustained effort to reorient the PNC's approach to gang control. Rather, staff privately expressed their disappointment that more cases did not achieve a positive outcome for the victims. A PDDH representative stated that although some investigations had confirmed the occurrence of police abuse, in other cases, gang members had been lawfully arrested and charged.[41]

HU staff spent much of their time, often without success, visiting police stations to track down recently arrested gang members and secure their release from custody. Generally, staff members were keen to demonstrate support for their detained peers, but they avoided advocacy activities that might actually have improved the situation of gang members. Homies Unidos's reaction to the arbitrary prison transfer of one Dieciocho member illustrates this point. Staff were notified that the authorities, who suspected Carlos Barahona ("el Chino Tres Colas") of being a Dieciocho leader, had decided to move him from Chalatenango to Cojutepeque. At the time, both prisons were reserved for members of the Dieciocho, and officials hoped to ascertain the extent of his power within the gang.

Homies Unidos, aware of intra-gang disputes, was concerned about Carlos Barahona's welfare in the new setting. Staff decided to go to Cojutepeque and maintain a presence outside the prison. HU members watched as he was led into the building, whereupon everyone returned to the capital and no further action was taken in the case. While this display of solidarity may have encouraged Carlos Barahona personally, it amounted to nothing more than the sum of several unproductive hours spent away from the office.

Overall, Homies Unidos's human rights program was perhaps the one element of its work that most clearly offered scope for lobbying the government, for media outreach, or to collaborate with other NGOs. Media work could have publicized abusive police practices to promote rights-respecting gang control. Civil society–based alliances could have strengthened the political voice of Homies Unidos. However, such collaborative efforts stalled as a result of HU's poor reputation and weak leadership. HU staff did not seek out opportunities to network or make alliances, except to solicit help to resolve the immediate problems of their peers. The group failed even to build an advocacy partnership with Homies Unidos–Los Angeles, with which it had strained relations.

The Homies Unidos Empowerment Strategy in Practice

As part of its empowerment strategy, Homies Unidos implemented a prevention program whereby staff used their firsthand experiences of gang life to warn young people about its perils and insist on the need for prevention. These public speaking engagements, generally performed in schools and seminars on gang violence, sought to raise audience awareness and constituted a form of information politics.

Information Politics

The term "information politics" refers to the provision of "information that would not otherwise be available, from sources that might not otherwise be heard."[42] In the case of Homies Unidos, it refers to facts or personal stories about the gang problem that could help alter the policy context and increase pressure for comprehensive gang control.

Information politics had the potential to advance HU advocacy, and the staff spoke of organizing more such public appearances in the months ahead. The talks never got beyond the planning stage, however, partly due to renewed funding difficulties that made organizational survival a greater priority and partly because the arrest of a staff member temporarily displaced any concern for agency work. The practice of information politics requires no particular funds or preparation and is easily implemented despite resource constraints. Nevertheless, the lost opportunities for advocacy were numerous.

The speaking engagements were to take the form of a *testimonio*, or testimonial story.

> The *testimonio* is . . . told in the first person by a narrator who is also a real protagonist or witness of the events he or she recounts, and whose unit of narration is usually a "life" or a significant life experience. . . . The situation of narration in *testimonio* has to involve an urgency to communicate, a problem of repression, poverty, subalternity, imprisonment, struggle for survival, and so on.[43]

The tradition of *testimonio* offers a true story previously obscured by official history. It is less concerned with the life of the narrator than with a problematic collective social situation that the speaker shares with the audience—in the case of Homies Unidos, usually students or gang prevention workers.[44] The "witness" implicit in its convention lends the *testimonio* both a "flesh-and-blood authenticity" and an aura of truth, which the audience is meant to respect.[45] At the same time, the firsthand experience affords the narrator authority. The main objectives of the genre are the self-representation of the voiceless, the raising of awareness, the condemnation of injustices, and the placement of issues within the domestic political agenda.[46] *Testimonio* engages listeners, and sometimes readers, to win their support for a cause. It has played an important role in the development of international human rights and solidarity movements.[47]

Narratives related by ex–gang members permit outsiders a glimpse of an experience that is removed from that of most people and difficult to access. The account is often transmitted orally, which is the option Homies Unidos had chosen. However, there also exists a growing number of print versions by "reformed characters" who decided to publicize details of their time in the gang as a way of warning others about the violence that accompanies this lifestyle.[48] Generally, such accounts describe the personal circumstances that led the narrator to join a gang, offer a stomach-turning description of gang life, and then depict his or her return to the conventional world. The stories address what it means to be a gang member and draw attention to the conditions of social marginality facing gang youths. As an advocacy tool, a gang *testimonio* not only illustrates the possibility of positive change, but also underscores the need to prevent the destruction of more human lives.

Although these stories are intended to contribute to gang control, scholars disagree on their impact. Some researchers find that talks aiming to educate young people about the consequences of gang involvement are unlikely to have a deterrent effect because they fail to target those who are at risk of joining a gang.[49] Others argue that accounts by ex–gang members can help to drive home the dangers of gang life and empower young people to transform their own lives.[50]

Here again, the goal is not to assess the extent to which HU staff may have helped reduce gang violence in El Salvador, but to emphasize that organizational weaknesses precluded it from making more frequent and effective use of a valuable advocacy tool. Media work—for example, the use of blogs and videos or a campaign developed with alternative media outlets or universities—could have delivered the information to a wider audience, educated the public about the nature of the gang problem, and advocated for an alternative gang policy. By influencing public opinion on the subject, Homies Unidos could then have applied greater political pressure for the adoption of prevention and rehabilitation programs. Instead, the group's internal weaknesses distracted from and undermined its ability to concentrate on advocacy efforts.

The Bakery in La Campanera

Homies Unidos provided access to a variety of services in an attempt to reach out to gang youths and persuade them to abandon drugs and violence. Whenever possible, the NGO worked with gang members in their own milieu as a way to both show respect for their lifestyle and facilitate their attendance at the organization's workshops.[51]

The empowerment strategy also covered skills and job development. Homies Unidos placed a number of ex–gang members in vocational training institutes, where they took classes in computing, automobile mechanics, and carpentry.[52] Employment opportunities were more difficult to secure, however, due to the lack of meaningful jobs in El Salvador generally, and the reluctance of the private sector to hire gang members. Self-employment in the form of a microenterprise therefore can be a valuable source of income for individuals with tattoos or a criminal record.

In 2006, Homies Unidos participated in one such experiment, a bakery, in La Campanera, Soyapango, an industrial hub bordering the capital and the country's third-most-populous city. In January that year, Christian Poveda, a Franco-Spanish photographer who had covered the Salvadoran civil war, began filming his documentary, *La vida loca*, much of it set in La Campanera. Although Homies Unidos claimed credit for the bakery, Poveda had financed its installation in order to capture gang members' self-employment capacity for the big screen.[53] Homies Unidos supported the bakery and also offered to organize a series of workshops on issues such as HIV/AIDS and human rights for the clique.

La Campanera is a community of some ten thousand inhabitants, where dozens of narrow residential passages are interspersed with corner shops, several evangelical churches, and a soccer field. In appearance unremarkable, the place has long been so stigmatized for its gang activity that all its youths are suspects in the eyes of police and rival gangs, and residents have little choice but to include a different address on their resumes.[54]

On a visit to La Campanera in March 2006, we toured the bakery, which had been launched just a few weeks earlier. We were accompanied by Heriberto "Eric Boy" Henríquez, who at the time was director of rehabilitation, tasked with engaging gang youths in the communities and seeking their release from police custody. In his account of his life, Heriberto left wartime El Salvador for the United States soon after he was recruited by the army at age fourteen. In Los Angeles, Heriberto became entangled in Dieciocho gang life and drug use, was sent to prison, and eventually was deported. His tattoos and a defiant attitude persisted through the intervening years; after being injured in a 2005 shooting incident, Heriberto regularly carried a weapon in the field for self-defense.

In La Campanera, we drove down the long entrance road of the community and parked the car outside the bakery. By the time of this visit, the gang graffiti had largely disappeared, but the place, still affected by extortions and other crime, had a heavy police presence. Upon our arrival, after a police patrol had gone out of sight, the community seemed eerily quiet. Then one gang member after another emerged from hiding, as if to illustrate the ineffectiveness of gang deterrence. A small group surrounded us while others sauntered down the road. Nearby, a girl with a large "18" tattooed across her face cuddled her toddler daughter. Remarking on this rare display of gang loyalty by a female, Heriberto, nodding in her direction, said with unconcealed pride, "*¿Viste eso?*" ("Did you see that?")

That day Heriberto exchanged respectful greetings with the gang members. The bakery, however, which had an apparently successful start, was closed. A baker had been hired to train the gang members, and they were expected to prepare a daily quota of bread and pastries. Non-tattooed helpers would then sell the product on their behalf. To turn the bakery into a lasting and self-sustainable project, gang members had been given a crash course in business administration. Some of the youths had been arrested, however, and the work had come to a standstill. Heriberto promised to stop by the police station in nearby Ilopango, where the gang members were likely being held.

Along the way, the stereo in his pickup truck blasted out music by American rapper 50 Cent. "*¡Bonita historia!*" ("Nice story!"), Heriberto shouted over the noise, nodding at the CD player. It seemed he still harbored an emotional attachment to gang culture, despite his reformed status. At the police station, the commanding officer was unavailable, so we returned to the HU office, where the rest of the afternoon was spent chatting over coffee and cheesecake.

Over the coming months, the gang members who worked in the bakery were harassed by police and arrested on several occasions. Homies Unidos repeatedly requested an appointment with the PNC's director-general, and when all these requests were ignored, HU sought to compel his appearance before a legislative committee. That tactic was also unsuccessful, suggesting that the organization lacked the stature to gain access to, much less exercise influence over, officials or to force changes in policing practices.

The bakery was to encounter greater problems, but now Homies Unidos faced an internal crisis of its own that temporarily distracted from the pursuit of advocacy activities. The arrest and subsequent conviction of Heriberto—and Homies Unidos's reaction to it—are instructive in that they revealed staff priorities and highlighted the group's neglect of media work, despite the negative publicity of these developments.

Shadows of the Gang World: The Case against Heriberto

One morning in mid-May 2006, police arrived at the NGO's office and arrested Heriberto for the July 2005 murder of a Dieciocho member at a nearby nightclub.[55] Routine tasks were set aside as staff began to mobilize support for him. The IDHUCA was approached for legal assistance and responded positively to the request. However, in a lineup, a witness for the FGR identified Heriberto as one of the gunmen. The court ordered that the case proceed to the pretrial phase; although Heriberto was released on bail, the judicial order was revoked a week later and Heriberto was sent to Chalatenango prison. The IDHUCA, which defends victims but not suspected perpetrators, withdrew at this point. HU volunteer Geovany, who had coordinated the health program, resigned in the midst of these developments and reportedly started working in a call center.

Salvadoran media quickly seized on the case, and Homies Unidos's international donors called to follow up on some of these reports. News of the arrest quickly spread and further dented Homies Unidos's reputation. A number of individuals from NGOs and public institutions expressed their wariness of an organization that had already been perceived as biased and unreliable.[56] Strangely, HU staff were less troubled by the events than one might have expected under the circumstances, remaining focused on Heriberto's welfare. They made no public relations effort to restore some of the NGO's previous status. Instead, HU members sought to use the situation to further their gang outreach and enlisted Heriberto for an arts workshop inside the prison.[57]

In July 2006, Heriberto was moved from Chalatenango to the maximum-security prison in Zacatecoluca, although he had yet to face trial. The authorities justified the transfer by alleging acts of intimidation committed behind bars.[58] The court delivered its judgment in February 2007, finding Heriberto and the co-defendant, Dieciocho leader Carlos Barahona, guilty of the murder of José "el Cranky" Cortez. The killing of this Dieciocho shot caller is thought to have been one of the factors in the rupture of the Dieciocho and is examined in an investigative piece by *El Faro*.[59]

Heriberto always denied any wrongdoing, calling the accusations against him a campaign of harassment launched by the authorities.[60] For its part, Homies Unidos publicly maintained that on the night of the shooting, it had hosted a dinner party for the director of Homies Unidos–Los Angeles, Silvia Beltrán, at which Heriberto was in attendance. The group left the restaurant at around 1:30 a.m., a half-hour after witnesses said the killing took place, and Heriberto gave his colleagues a lift home. Therefore, he could not have been at the crime scene.[61]

Silvia resigned shortly after the trial and was initially not available for comments. When contacted again years later, she professed that Heriberto's conviction had been a major emotional blow to her, since they had known each other for a long time. Silvia confirmed that she had attended the dinner but said she had left early and could not say when the rest of the group had departed. To this day, she believes Heriberto could not have been capable of murdering another Dieciocho member.[62]

When the proceedings progressed to the trial phase, in early 2007, the FGR presented a whole range of evidence against the defendants, including a ballistics test that confirmed that five out of more than sixty cartridge cases found at the crime scene had been fired by Heriberto's semiautomatic pistol. A key part of the prosecution's evidence was the testimony of a protected witness, "Armando" (a pseudonym), who identified Heriberto Henríquez and Carlos Barahona as regular customers of the bar and swore that he saw them shoot the victim.

The defense maintained their previous line of argument and presented four witnesses to the killing, including Miriam, Geovany, and a gang member who claimed to have been injured in the incident but insisted that the defendants had not been present and thus not involved in the death of José Cortez. The judges, however, admitted the FGR's evidence in full and found no irregularities in it, whereas the witnesses for the defense had become entangled in contradictions and were seen to be biased. Heriberto Henríquez and Carlos Barahona were each sentenced to sixteen years.

The verdict and Homies Unidos's role in the case are instructive for two reasons. First, the organization's leadership still did not screen recruits rigorously enough to ensure that the staffing problems of the early years would not repeat themselves and continue to weaken the organization. Second, staff remained unconditionally supportive of Heriberto despite learning that he had not abandoned crime and was an inappropriate choice as a spokesperson for Homies Unidos's cause.

While the NGO's support for one of their own is understandable, it showed that HU personnel once more put the welfare of gang members above the welfare of the organization and the advocacy work it was designed to perform. These attitudes continued to be reflected in Homies Unidos's failure to incorporate the Campanera bakery into a broader advocacy strategy or prevent it from collapsing.

Empowerment in La Campanera?

The bakery in La Campanera lost staff and would soon struggle to continue its work in the face of increased police harassment. The story of Homies Unidos's activities in La Campanera further illustrates the organization's strategic limitations, which contributed to the premature end of the project and undermined the effectiveness of the group's advocacy role.

One morning in July 2006, I accompanied Miriam and Luis as they travelled to La Campanera, where they planned to hold an HIV/AIDS awareness workshop. This would be the first in a series of thematic talks for which Homies Unidos had enlisted expert speakers. Prior to the event, we stopped by the bakery. Pastries were in the oven, but it was apparent that the microenterprise was experiencing difficulties. José "Moreno" Rosales, the gang member who managed the bakery, voiced his frustrations, explaining that the business was losing money. He said that several workers tended to disappear during the day, forcing him to work extra hours to get the work done. Luis seemed genuinely surprised, but merely instructed the youth to share his responsibilities with another team member.

Outside the bakery, we sat down for lunch while a street vendor prepared the meals that the workshop participants would receive. By the time we arrived at the nearby church, where the gang members often met to avoid police harassment, the workshop was already well under way.

Depending on the funding situation, Homies Unidos distributed pamphlets with HIV/AIDS prevention messages in the gang vernacular and helped organize HIV testing sessions. That particular day, the goal was more limited. Some fifty male gang members, mostly bare-chested and tattooed, lolled on the chairs and listened with moderate attention while HU staff filmed the event for the archive that chronicled the NGO's work. After the expert's talk, Luis addressed the crowd, and Miriam distributed a generous amount of condoms. Their visit to the community ended soon afterward.

The nature of the event raised doubts about Homies Unidos's ability to empower, or their commitment to empowering, individual gang members to abandon drugs and violence or to promote nonpunitive gang control policies. A number of observations can be made about what was, as things turned out, both the first and last HU workshop in La Campanera. First, if HU staff were trained to conduct health-related workshops, why hire outside speakers? The episode might suggest that they were happy enough to claim credit for the talk, but were not prepared to do the work it entailed. Second, none of the film or photographs of the event were used in a media strategy to raise public awareness of gang members' needs. The limited use of photos and videos implied that they had no purpose other than to show Homies Unidos in action to donors and other potential supporters of the NGO. Finally, the distribution of food and condoms might have encouraged gang members to attend HU workshops, but it remained unclear whether these activities helped reduce gang violence. This vital question remained unanswered because Homies Unidos never followed up to find out whether the gang members actually turned to a more conventional lifestyle. In light of this failure, it appears that HU staff were primarily concerned with the social welfare of their peers, rather than looking for ways to convert the rhetoric of gang empowerment and alternative gang control into a more powerful advocacy agenda.

On a later visit to La Campanera, I accompanied two probation officers and found the community literally under siege and the bakery closed. A police checkpoint was manned at an entrance to the area, and the police and military presence was palpable. A number of youths in full gang attire waited outside the bakery in anticipation of a press conference convened by Homies Unidos to publicize concerns about police harassment and interference with the rehabilitation project. HU joined the gang members in condemning police abuse, raids, and repeated arrests and blamed the PNC for the closure of the bakery and thus the breakdown of the project.[63] The police, however, would defend their entry into the building by arguing that they were pursuing criminals who sought refuge there.[64]

In previous weeks, the situation in La Campanera had become increasingly tense due to persistent police harassment, beatings, and death threats. One policeman in particular had attracted the ire of the gang members, and in early July 2006, one shot and killed him during a police chase.[65] The PNC increased its presence in the area and on one occasion raided a nearby church where close to two hundred gang members were holding a wake for a friend.[66] During the operation, heavily armed police forced all the young men to strip down to their underwear, shouted obscenities, and beat them before placing them under arrest.[67]

That incident offered HU staff an opportunity to highlight police abuse against gang members and press for more rights-respecting law enforcement. Instead, Homies Unidos shut down the Campanera bakery and ceased all its activities in the community, claiming that gang suppression had made its work there impossible.[68] Homies Unidos never returned to the community, and Christian Poveda was shot to death in September 2009 by Dieciocho members. Although eleven people were convicted of the crime, it has never been conclusively investigated.[69] La Campanera, despite the great need for social interventions, has remained virtually forgotten by NGOs and state institutions.[70]

In late 2006, not long after the events above, HU launched another, similar microenterprise in Chalchuapa, a small town near the Guatemalan border. The Chalchuapa bakery once again brought together a small group of Dieciocho members to run it. They told reporters of their continued emotional ties to the gang and admitted taking drugs and hanging out much as before.[71] Homies Unidos later acknowledged that its attempts to create rehabilitation projects of this kind had not prospered.[72]

The abrupt closure of the Campanera bakery raises several concerns about the viability of these self-employment opportunities. First, although Homies Unidos officially maintained that the government needed to implement comprehensive and rights-respecting gang control, in reality, the organization's empowerment strategy pursued only indirect policy influence. Homies Unidos could have used a media outreach campaign to publicize the Campanera bakery, explain that reducing gang violence meant giving young people employment opportunities, and show that the NGO offered a way to address the problem. Such an initiative could have helped to alter the policy context and put pressure on the authorities to pursue an alternative to Mano Dura.

Second, Homies Unidos did not try very hard to persuade the authorities to change their policing tactics and stop their interference with the bakery. The government's unjustified assumption that gang members inevitably scorn rehabilitation and continue to commit crimes was one reason for the heavy-handed operations to shut down the Campanera bakery.[73] However, the fact that HU staff identified with and were protective of gang youths, regardless of their delinquent behavior, could not have helped the project. Police abuse, the evidence indicates, did occur in La Campanera and deserved to be publicly condemned. But the question remains how some gang members might have pulled away from violence and drugs as long as they remained routinely exposed to the influence of peers still committed to gang life. Although Homies Unidos could not work with gang members while also notifying the police of any illicit activities, the organization could have tried to bring other actors on board. A broader community intervention, bringing together a wide range of social and state institutions, not only would have been able to provide a greater range of services and thus respond more effectively to gang members' manifold needs, but also might have offered a better way of dealing with gang members who rejected these opportunities and kept breaking the law.

Third, and perhaps most importantly, Homies Unidos did not monitor the bakery to determine whether participants actually were withdrawing from their old lives of crime and violence. Nor did the NGO develop strategies to deal with backsliders. Skills training and job opportunities do not automatically lead to gang desistance. Also, Mano Dura had encouraged an increasing number of gang members to approach Homies Unidos with requests for a rehabilitation initiative.[74] Although the organization believed these requests boosted its outreach possibilities, the risk was that gang members might seek out such programs to hide from the police, but not to abandon gang life. A self-employment option would make this easier precisely because of its independent nature. It cannot be assumed that none of the youths of the Campanera bakery were interested in rehabilitation or that the entire group merely sought to convert the place into a gang hangout. The Campanera gang members, however, were left unsupervised and unaccountable for much of the time, and apparently continued to use drugs at the site.[75]

Had Homies Unidos exercised greater supervision over the youths' activities, it might have helped mitigate growing tensions between the clique and the police. While the organization was happy to support a rehabilitation project, it seemed to lack the creativity or motivation to design a professional project that might have fulfilled the dual purpose of rehabilitation and gang-related advocacy. The Campanera project suggests that Homies Unidos was interested in improving the life and welfare of gang youth in the short term, but was not driven to develop the capacity to advocate alternative gang control, rhetorical commitments notwithstanding.

Conclusion

As a peer rehabilitation NGO, Homies Unidos aimed to empower gang members by uniting former rivals who would propose their own solutions to the problems of their peers, and reach out to gang youth to encourage them to abandon drugs and violence. The organization's work was informed by the view that gang violence could not be reduced through Mano Dura but rather required the implementation of a comprehensive and rights-respecting gang policy. However, political and social constraints—notably, elite influence, the nature of the ruling ARENA party, and an oligarchic media system—were likely to hinder their accomplishments. The group's strategic choices therefore were crucial if it was to bring real change to policy making and policing practices. Homies Unidos's programs used prevention and information politics, helped provide access to services and school or job placements, and promoted human rights. A key objective for the organization was to act as a bridge between gang members and the conventional world, thus facilitating the integration between the two.

Although the group's advocacy activities did little to directly influence policy, they had the potential to alter the policy context and create incentives for the implementation of gang prevention and rehabilitation and more targeted law enforcement. In practice, however, they contributed little toward those ends. Exogenous factors played a role, but so did Homies Unidos's strategic choices, shaped by staff ideology and group characteristics.

Magdaleno Rose-Ávila's ideas, logistical support, and fund-raising were critical in the 1996 creation of Homies Unidos, and he guided it through its establishment phase. The gang study that Magdaleno helped the IUDOP carry out inspired Homies Unidos's programs before the NGO developed an organic capacity for gang rehabilitation and empowerment. These early activities constituted the foundational ideology of Homies Unidos. It was to be run by gang members in the belief that they could reach out to gang youth more effectively because of their shared experience. Magdaleno's departure left a leadership vacuum, however, and how HU staff managed to fill it had important consequences for their advocacy work.

HU staff publicly presented themselves as ex–gang members, but they were *pandilleros calmados* (retired gang members) who remained emotionally attached to their gangs and identified with gang culture and values. Given their continued ties to their gang pasts, HU staff believed in the positive functions of gangs and preferred to see their peers withdraw from drugs and violence rather than leave the gang altogether. Their status as *pandilleros calmados* was known in NGO and official circles, where people viewed Homies Unidos's ideological position with some skepticism. This wariness not only diminished the organization's possibilities for networking or alliance building, but also restricted its access to government and police authorities.

The Salvadoran government and law enforcement categorized gang members as criminals, a position that strained their already limited relationship with Homies Unidos. The NGO, however, did little to ease this antagonism. At the same time that they publicly exposed police harassment of gang members, HU staff were protective of gang members who apparently had committed crimes. Homies Unidos could have asked other social and state institutions to work with it on broader, more holistic community interventions. Such collaborative efforts could have responded more effectively to gang members' needs in areas such as health care, education, vocational training, and employment, as well as fostered dialogue and reconciliation between gang members and aggrieved communities. In addition, such a comprehensive approach might have offered a means to more effective law enforcement—even the possibility of promoting rights-respecting gang policing. It is difficult to know to what extent such steps toward wide-ranging community interventions would have met with success, given the repudiation that Homies Unidos itself experienced in Salvadoran society. But the absence of these efforts raises doubts about Homies Unidos's capacity or commitment to real gang control.

HU advocacy was also affected by a series of institutional sustainability problems, principally financing and staffing issues. The agency's lack of grant-seeking skills, along with such external factors as project-driven donor support and a hostile domestic funding environment, made it difficult for Homies Unidos to raise sufficient revenue to keep working. Although the NGO managed to survive repeated resource shortfalls, the constant financial insecurity considerably weakened the organization and limited its work both quantitatively and qualitatively.

Given the nature of its recruits, Homies Unidos experienced frequent staff turnovers and serious skills shortages. HU members' firsthand experience of gang life was meant to make them the ideal spokespersons for their cause. However, they seemed more concerned with internal power struggles than with staff professionalism. Despite Homies Unidos's skills deficit, staff resisted the recruitment of qualified non–gang members whose presence and supervision might have helped improve the group's work. Instead, the NGO's reputation and legitimacy were further eroded by the arrest and subsequent criminal conviction of a staff member. Due to inability or to frustration with difficult work, staff struggled to perform routine jobs as well as substantive activities. For example, the Campanera rehabilitation project, which could have served HU advocacy purposes, was not incorporated into a broader strategy.

Finally, strategic constraints limited the potential impact of HU advocacy. Its human rights program served to alert the PDDH to police abuse against gang members and enabled it to pursue a number of individual cases. Even these, however, were not followed up with advocacy work designed to draw attention to the findings of abuse or to increase pressure for rights-respecting gang enforcement. Testimonial stories and information politics could have raised awareness of the gang problem and the need for gang prevention and rehabilitation. Yet, speaking engagements, though easy to organize, became increasingly rare.

The media could have been used to publicize the Campanera bakery and thus highlight the role of job opportunities in gang rehabilitation, as well as to create pressure for an alternative to Mano Dura. Although Homies Unidos supported the development of the project, it failed to prevent continued gang activity by its participants. As a result, suppressive policing eventually caused the collapse of the project.

Overall, HU staff were too concerned with organizational survival and the welfare of their peers to conduct gang advocacy more effectively. They pursued a strategy that, without lobbying and media work, was unlikely to stimulate policy change by a government opposed to comprehensive and rights-respecting gang control.

CHAPTER 6

Reason, Religion, and Loving-Kindness

The Polígono Industrial Don Bosco (Don Bosco Industrial Park, or Polígono/PIDB) was founded in 1988 and directed by Father José Moratalla, a Spanish Salesian priest, to assist marginalized Salvadoran youth in obtaining job skills and opportunities for a better life. Located in La Iberia, a gang-affected community in eastern San Salvador, the Polígono initiated a residential education and training program for at-risk youth and gang members. It became widely respected for modeling successful social reintegration.

The Polígono's leadership maintained that the gang problem would not be resolved with Mano Dura, but required an alternative response that combined law enforcement with prevention and rehabilitation. Social and political constraints in the form of elite influence in policy making, the ruling ARENA party's status quo nature, and an oligarchic media system conspired against the promotion of comprehensive gang control. The adoption of a creative advocacy strategy was critical if the official suppressive approach was to be reshaped.

The Polígono sought to stimulate change by implementing an innovative program and demonstrating to the government a better way to deal with the gang situation. The assumption was that a viable initiative could serve to increase pressure on the authorities to abandon single-minded gang suppression and shift their focus to comprehensive gang control. The goal of this chapter is to highlight the program's main premises and characteristics, which will help explain why the Polígono's constructive criticism was unlikely—and, in fact, failed—to yield the anticipated policy outcome.

This chapter begins by tracing the Polígono's emergence as a community-based development organization, underpinned by the Salesians' special concern for marginalized youth, and describes the organization's contemporary characteristics. The chapter then reviews the program content, particularly in education, as well as job training and development, with particular attention to the philosophy behind this approach and its implications for gang-related advocacy. Both the PIDB participant selection criteria and organizational capacity to rehabilitate gang members raise questions about the nature of the presumed model gang program and explain why the Polígono promoted its work the way it did. Lastly, the chapter describes how the Polígono showcased its initiative to officials and publicized its position through limited media work in an attempt to reorient gang policy. It sought to address the gang problem in its own community and to strengthen its political voice by building an alliance of advocacy actors.

A lack of systematic evaluations allowed the Polígono to portray itself as a successful gang program, and it used this image to persuade the government to implement prevention and rehabilitation programs. The model initiative, for its part, proposed self-reliance rather than pushing for improvements in the social environment. Its uncontroversial goals enabled the Polígono to gain access to policymakers and state funding. This relationship in turn helped relieve the government of its responsibility for gang prevention and rehabilitation. The organization also limited itself to lobbying the government with quiet pressure. It failed to pursue proactive media work, mobilize community residents, or construct strategic alliances to bolster its advocacy efforts. Ultimately, the showcasing of a model gang program had the effect of raising the institutional profile, but was an ineffective advocacy strategy.

The Salesian Roots of the Polígono

The development of the Polígono is largely due to the creativity and fund-raising efforts of its founder and director, Father José Moratalla. A member of the Salesian congregation, "Padre Pepe," as he is called, designed the institution to meet the particular needs of the local community where it is based, but retained the Salesians' traditional concern for the most underprivileged youths in society.

The Salesian credo derives from the preventive system developed by Saint John Bosco (1815–1888), an Italian priest who established the religious order in 1859. Giovanni (John) Bosco's childhood in the countryside near the northern Italian city of Turin was marked by deep poverty. His desire to help the neediest children was strengthened when he moved to Turin soon after his ordination, in 1841. There he witnessed the serious social dislocations that the early industrial revolution had triggered. While ruthless entrepreneurs greatly increased their wealth, the workers remained trapped in conditions of poverty and exploitation. Determined to ensure the spiritual and material welfare of the youths he saw languishing in prison and on the streets, Don Bosco devised a pastoral education system directed at their comprehensive development.[1] The pillars of this system were reason, religion, and loving-kindness.

The first element stressed human and Christian values, while the second aimed to familiarize these youths with the message of Jesus and the sacraments. "Loving-kindness" referred to an educational style whereby the teacher was not thought of as a superior, acting instead like a father, brother, or friend who offered advice and corrected misbehavior in a respectful but firm manner.[2] The Salesian education system is based on trust between teachers and students, which is built in an atmosphere of family spirit, informality, and dialogue. Personal relations and recreational activities were central to this approach, both to prevent boredom and to create a stimulating learning environment.[3]

Since Don Bosco founded the new religious order in 1859, Salesians have worked among the poorest and most disadvantaged youths in many countries around the world, where they run schools, oratories, and parishes. In El Salvador, the Salesians started their operations in 1897 by transforming a public agricultural school into a vocational training institute.[4] The Polígono is one of their projects.

La Iberia

Father Moratalla's attempts to alleviate the social marginalization facing Salvadoran children began in 1985, when he started teaching at the Salesian School Don Bosco in La Iberia. Situated in eastern San Salvador, the community originated as a temporary settlement for the homeless following a 1965 earthquake. Initially conceived as a short-term solution for low-income families who sought shelter there, the area over time became permanent housing. For years, the terrain was covered with *champas* (cardboard or laminate shacks) erected along dusty paths and lacking basic services. During the civil war, the overcrowding in La Iberia worsened as hundreds of families fled the violence in the countryside and took refuge there and in other marginal zones.[5]

Upon his arrival in 1985, Father Moratalla found a community rife with alcoholism, drug consumption, and high levels of crime and violence. The absence of worthwhile jobs forced many girls into prostitution, while boys became involved in criminal gangs. Father Moratalla felt he needed to do more than teach classes, and for the next two years, he spent most of his evenings visiting with the locals and listening to their stories and concerns. Over time, he realized that education and job training alone were not enough to secure people decent employment. A possible solution to this problem was to create cooperative enterprises, which would provide jobs and enable people to overcome a culture of dependency and hopelessness.

The Salesian school building was damaged by an earthquake in 1986, and the school relocated. Father Moratalla, however, remained in La Iberia to help establish the Polígono.[6] The mayor of San Salvador was persuaded to offer a piece of land with a ninety-nine-year ground lease. On what was then the municipal rubbish dump, the youths started to build their future workplace. In 1988, the Polígono commenced its operations with ten small, mostly industrial, cooperatives. In 1994, it also opened an educational institute in a multi-storey building on the land.[7]

A picture of progress greets today's visitors to La Iberia. The roads are paved; shacks have largely been replaced by more durable housing made of mixed-system materials; most residents possess legal housing titles; and there is better access to water, sanitation, and electricity.[8] Social problems nevertheless have persisted in this community of some seventy-five hundred inhabitants.[9] Bordered by a defunct railway line, factories, a market, and one of San Salvador's main bus terminals, the area has only a few—for the most part, neglected—parks and sports grounds. In addition to noise and air pollution, residents experience overcrowding and the illnesses associated with unhealthy living conditions.[10] As of 2006, at least 80 percent of the families worked in the informal sector and received only subsistence-level wages.[11] As of 2010, this situation had not substantially changed.[12] A lack of decent jobs has pushed many residents to migrate to the United States, and as a result, the majority of homes became single-parent households.[13] By 2014, many houses had been abandoned.[14]

Perhaps the most acute problem is the persistence of gang activity. At least until the 2012 gang truce, La Iberia was one of the most stigmatized communities in the capital, if not the country. The area is associated with a variety of crimes, notably homicides, extortion, drug sales, robberies, and rapes. But while residents experience high levels of insecurity, reported victimization rates are low. The most recent study on La Iberia suggests the reasons are fear and institutional mistrust.[15] However, low victimization may also speak to the social bonds and the climate of coexistence that over the years have developed between gang members and the community.

The gangs have carved up the area so that the Dieciocho (now divided into Revolucionarios and Sureños) dominates the western part, while Mara Salvatrucha controls the eastern sector, which hosts the Polígono. Staff and students have been the targets of harassment and extortion attempts by MS gang members. Nevertheless, Father Moratalla and his team continue to carry out their work, despite the difficulties and security risks it entails.

Although the Polígono is situated in a gang-affected community and claims to have developed an innovative gang program, it has done its work exclusively within the agency's residential setting. The organization's failure to address the gang situation outside its doors raises doubts about the Polígono's capacity for gang work and has undermined its attempts to influence the government's policy by showcasing a model initiative.

The Polígono Today

Shielded by high walls, the Polígono is an oasis of tranquility in a gray urban landscape. A large parking lot separates the school and boarding houses from the cooperatives, offices, verdant open-air canteen, and large athletic field. There is also a health clinic that offers treatment to the local population for a reduced charge.[16] On weekdays, the grounds are alive with the faint sound of machines and the voices of youths walking to their classes. Despite its reputation as a gang prevention and rehabilitation center, the PIDB remains a development organization that works to generate meaningful jobs and prevent the poor from turning to gangs and crime. A residential program for at-risk youths and gang members, not part of the original plan, was only one component of the Polígono's commitment to help the neediest members of society.

In 1992, Father Moratalla and his staff began working with street children they befriended in bus terminals and public squares. Increasing deportations of gang members from the United States gave the gang problem in El Salvador a different dimension, however, and the street children became largely absorbed into this new, more violent culture. In 1995, UNICEF–El Salvador suggested that the Polígono institute a scholarship-based alternative to the ineffective rehabilitation process that existed in youth detention centers.[17] In the proposal, juvenile courts would identify appropriate candidates and the Supreme Court of Justice—through a grant program of its Juvenile Justice Unit—would release UNICEF funds to the Polígono, where the selected individuals would spend the remainder of their sentences.[18] This agreement was in place between 1996 and 2011, and since some 80 percent of juvenile offenders belonged to gangs, this was how the Polígono came to work with gang members.[19]

Over the years, staff recognized that gang rehabilitation was difficult and therefore decided to limit entry to applicants who declared their intention to leave the gang and change their lives.[20] Polígono staff were trained as educators or in similar professions, but had no specific gang expertise. Despite these limitations, the agency gained a reputation as a successful gang rehabilitation center. The mainstream media repeatedly highlighted the Polígono's experience. Its status was such that Salvadoran and foreign officials alike toured the facility.[21] Antonio Saca and Rodrigo Ávila, ARENA's candidates for the presidency in 2004 and 2009, respectively, both visited the Polígono during their campaigns and expressed their interest in reproducing the Polígono model.[22] Colombian pop star and UNICEF goodwill ambassador Shakira, visiting El Salvador to support a campaign against violence, even invited Father Moratalla onto the concert stage.[23]

Before examining the Polígono's programs and its relationship to the government, it is revealing to look at its sources of revenue. Like many NGOs, the Polígono experienced recurrent financial difficulties. For example, when in 1992 resources were depleted and salaries went unpaid over a four-month period, twenty-five of twenty-seven technical staff resigned. A similar three-month crisis in 1998 prompted more staff flight.[24] Eventually, however, the Polígono was able to overcome these challenges and developed a fairly strong donor base. The organization accepts private donations in cash and kind, but has relied for much of its revenue on contributions from UNICEF, the Inter-American Development Bank, and the Spanish and Salvadoran governments. At the time of this research, more than 60 percent of the Polígono's income came from the Salvadoran authorities, including the CNSP, but had to be renewed each year.[25] Collaboration of this kind had benefits for both sides. It helped the Polígono to ensure the sustainability of its project, and the government to off-load its responsibility for gang prevention and rehabilitation and the social reintegration of juvenile offenders.

The public funding also, however, imposed constraints on the Polígono's gang-related advocacy, threatened the organization's independence, and dampened its criticism of Mano Dura. In addition, public funding meant that the government could support small-scale efforts and publicize its commitment to gang prevention and rehabilitation without any involvement of its own. Not only did the Polígono pursue an ineffective strategy to persuade the government to reorient its gang policy, but its cooperative attitude also probably lessened the pressure on the authorities to make real change.

The Polígono's Residential Program

The Polígono's work with at-risk youths and gang members was structured around a residential education and job-training project, including specialized components for girls. The Miguel Magone and Laura Vicuña Program is intended for youths aged fourteen to eighteen years, although the upper limit is occasionally extended to allow individuals to complete their education.[26] Scholarship holders join the Polígono following a lengthy admissions process, which culminates in the signing of a mutual contract, in which the Polígono, the applicants, and their parents or sponsors all pledge to honor their respective commitments. Resident life in the Polígono is tightly organized and monitored, based on guidelines designed to maintain order and promote morality. Recurring violations on the part of the students can lead to their expulsion from the institution. In the case of juvenile offenders, dismissal sends them back to a detention center.

Staff also meet with parents once a month and conduct house calls four times a year in an effort to strengthen the parents' moral and spiritual values and to help them improve their parenting skills. To facilitate their social reintegration, the boys and girls are required to spend weekends with their family. Progress is monitored and recorded in the students' files, which staff use to produce a quarterly evaluation of each student and, if necessary, undertake corrective measures.

At the heart of the Polígono are the Instituto Técnico Obrero-Empresarial (Technical Institute for Entrepreneurial Workers, or ITOE) and the largely industrial cooperatives, which provide employment and income to their workers and owners. The ITOE offers education from the preschool level to the *bachillerato* (high school) and serves more than three hundred students, including both boarders and day students.[27] The curriculum emphasizes technical training and business administration. It requires those in secondary education to attend vocational workshops, while the boarders studying for their *bachillerato* must join one of the cooperatives as unpaid apprentices. Like many others, Father Moratalla believes the key problem in gang rehabilitation and social reintegration is the lack of job opportunities in El Salvador.[28] So by design, Polígono educational programs prepare students for self-employment in the form of either a cooperative or a microenterprise. The Polígono's approach reflects its motto, "Education for work," and is based on the preventive system of Don Bosco, which is intended to mold young people into upright citizens and good Christians.[29] The PIDB built on these ideas to craft both a new entrepreneurial paradigm and a novel technical-academic education model: *empresarios solidarios cristianos*. This model is meant to create not qualified labor, but entrepreneurs who embrace discipline, solidarity, and a Christian spirit of self-reliance.

The Polígono's philosophy, though based on Salesian principles and Father Moratalla's pragmatism, nevertheless coincides with the neoliberal values espoused by ARENA. The organization's model program does not propose to address the structural factors associated with the gang problem but rather prepares youths to function within the limitations of the existing social and economic systems. Because the goals of the Polígono's project overlapped with the neoliberal emphasis on individualism and self-reliance, they were uncontroversial in official circles and gave the organization access to the policy-making process and public funding. The Polígono's program and its promotional advocacy strategies made it unlikely that the government would feel pressure to implement a comprehensive gang policy.

Polígono Cooperatives and Microenterprises: An Alternative to Gang Life?

The organization tries to demonstrate the viability of its model with cooperatives that provide employment and income to residents of La Iberia, focusing specifically on workers' and industrial co-ops. A cooperative is a voluntarily organized firm that is owned, capitalized, and controlled by member-owners, who share risks and benefits proportional to their participation.[30] These enterprises can constitute a platform for job security and contribute to the social development of local communities that have limited employment prospects.

Despite the relative merits of a group enterprise, co-ops are difficult to operate. Like for-profit corporations, they require adequate capital to operate effectively and grow, but their particular structures and practices make it more difficult to raise capital. Most critically, they have to be competitive and achieve the profitability essential for their continued existence.

The ten co-ops established by the Polígono in 1988 primarily fabricated goods with easy commercial potential. With a focus on craft and industrial production, the Grupo Empresarial Don Bosco (Don Bosco Business Group) included aluminum, furniture-making, shoe manufacture, die-stamping, plastics, bakeries, mechanics, ceramics, metal production, and printing operations. All were integrated into a co-op federation led by a Federative Council that owned the firms' physical infrastructure, as a way to keep operation costs down and provide better products than if the co-ops functioned as individual enterprises.

The Polígono's Fundación Salvadoreña Educación y Trabajo (Salvadoran Foundation for Education and Work, or EDYTRA) is tasked with providing the co-ops with the necessary support services. As their legal representative and fund-raising department, EDYTRA administers donations for machinery, provides centralized marketing facilities, and locates outside experts who provide co-op members with business administration training.[31]

Of the ten co-ops listed above, two ceased operations for failure to compete effectively, while the ceramics factory closed due to staff flight.[32] The seven remaining firms provide work to some 250 individuals, including members, workers, and the boarders who train as unpaid apprentices.[33] In 2005, they had a joint annual gross turnover of US $724,600.[34] However, if they were operating as regular businesses, each would have had to spend significant portions of revenues for nonwage business expenses, such as the acquisition of raw materials and reinvestment in the maintenance of factories and equipment. The average workforce of twenty-eight individuals per enterprise made it unlikely that the co-ops could pay employees more than the minimum wage.[35] Overall output performance was moderate despite the incentives that the Polígono offered the co-ops, which included leased land, donations for buildings and modern machinery, marketing and training, and support for the unpaid apprentices.

The co-ops' difficulties appear to be related both to their particular manufacturing sectors and to the economic environment of El Salvador. Unfortunately, due to a restructuring of the Salvadoran economy in favor of the service sector, the manufacturing industry lost its dominance and left the Polígono with a small market to supply. Furthermore, the co-ops face significant competition from large domestic and transnational companies, which can manufacture at lower costs or import and sell products more cheaply.

All these downsides do not mean that the Polígono workers find such cooperative employment and its income opportunities unsatisfying. Yet, the constraints on the co-ops and the modest salaries they offer raise questions about the efficacy of the Polígono's program for gang rehabilitation. To what extent does the cooperative model constitute a feasible alternative for young people who can potentially earn more money with extortion or drug sales than with licit activities? The idea of self-employment afforded the Polígono official support for its programs and allowed it, based only on anecdotal evidence, to promote itself as a feasible gang policy choice. Evaluations could document the weaknesses of both the cooperative and microenterprise models used by the Polígono, but in their absence, the organization has been able to use an anecdotal success story for its advocacy of gang prevention and rehabilitation.

Microenterprises are another self-employment option tried by the Polígono to give young people a way to escape the lure of gang life and crime. Most microenterprises produce and distribute goods and services with little or no capital, functioning primarily as survival strategies. The low level of initial capital investment characteristic of this business model generally permits only limited labor productivity, low incomes, and minimal profits to reinvest in growth. They generally start as one-person firms dedicated to economic activities with the lowest barriers to entry. Because their growth is constrained by a lack of markets and finance, they often struggle to be efficient or profitable.[36]

The following example illustrates the weaknesses of a program that expects young, uneducated gang members to turn their lives around essentially on their own. Nineteen-year-old Carlos (a pseudonym) was permitted to transfer to the Polígono to complete a sentence for homicide. Having joined a gang at eleven years old, he had completed only four years of formal education prior to joining the Polígono. Carlos spent close to two years there before security concerns prompted his relocation. His facial tattoos prompted officials to convert his sentence into house arrest and to encourage him to start his own microenterprise, a bakery.

Like every Polígono boarder, Carlos had been required to open a savings account. These accounts are administered by the institution and released upon completion of the program as seed capital for a microenterprise or for university studies. At the time of this research, Carlos had already spent some six months working in his bakery, installed in the home of a relative. The bakery had been set up in a laminate shack with only rudimentary equipment and under rather insanitary conditions. Together with an assistant, Carlos prepared assorted breads and pastries and had another assistant deliver them to customers. Ostensibly, this was a functioning business, but Carlos acknowledged that his savings were insufficient to expand his bakery and that he did not know how to raise more investment capital.

The Polígono proposed its job training and development program as an alternative to gang life and because gang members stand little chance of being recruited for the limited employment opportunities that exist. In terms of employment creation and poverty alleviation, a microenterprise requires people to manage their own welfare through active participation in the market economy. Microenterprise development, like cooperatives, thus is consistent with neoliberal values and paves the way for a sponsoring organization like the Polígono to receive governmental backing. Despite the program's inherent problems, the Polígono supports microenterprise because it can provide individuals with a minimum level of income where job opportunities are scarce. In Carlos's case, it was too early to tell whether a modestly performing business would enable him to leave gang life. (By 2014, he had migrated to the United States after years of hiding from both his own and the rival gang. The bakery never developed into a functioning business.) It is also unclear whether a small-scale program of the kind the Polígono promotes can meet young people's income needs sufficiently to encourage their reintegration into society.

To be fair, the PIDB presented its program as an option, not a panacea, for gang control. In the absence of empirical evaluations of its work, however, the organization can present the project as a successful initiative and make its case for gang prevention and rehabilitation through small-scale entrepreneurship.

Showcasing the Polígono's Gang Program

After its initial work with street children, the Polígono focused on three target groups: at-risk youth, gang members, and juvenile offenders. For the purposes of its program, the Polígono defined these terms as follows:[37] "At-risk youth" refers to adolescents who live in a marginal community where gangs often are present, come from low-income and/ or dysfunctional families, and may have siblings or relatives in a gang.

"Gang members" are youths who wear tattoos and baggy clothes, paint territorial graffiti, communicate in signs and special argot, congregate with other gang members, live in *destroyers*, listen to rap or hard rock, display postures of toughness, and use weapons to commit crimes. "Juvenile offenders" were under eighteen years old when they committed a crime and were given permission to complete their sentence in the Polígono.

The Polígono does not reach out to individuals for its services, but receives referrals (juvenile offenders and gang members) or, as is currently the case, self-referrals (at-risk youth). The agency developed a screening mechanism to filter candidates who seek admission to the residential program. The selection process includes a guided tour of the campus, an interview with the applicant and the parents, and a psychometric evaluation designed to measure the candidate's IQ, attitudes, and personality. Of particular significance is the interview and test phase, which allows Polígono staff to study applicants and their professed commitment to education and work and to exclude those they consider unsuitable. Admission is followed by a one-month probation period that is designed to establish whether the new student can adapt to the daily life and rules of the institution.

It appears that after the Polígono's first intake of juvenile offenders and gang members in the 1990s, it tightened its admissions criteria to exclude the more difficult cases. The Polígono started barring youths with a nuclear family, a drug addiction, a low IQ or special learning needs, male or female homosexuality, or active gang membership or continued identification with a gang. At the same time that these strict criteria barred those most in need of treatment, there was a tendency for "net-widening," in which services were extended to youths who might not require them as much.

For example, one MS member was not accepted for his refusal to say his age (eighteen), whereas another gang member was expelled when he was found to have written "MS" on his computer.[38] At the same time, the Polígono admitted individuals who were disadvantaged but did not appear at risk for joining a gang.[39] For instance, one young woman who had experienced domestic violence and turned to prostitution was funded by the Polígono so that she could complete her university education. Another came from a single-parent household and had to help her mother at work rather than attend school. She seemed to possess all the requisites of a model student and apprentice, and her request to be granted the opportunity for further study was readily granted. This is not to deny the importance of the Polígono's work with needy youths, but to show that its program did not target gang-prone youths and, in fact, largely excluded gang members.

By the Polígono's own account, when this research began, up to 60 percent of boarders were at-risk youth, while 40 percent were juvenile offenders, including gang members.[40] According to available statistical information, of the more than 900 individuals who joined the program over the years, 155 were gang members.[41] However, an earlier, incomplete data set combined the numbers of gang-prone youths and gang members under the total figure for gang members.

These contradictions make it difficult to ascertain how many gang members entered the institution and graduated from it. Furthermore, given the lack of independent evaluations, it is impossible to determine how many of those who were in gangs ultimately abandoned gang life as a result of joining the Polígono. The boarders interviewed could only confirm that the number of gang youths had declined over the years.[42] At the time of a 2006 research visit, only one gang member was enrolled in the program. A CNSP rehabilitation officer, who called on the Polígono to verify whether forty scholarships earmarked for gang rehabilitation were spent accordingly, was reportedly denied access to all forty target youths, supposedly for reasons of scheduling and illness.[43] The CNSP's lack of monitoring and evaluation permitted what appears to have been a misappropriation of gang program funds.

For some prospective applicants, the presence of gangs in La Iberia may have reduced the Polígono's appeal as a rehabilitation center, which may explain the decline in the number of gang members in the program. Local MS members had previously sought to kill three participants and, in 2005, actually followed one gang youth onto the agency's premises and murdered him there.[44] The Polígono's gang program, with its screening mechanism and requirement of prior value transformation, nevertheless raises questions about the organization's technical preparation for gang rehabilitation.

The Polígono was well aware of the criticism expressed by some of the judges who authorized the transfer of juvenile offenders to the institution. Aída Santos, sentence enforcement judge and later president of the CNSP (2009–2011), complained that the agency preferred to work only with "good kids" and rejected more difficult cases.[45] Father Moratalla insisted that the Polígono had established rules that helped maintain a violence-free environment and facilitated work in a residential setting. Gang members, he pointed out, needed to leave behind all ideological baggage to be receptive to the Polígono's education and training activities. Father Moratalla also asserted that critical judges inappropriately interfered with pedagogical issues and wanted to destabilize the Polígono.[46] Judges preferred to move juvenile offenders to the Polígono, despite its limitations, because its residential program was more comprehensive and rigorous than the rehabilitation process carried out in state-run youth detention centers.[47]

The Polígono was aware that it had assumed a responsibility of the state. Nevertheless, it did not want to close the only alternative space for juvenile offenders, preferring to collaborate with the government to solve a problem that overwhelms state institutions.[48] The PIDB response to this dilemma had important implications for its attempts to advocate alternative gang control. The government used the Polígono's work with juvenile offenders and gang members to demonstrate its support for prevention and rehabilitation without having to make long-term policy and resource commitments to the problem. In other words, the Polígono's strategy did not put greater political pressure on the government but may instead have inadvertently decreased it.

The Polígono may have had a number of reasons for not evaluating its activities, such as Father Moratalla's preference for action over research. What seems likely, however, is that the organization chose not to produce and publicize formal assessments because they would have revealed program limitations and undermined the positive reputation of both the organization and its initiatives.

Had the program, in truth, been more gang-specific than it actually was, documented examples of the agency's contributions to gang prevention and rehabilitation could have bolstered its advocacy. Instead, the organization relied only on anecdotal evidence to support its policy option and promote alternative gang control. Superficial perceptions of staff competence were largely taken for granted and allowed the Polígono to become a prominent advocate of gang prevention and rehabilitation. Its status ultimately served the organization more than its activism.

Encouraging Gang Desistance

As indicated earlier, the Polígono's admissions criteria exclude individuals who remain identified with their gang. The institution did, however, admit some gang youths who had signaled their intention to change but had yet to do so. Two of these cases, described below, highlight the agency's difficulties with achieving gang members' emancipation and contrast the actual outcomes with the program's public image. Despite its apparent lack of gang expertise or objective evidence of successful gang rehabilitation, the Polígono was able to sustain its positive reputation and its advocacy activities.

Pedro and Carlos (fictitious names) had both been members of the Mara Salvatrucha. They were moved to the Polígono from a detention center where they had begun serving sentences for homicide.[49] Pedro joined the gang at fifteen years of age and had been a member for two years when he was admitted to the Polígono, in mid-2003. In his application, the teenager expressed his desire to adopt a different lifestyle, but his initial personality test identified a tendency to lie and manipulate, as well as a weak commitment to renouncing the gang. The first report highlighted academic difficulties and persistent identification with the MS. Two years later, he continued to use intimidating behavior toward classmates and show emotional attachment to the gang, conduct that caused a psychologist to express his concern. In 2006, Polígono staff acknowledged that Pedro was a difficult case, but insisted that he was committed to leaving the gang. Their opinion was based on observations that he had improved his posture and language and no longer identified with the gang through hand signs or writings.[50] In an interview, he made sure to shake hands and answered questions eloquently. Nevertheless, he maintained a defiant attitude, was opposed to having his tattoos removed, and had no regrets about his gang experience. He observed that compliance with the Polígono's internal regulations required only adaptation. In a subsequent court hearing, Pedro's supervisors attested to his good conduct, and he requested his discharge from the Polígono. To his apparent dismay, the judge ordered that he continue with the program. Pedro eventually went to live with his brother, but the pervasive gang presence in the area prompted them to move. The family has not been heard from since.

Carlos, whose bakery microenterprise was described earlier, was initially rejected by the Polígono for his facial tattoos. A former gang leader, he was admitted, however, after UNICEF intervened.[51] His psychometric test revealed insincerity, impulsiveness, egocentricity, and a lack of self-control as key characteristics. During his time in the Polígono, Carlos often listened to Christian messages—apparently to make a good impression. In his dealings with staff, the young man appeared serious and humble, yet toward fellow students, he was intimidating and demanded respect for his gang experience. Prior to quarterly reports and court hearings, he acted pleasantly in order to gain approval. Nonetheless, regular psychological assessments confirmed that Carlos retained emotional ties to his gang. During two interviews with him, the ambivalent behavior that Polígono staff had noted was readily apparent. In the presence of authority figures, Carlos assumed a quiet and docile stance, but when interviewed alone, his attitude was one of indifference and disdain that quickly became aggressive.

Both young men were unapologetic about their gang experience and remained attached to Mara Salvatrucha. Attitude and value change is no fast and easy process, but it can be argued that the Polígono was unable to weaken their gang identity for reasons related to technical capacity and the residential setting. This is not to suggest Polígono staff lacked other professional skills, but they had no gang expertise. The agency assumed that the Salesian principles of reason, religion, and loving-kindness could be applied to the gang program and that youths would improve their conduct if educators maintained regular dialogue with them and helped fulfill their apparent emotional needs. One Polígono psychologist insisted that initially gang members found it difficult to adapt to life in the institution, but they changed completely after a few months. Realistically, the change may have reflected not real transformations but rather adaptation, as Pedro suggested, to the behavior modification that was pursued in the residential setting.

Polígono staff regularly monitors the students and, if required, summons them to a meeting to discuss any problems. Depending on the case, behavior is rewarded or penalized with favorable or unfavorable quarterly reports. Juvenile offenders in particular are interested in obtaining a positive assessment. Therefore, individuals quickly learn to self-censor their speech and actions to avoid criticism and potential expulsion from the institution. Nevertheless, behavior modification is a simplistic and ineffective approach to gang rehabilitation. As a form of reward-punishment social control, this technique tends to elicit short-term compliance but no long-term changes in personality or behavior.[52] In other words, gang youths conformed to the Polígono's rules to make life easier, but may not have maintained a reformed lifestyle after their graduation.

Without formal objective evaluations of the PIDB programs, its contribution to gang prevention and rehabilitation is unclear. According to its own estimates, 90 percent of participants changed, while 10 percent re-offended or were killed. In addition, many grateful graduates have reportedly remained in contact with Father Moratalla and his team.[53]

A "Contagion" of Reality?

By modeling an alternative gang prevention and rehabilitation program, the Polígono sought to demonstrate to the government a more appropriate solution to the gang problem. As a form of indirect influence, this kind of strategy can alter the policy context, especially if combined with lobbying or media work. The Polígono's advocacy approach was shaped by Father Moratalla's belief that a collaborative attitude toward the state is preferable to an adversarial relationship. In his view, democracy requires civil society to engage political leaders through dialogue and consensus rather than opposition or protest. Therefore, it was right for the Polígono to cooperate with the authorities. In the most optimistic view, since the Salvadoran government is popularly elected, it would have to consider implementation of the proposals that were being presented to it.[54]

The Polígono's primary objective was to consolidate its work and turn it into a model that could be replicated by others. Father Moratalla imagined the Polígono to be an experiment of Salvadoran society because society itself needed to reflect on how to develop an effective response to gang violence. The priest and his team hoped that the initiative they had built might "infect" the reality around them and transform it.[55] The Polígono aimed not merely to express its disapproval of the existing gang policy, but also to provide constructive criticism and share an alternative approach with the authorities. By doing so, the agency implicitly rejected Mano Dura.

Father Moratalla acknowledged that his program could be interpreted in different ways. A government committed to the poor would respect and support the initiative, while one that adhered to other political or ideological criteria might reject it. The Polígono has in fact been able to cooperate with some government ministries. For example, it provided education and training services and promoted the creation of achiote cooperatives, although the government claimed full credit for what were joint activities.

In other cases, the Polígono found it more difficult to influence an administration that did not share the agency's commitment to marginalized sectors. According to Father Moratalla, the Polígono sometimes faced a lonely struggle. At the same time, he considered it positive that when the government authorized and funded the agency's work, it demonstrated tacit approval of the initiative. In the long term, Father Moratalla believed, action would force action, and the Polígono's work would persuade the authorities to implement a governmental gang prevention and rehabilitation program.

The Polígono pursued three methods to showcase its project and promote an alternative gang policy. First, it sought to create a professional and sustainable model such that its positive public reputation would speak for itself and persuade others of the model's benefits. Because the Polígono emphasized this tactic, the organization made few proactive attempts to advocate other means to reduce gang violence. Father Moratalla also sought to assist the authorities—for example, by alerting them to suspected gang infiltration of the PNC.

Second, the Polígono gained respect and credibility over the years. As a result, Father Moratalla's opinion was frequently solicited by the media. Following the launch of Mano Dura, for example, *La Prensa Gráfica* invited the priest to a roundtable discussion on the gangs, the Ley Anti Maras, and the importance of prevention and rehabilitation. Father Moratalla expressed his concern that the anti-gang legislation might allow the police to commit human rights violations and insisted that everyone needed to contribute to the search for alternative solutions.

Although his statements were important for highlighting the limitations of the government's gang policy, they were weakened by his unfounded contention that the gangs had evolved into organized crime groups. As explained in chapters 2 and 3, such a depiction of the street gangs favors law enforcement action and delegitimizes responses that would address the structural factors underlying gang development. Father Moratalla may have had the best of intentions at the time, but such uninformed or unconsidered comments undermined his arguments for prevention and rehabilitation. His message reflected his belief that society must collaborate with the government to achieve more effective gang control. His argument was ineffectual because he made a generalized call for prevention and rehabilitation, but he failed to insist that the government take responsibility for implementing a comprehensive gang policy or improving public security.

Third, the Polígono was invited to present its program in gang-related forums in El Salvador and abroad. PIDB staff participated in information exchanges on street gangs in the United States and Spain, for example, where they stressed the need for a comprehensive gang policy. The Salvadoran government also invited the Polígono to the 2004 Anti-Gang Forum and the second of the annual gang conferences in 2006 to explain its rehabilitation program. One problem with these official events, as chapter 2 indicates, was that they privileged law enforce-

ment cooperation and signaled no public interest in developing comple-
mentary strategies. Including a talk by Polígono on gang prevention and
rehabilitation allowed the government to claim a commitment to these
options without having to do anything substantive.

The principal difficulties with the Polígono's advocacy approach
are illustrated by a presentation made by a staff member at a domestic
conference in June 2006. Raúl Ramírez, the director of education, explained the nature of the gang problem, including a number of myths
such as the purported link between street gangs and organized crime.
Given the enormous economic cost of violence in El Salvador, he asked
whether this was evidence of an effective response or required a different strategy. Raúl reminded the audience of the obstacles to addressing
a problem of that magnitude with only the small projects that existed in
the country. He then introduced the Polígono's philosophy and reiterated its belief that education and job development programs are an important option. He ended with anecdotal evidence of two success stories, including Carlos's bakery. In the subsequent question-and-answer
session, one person described the presentation as an optimistic one that
presented the Polígono's achievements, but not the limitations of its
work. Raúl acknowledged that shortcomings existed, but maintained
that the Polígono constituted an option, however modest.

The talk demonstrated the NGO's preference for questioning the
government's gang policy only indirectly, through showcasing a model
alternative. The Polígono's reputation permitted it to present its project to different audiences, including public officials. The organization
was able to share ideas and highlight alternative policy choices, but quiet
advocacy was unlikely to reorient the government's existing approach
to gang control. A more confrontational strategy, in combination with
lobbying or media work, might have been more powerful. As a largely
state-funded agency, the Polígono was effectively inhibited from criticizing the authorities in more explicit terms. This nonadversarial style
provided the NGO with certain benefits and therefore an incentive to
maintain it. Showcasing the Polígono model raised the institutional
profile, but fell short as an effective advocacy strategy.

Civil Society Coordination or Confrontation?

The Polígono is located within a gang-affected community and is ideally positioned to develop a response to the gang situation outside its
doors. Instead, it designed an in-house program for nonlocal individ-

uals from around the country. If the Polígono had targeted neighborhood gang members and the community factors that help spawn the local groups, it might have had a greater impact than that from its residential program alone.

An attempt to effect change in the streets would have been in the organization's interest because the continued gang presence constituted a security risk to staff and boarders alike. The fact that the Polígono did not or could not mitigate the local gang problem became embarrassingly obvious. In November 2005, police discovered that members of the local gang had created a clandestine cemetery behind the Polígono's athletic field to bury their victims.[56] Then, some of the youths painted the wall surrounding the Polígono with characteristic Mara Salvatrucha graffiti. When the symbols were removed, they simply "retook their territory" by re-inscribing the letters within the painted-over patch (the graffiti was again erased during the 2012 gang truce).

Father Moratalla admitted that the Polígono failed to help control the local gang problem. He said that the challenge was one of gaining greater organizational and resource capacity. More importantly, however, the NGO neglected to mobilize community residents and thus create greater pressure for policy change. The Polígono's program for gang prevention and rehabilitation might have stood a greater chance of stimulating government action had it been backed by popular support. For the Polígono, this would have meant investing time and resources in activities that involved the local community in the development of policy goals. Since La Iberia residents experienced the gang's presence on a daily basis, it was in their interest to seek a workable solution and to join the Polígono's advocacy efforts. The organization did undertake some community organizing, but it concerned improvements to local infrastructure and housing and was unrelated to the reduction of gang violence.

The Polígono recognized that its project was of limited reach and that effective gang control required a national gang strategy coordinated by the government. While Father Moratalla participated in a number of civil society initiatives to design a comprehensive response to the gang problem, alliances with other organizations could have made the Polígono a politically more powerful advocate of gang prevention and rehabilitation. Unfortunately, such collaborative efforts were not realized.

Father Moratalla's experiences, notably in reaction to the launch of Mano Dura, offer lessons for NGO promotion of an alternative gang policy. For a while, he worked with a network of advocates on children's issues, but reportedly withdrew because he felt the mechanism was a talking shop that produced no concrete results.[57] Following the introduction of Mano Dura, civil society groups and government officials met for a few months in a roundtable forum on the gang problem.[58] These discussions suggested the creation of a national body that would design and coordinate a comprehensive gang control strategy, while government, the private sector, and civil society actors would provide resources and carry out gang enforcement, prevention, and rehabilitation. A UNICEF consultant prepared a written proposal based on these ideas, which was submitted to then-minister of gobernación René Figueroa in late 2004. He pledged to incorporate the ideas into the Súper Mano Dura plan. The document, however, was shelved, and thereafter the forum ceased to function.[59]

In 2006, some of the individuals who participated in the roundtables, and were disappointed at the continued failure to develop a full-fledged gang policy, decided to make another attempt to work toward the formation of a coordinated gang control strategy. This included the directors of the Polígono, FESPAD, the IDHUCA, and the IUDOP, as well as the head of the PNC's Division of Juvenile Services, members of UNICEF, and the Archdiocese of San Salvador. The group intended to meet on a private basis until it developed some concrete ideas, but it soon disintegrated. Father Moratalla apparently had caused some discontent with his unauthorized decision to invite PNC chief Rodrigo Ávila, a Mano Dura proponent, to future meetings.[60]

According to some of the participants, the initiative failed for the following reasons. First, although many individuals and organizations in El Salvador were committed to reducing gang violence, there was no consensus about the nature of the problem and possible solutions. Second, a lack of common objectives prevented NGOs and other actors from coordinating their activities. Their desire for publicity and to enhance their organizational profile (and thus to attract more funding) had simply been a greater priority. Third, the alliance-building process had included individuals in their personal capacity, not as representatives of institutions who were authorized to make the necessary policy and resource commitments. Fourth, it can be argued that different organizations had managed to rally around the need for alternative solutions to the gang problem, but lacked the leadership to unite them for advocacy purposes. Fifth, the NGOs and their allies had not developed the strategies and skills required for the effective articulation of political demands.[61] Gang control continued to be seen as a technical issue (to be resolved through proposal making), rather than a political one (to be addressed through more creative and confrontational advocacy strategies). In the end, the Polígono and other actors—including NGOs, church groups, and research institutes—failed to set aside their differences and press collectively for the implementation of an alternative gang policy. The ongoing challenge for gang-related NGO advocacy was to better understand the power dynamics in El Salvador and find ways to persuade the economic and political elite to make greater concessions on gang prevention and rehabilitation.

Conclusion

Father Moratalla, a Spanish Salesian priest who founded and directed the Polígono, wanted to design a solution for the education and employment needs of the youths in one of San Salvador's marginal communities. The vision and creativity of this organizational entrepreneur permitted the Polígono to consolidate itself institutionally and financially and to develop a widely respected gang prevention and rehabilitation initiative.

Although the agency had originally not intended to assist ex–gang members, it turned to developing what it considered a suitable program because the need was apparent and the staff was committed to working with disadvantaged young people. This project combined the Salesians' special concern for the neediest youth with the preventive system of Don Bosco, based on the principles of reason, religion, and loving-kindness. The residential education and training program sought to convert participants into responsible Christians and to prepare them for self-sufficiency through self-employment. While the goal was to change the perceived culture of dependency among poor people, an independent income-generating activity could enable gang members to overcome the difficulties they faced to secure stable employment.

With its residential training program, the Polígono sought to demonstrate to the government a more effective way of tackling the gang problem and to persuade officials to implement comprehensive gang control. Its choice of an advocacy strategy relied on indirect policy influence. This could have altered the policy context, particularly if combined with lobbying or media work. However, contextual factors—notably elite influence over policy making, the authority of ARENA as the guardian of conservative interests, and the absence of a pluralistic media system—constituted critical barriers to the promotion of gang prevention and rehabilitation. Opposition to the Polígono's advocacy agenda was expected, which meant its strategic choices were critical in order to make advances in promoting alternative policies.

The Polígono's criticism of Mano Dura and showcasing of an alternative approach to gang control encouraged the Saca administration to adopt less punitive rhetoric and, ostensibly, a different policy. One example was the *granja-escuela*, the rehabilitation center established in 2005 by the National Council of Public Security. The *granja* resembled the Polígono's project to offer ex–gang members job training and development. What the government did not implement was a long-term, comprehensive, and sustainable gang control strategy. Instead, it continued to privilege suppression.

The Polígono's advocacy efforts were valuable because they demonstrated the importance of providing at-risk and gang youth with education and employment opportunities. Yet, its indirect strategy put insufficient pressure on the government to alter its approach to gang violence reduction and may even have decreased this pressure. The government chose to financially support the organization, thereby effectively devolving some of its responsibilities for rehabilitation, notably as regards juvenile offenders and gang members, onto the nonprofit sector. What becomes apparent is that the Polígono's policy influence was affected by exogenous factors and strategic choices, which in turn were shaped by its identity and internal characteristics.

The Polígono's program was based on both Salesian principles and simple pragmatism, yet the individualism and self-reliance it championed coincided with the neoliberal values espoused by ARENA. Unsurprisingly perhaps, the government was prepared to fund much of the Polígono's work, which the agency interpreted as a sign that the government recognized the importance of gang prevention and rehabilitation. Staff members, however, had no gang expertise. There was little proof that they successfully encouraged young people to leave gangs or worked to any great extent with gang members, given the agency's exclusive admissions criteria. The Polígono was able to promote its program on the basis of anecdotal evidence of success, which earned it respect and credibility as a gang rehabilitation center. Popular credibility permitted the Polígono to tout its initiative to policymakers and to be consulted by the media on the gang problem.

The Polígono's strategic choices also limited the potential impact of its advocacy. Despite the limitations of the program, its existence served to introduce fresh ideas into the Salvadoran policy context and to stimulate the identification of policy options. The ways in which the agency tried to demonstrate a better way of reducing gang violence, however, were too subtle to force the anticipated policy change. Its indirect advocacy method was unlikely to apply enough pressure on the authorities unless combined with other activities, such as media work or lobbying. Although the Polígono was accessible to the press, it had no explicit media strategy. It enjoyed sufficient public visibility to share its position with a wider audience, but made no proactive attempts to influence public opinion and thus create more popular political support for alternative gang control. The NGO also responded to invitations to showcase its program at official events, but these mostly promoted gang suppression and did not signal a real interest in gang prevention and rehabilitation. Citizen mobilization, which could have been a powerful tool to back up the PIDB's advocacy efforts and its push for an alternative gang policy, was neglected.

The organization attempted to build alliances with other civil society actors, and if they had been successful, these activities could have strengthened its advocacy position. The cooperative interagency initiatives in which the Polígono participated, however, soon disintegrated, largely because potential allies lacked unifying leadership or clarity about the gang problem and had no common objectives to sustain their cooperation. The Polígono relied on quiet pressure and indirect advocacy, and this could not overcome the government's lack of political will to move away from Mano Dura.

Conclusion

This book was inspired by the desire to develop a better understanding of NGO practices. The existing literature tends to study these organizations in isolation from their socio-political environment and as such does not capture the ways in which NGO behavior is shaped by exogenous factors. Furthermore, these studies generally leave aside the internal dynamics of these agencies, glossing over the extent to which human relations shape the organizations' activities and influence. In short, to grasp why NGOs act the way they do, it is necessary both to situate them more firmly within their environment and to examine their inner workings.

To meet this goal, the book explored how three Salvadoran NGOs— a legal advocacy organization, a peer rehabilitation group, and a Catholic development agency—sought to promote alternative gang control and why their advocacy efforts were largely ineffective. The Mano Dura plan, introduced by the outgoing Francisco Flores government in 2003, proposed to lower the country's homicide rate by cracking down on street gangs. It allowed the arrest of suspected gang members on the basis of their physical appearance. The mass media legitimized the initiative by fanning a gang panic and increased public support for it by depicting suppression as the most appropriate response. Widespread opposition to the measure prompted the Antonio Saca administration to incorporate prevention and rehabilitation language into its Súper Mano Dura plan, but officials continued to resist the implementation of a comprehensive gang policy. Mano Dura constituted a populist ploy that was introduced chiefly to enhance ARENA's electoral appeal. It was subsequently modified only to deflect criticism and avoid addressing the structural factors associated with the proliferation of gangs.

The research for this book highlighted a contemporary El Salvador characterized by historical patterns of economic and political dominance by elite alliances, which successfully neutralized efforts to reorient the gang policy pursued between 2003 and 2006. Three specific societal factors were found to be critical barriers to a comprehensive gang control strategy: elite influence over the state, ARENA's protection of the elite, and the absence of a pluralistic media system. The NGOs' strategies—which included legal and policy advocacy, gang empowerment and rehabilitation, and the development of a model gang program—differed in their tactical style, but all failed to generate sufficient pressure to motivate a genuine change in gang policy.

The Continuity of Authoritarianism and Elite Influence

El Salvador has a long tradition of authoritarianism and reliance on institutionalized violence to maintain order and defend elite privileges. During colonial times, *campesino* protests against the economic structures that excluded them were crushed, while the republican years saw the continued use of force to deal with social problems. Periodic indigenous uprisings in response to deep-seated social injustices were brutally repressed, notably during the 1932 *matanza*, when thousands of *campesinos* were killed. Decades later, the state waged a devastating counterinsurgency war against a guerrilla movement that sought to create a fairer and more equal society. However, even prior to the outbreak of the civil war, every actual or potential challenge to the status quo was portrayed as a communist-inspired subversion aimed at undermining the institutions that had brought progress to the country.

The military, which held the reins of state power for close to five decades, played an important role in the suppression of social and political conflict. State-sponsored terror was also enforced through an extensive public security apparatus; the militarized police corps did not protect ordinary citizens, but rather kept the rulers safe from the ruled. Death squads, created by Roberto D'Aubuisson, the founder of the right-wing ARENA party, and made up in large part of military and police personnel, eliminated sources of dissent and sowed fear among the urban population. Equally insidious were the various paramilitary groups that infiltrated rural communities and destroyed local social networks. Over time, violence became the principal tool for managing state-society relations, and this remained the case in the 2000s. As a result, ARENA governments preferred punitive measures to suppress the gang problem instead of addressing the structural factors that contributed to its emergence.

The 1992 Chapultepec Peace Accords ended El Salvador's civil war and introduced democracy, but the authoritarian patterns of the past survived this transition. Both elite and ordinary Salvadorans continued to harbor authoritarian attitudes, favoring law and order over respect for human rights. The postwar period was marked by a climate of insecurity, which conservative politicians exploited to foster nostalgia for authoritarianism and to justify the adoption of tougher laws and militarized policing. Thus, the 2003 Mano Dura anti-gang initiative enjoyed considerable popularity precisely because the groundwork for such a fundamentally suppressive policy was already prepared. The plan only deepened society's preference for punitive responses.

Mano Dura nevertheless was largely a populist policy designed to enhance ARENA's electoral image in the run-up to the 2004 presidential contest. It also reinforced El Salvador's authoritarian legacy by inflating the seriousness of the gang threat, encouraging popular demands for gang suppression, and instituting discriminatory legislation and suppressive tactics that the right-wing media helped legitimize. Governments across the world can and do adopt populist anti-crime measures like Mano Dura because citizens who live in constant fear of victimization are likely to applaud a strong stance against crime. Such policies, embodying the ideological preferences of those forces with no interest in the construction of a democratic society, are of even greater concern in fragile democracies where authoritarianism may again creep into the social fabric. By encouraging an alarming mix of social profiling, greater insecurity, and a lingering nostalgia for authoritarianism, Mano Dura may actually have constituted a greater threat to society than the gangs themselves.

Central to Mano Dura was the role of the Policía Nacional Civil. Designed to replace the old security forces following the civil war, the PNC was conceived to be the civilian, apolitical, professional, and rights-respecting police that a democratic El Salvador required. The right, however, sought to gain control over what it saw as a key instrument of state power and social control by ensuring that conservative elements dominated the force. This maneuvering was to some extent neutralized as long as international monitoring and donor assistance pressured the government to comply with the peace agreement. However, after the departure of foreign observers, the new police force suffered further institutional corrosion. The ex-military personnel who oversaw its transformation controlled the PNC's command structure, turning it into a corrupt and abusive institution without investigative capacities or respect for human rights, one that embraced social cleansing groups and a commitment to suppression.

The country's conservative sectors mounted resistance against all public security reforms, suggesting that this was also their favored approach. One risk from such a persistent display of state violence is that the population comes to accept it as the normal way to deal with crime, a mindset that poses serious obstacles to democratic consolidation. For their part, NGOs found it difficult to successfully advocate alternative gang control in this atmosphere of official indifference to human rights and investigative policing.

The Power Structure of Salvadoran Society

The ARENA government continued its suppressive gang strategy even after Súper Mano Dura had become a political liability and was withdrawn. While the introduction of the original plan had been politically driven, the basic punitive approach was not changed because it allowed the Saca administration to demonstrate its commitment to gang control without addressing the structural factors that fostered gang culture. This preference for suppression over other strategies, despite the evident need for a comprehensive policy, arose directly from the domestic power structure that centered on the country's economic elites and their influence over ARENA and the right-wing media.

El Salvador's economic and political affairs have historically revolved around the first element of that power structure, the oligarchy. This elite began building its fortunes through coffee growing while most of the working population lived in poverty. By virtue of its vast financial and social power, the oligarchy always enjoyed substantial influence over state institutions and public policy making. In the early republican years, the wealthiest families took turns exercising direct political control, but in the early 1930s, they ceded the reins of government to the military, which defended conservative upper-class interests until the outbreak of the civil war in 1980. Over the decades, the configuration of the wealthy ruling elite changed with successive periods of economic diversification, the neoliberal reforms of the 1990s, and a structural shift toward a new regional growth pattern that saw the emergence of globalized economic power groups. These transformations notwithstanding, the oligarchy never once relaxed either its political influence or its rigid hostility toward even the most moderate reform efforts. These traditional power structures survived El Salvador's transition to democracy, though under a different guise, and constituted a key obstacle to the advocacy of an alternative gang policy.

The progressive army officers' coup of October 1979 effectively ended the long-standing military-oligarchy alliance. Its wealth and privileges at stake, the right sought to reassert its dominance by creating its own political party. Founded in 1981 with a pro-capitalist/anti-communist ideology, the Alianza Republicana Nacionalista constituted the second element of the power structure and a political project that the country's elite families could rally around despite their divergent economic interests. With ARENA's victory in the 1989 presidential elections, the right returned to a dominant position from which to perpetuate the status quo. Because the civil war had destroyed the economy and ended the wealthy class's historic way of life, the relatively moderate ARENA leadership entered peace negotiations with the FMLN and oversaw the advent of democracy as mandated by the Peace Accords of 1992. Despite their increased tolerance of democratic norms, however, the right as a whole remained opposed to structural reforms that might redress the perpetual imbalance of social and economic power.

In the intervening years, ARENA was the main vehicle for elite political participation. The policies of the four administrations until 2009 tended to favor that small, economically powerful segment of Salvadoran society. The most influential groups enjoyed privileged access to the highest authorities. Although their pressure did not always achieve the desired results, it was nonetheless so pervasive that it amounted to a capture of the state. Given the partisan nature of ARENA governments, the groups advocating gang prevention and rehabilitation were unlikely to find a receptive ear, a situation exacerbated by the highly undemocratic and exclusive policy-making process, itself the product of the elite's readiness to circumvent formal channels. This scenario raised doubts not only about the possibilities for policy advocacy of any kind, but also about the prospects for democratic consolidation and the creation of a fairer society.

The third element in the power structure of Salvadoran society is the country's conservative media. In the decades prior to the Peace Accords, independent media outlets faced state censorship or were driven out of existence by political violence. The news organizations that survived those years inevitably maintained a proregime stance. The political openings of the early 1990s ushered in a more hospitable environment for journalistic work, but twenty years later, media independence remains elusive. Social media provide new space for the expression of a diverse range of opinions and criticisms, but given limited Internet access in El Salvador, the reach of online content remains limited.

A content analysis of gang-related coverage by the two leading dailies, *La Prensa Gráfica* and *El Diario de Hoy*, revealed a clear informational bias toward the ARENA governments' policy agenda. Although the papers displayed subtle ideological differences, both fanned a gang panic and amplified the official interpretation of the gang problem by promoting negative, dehumanizing stereotypes of gang members. Research suggests that this biased reporting helped lead the Salvadoran public to perceive the gang problem as more serious than it was. It also prompted support for Mano Dura policies despite their demonstrated ineffectiveness and harm to human rights. The distorted coverage was partly the outcome of poor journalistic practices, but the concentration of media ownership, the political use of advertising, and reportorial self-censorship also served to produce uncritical news content. This environment made it difficult for opponents of Mano Dura to disseminate their ideas to a wider audience.

NGO Advocacy Strategies in Comparison

A combination of exogenous and endogenous factors explains why NGO advocacy strategies were relatively ineffective in promoting alternative gang control. The withdrawal of special anti-gang legislation and President Saca's public commitment to gang prevention and rehabilitation— through, for example, programs such as Mano Amiga and Mano Extendida—might have been interpreted as successes by advocates. However, both the continued preference for suppression and the limited nature of the programs suggest that the government remained unenthusiastic about true gang mitigation and had adopted these new initiatives only to deflect further criticism.

Given the socio-political constraints on NGO advocacy in El Salvador, it might be argued that the possibilities for achieving the organizations' stated policy objectives were always slim. While no ARENA administration was likely to accede to NGO demands without resistance, the political environment was not so hostile that all advocacy activities were simply futile from the start. The fact that the executive felt compelled to assume a different policy stance on the gang issue at all indicates that coordinated efforts could produce meaningful advances. One purpose of describing the three NGOs that are the subject of this book within their domestic context was to highlight the dynamic interaction among them. Democratic social and political change can develop only through a persistent action-reaction cycle in which the government incorporates the demands of the governed. As the analysis revealed, however, the NGOs' advocacy strategies were shaped by organizational characteristics and tactical choices that weakened the political pressure they could bring to bear in favor of alternative gang control.

Organizational Characteristics

The agencies' capacity for activism and the approaches they pursued depended on internal factors, including how they were formed and how well they were able to sustain themselves. Origin and identity can help explain why an organization will adopt certain strategies and why some agencies may be politically more influential than others. FESPAD was established and directed by Salvadoran legal scholars to promote human rights and the rule of law. It was logical, then, that it would contest Mano Dura through legal and policy advocacy. The Polígono began as a religious development organization that responded to the education and employment needs of marginalized youth. It subsequently applied its education-for-work paradigm to a model gang program. The peer rehabilitation group Homies Unidos was founded to give gang members the opportunity to design solutions to their own problems and empower other gang members to abandon drugs and violence. Gang empowerment and rehabilitation remained Homies Unidos's tactical priority even when the agency began to promote alternative gang control.

The strategies that the NGOs adopted were also informed by their different ideological standpoints on the advocacy issue and on the degree of antagonism with which each approached the authorities. While each group agreed on the need for gang prevention and rehabilitation programs, they disagreed on the issue of whether gangs should be disbanded altogether. FESPAD and the Polígono endorsed the official view that gang offenders should be prosecuted and all gang members encouraged to leave the gang. Both of these organizations could therefore at least gain access to policymakers and directly convey to them the importance of rights-respecting gang enforcement and social intervention, even though these efforts produced only mixed results. By contrast, the *pandilleros calmados* of Homies Unidos still identified with gang values and argued that street gangs had positive functions. According to these retired gang members, young people should therefore be required only to abandon drugs and violence, but not the gang itself. Since this standpoint, and the very identity of Homies Unidos as an organization of former gang members, conflicted with the government's perception of gang members as socially undesirable and expendable individuals, the NGO predictably found it more difficult even to meet with the authorities.

In their relationship with the state, each NGO had developed a preference for either confrontation or collaboration. Homies Unidos was the only organization that maintained an explicitly antagonistic stance, although less for tactical reasons than because of staff members' attachment to the gang and its oppositional culture. FESPAD and the Polígono, in contrast, both rejected a purely adversarial relationship. Instead, these NGOs sought to assist the government in developing more effective gang policies, FESPAD through legal and policy proposals and the Polígono by showcasing a rehabilitation program. Polígono director Father Moratalla and his team were reluctant to openly criticize Mano Dura, but Homies Unidos and FESPAD protested its human rights violations in various ways, the latter particularly through *denuncia* (public condemnation). Collaboration with officials gave the organizations an opportunity to influence the government through policy alternatives, rather than to merely expose the limitations of the existing approach.

Importantly, however, none of the NGOs combined their confrontational or collaborative efforts with activities that would effectively increase political pressure for the implementation of alternative gang control. Because the government lacked the incentives either to counter police abuse or to pursue nonpunitive gang mitigation programs, it was unlikely to respond to advocacy demands unless compelled to do so. The organizations that had embraced collaboration may well have believed it to be more viable than confrontation. Perceptions of what constituted legitimate political behavior in a society with fragile democratic institutions, however, only weakened the NGOs' strategies insofar as they discarded adversarial tactics when the advocacy situation seemed to require it.

Funding, Access, and Advocacy

Agencies that possess a positive public reputation, often acquired through demonstrated competence, are more likely to be consulted by the media and able to participate in the policy process. However, they must also have the capacity to both sustain themselves and conduct their operations. NGOs require a reliable flow of income, which is conditioned by the availability of funding but also by the organizations' grant-seeking abilities. At the same time, staff must have the professional skills and knowledge required to advance their advocacy agenda. Deficits in any of these areas affect an NGO's ability to create policy change and may even threaten organizational survival.

It follows that for those NGOs that enjoyed a positive public image, access to both the authorities and the media was comparatively easier. Both FESPAD and the Polígono, which were widely respected for their professional work, were repeatedly approached by journalists and invited to official events on the gang problem. By contrast, HU staff received little media attention, and their status as ex–gang members strained relations with both the government and the police. Homies Unidos's public reputation was further tarnished when one of the directors was arrested and convicted for homicide.

All three organizations had experienced severe financial crises at some point. Short-term donor contracts and the limited availability of grants were a general challenge, but FESPAD and Homies Unidos faced additional constraints because the domestic funding environment was unfavorable for both a critically minded NGO and one run by ex–gang members (synonymous, for many Salvadorans, with "criminals"). However, some of the organizations dealt with fund-raising concerns more successfully than others. While the Polígono was able to receive funding from the government and international donors to whom its micro-enterprise model appealed, FESPAD relied on a membership program and a series of commercial activities such as legal services and publication sales. Homies Unidos's staff, in contrast, had neither developed appropriate grant-seeking skills nor, for more than a decade, managed to obtain legal status for the group, which left staff too preoccupied with organizational survival to devote much time to advocacy work.

The NGOs could draw on diverse kinds of expert knowledge to carry forward their advocacy. For instance, HU staff could use their firsthand experience of gang life to warn publicly about its perils and insist on the need for alternative responses. However, the agency's staff did not display the capacity for or the interest in either conducting effective gang prevention and rehabilitation or tying their work to a broader advocacy strategy. The Polígono, for its part, was qualified to provide young people with education and job training, but lacked specialized gang intervention skills. However, because the NGO was never asked to provide more than anecdotal evidence of program outcomes, it was able to maintain its reputation as a successful gang rehabilitation center and to use its standing to advocate alternative gang control. FESPAD, on the other hand, possessed extensive legal expertise that enabled staff to criticize the anti-gang law and help draft appropriate legislation that did not infringe on constitutional principles. The lawyers also lacked gang expertise, which meant that their proposal for gang violence prevention yielded only broad policy recommendations that would not have substantially advanced alternative gang control even if implemented.

Skillful media work could have served to educate the public and/or shape public opinion on the gang issue, thus creating political pressure for a comprehensive gang policy. This capacity remained underdeveloped in all three NGOs. Homies Unidos did not undertake any media work, citing biased reporting as the reason. Father Moratalla, for his part, responded positively to interview requests, but otherwise preferred to focus on the creation of job training and development programs. The FESPAD media strategy, involving paid ads and press conferences, was critical for its human rights work, but was not enough to counter all the negative reporting on gangs in the mainstream media. The news coverage that it did receive served to raise FESPAD's institutional profile, but did not turn the biased news about Mano Dura into ideologically contested terrain.

Finally, and most importantly, all NGOs need advocacy planning skills to effectively promote their policy objectives. This requires an analysis of the political environment, its power relations, and its possibilities and limits for advocacy, as well as the subsequent mapping of a strategy that reflects these dynamics. Interestingly, the staff of each of the three agencies was familiar with the characteristics of the domestic Salvadoran context, particularly the persistence of its established power structures. Each NGO was reasonably clear about the outcome it hoped to achieve. None, however, tailored its strategy to the intricacies of the advocacy issue within this political context. Committed to showcasing its gang program and applying "quiet pressure" to the government, the Polígono seemed unprepared to consider the adoption of a different tactical style, despite the inefficacy of its existing approach. Both Homies Unidos and FESPAD not only failed to anticipate some of the barriers to their advocacy, but also proved unable to deal with obstacles when they arose. FESPAD's experience demonstrated these strategic limitations perhaps most clearly: for example, when a newly elected ARENA mayor remained indifferent to a gang policy proposal approved by his FMLN predecessor or when its legal aid case related to police abuse did not proceed due to the arbitrariness of the criminal justice system. The second incident in particular provoked a feeling of powerlessness among the lawyers, who acquiesced to this setback and seemed unsure how to reorient their strategy. In all three NGOs, weaknesses in their advocacy planning were reflected in their choices of advocacy tools and targets.

Advocacy Tools and Targets

The organizations' efforts to contest Mano Dura differed considerably in terms of strategy and policy influence (whether direct or indirect). Notwithstanding the broader tactical style, their success depended to a great extent on the methods they adopted (and how they were used) and the actors that were targeted (and how they were approached). To promote alternative gang control, the NGOs selected among four tools (*testimonio*/information politics, legal mechanisms, *denuncia*/public condemnation, and proposals) and four targets (government, the private sector, the media, and civil society).

ADVOCACY TOOLS

Testimonio/information politics was a key element of Homies Unidos's prevention program. Staff talked publicly about their own gang experiences to raise awareness of the nature of the gang problem, put human faces to the stereotypes of gang members, and emphasize the need for alternative responses. These speaking engagements could have helped to increase the pressure for comprehensive gang control, particularly if they had been combined with media work, but organizational weaknesses precluded Homies Unidos from making regular use of this advocacy tool.

FESPAD relied exclusively (and unsuccessfully) on legal mechanisms when seeking to obtain redress for an ex–gang member who was the victim of police harassment. The lawyers subsequently also tried to challenge Mano Dura based on this representative case. Given the organization's mandate to promote the rule of law, the staff felt obliged to use formal legal channels in their own work. At the same time, this decision was surprising because official unresponsiveness to such approaches is a well-known problem that FESPAD itself repeatedly documented in its reports. The experience clearly demonstrated that legal mechanisms were not a viable advocacy tool in a country where the political class had thus far shown little interest in strengthening the rule of law and the independent judiciary this required. If anything, the NGO's inability to recognize the limitations of this approach suggested some degree of political inexperience.

Denuncia/public condemnation of human rights violations attributable to Mano Dura was important to the work of both Homies Unidos and FESPAD. While the former preferred to alert the PDDH to perceived abuses, the latter aimed to shame the government into adopting a rights-respecting gang policy by exposing violations through published reports. Important as these activities were, *denuncia* itself does not necessarily motivate a change in state behavior, as the case of gang advocacy amply demonstrates. The effectiveness of this methodology depended to a large extent on the media's willingness to reveal abuses and the authorities' vulnerability to such publicity. The government was perfectly aware of the illegalities committed under Mano Dura but felt no need to remedy them. So increasing political pressure was a vital strategy. This was a challenge because the mass media created a climate that supported suppression and in which gang members were widely seen as perpetrators rather than victims. The NGOs, however, did not continue to trigger the "boomerang pattern" (the activation of advocacy mechanisms abroad to create pressure for change at home), which had some effect in the early advocacy phase. Nor did they explain to the skeptical public that human rights activism was no obstacle to gang control but, rather, helped improve it.

The Polígono and FESPAD both adopted a collaborative attitude toward the government and aimed to provide constructive criticism of Mano Dura; the former, by modeling a gang program and the latter, through the development of legal and policy documents. A proposal-making capacity can strengthen advocacy efforts, and in other Latin American countries, NGOs could in fact increase their influence by offering realistic policy options.[1] However, proposals are unlikely to induce change in the absence of the necessary political will. Both organizations seemed to perceive gang control as a technical issue that could be resolved merely by presenting alternatives to Mano Dura; they both underestimated the need for a more assertive advocacy style. Indeed, by not effectively balancing the tension between confrontation and collaboration, the NGOs were co-opted into a partisan cause: FESPAD, by participating in the Anti-Gang Forum and permitting the government to appear consultative even though it had no intention of abandoning gang suppression; the Polígono, by accepting official funding and partially assuming the state's responsibility for the rehabilitation of gang members and juvenile offenders.

ADVOCACY TARGETS

Given the government's responsibilities in areas as diverse as laws, policies, budgets, and institutional practices, it was inevitable that the NGOs would approach successive administrations to promote constitutional anti-gang legislation, prevention, rehabilitation, and responsible policing. Yet, notwithstanding the importance of policy engagement at the highest level, it was surprising that the agencies focused extensively on the government, knowing, as they did, that decision making occurred largely behind closed doors and that the economic elite remained the de facto power in El Salvador. Activities aimed at improving laws and policies could not, and did not, change the structures, values, and behavior that subverted democratic institutions and conspired against the implementation of alternative gang control.

Conversely, it was startling that none of the NGOs targeted the private sector, especially the economic elite that exercised substantial influence over policy making. Each had recognized the importance of economic opportunity for gang prevention and rehabilitation, including job creation and the end of recruitment practices that generally discriminated against gang members. However, the NGOs dealt with this situation in ways that disregarded, by omission or commission, the complicity of the business sector. Homies Unidos and the Polígono both chose, on the one hand, to work within the existing structural constraints and offered youths self-employment training. These efforts, no matter how positively they may have affected individual lives, were inadequate given the magnitude of the problem. Yet, this awareness prompted no change in strategy. FESPAD, on the other hand, expected the government to take the necessary measures, but never challenged the elite interests that maintained the status quo. By not targeting those with the power to support or veto economic, fiscal, and redistributive policies, the NGOs neglected precisely those actors who could have helped improve the structural conditions that foster gang development and create the resources required for prevention and rehabilitation programs.

Given the media's functions of providing information, fostering debate, and shaping public opinion, NGOs that worked with journalistic outlets could seek to publicize their policy position, alter popular perceptions of the gang problem, and create pressure for alternative gang control. FESPAD was the only agency that developed a media strategy, involving standard activities such as paid advertisements and press conferences. With its periodic public pronouncements against Mano Dura, FESPAD did gain some visibility, but it largely targeted the mainstream press in its desire to reach a wide audience. Although this allowed the organization to engage the political class, the right-wing media were controlled and operated by owners who wanted to promote the status quo, not challenge it. The voice of FESPAD was therefore largely drowned out by the abundant pro–Mano Dura coverage. Furthermore, the organization considered the media to be a site for advocacy, but did not confront them directly, for example, to demand that they improve their reporting practices. Since journalistic work was shaped by the political and business interests of the media owners, only substantive changes in the sector itself could have led to more responsible news reporting and a more pluralistic debate on gang control.

Given both the complexity of the advocacy issue and chronic resource constraints, individual NGOs could hope to advance alternative gang control only to a limited extent. Building alliances with other civil society groups, however, would have permitted them not only to share advocacy tasks, but also to amplify their political voice and influence. Each of the NGOs attempted some form of networking or alliance building, but for different reasons and with different outcomes. HU staff did not seek out opportunities for collective action except to solicit help to resolve the immediate problems of their peers. Networking possibilities for Homies Unidos had also diminished over time because the organization's staffing bias in favor of the Dieciocho elicited skepticism among potential allies. Further, its reputation was damaged by the criminal conviction of a senior member. Father Moratalla withdrew the Polígono from a network when he decided the mechanism was a talking shop that produced no concrete results.

Together with FESPAD and other organizations, the Polígono also tried to launch a civil society–based initiative aimed at promoting a nationally coordinated gang policy. This incipient coalition also disintegrated, largely because participants disagreed on the nature of the gang problem and its solution and thus lacked common objectives. FESPAD, however, recognized the importance of strategic alliances. It helped form an activist coalition aimed at addressing human rights and social justice issues in El Salvador and inducing a shift from protest behavior to proposal making. The alliance became dormant, however, when several NGO leaders went to work for the Funes government.

Overall, the strategies of the three organizations differed in style, yet were similar insofar as they failed to create sufficient political pressure for the implementation of alternative gang control. Both the exogenous and endogenous factors that affected their advocacy suggest some broader conclusions about democracy and civil society in contemporary El Salvador.

Democracy and Civil Society in El Salvador

The strategies of the three NGOs were aimed at specific legal and policy transformations, rather than the structural conditions in which the advocacy unfolded. However, their attempts to contest Mano Dura encountered obstacles partly because of the characteristics of El Salvador's democracy. Thus, one of the implications of this study is that the political system itself needs to become the object of reform. The Peace Accords that ended the civil war permitted greater political inclusion and freedom of expression, but the possibilities for promoting human rights and social justice issues remained limited until 2009 because politics under ARENA rule reverted to its previous exclusionary patterns. While it is understandable that a country with an established authoritarian tradition could not develop into a full-fledged democracy overnight, the elite who were indispensable to the democratic transition did not subsequently support its consolidation. This is not to deny the importance of civil society's contribution to this process. Yet, the elite played a key role in the deepening of El Salvador's democracy, including in the creation of a new political culture, the formation of democratic institutions, and the exercise of power. Since the right had a stake in the prewar system, it could be expected to try to re-establish previous patterns of control and domination. Perhaps the most evident sign of the democratic subversion that occurred in the postwar period is the politicization of public institutions.

The appointment of individuals loyal to the right may have been most conspicuous in the criminal justice system, but it reflected a much wider trend aimed at maintaining partisan influence over the state. Thus, the institutional limitations that are often attributed solely to insufficient resources and training can also be interpreted as a deliberate outcome of this politicization. In other words, what appears to be a weak state may in fact be one that *is* functioning, albeit for a nondemocratic purpose, namely that of ensuring impunity for, and protecting the privileges of, the country's economic and political ruling class. Although El Salvador has been governed since 2009 by ostensibly more progressive administrations, this does not mean that certain practices ingrained in the country's political culture will necessarily be abandoned.

While the right understood how to manipulate democracy to further its own interests, this scenario also implies that El Salvador's democracy will not be consolidated until its institutions are permitted to fulfill the mandate under which they were created. Every state must have the autonomy and capacity to implement policies and to allocate resources in a way that responds to the needs of the entire population, not to the demands of a minority. While this study has highlighted the nexus between elite behavior and democratic development, it has paid comparatively little attention to the role of other actors in this process. Future research could explore how it was possible for democracy building to be thwarted without major popular resistance.

Since current leaders will not strengthen the political system unless compelled to do so, pressure for change needs to come from elsewhere. Two sources of change are the media and society itself. The media have a vital role to play in a democracy by, for example, monitoring the state and promoting accountability, providing information to the public, and fostering critical opinion and debate. The press can perform these tasks adequately, however, only if it enjoys the necessary independence from political control. Since the commercial interests and/or ideological preferences of certain Salvadoran media owners interfere unduly with reporting, the principal news organizations do not currently contribute to the construction of a democratic society in any meaningful way. Investigative journalism is practically nonexistent (*El Faro* being the exception) to the point that vital issues such as public corruption, organized crime, and extrajudicial executions remain shrouded in silence. News treatment of the street gangs and other aspects of the national reality could improve only if the press took its social function more seriously. Ideally, the demand for critical and independent journalism should come from the citizens, but education and democratic citizenship are poorly promoted, and many Salvadorans do not question the quality of news reporting. The social and political polarization means that the average citizen does not seek or demand critical journalism, but prefers media content that feeds their stereotypes.

Under the current circumstances, the following measures might be more feasible to improve the conditions under which journalists work and, ultimately, the news products themselves. First, existing collegiate bodies could be strengthened in order to protect the rights and interests of journalists and pose a greater counterweight to the power of media owners and editors. Public debates might foreground the need for critical journalism, while a journalist protection law might shield reporters against reprisals. Such steps, however, are unlikely to have any significant impact as long as media companies determine editorial policies, and job security for journalists remains precarious. Second, the country could adopt advertising regulations to prevent media outlets from being punished for critical reporting through the withdrawal of advertising revenue. Third, civil society groups need to promote the further development of alternative media to provide unbiased sources of the information that is too often distorted or suppressed in the mainstream press. Existing examples include the electronic newspapers *El Faro*, *Revista Factum*, and *Diario1*, as well as numerous blogs. The existence of these media is encouraging, but they will need to reach a much larger audience than is currently the case if they are to stimulate greater debate in society.

In the long term, democracy is more likely to be entrenched if ordinary Salvadorans participate in this process. This requires citizens who are socialized to democratic values, understand their rights and obligations, and participate in politics through activities as fundamental as voting, demonstrations, and lobbying. Citizens must be educated to be able to articulate demands, propose concrete solutions, and claim as their entitlements those goods that have traditionally been regarded as privileges in the country.

If this is to occur, however, Salvadoran society will first need to overcome a series of dilemmas. First, declining job prospects in recent years have prompted a growing number of Salvadorans to emigrate. As long as people believe they lack the power to improve domestic conditions, they will prefer the risks of migration over political participation at home. Second, both the postwar consumer culture and the climate of insecurity have encouraged many Salvadorans to retreat into the private sphere. Individuals who are focused on improving their social status or, from fear and mistrust, shun cooperation with others are unlikely to actively seek social and political change. Third, a generalized perception that successive governments have done little to lower crime rates and address economic problems has led to widespread democratic disenchantment and political apathy. Unless current levels of political indifference are reversed, democracy will not deepen, and popular needs and expectations will remain unfulfilled. Fourth, decades of authoritarianism instilled a culture of submission and conformism that has survived to this day. As a result, most citizens are averse to organizing in defense of their rights and interests. Fifth, the persistence of an authoritarian culture has meant that many Salvadorans not only favor the continuation of state suppression—if not vigilante justice—but would also willingly discard their recently won political freedoms in exchange for what they perceive to be greater security. These "un-civic" tendencies in society undermine the construction of democratic values and, together with citizen alienation and passivity, pose serious obstacles to democratic consolidation. Reversing these trends is a long and difficult process that depends on active civil society involvement.

Civil Society: Challenges and Possibilities

In the final years of the authoritarian era, the Salvadoran social movement was at the forefront of calls for peace and democratization. However, once these objectives were achieved and the state ceased to be the enemy, the social movement lost its unity and sense of purpose. While freedom of expression increased and civic activity flourished in some ways through the proliferation of NGOs, the social movement in recent years has lacked leadership, analytical and strategic capacity, and a common agenda. If anything, this situation worsened with the FMLN's rise to power in 2009. The social movement saw its leadership even more reduced when some of its members joined the government. The reluctance of many organizations to criticize FMLN administrations impedes the creation of a common agenda. The growth of the NGO sector, itself stimulated by the early postwar influx of international donor assistance, has led to the fragmentation of El Salvador's civil society into small, competing organizations. While the sheer diversity of these actors and their concerns might appear positive, this pluralism is now so extreme that it has become disempowering.

If NGOs and other civil society actors are to remain relevant and effective, they will need to evolve institutionally and to adapt to an altered political environment. This requires them both to review their organizational missions, priorities, and structures and to reconsider the ways they engage the state. Repressive rule ended fairly recently, and many NGOs have maintained their confrontational stance toward the state. While civil society can, and should, continue to monitor and criticize the state, it can also seek to strengthen it through objective analyses and professional proposals. To be valuable civil society actors, the organizations must find ways to ensure that their voices not only are heard, but also are taken into account at the time of decision making.

There are three specific areas that offer opportunities for NGOs to be directly involved in the country's democratic project. First, access to information is vital to improve state transparency and accountability and end the abuse of power. Given the Salvadoran media's current limitations, NGOs could conduct their own investigations into reports of misuse and abuse of power, perhaps in collaboration with academic institutions, and publicly disseminate the findings. In addition to bringing governmental affairs into the full light of public scrutiny, such access to information could empower citizens in defense of their rights and interests. Second, NGOs could undertake civic education programs to familiarize both young people and adults with democratic values and practices. Such programs would also promote a wider understanding of the obligations and rights of democratic citizenship. This requires sustained and systematic community-based efforts aimed at generating a demand for democratic consolidation. Activities of this kind can, over time, create real cultural transformation and stimulate greater political participation. Third, rather than seeking specific policy and legal changes, NGOs could play a more explicit role in shaping broader issues, such as institutional reforms, the rule of law, respect for human rights, and governmental transparency and accountability. In particular, they could work to mobilize much-needed public pressure, which is the best, if not the only, way of countering persistent patterns of inequality and exclusion and enhancing the quality of democracy.

Toward Comprehensive Gang Control in El Salvador

While not a gang study per se, this book makes a number of policy-relevant observations concerning street gangs. Most importantly, it shows that gang development is associated with individual, community, and structural factors, and that Mano Dura, despite its political utility, was an ineffective, even counterproductive approach to the gang problem. While this research focused on Mano Dura policies (2003–2006), it also showed that the Saca administration continued to rely to some degree on gang suppression and failed to adopt and implement a comprehensive and rights-respecting gang policy. As the epilogue shows, this situation continued under the FMLN administrations that have been in power since 2009. The purpose of this final section is to point out avenues for comprehensive gang control in El Salvador. Gang control is complex, however, and this study can do no more than suggest the basic steps toward this goal.

Two broad areas, research and programs, need to be addressed together. First, future research into El Salvador's street gangs might explore members' involvement in drug trafficking, particularly their relationship with more powerful actors; the gangs' transnational ties, notably from inside the prisons and to their counterparts in the United States; and the prevalence and nature of the social networks in the communities, including the use of illicit economies as survival strategies. Second, the development of gang programs must be based on comprehensive gang research. Such research could explore, for example, the motivations for gang joining; gang prevalence, structures, and organization; crime patterns; and community contexts. The gang literature has grown substantially, and certain works in this field can help researchers understand gang dynamics and gang policy options in El Salvador.[2]

Nonetheless, there is a need for more local research, particularly studies that mix methods and, ideally, incorporate observation in gang-affected communities. This is currently impossible due to gang members' suspicions toward outsiders, but rich empirical information could also be obtained through interviews of individuals living and/or working in these communities. This research could help explore aspects such as young people's strategies to resist gang joining; community strategies to prevent the emergence of gangs; ways of weakening the gangs' influence in schools and communities, as well as preventing their regeneration; and ways of offering better rehabilitation in adult and juvenile detention facilities, including psychological and psychiatric care.

There are, so far, few, if any, successful gang programs that might be adapted to the Salvadoran context, but the available policy choices are clear.[3] First, three gang control strategies—prevention, law enforcement, and rehabilitation—can each be applied at the individual, community, and societal levels. Most programs target the individual level (the gang-prone youth or gang member) with prevention and rehabilitation activities, such as counseling, educational services, and job training and placement. While these efforts can positively affect the lives of some young people, given the magnitude of the problem, they do virtually nothing to reduce gang crime and violence. The societal level concerns issues such as social exclusion, defective educational services, and unemployment/underemployment. These problems are difficult to alleviate as long as the most powerful stratum of Salvadoran society protects the status quo. Gang scholars therefore suggest focusing efforts at the community level, where the gangs emerge.[4] The objective would be not only to implement the aforementioned strategies, but also to empower residents to contain the gang problem. The challenge is how to achieve this in places where social capital is weak or fear and insecurity appear overwhelming.

Ethnographic research elsewhere in Latin America has shown that residents in conflictive communities can and do stand up to violence by state and nonstate actors. But what makes such forms of resistance possible in some contexts and not in others? In El Salvador's gang-controlled territories, inhabitants have also adapted different responses to threats and violence, including restricted mobility and socialization, an uneasy coexistence with the gangs, or migration. Open and organized opposition to the gangs, however, is practically unheard of. There is thus a need for comparative studies of these dynamics.

Second, the government needs to develop a comprehensive gang policy. So far, the Salvadoran authorities have preferred law enforcement (albeit Mano Dura policing), deeming prevention and rehabilitation to be essentially secondary elements. In reality, these three strategies need to be combined and given equal weight. Prevention and rehabilitation programs require the administration to commit resources, which sounds costly on the surface, but in the long term the country will pay a far higher price if it continues to incarcerate its youth and fails to invest in its citizens. To be sure, the Salvadoran government faces financial constraints. It would therefore need to expand its resource base (through economic growth, effective taxation, and control of tax evasion) and avoid the possible duplication of institutions, as might be the case with the National Youth Institute, the National Council for Children and Adolescents (CONNA), and the Salvadoran Institute for the Comprehensive Development of Children and Adolescents.

Law enforcement needs to shift from suppression to a policing strategy that might combine intelligence-led policing (the use of data analysis and crime intelligence to target prolific and serious offenders) with community policing (the requirement that officers work with local residents to address security problems and emphasize crime prevention). The challenge is how to achieve this when the PNC has yet to abandon abusive practices and reduce the rampant corruption within its ranks.

Third, all gang programs and policies, once implemented, must be systematically monitored and independently evaluated to gauge their effectiveness and ensure that they do not in fact exacerbate the existing situation. Fourth, the Salvadoran government needs to assume overall responsibility for gang control. Civil society groups may contribute to this effort but cannot and should not be expected to do it largely on their own. Unfortunately, I found little evidence of a domestic capacity for gang control at the beginning of this research or during subsequent research visits. El Salvador could begin by consulting outside experts on gang control, but the long-term objective must be to foster local expertise.

The street gangs have developed into a growing and serious social problem in El Salvador, partly because gang violence was for so long ignored by the authorities and subsequently addressed through suppression. Despite the human and economic costs—not only for gang members, but also for the gang-affected communities and society at large—no administration has so far displayed the necessary political will to seriously address the gang situation. Indeed, it was the failure of the NGOs to recognize the politics of gang control that partly prevented them from more effectively advocating an alternative to Mano Dura. Thus, although street gangs are not a recent problem, a long-term, comprehensive gang policy remains to be developed. Unless El Salvador puts such a policy in place in the near future, gang violence will continue to devastate Salvadoran society for a long time to come.

Epilogue

For the three NGOs in this study, gang policy advocacy and intervention in the post–Mano Dura era remained full of twists and turns, in part because of the FMLN administrations' gang strategies and their implications.

In March 2009, through an electoral alliance between former television journalist Mauricio Funes and the FMLN, this party secured its first presidential victory. Acknowledging the failure of the Mano Dura plans of the ARENA administrations, the Funes government pledged to adopt a different approach to gangs and crime. Its Política Nacional de Justicia, Seguridad Pública y Convivencia (National Policy of Justice, Public Security, and Coexistence) contained no explicit gang strategy, but instead proposed to tackle crime in all its forms through social prevention, law enforcement, rehabilitation, victim support, and institutional and legal reforms.[1]

Initially, President Funes also promised to fight organized crime and create a mechanism modeled on the International Commission against Impunity in Guatemala. In a remarkable U-turn, however, the government dropped organized crime from the public discourse, and the gangs were again depicted as the main security threat. The official who perhaps endorsed this idea the most was General David Munguía Payés, the minister of defense and architect of the gang truce that emerged in March 2012.

From the outset, the Funes administration faced a series of challenges that would trigger a reversal in the security strategy. The policy faced financing problems due to empty state coffers, which were the result of a low tax base, high debt levels, and past corruption. Attempts to introduce a special security tax were vehemently opposed by the private sector. In October 2009, the homicide rate surged, unexpectedly so it seemed, given a sustained decrease in murders between 2007 and 2008. Before long, ARENA, the mainstream media, and the business sector criticized the authorities as incompetent. The pressure on the Funes government to develop a drastic response to crime and violence intensified, and its security strategy came to resemble the earlier Mano Dura approach to gangs.

In November 2009, the president authorized the deployment of soldiers to the most crime-ridden communities. Although the Armed Forces had been participating in public security tasks since 1993, they were now given broader powers that permitted them, independently of the PNC, to conduct patrols, carry out stop-and-search procedures, and arrest criminals caught red-handed. In addition, soldiers were dispatched to previously unguarded border areas, as well as to gang prisons, where they would secure the perimeters and search personnel and visitors upon entering and exiting the facilities.

Human rights defenders rejected military involvement in public security not only for its contravention of the Peace Accords, but also because of reported abuse and denigrating treatment during the strip searches of prison visitors.[2] In April 2012, one month into the gang truce, the soldiers were withdrawn from the penitentiaries. The military, however, has continued to play a supporting role in public security and, other abuses aside, has also been implicated in forced disappearances in gang territories.[3]

In June 2010, a massacre of unprecedented brutality in the postwar period further toughened the government's stance toward the gangs. On 20 June, Dieciocho members opened fire on a microbus in Mejicanos, a municipality bordering San Salvador, killing three people. Later that night, members of the same gang targeted another microbus in the area, this time murdering the driver before dousing the crowded vehicle with gasoline and setting it ablaze. Seventeen people perished in the event, and eleven more were hospitalized with serious burn injuries. The callousness of the attacks stunned a population accustomed to high levels of violence and prompted the government to propose a new anti-gang act.[4] The gangs threatened reprisals against the collective transport sector, hoping to prevent, unsuccessfully, the adoption of the law. A gang rehabilitation law was also contemplated but later shelved.

In November 2011, Manuel Melgar, the minister of justice and public security and a former guerrilla commander, abruptly left his post. In a move that would facilitate the implementation of the gang truce, President Funes granted the portfolio to General Munguía Payés, hitherto the minister of defense. This appointment triggered an extensive overhaul of both the security cabinet and policy. The key official to be replaced in January 2012 was ex–guerrilla commander Carlos Ascencio, whose post as PNC director-general was filled by General Francisco Salinas, previously the deputy minister of defense. General Salinas reshuffled the police leadership, swapping officers perceived as committed to a holistic crime strategy with officers who favored suppression. Before long, FESPAD and other civil society groups filed a claim of unconstitutionality against the generals' appointments. In May 2013, these were declared unconstitutional, and General Munguía Payés returned to the ministry of defense.[5]

At the start of his tenure as minister of justice and public security, General Munguía Payés asserted that 90 percent of El Salvador's homicides were being committed by the street gangs.[6] The claim was based on the "observations" of soldiers who patrolled gang-affected communities, as was the minister's assertion that the gangs' "social base" had grown to comprise some four hundred thousand individuals, in addition to some sixty thousand active gang members nationwide.[7] Resolutely, General Munguía Payés vowed to reduce the murder rate by 30 percent.[8]

Early in the Funes administration, the PNC reportedly tried to strengthen its investigative capacity and community policing, efforts that had not advanced under conservative directors. The new PNC inspector-general, human rights defender Zaira Navas, began investigating officers implicated in corruption and serious crime. Navas, however, resigned when General Salinas was appointed to head the PNC, and internal investigations have since not been conducted with the same enthusiasm. A cornerstone of the Funes government's security policy, however, turned out to be a gang truce.

In March 2012, *El Faro* revealed that the government had negotiated a truce with Mara Salvatrucha and the Dieciocho so as to lower the homicide rate. The deal reportedly included large cash payments to gang leaders, some thirty of whom were transferred from the maximum security prison to less restrictive facilities where they could receive family visits and order street-based gang members to cease killings.[9] Through a series of communiqués, gang leaders announced a reduction of homicides and an end to school-based gang activity, forced recruitment, and violence against women. In return, they asked the government for an end to police operations and abuse, the repeal of the anti-gang law, and better prison conditions, as well as education and job opportunities. Gang members carried out symbolic disarmaments, and the mediators of the truce, ex–guerrilla commander Raúl Mijango and military bishop Fabio Colindres, helped create a humanitarian foundation that sought the support of the private sector. Businesses were reluctant to get involved, however, unless the government itself committed fully to the truce.[10]

The truce coincided with a sharp decline in homicides, from a daily average of fourteen to five murders.[11] However, the gangs maintained their stranglehold over local territories, occasioned continued forced displacement, and refused to discontinue extortions.[12] As time went by, a series of clandestine graves were found where the gangs had buried their victims during the truce. The discoveries suggest that the gangs had not substantially diminished their murders, but rather changed their modus operandi.

Salvadoran society remained skeptical of the truce, largely because of its lack of transparency and the uncertainty about the nature of the government's association with it.[13] The Funes administration strenuously denied any involvement, but *El Faro* later disclosed that General Munguía Payés and Raúl Mijango had in fact pushed for the initiative.[14]

Questions also remained as to the actual viability of the truce. Similar schemes have been attempted elsewhere, sometimes with success. Researchers, however, find that such truces often fail and may even result in greater violence because the rebellious nature of gang youths and the tenuous nature of gang leadership make it difficult to control members and ensure their compliance with a ceasefire.[15]

The repeated denials of involvement allowed the Funes government to distance itself from the truce if it backfired, as well as to shield itself from a possible backlash for a perceived negotiation with criminals. At the same time, the ceasefire permitted the government to claim credit for a lowered homicide rate. In July 2013, however, a few weeks after Ricardo Perdomo had replaced David Munguía Payés at the Ministry of Justice and Public Security, El Salvador's murder rate rose sharply, suggesting that the truce was showing signs of crumbling.

Reduced levels of violence were politically convenient for the government, but, as in some other contexts, may also have been motivated by other dynamics. Medellín's unprecedented decline in homicides in 2003 and 2008, for example, was the result both of important investments in public infrastructure and social services in the city's marginal neighborhoods and of changes in the structure of the criminal underworld. Diego Murillo ("Don Berna"), a paramilitary leader whose faction solidified control over the *comunas* (wards), ordered the gangs under his command to commit the least possible violence and thus deflect attention from the drug business.[16] (Murillo was extradited to the United States in 2008 to face drug trafficking charges.)

El Salvador's gang truce, had it been followed by greater social and economic opportunities, could have developed into a sustainable response to the gangs. Instead, it may have contributed to the gangs' continued evolution. Notwithstanding any positive outcomes, such as isolated job creation projects and local community dialogues, the truce sent the message that the state was unable to control violence by institutional means. Further, it made the gangs acutely aware of their political power. This legacy would haunt the Sánchez Cerén government that took power in June 2014.

Three candidates participated in that year's contest: Salvador Sánchez Cerén of the FMLN, a former schoolteacher and guerrilla commander, who served as vice president under Mauricio Funes; former President Antonio Saca, expelled from ARENA in 2009 and founder of the more moderate right-wing Gran Alianza por la Unidad Nacional (Great Alliance for National Unity, or GANA), who ran on a coalition ticket; and Norman Quijano, the ARENA mayor of San Salvador (2009–2015). Antonio Saca turned out to be a weak contender, and the election runoff in March 2014 pitted ARENA against the FMLN.

While Norman Quijano proposed to militarize public security and rejected a gang truce, Salvador Sánchez Cerén promised to "deepen the change" begun by the Funes government, offering to counteract extortion and work toward the social prevention of crime and violence.[17] In an attempt to discredit its opponent ten days prior to the first round of elections, ARENA disseminated "leaked" documents that purported to show that Mauricio Funes and the FMLN had agreed to a voter mobilization with the gangs for the 2009 presidential contest.[18] (It later emerged that after the first round, Norman Quijano proposed a deal to the gangs if they refrained from predisposing voters against ARENA in the runoff election.)[19]

Widespread satisfaction with the Funes government's social policies, corruption allegations against former President Francisco Flores—who died in January 2016—and opinion polls that pointed to the FMLN's clear lead over ARENA created enormous expectations that the left would achieve a landslide victory. However, a combination of factors led to a tight race, including the limited electoral appeal of Salvador Sánchez Cerén; the political instability in Venezuela, a country with which an FMLN government would seek close relations; President Funes's repeated and unlawful campaigning in favor of the FMLN; and ARENA's striking capacity to mobilize voters. Preliminary results suggested a victory for the FMLN, but ARENA claimed massive irregularities had been committed and called on the Armed Forces to intervene and prevent a fraud. The military high command publicly declared that no coup was being plotted, but this tense ending to the electoral process was perhaps a foreboding of the volatile security situation that would await the Sánchez Cerén administration.

A cornerstone of the government's security policy is the Consejo Nacional de Seguridad Ciudadana y Convivencia (National Council of Citizen Security and Coexistence, or CNSCC). Created in September 2014, the Council brings together the state, the private sector, and churches in an effort to facilitate dialogue and consensus on security and justice policies. Its main accomplishment to date has been the development of Plan El Salvador Seguro (Plan for a Safe El Salvador, or PESS), which concentrates on the fifty most violent municipalities.[20] It proposes to recover public spaces, strengthen municipal capacities for the social prevention of crime and violence, create gun-free zones, promote youth employment, and expand community policing. Given very limited public resources, the government unsuccessfully tried to enhance tax collection, even going so far as to publish a treasury list of the largest tax debtors.[21] In the face of corporate resistance, it created a 5 percent telecommunications tax meant to help finance the PESS.

The administration also drafted the Special Law for the Reinsertion of Gang Members and the Prevention of Individuals at Risk, which, if adopted, would offer scholarships, jobs, microcredits, and housing credits, as well as psychological and drug treatment. Its potential impact is unclear, however, given that it would require the target population to be ex–gang members or *pesetas* (those considered traitors by active gang members) and that the private sector has proved reluctant to hire them. In practice, the Sánchez Cerén government's security strategy has not only lacked direction but also embraced Mano Dura even more than its predecessor.

The possibility of a gang truce was rejected, and the breakdown of the initiative saw an escalation of the murder rate throughout 2014 and 2015. Massive prison transfers of gang members aim to isolate them from their social networks on the outside, and the deployment of army elite battalions seeks to support the fight against the gangs. Since the end of the truce, gang attacks on police, and to some extent on soldiers, increased sharply. As of 18 December 2015, sixty-two police officers had been killed, compared to thirty-nine in 2014.[22] Scores of gang members have died in supposed "confrontations" with the security forces, yet the police rarely sustain injuries, much less casualties, in these operations. Although the PNC has insisted that its officers are acting in self-defense, crime scene photos circulating in the social media have raised suspicions that extrajudicial executions of gang members are being disguised as clashes. Journalistic investigations suggest that, at least in some cases, unlawful killings have taken place.[23]

In this polarized social and political environment, the gang policies and programs of the three NGOs in this study have taken very dissimilar paths. FESPAD participated in the forums that prepared the PESS, but not in the Council, which excludes civil society groups from its sessions. Despite a difficult funding context, the organization resumed more of its earlier monitoring and reporting activities. It also began participating in the Civil Society Working Group on Forced Displacement to show that it does not coddle criminals. For the first time, FESPAD also worked with gang members, employing a restorative justice methodology to promote dialogue between the youths and the local community. Residents developed greater trust in the gang members when they were willing to address existing security problems, and the NGO subsequently helped create job projects (a chicken farm and a greenhouse) for the youths. FESPAD continues not only to give human rights workshops to the police, but also to deal with cases of police and military abuse in its legal aid clinic.

Homies Unidos kept working on HIV/AIDS prevention and the culture of peace. After continued difficulties with bakery projects, HU began creating call centers for *pandilleros calmados*. Due to a lack of marketing and soft skills, however, these ventures did not thrive. Full-fledged evaluations of Homies Unidos's work were never carried out because the staff of donor agencies declined to visit gang-affected communities.[24] A change in donor policies deprived the NGO of further funding possibilities, forcing it to close its doors permanently in 2012. Luis continues to share Homies Unidos's experience when invited to events abroad and otherwise survives on odd jobs. With the help of church donations, he has created two basic drug treatment centers for gang and non-gang members. Heriberto, a member of the Dieciocho-Sureños faction, was one of the gang leaders who promoted the truce. Since its collapse, he has been transferred back to the maximum security prison, where he will spend the remainder of his sentence. Miriam reportedly converted to evangelicalism and is working in gang intervention, while María José

(Luis's sister) headed a lesbian rights group. Ultimately, Homies Unidos never learned to function as an NGO, but it served to promote the idea of gang intervention and to help outsiders gain access to gang members. Despite its limitations and its closure, it continues to feature in the best practices brochures of donors.

For the Polígono, gang evolution in La Iberia and elsewhere has necessarily affected the organization's work. With the arrests of many local gang members in the Mano Dura era, staff believe that the community became quieter. But with the release of some gang members, and changing leaderships, La Iberia is also changing. Attitudes toward the Polígono are more antagonistic than in the past. Although gang members are no longer admitted as boarders, they send their families to the Polígono's health clinic and their children to its school as day students. Father Moratalla hopes to keep expanding the educational and cultural activities available to youths from marginal communities. He has created a youth orchestra and choir for students from both the Polígono and public schools in Greater San Salvador. Periodic funding problems, however, have complicated staff retention and program development.

El Salvador's panorama presents many challenges for its citizens and institutions, and it is difficult to see the direction of change. The lack of dignified job opportunities continues to prompt many people to abandon the country, and the gangs continue not only to defy the state more openly, but also to welcome adolescents who find no place in society. Organized crime has, to all appearances, found ample space to operate, but only effective judicial investigations can reveal the nature of these criminal networks and the ways in which they have expanded within the state. For now, parties across the political spectrum have shown little enthusiasm either for appointing an attorney-general with integrity or for seriously considering the creation of an independent investigative mechanism. Rather than leave the fight against corruption and impunity to actors who might have a vested interest in preventing it, Salvadorans need to find new ways of exercising their citizenship and to demand better of those who hold the country's fate in their hands.

Notes

Introduction

1. Although some researchers distinguish between *pandillas* and *maras*, the terms may be used interchangeably. In El Salvador, the word "*mara*" originally denoted a group of people, such as friends or coworkers. Over time, the term became associated with Mara Salvatrucha and Calle Dieciocho in order to distinguish groups with a foreign origin from local street gangs. However, there is great variety among and within all street gangs, and the label "*mara*" is not useful for understanding the characteristics of MS-13 and the Dieciocho. Indeed, the word has acquired a negative connotation, and the Dieciocho rejects its indiscriminate use as being discriminatory.

2. IUDOP, "La delincuencia urbana: Encuesta exploratoria," *ECA* 534–535 (1993): 477.

3. Wim Savenije and Chris van der Borgh, "Youth Gangs, Social Exclusion and the Transformation of Violence in El Salvador," in *Armed Actors: Organized Violence and State Failure in Latin America*, ed. Kees Koonings and Dirk Kruijt (London: Zed Books, 2004), 168.

4. Wim Savenije and Chris van der Borgh, "San Salvador: Violence and Resilience in Gangland—Coping with the Code of the Street," in *Violence and Resilience in Latin American Cities*, ed. Kees Koonings and Dirk Krujt (London: Zed Books, 2015).

5. Sonja Wolf, "Street Gangs of El Salvador," in *Maras: Gang Violence and Security in Central America*, ed. Thomas Bruneau, Lucía Dammert, and Elizabeth Skinner (Austin: University of Texas Press, 2011): 43–69.

6. Juan Gómez Hecht, "El crimen organizado en las cárceles: Las extorsiones desde los Centros Penales en El Salvador (2008–2009)," *Revista Policía y Seguridad Pública* 3.1 (2013): 131–171.

7. Maestría en Psicología Comunitaria de la UCA, *Diagnóstico Sobre la Caracterización de la Población Salvadoreña Retornada con Necesidades de Protección* (San Salvador: UCA, 2014).

8. Jeannette Aguilar and Lissette Miranda, "Entre la articulación y la competencia: Las respuestas de la sociedad civil organizada a las pandillas en El Sal-

vador," in *Maras y pandillas en Centroamérica: Las respuestas de la sociedad civil organizada*, ed. José Miguel Cruz (San Salvador: UCA Editores, 2006), 58.

9. This book is based on nine months of fieldwork conducted in El Salvador between 2005 and 2006. The research included a content analysis of gang-related press coverage, and more than 180 semistructured interviews with government and law enforcement officials, academics, judges, journalists, NGO workers, and ex-gang members. Additional research visits to El Salvador were carried out between 2010 and 2016.

10. See Kerstin Martens, "Mission Impossible? Defining Nongovernmental Organizations," *Voluntas: International Journal of Voluntary and Nonprofit Organizations* 13 (2002): 277–278.

11. James Petras, "Imperialism and NGOs in Latin America," *Monthly Review* 49 (1997): 10–33.

12. Margarita Bosch, "NGOs and Development in Brazil: Roles and Responsibilities in a 'New World Order,'" in *NGOs, States and Donors: Too Close for Comfort?* ed. David Hulme and Michael Edwards (London: Macmillan, 1997); Jenny Pearce, "NGOs and social change: Agents or facilitators?" *Development in Practice* 3 (1993): 224–227.

13. Michael Edwards and David Hulme, "Too Close for Comfort? The Impact of Official Aid on Nongovernmental Organizations," *World Development* 24 (1996): 961–973.

14. David Hulme and Michael Edwards, "Conclusion: Too Close to the Powerful, Too Far from the Powerless?" in *NGOs, States and Donors: Too Close for Comfort?*, ed. David Hulme and Michael Edwards (London: Macmillan, 1997).

15. William Fisher, "Doing Good? The Politics and Antipolitics of NGO Practices," *Annual Review of Anthropology* 26 (1997): 439–464; P. J. Simmons, "Learning to Live with NGOs," *Foreign Policy* 112 (1998): 82–96; Shirin Sinnar, "Mixed Blessing: The Growing Influence of NGOs," *Harvard International Review* 18 (1995–1996): 54–57.

16. Michael Edwards and David Hulme, eds., *Making a Difference: NGOs and Development in a Changing World* (London: Earthscan, 1992); Alan Fowler, *Striking a Balance: A Guide to Enhancing the Effectiveness of Non-Governmental Organisations in International Development* (London: Earthscan, 1997).

17. Michael Edwards and David Hulme, eds., *Beyond the Magic Bullet: NGO Performance and Accountability in the Post-Cold War World* (West Hartford, CT: Kumarian Press, 1996).

18. Alnoor Ebrahim, "Accountability in Practice: Mechanisms for NGOs," *World Development* 31 (2003): 813–829; Margaret Gibelman and Sheldon Gelman, "Very public scandals: Nongovernmental organizations in trouble," *Nonprofit and Voluntary Sector Quarterly* 12 (2001): 49–66.

19. Michael Edwards and David Hulme, "Introduction: NGO Performance and Accountability," in *Beyond the Magic Bullet: NGO Performance and Accountability in the Post-Cold War World*, ed. Edwards and Hulme.

20. Sarah Lister, "The consultation practice of northern NGOs: A study of British organizations in Guatemala," *Journal of International Development* 13 (2001): 1071–1082.

21. Iain Atack, "Four Criteria of Development NGO Legitimacy," *World*

Development 27 (1999): 855–864; John Saxby, "Who Owns the Private Aid Agencies?" in *Compassion and Calculation: The Business of Private Foreign Aid*, ed. David Sogge, Kees Biekart, and John Saxby (London: Pluto Press, 1996).

22. Sarah Lister, "NGO Legitimacy: Technical Issue or Social Construct?" *Critique of Anthropology* 23 (2003): 175–192.

23. Marlon Carranza, "Del asistencialismo a la incidencia y el cabildeo: Las diversas respuestas de la sociedad civil organizada al fenómeno de las pandillas en Honduras," in *Maras y pandillas en Centroamérica: Las respuestas de la sociedad civil organizada*, ed. José Miguel Cruz (San Salvador: UCA Editores, 2006); Emilio Goubaud, "Mesas de mediación y negociación de conflictos con líderes juveniles: El caso de Villa Nueva," in *Juventudes, violencia y exclusión: Desafíos para las Políticas Públicas*, ed. Javier Moreno (Guatemala City: Magna Terra Editores, 2006).

24. Vanessa Johnston, "An Ecuadorian Alternative: Gang Reintegration," in *Small Arms Survey 2010*, ed. Small Arms Survey (Cambridge: Cambridge University Press, 2010); Glaister Leslie, *Confronting the Don: The Political Economy of Gang Violence in Jamaica* (Geneva: Small Arms Survey, 2010); Alfredo Santillán and Soledad Varea, "Estrategias y políticas de inclusión (¿asimilación?) de pandillas en Ecuador: Dos modelos de ciudades, dos visiones sobre las potencialidades de los/as jóvenes pandilleros/as," *URVIO, Revista Latinoamericana de Seguridad Ciudadana* 4 (May 2008): 81–99.

25. Adam Baird, "Negotiating Pathways to Manhood: Rejecting Gangs and Violence in Medellín's Periphery," *Journal of Conflictology* 3.1 (2012): 30–41.

26. Michal Almog-Bar and Hillel Schmid, "Advocacy Activities of Non-profit Human Service Organizations: A Critical Review," *Nonprofit and Voluntary Sector Quarterly* 43.1 (2014): 11–35; Sabine Lang, *NGOs, Civil Society, and the Public Sphere* (New York: Cambridge University Press, 2013).

27. Paul Nelson and Ellen Dorsey, *New Rights Advocacy: Changing Strategies of Development and Human Rights NGOs* (Washington, DC: Georgetown University Press, 2008).

28. Mari Fitzduff and Cheyanne Church, eds., *NGOs at the Table* (Lanham, MD: Rowman and Littlefield, 2004).

29. Peter Gourevitch, David Lake, and Janice Gross Stein, eds., *The Credibility of Transnational NGOs: When Virtue Is Not Enough* (New York: Cambridge University Press, 2012); Amy Risley, *Civil Society Organizations, Advocacy, and Policy Making in Latin American Democracies: Pathways to Participation* (New York: Palgrave Macmillan, 2015); Wendy Wong, *Internal Affairs: How the Structure of NGOs Transforms Human Rights* (Ithaca and London: Cornell University Press, 2012); Xueyong Zhan and Shui-Yan Tang, "Political Opportunities, Resource Constraints and Policy Advocacy of Environmental NGOs in China," *Public Administration* 91.2 (2013): 381–399.

30. Barbara Rugendyke, ed., *NGOs as Advocates for Development in a Globalising World* (London and New York: Routledge, 2007).

31. Victoria Bernal and Inderpal Grewal, eds., *Theorizing NGOs: States, Feminisms, and Neoliberalism* (Durham and London: Duke University Press, 2014).

32. David Lewis and Paul Opoku-Mensah, "Moving forward research agen-

das on international NGOs: Theory, agency and context," *Journal of International Development* 18 (2006): 671.

33. Dorothea Hilhorst, *The Real World of NGOs: Discourses, Diversity and Development* (London: Zed Books, 2003); Stephen Hopgood, *Keepers of the Flame: Understanding Amnesty International* (Ithaca, NY: Cornell University Press, 2006).

34. Malcolm Klein and Cheryl Maxson, *Street Gang Patterns and Policies* (New York: Oxford University Press, 2006), 4.

35. Interview with Milton Vega, rehabilitation officer, CNSP, San Salvador, 7 April 2006.

36. See Tim Delaney, *American Street Gangs* (Upper Saddle River, NJ: Pearson, 2006), ch. 2.

37. James Diego Vigil, *A Rainbow of Gangs: Street Cultures in the Mega-City* (Austin: University of Texas Press, 2002), 36.

38. Originally worn by black urban youths, the zoot suit, with its high-waisted pants and long coat, was adopted by Mexican-Americans in the 1940s. The 1943 riots involved hundreds of Anglo servicemen and citizens who attacked zoot-suited Chicanos. In the aftermath of these violent clashes, many young Mexican-Americans began to idolize the gang members who had defended their neighborhood against the aggressors.

39. Herbert Covey, *Street Gangs Throughout the World* (Springfield, IL: Charles C. Thomas, 2003), 51.

40. Mary Johnson, "National Policies and the Rise of Transnational Gangs," Migration Policy Institute, April 2006, www.migrationpolicy.org /article/national-policies-and-rise-transnational-gangs.

41. Vigil, *A Rainbow of Gangs*, 135–136.

42. On the origins and transformations of Mara Salvatrucha, see T. W. Ward, *Gangsters Without Borders: An Ethnography of a Salvadoran Street Gang* (New York and Oxford: Oxford University Press, 2013).

43. Washington Office on Latin America, *Youth Gangs in Central America* (Washington, DC: WOLA, 2006), 3.

44. Al Valdez, "The Origins of Southern California Latino Gangs," in *Maras: Gang Violence and Security in Central America*, ed. Thomas Bruneau, Lucía Dammert, and Elizabeth Skinner (Austin: University of Texas Press, 2011), 24–26.

45. José Miguel Cruz and Nelson Portillo, *Solidaridad y violencia en las pandillas del gran San Salvador: Más allá de la vida loca* (San Salvador: UCA Editores, 1998), 57–58.

46. The 1996 Illegal Immigration Reform and Immigrant Responsibility Act (IIRIRA) expanded the definition of an aggravated felony, thus triggering mandatory deportation, and was applied retroactively. Any non-US citizen could be repatriated either immediately or after a prison sentence.

47. Elana Zilberg, "Fools Banished from the Kingdom: Remapping Geographies of Gang Violence between the Americas (Los Angeles and San Salvador)," *American Quarterly* 56 (2004): 759–779.

48. Marcela Smutt and Lissette Miranda, *El Fenómeno de las Pandillas en El Salvador* (San Salvador: UNICEF and FLACSO, 1998), 36, 59.

49. Covey, *Street Gangs Throughout the World*, 117.

50. José Luís Rocha, "Violencia y políticas públicas hacia los jóvenes: Las pandillas en Nicaragua," in *Juventudes, Violencia y Exclusión: Desafíos para las Políticas Públicas*, ed. Javier Moro (Guatemala City: MagnaTerra Editores, 2006), 181–182, 195.

51. Frédéric Faux, *Les maras, gangs d'enfants* (Paris: Éditions Autrement Frontières, 2006), 128.

52. On "transnational," see Wim Savenije, "La Mara Salvatrucha y el Barrio 18 St. Fenómenos sociales trasnacionales, respuestas represivas nacionales," *Foreign Affairs En Español* (April–June 2004), www.foreignaffairs-esp.org; on "criminal," see Jorge Fernández and Víctor Ronquillo, *De los Maras a los Zetas: Los secretos del narcotráfico, de Colombia a Chicago* (Mexico City: Random House Mondadori, 2006), 40.

53. World Bank, *El Salvador: Estudio institucional y de gasto público en seguridad y justicia* (Washington, DC: World Bank, 2012), 30.

54. Ibid.

55. Jeannette Aguilar, *Pandillas juveniles transnacionales en Centroamérica, México y Estados Unidos: Diagnóstico de El Salvador* (San Salvador: IUDOP, 2006), 12–17.

56. Telephone interview with Jeanne Rikkers, program director, Fundación Cristosal, San Salvador, 3 December 2015.

57. María Santacruz and Elin Ranum, *"Seconds in the Air": Women Gang-Members and their Prisons* (San Salvador: IUDOP, 2010), 208.

58. Juan José Martínez, *Ver, oír, callar: En las profundidades de una pandilla salvadoreña* (San Salvador: AURA Ediciones, 2013).

59. Mo Hume, "Mano Dura: El Salvador responds to gangs," *Development in Practice* 17.6 (2007): 739–751.

60. Telephone interview with Roberto Valencia, journalist, *El Faro*, San Salvador, 12 December 2015.

61. Smutt and Miranda, *El Fenómeno de las Pandillas*, 143.

62. Joan Moore, *Going Down to the Barrio: Homeboys and Homegirls in Change* (Philadelphia: Temple University Press, 1991), 31.

63. Aguilar and Miranda, "Entre la articulación y la competencia," 43.

64. Ibid., 51–52.

65. Cristian Díaz, "Ministro Payés confirma que militar capturado vendió arma y municiones por $900," *La Prensa Gráfica*, 18 October 2015. www.laprensagrafica.com/2015/10/18/ministro-payes-confirma-que-militar-capturado-vendio-arma-y-municiones-por-900.

66. Cruz and Portillo, *Solidaridad y violencia en las pandillas*, 59.

67. Robert Brenneman, *Homies and Hermanos: God and Gangs in Central America* (New York: Oxford University Press, 2012).

68. Cruz and Portillo, *Solidaridad y violencia en las pandillas*, 155–162.

69. Terence P. Thornberry et al., *Gangs and Delinquency in Developmental Perspective* (Cambridge: Cambridge University Press, 2003), 73.

70. Malcolm Klein, *The American Street Gang: Its Nature, Prevalence, and Control* (New York: Oxford University Press, 1995), 27, 80.

71. María Santacruz and José Miguel Cruz, "Las maras en El Salvador," in

Maras y pandillas en Centroamérica, vol. 1, ed. ERIC, IDESO, IDIES, IUDOP (Managua: UCA Publicaciones, 2001), 37–42.

72. Telephone interview with Jeanne Rikkers, program director, Fundación Cristosal, San Salvador, 3 December 2015.

73. Klein, *The American Street Gang*, 231.

74. Vigil, *A Rainbow of Gangs*, 7.

75. Savenije and van der Borgh, "Youth Gangs," 167.

76. Cruz and Portillo, *Solidaridad y violencia en las pandillas*, 68–69.

77. Smutt and Miranda, *El Fenómeno de las Pandillas*, 137.

78. Shamima Ahmed and David Potter, *NGOs in International Politics* (Bloomfield, CT: Kumarian Press, 2006), 25.

79. John Casey, "Third sector participation in the policy process: A framework for comparative analysis," *Policy & Politics* 32 (2004): 251.

80. On this distinction, see Margaret Keck and Kathryn Sikkink, *Activists Beyond Borders: Advocacy Networks in International Politics* (Ithaca, NY: Cornell University Press, 1998), 25.

Chapter 1

1. Jenny Pearce, *Promised Land: Peasant Rebellion in Chalatenango El Salvador* (London: Latin America Bureau, 1986), 15–16.

2. James Dunkerley, *Power in the Isthmus: A Political History of Modern Central America*, 2nd ed. (London: Verso, 1988), 16.

3. James Mahoney, *The Legacies of Liberalism: Path Dependence and Political Regimes in Central America* (Baltimore: Johns Hopkins University Press, 2001), 12.

4. Ibid., 127, 130.

5. James Dunkerley, *The Long War: Dictatorship and Revolution in El Salvador* (London: Junction Books, 1982), 12.

6. Elisabeth Jean Wood, *Insurgent Collective Action and Civil War in El Salvador* (Cambridge: Cambridge University Press, 2003), 22.

7. Tommie Sue Montgomery, *Revolution in El Salvador: From Civil Strife to Civil Peace*, 2nd ed. (Boulder, CO: Westview Press, 1995), 30.

8. Ibid., 30–32.

9. Mahoney, *The Legacies of Liberalism*, 36.

10. Thomas Anderson, *Matanza*, 2nd ed. (Willimantic, CT: Curbstone Press, 1992), 62–88.

11. Patricia Parkman, *Nonviolent Insurrection in El Salvador: The Fall of Maximiliano Hernández Martínez* (Tucson: University of Arizona Press, 1988), 16–17, 25–26.

12. William Stanley, *The Protection Racket State: Elite Politics, Military Extortion, and Civil War in El Salvador* (Philadelphia: Temple University Press, 1996), 6–7.

13. Héctor Lindo-Fuentes, Erik Ching, and Rafael Lara-Martínez, *Remembering a Massacre in El Salvador: The Insurrection of 1932, Roque Dalton, and the Politics of Historical Memory* (Albuquerque: University of New Mexico Press, 2007), 2.

14. Erik Ching, "Patronage and Politics under General Maximiliano Hernández Martínez, 1931–1939," in *Landscapes of Struggle: Politics, Society, and Community in El Salvador*, ed. Aldo Lauria-Santiago and Leigh Binford (Pittsburg, PA: University of Pittsburgh Press, 2004), 51–52.

15. Lindo-Fuentes, Ching, and Lara-Martínez, *Remembering a Massacre in El Salvador*, ch. 1.

16. Mario Lungo, *El Salvador in the Eighties: Counterinsurgency and Revolution* (Philadelphia: Temple University Press, 1996), 11.

17. Anderson, *Matanza*, 176.

18. Ibid., 114–115.

19. Ibid., 205.

20. Wood, *Insurgent Collective Action*, 24.

21. Roxana Martel, "Las maras salvadoreñas: Nuevas formas de espanto y control social," *ECA* 696 (2006): 961–962.

22. Parkman, *Nonviolent Insurrection in El Salvador*, chs. 5–6.

23. Mahoney, *The Legacies of Liberalism*, 47.

24. Wood, *Insurgent Collective Action*, 25.

25. Walter Lafeber, *Inevitable Revolutions: The United States in Central America*, 2nd ed. (New York: W. W. Norton, 1993), 151, 175.

26. The "Soccer War" was a four-day armed confrontation. In July 1969, land reforms in Honduras forced Salvadoran immigrants to return home, and El Salvador responded with force to claim the seized land as its own. The clashes occurred in the context of the 1970 World Cup qualifying matches.

27. Pearce, *Promised Land*, 24–33.

28. Lungo, *El Salvador in the Eighties*, 11, 117–119.

29. Leigh Binford, *The El Mozote Massacre: Anthropology and Human Rights* (Tucson: University of Arizona Press, 1996), 39, 45–46.

30. Mo Hume, *Armed Violence and Poverty in El Salvador*: A Mini Case Study for the Armed Violence and Poverty Initiative (Bradford: University of Bradford, 2004), www.bradford.ac.uk/acad/cics/publications/AVPI/poverty/AVPI _El_Salvador.pdf, 24.

31. William LeoGrande, *Our Own Backyard: The United States in Central America, 1977–1992* (Chapel Hill: University of North Carolina Press, 1998), 48–49.

32. Charles Brockett, *Political Movements and Violence in Central America* (New York: Cambridge University Press, 2005), 232.

33. Dirk Kruijt, *Guerrillas: War and Peace in Central America* (London and New York: Zed Books, 2008), 35–36.

34. Charles Brockett, *Land, Power, and Poverty: Agrarian Transformation and Political Conflict in Central America* (Boulder, CO: Westview Press, 1998), 135.

35. Wood, *Insurgent Collective Action*, 25, 90.

36. Brockett, *Land, Power, and Poverty*, 137.

37. LeoGrande, *Our Own Backyard*, 39.

38. Jeffery M. Paige, *Coffee and Power: Revolution and the Rise of Democracy in Central America* (Cambridge, MA: Harvard University Press, 1997), 34.

39. LeoGrande, *Our Own Backyard*, 40–42.

40. Elisabeth Jean Wood, "An Insurgent Path to Democracy: Popular Mo-

bilization, Economic Interests, and Regime Transition in South Africa and El Salvador," *Comparative Political Studies* 34 (2001): 870–871.

41. Dunkerley, *Power in the Isthmus*, 401–402.

42. Americas Watch, *El Salvador's Decade of Terror: Human Rights Since the Assassination of Archbishop Romero* (New Haven, CT: Yale University Press, 1991), 119.

43. Binford, *The El Mozote Massacre*.

44. LeoGrande, *Our Own Backyard*, 58.

45. Montgomery, *Revolution in El Salvador*, 132–133.

46. Amnesty International, *El Salvador: "Death Squads"—A Government Strategy* (London: Amnesty International, 1988), 9–10.

47. Truth Commission for El Salvador *From Madness to Hope: The 12-Year War in El Salvador*, UN Security Council (S/25500), 15 March 1993, 358.

48. Americas Watch, *El Salvador's Decade of Terror*, 21.

49. LeoGrande, *Our Own Backyard*, 235.

50. Dunkerley, *The Long War*, 203.

51. Clara Nieto, *Masters of War: Latin America and U.S. Aggression from the Cuban Revolution Through the Clinton Years* (New York: Seven Stories Press, 2003), 375–376.

52. Americas Watch, *El Salvador's Decade of Terror*, 127.

53. LeoGrande, *Our Own Backyard*, 279.

54. Lisa Hall MacLeod, *Constructing Peace: Lessons from UN Peacebuilding Operations in El Salvador and Cambodia* (Oxford: Lexington Books, 2006), 18–19.

55. Montgomery, *Revolution in El Salvador*, 191–192.

56. Teresa Whitfield, *Paying the Price: Ignacio Ellacuria and the Murdered Jesuits of El Salvador* (Philadelphia: Temple University Press, 1995), 252–253, 317–320.

57. Stanley, *The Protection Racket State*, 241.

58. Lungo, *El Salvador in the Eighties*, 24.

59. Martha Doggett, *Death Foretold: The Jesuit Murders in El Salvador* (Washington, DC: Georgetown University Press, 1993), 37.

60. Whitfield, *Paying the Price*, 1–14, 79, 188.

61. See Hall MacLeod, *Constructing Peace*, 21–28.

62. GOES and FMLN, "Peace Agreement between the Government of El Salvador and the FMLN signed on 16 January 1992," reprinted in *The United Nations and El Salvador 1990–1995*, United Nations Blue Book Series, vol. 4 (New York: United Nations, 1995).

63. Hall MacLeod, *Constructing Peace*, 45.

64. CIDAI, "Los acuerdos de paz, diez años después," *ECA* 641–642 (2002): 220–225.

65. Priscilla Hayner, *Unspeakable Truths: Transitional Justice and the Challenge of the Truth Commissions* (New York: Routledge, 2001), 93.

66. Philip Williams and Knut Walter, *Militarization and Demilitarization in El Salvador's Transition to Democracy* (Pittsburgh, PA: University of Pittsburgh Press, 1997), 156–175.

67. Truth Commission, *From Madness to Hope*, 311.

68. Ibid., 357, 359.

69. Ibid., 380, 382.

70. Doggett, *Death Foretold*, 264–266.

71. Hayner, *Unspeakable Truths*, 91.

72. FESPAD, *Estado de la Seguridad Pública y la Justicia Penal en El Salvador, Enero-Agosto 2005* (San Salvador: FESPAD Ediciones, 2005), 64–66.

73. Jack Spence and George Vickers, *A Negotiated Revolution? A Two-Year Progress Report on the Salvadoran Peace Accords* (Cambridge, MA: Hemisphere Initiatives, 1994), 4.

74. Joint Group for the Investigation of Politically Motivated Illegal Armed Groups, *Report of the Joint Group for the Investigation of Politically Motivated Illegal Armed Groups in El Salvador*, UN Security Council (S/1994/989), 28 July 1994, 24.

75. Ibid., 22–23.

76. Ibid., 59.

77. Margaret Popkin, *Peace Without Justice: Obstacles to Building the Rule of Law in El Salvador* (University Park: Penn State University Press, 2000), 26–27.

78. Gino Costa, *La Policía Nacional Civil de El Salvador (1990-1997)* (San Salvador: UCA Editores, 1999), 134.

79. William Stanley, *Risking Failure: The Problems and Promise of the New Civilian Police in El Salvador* (Cambridge, MA: Hemisphere Initiatives, 1993), 15.

80. GOES and FMLN, "Peace Agreement," ch. 2.

81. Costa, *La Policía Nacional Civil*, 195–199.

82. José Miguel Cruz, "Violencia, inseguridad ciudadana y las maniobras de las élites: La dinámica de la reforma policial en El Salvador," in *Seguridad y reforma policial en las Américas*, ed. Lucía Dammert and John Bailey (Mexico City: Siglo XXI Editores, 2005), 240.

83. Costa, *La Policía Nacional Civil*, 189.

84. Ibid., 141, 183–190.

85. Cruz, "Violencia, inseguridad ciudadana y las maniobras de las élites," 256.

86. William Stanley, *Protectors or Perpetrators? The Institutional Crisis of the Salvadoran Civilian Police* (Washington, DC: WOLA and Hemisphere Initiatives, 1996), 10.

87. Costa, *La Policía Nacional Civil*, 203.

88. Ibid., 235, 278–279.

89. Ibid., 237 (note 13), 242, 262, 272.

90. Ibid., 204, 211.

91. Manuel Antonio Garretón, *Incomplete Democracy: Political Democratization in Chile and Latin America* (Chapel Hill: University of North Carolina Press, 2003), 47.

92. Álvaro Artiga, Carlos Dada, David Escobar, and Hugo Martínez, *La polarización política en El Salvador* (San Salvador: FUNDAUNGO, 2007).

93. Ricardo Córdova Macías, Carlos G. Ramos, and Nayelly Loya Marín, "La contribución del proceso de paz a la construcción de la democracia en El Salvador (1992–2004)," in *Construyendo la democracia en sociedades posconflicto: Guatemala y El Salvador, un enfoque comparado*, ed. Dinorah Azpuru et al. (Guatemala City: F&G Editores, 2007), 146–149.

94. Jack Spence, *War and Peace in Central America: Comparing Transitions Toward Democracy and Social Equity in Guatemala, El Salvador, and Nicaragua* (Brookline, MA: Hemisphere Initiatives, 2004), 4; Nataly Guzmán, "Las elecciones presidenciales de 2004: Un estudio desde la prensa escrita," *ECA* 667 (2004): 419–438.

95. Córdova Macías, Ramos, and Loya Marín, "La contribución del proceso de paz," 159–169.

96. FESPAD, *Estado de la Seguridad Pública y la Justicia Penal en El Salvador, Julio 2002–Diciembre 2003* (San Salvador: FESPAD Ediciones, 2004), 114–120.

97. Córdova Macías, Ramos, and Loya Marín, "La contribución del proceso de paz," 145.

98. PDDH, *Violaciones a los derechos humanos por responsabilidad de la Policía Nacional Civil de El Salvador* (San Salvador: PDDH, 2007), 9.

99. José Miguel Cruz, "Los acuerdos de paz, diez años después: Una mirada desde los ciudadanos," *ECA* 641–642 (2002): 237.

100. Latin American Public Opinion Project (LAPOP), *The Political Culture of Democracy in the Americas, 2014* (Nashville, TN: Vanderbilt University, 2014).

101. Córdova Macías, Ramos, and Loya Marín, "La contribución del proceso de paz," 257–258.

102. PNUD, *Informe sobre Desarrollo Humano, El Salvador (IDHES) 2003* (San Salvador: PNUD, 2003), 23.

103. PNUD, *Informe sobre Desarrollo Humano, El Salvador (IDHES) 2001* (San Salvador: PNUD, 2001), 90.

104. DIGESTYC, *Encuesta de Hogares y Propósitos Múltiples 2003* (San Salvador: Ministerio de Economía, 2004), 523.

105. DIGESTYC, *Encuesta de Hogares y Propósitos Múltiples 2014* (San Salvador: Ministerio de Economía, 2015).

106. Ibid., 2.

107. PNUD, *IDHES 2003*, 14.

108. PNUD, *Informe sobre Desarrollo Humano, El Salvador (IDHES) 2013* (San Salvador: PNUD, 2013), 104.

109. Telephone interview with Alexander Segovia, economist, San Salvador, 8 December 2015.

110. Secretaría Técnica y de Planificación de la Presidencia de la República (STPP) and Ministerio de Economía-Dirección General de Estadística y Censos (MINEC-DIGESTYC), *Medición Multidimensional de la Pobreza* (San Salvador: STPP and MINEC-DIGESTYC, 2015).

111. PNUD, *Informe sobre Desarrollo Humano, El Salvador (IDHES) 2005* (San Salvador: PNUD, 2005), 34.

112. Pew Research Center, "Hispanics of Salvadoran Origin in the United States, 2013," 15 September 2015, www.pewhispanic.org/2015/09/15/hispanics-of-salvadoran-origin-in-the-united-states-2013/.

113. PNUD, *IDHES 2001*, 151; PNUD, *IDHES 2005*, 15.

114. PNUD, *IDHES 2013*, 304–305.

115. PNUD, *IDHES 2003*, 35.

116. José Miguel Cruz and Luís Armando González, "Magnitud de la violencia en El Salvador," *ECA* 588 (1997): 960.

117. See Roberto Valencia, "La cifra de salvadoreños asesinados se dispara

un 118% respecto al inicio de 2015," *El Faro*, 1 March 2016, www.elfaro.net /es/201603/el_salvador/18129/La-cifra-de-salvadoreños-asesinados-se-dispara -un-118--respecto-al-inicio-de-2015.htm.

118. PNUD, *¿Cuánto cuesta la violencia a El Salvador?* (San Salvador: PNUD, 2005), 58.

119. Carlos Acevedo, "Los costos económicos de la violencia en El Salvador," in *Economía Política de la Seguridad Ciudadana*, ed. Fernando Carrión and Manuel Dammert (Quito: FLACSO, 2009), 155.

120. Kees Koonings and Dirk Kruijt, "Fractured Cities, Second-Class Citizenship and Urban Violence," in *Fractured Cities: Social Exclusion, Urban Violence and Contested Spaces in Latin America*, ed. Kees Koonings and Dirk Kruijt (London: Zed Books, 2007), 7.

121. José Miguel Cruz, "Los factores posibilitadores y las expresiones de la violencia en los noventa," *ECA* 588 (1997): 989.

122. Cruz, "Violencia, inseguridad ciudadana y las maniobras de las élites," 248.

123. PNUD, *¿Cuánto cuesta la violencia a El Salvador?*, 26, 35.

124. Walter Murcia, *Las pandillas en El Salvador* (Santiago de Chile: Comisión Económica para América Latina y el Caribe, 2015), 22.

125. José Miguel Cruz, "El Salvador," in *La cara de la violencia urbana en América Central*, ed. Fundación Arias (San José: Fundación Arias, 2006), 130.

126. See Valeria Guzmán, "Policía desmiente versión del gobierno de que el 60% de víctimas de homicidios son pandilleros," *El Faro*, 13 July 2015, www .elfaro.net/es/201507/noticias/17173/Policía-desmiente-versión-del-gobierno -de-que-el-60--de-víctimas-de-homicidios-son-pandilleros.htm.

127. IUDOP, *La situación de la seguridad y la justicia, 2009–2014* (San Salvador: IUDOP, 2014).

128. See José Miguel Cruz, "Violencia, democracia y cultura política en América Latina," *ECA* 619–620 (2000): 519.

129. Ibid., 521.

130. Edgardo Amaya Cóbar, "Las políticas de seguridad en El Salvador 1992–2002," in *Seguridad y reforma policial en las Américas*, ed. Lucía Dammert and John Bailey (Mexico City: Siglo XXI Editores, 2005), 223–225.

131. IUDOP, *La situación de la Seguridad y la justicia*, 2.

132. Cruz, "El Salvador," 108, 135.

133. FESPAD, *Primer gobierno de izquierda: Una lectura de derechos humanos al Gobierno de Mauricio Funes (2009–2014)* (San Salvador: FESPAD Ediciones, 2014), 24.

134. Former Deputy Minister for Public Security and Director-General of the PNC Rodrigo Ávila is the owner of several gun shops and private security firms. See Hume, *Armed Violence and Poverty*, 17.

135. Sidney Blanco and Francisco Díaz, *Deficiencias policiales, fiscales o judiciales en la investigación y juzgamiento causantes de impunidad* (San Salvador: PNUD, 2007), 18.

136. Suchit Chávez and Jessica Ávalos, "Los países que no lloran a sus muertos," *La Prensa Gráfica*, 30 March 2014, www.laprensagrafica.com/2014/03/30 /los-paises-que-no-lloran-a-sus-muertos.

137. International Human Rights Clinic, *No Place to Hide: Gang, State,*

and Clandestine Violence in El Salvador (Cambridge, MA: Harvard Law School, 2007), 66–67.

138. Mauricio Sandoval (1999–2003) previously directed the state intelligence apparatus and was named in a confidential Truth Commission report in connection with death squad activities. He resigned from the PNC in 2003 to seek nomination as ARENA's 2004 presidential candidate. Ricardo Menesses (2003–2005) was a member of the Treasury Police and, in principle, barred from joining the PNC. Rodrigo Ávila (1994–1999 and 2006–2008) was previously an ARENA congressman and mayoral candidate and was its 2009 presidential candidate.

139. PDDH, *Violaciones a los derechos humanos*, 11.

140. Spence, *War and Peace in Central America*, 61.

141. IUDOP, *Evaluación Anual de la PNC, 2011* (San Salvador: UCA, 2012), ch. 3.

142. Anonymous interview AI-007, 28 July 2006.

143. Ibid.

144. Héctor Silva, *Infiltrados: Crónica de la corrupción en la PNC (1992–2013)* (San Salvador: UCA Editores, 2014).

145. Interview with Xochitl Marchelli, human rights instructor, ANSP, San Salvador, 4 May 2006.

146. Rachel Neild, "Sustaining Reform: Democratic Policing in Central America," *Citizen Security Monitor* 1.1 (Washington, DC: WOLA, 2002), 4.

147. Córdova Macías, Ramos, and Loya Marín, "La contribución del proceso de paz," 230.

148. PDDH, *Violaciones a los derechos humanos*, 78–79.

149. Nelson Rauda, "Aquí estamos en guerra," *La Prensa Gráfica*, 19 February 2015, www.laprensagrafica.com/2015/02/19/aqui-estamos-en-guerra.

150. PDDH, *Violaciones a los derechos humanos*, 23, 38.

151. Ibid., 9, 23.

152. Ibid., 60–61.

153. Óscar Martínez, "Aquí ya no caben más: Mátenlos," *El Faro*, 2 July 2015, www.salanegra.elfaro.net/es/201507/cronicas/17148/Aquí-ya-no-caben-más-mátenlos.htm.

154. *La Prensa Gráfica*, "Gobierno niega existencia de grupos de exterminio de pandilleros," 19 August 2005.

155. Anonymous interview AI-007, 28 July 2006.

156. Grupo Omega was run by retired army officers, including General Gustavo Perdomo (named in the Truth Commission report for human rights abuses), Major Óscar Peña Durán, and Captain Adolfo Tórrez. (Tórrez was a private security entrepreneur and ARENA's departmental director for San Salvador. In 2010, he was expelled from the party after it was revealed that he had asked a PCN legislator detained in the United States for half a million dollars to make his drug trafficking charges in El Salvador go away. A few weeks later, he was killed under mysterious circumstances.) The intelligence units were located, among other places, at the Interior Ministry, the Treasury, and the Vice Ministry of Transport. An ex-Guardsman, Commissioner García Funes previously acted as PNC deputy director of investigations, PNC deputy director of

specialized areas, and director of the Transnational Anti-Gang Center. He is currently the PNC's head of the Western Region. Commissioner Tobar Prieto is an ex-National Policeman and previously acted as PNC deputy director of investigations, PNC deputy director-general, and PNC director-general. He is currently an adviser in the Ministry of Justice and Public Security.

157. Dolores Albiac, "Los ricos más ricos de El Salvador," *ECA* 612 (1999): 841–864; Carlos Paniagua, "El bloque empresarial hegemónico salvadoreño," *ECA* 645–646 (2002): 609–693.

158. Alexander Segovia, "Integración real y grupos centroamericanos de poder económico. Implicaciones para la democracia y el desarrollo regional," *ECA* 691–692 (2006): 533–534.

159. Ibid., 539, 545.

160. Telephone interview with Alexander Segovia, economist, San Salvador, 8 December 2015. See also Efren Lemus, "La millonaria revolución de Alba," *El Faro*, 19 January 2014, www.elfaro.net/es/201401/noticias/14423/La-millonaria -revolución-de-Alba.htm.

161. Segovia, "Integración real," 550.

162. Ibid., 546.

163. IUDOP, "La transparencia en el Estado salvadoreño: La perspectiva de los empresarios," *Boletín de prensa* Año 20, No. 1 (San Salvador: IUDOP, 2005), 7–8.

164. Las Dignas, FESPAD, and IDHUCA, eds., *El Salvador por dentro* (San Salvador: UCA, 2005), 122–123.

165. See Paul Almeida, *Waves of Protest: Popular Struggle in El Salvador, 1925–2005* (Minneapolis: University of Minnesota Press, 2008), 213.

166. Luís Armando González and Roxana Martel, "Pobreza y sociedad civil: El caso de El Salvador," *ECA* 659 (2003): 897.

167. Aguilar and Miranda, "Entre la articulación y la competencia," 73.

168. Jenny Pearce, "From civil war to 'civil society': Has the end of the Cold War brought peace to Central America?" *International Affairs* 74 (1998): 599.

169. Ibid., 614.

170. Córdova Macías, Ramos, and Loya Marín, "La contribución del proceso de paz," 211.

171. Centre for International Studies, *Engagement with Civil Society in Central America: Perspectives of Central American CSOs* (Dublin: Dublin City University, 2007), 29–30.

172. Ibid., 20.

173. Ibid., 34.

Chapter 2

1. *El Diario de Hoy*, "Barrerán a las maras," 24 July 2003, 2–3.

2. *La Prensa Gráfica*, "'Mano Dura' contra mareros," 24 July 2003, 2–3.

3. IDHUCA, "Análisis de la Ley Antimaras," *Proceso* No. 1062, 27 August 2003, www.uca.edu.sv/publica/proceso/proc1062.html.

4. Asamblea Legislativa, *Ley Anti Maras*, Decreto No. 158 (*Diario Ofi-*

cial, 10 October 2003); *La Prensa Gráfica*, "Flores insiste en la ley antimaras," 13 September 2003, 18.

5. PDDH, *Demanda de inconstitucionalidad contra la Ley Antimaras* (San Salvador: PDDH, 2003), www.pddh.gob.sv. On the judges' position, see *La Prensa Gráfica*, "Jueces: ley no se puede aplicar," 10 October 2003, 13.

6. Corte Suprema de Justicia, *Sentencia de Inconstitucionalidad 52-2003/56-2003/57-2003*, 1 April 2004, www.jurisprudencia.gob.sv.

7. Asamblea Legislativa, *Ley para el Combate de las Actividades Delincuenciales de Grupos o Asociaciones Ilícitas Especiales*. Decreto No. 305 (*Diario Oficial*, 2 April 2004).

8. United Nations Committee on the Rights of the Child (UNCRC), *36th session, Consideration of reports submitted by states parties under Article 44 of the Convention. Concluding Observations: El Salvador*, CRC/C/15/Add.232, 30 June 2004, www.un.org, 15.

9. *El Diario de Hoy*, "Bajaron crímenes, asegura Menesses," 16 August 2003, 3.

10. Sydney Blanco, "Apuntes sobre la Ley Antimaras," *ECA* 663–664 (2004): 134–135.

11. FESPAD, *Estado de la Seguridad Pública y la Justicia Penal en El Salvador, 2004* (San Salvador: FESPAD Ediciones, 2005), 13.

12. José Miguel Cruz, "El Salvador," in *La cara de la violencia urbana en América Central*, ed. Fundación Arias (San José: Fundación Arias, 2006), 113.

13. Julian V. Roberts et al., *Penal Populism and Public Opinion: Lessons from Five Countries* (Oxford: Oxford University Press, 2003), 5, 66.

14. CIDAI, "Las elecciones municipales y legislativas del 16 de marzo de 2003," *ECA* 653–654 (2003): 178–184.

15. Consejo de Redacción, "Juicio político sobre las elecciones 2003," *ECA* 653–654 (2003): 169.

16. IUDOP, "Las preferencias políticas en octubre de 2003: la mano dura de ARENA," *ECA* 660 (2003): 1075.

17. Ibid.; IUDOP, "Opinión pública a finales de 2003 y preferencias electorales: encuesta de evaluación de fin de año," *ECA* 661–662 (2003): 1237.

18. IUDOP, "Las preferencias políticas en octubre de 2003," 1075.

19. IUDOP, "Los salvadoreños frente a las elecciones presidenciales de 2004," *Boletín de prensa* Año 18, No. 3 (San Salvador: IUDOP, 2003), 2.

20. Ibid., 4–6.

21. IUDOP, "Las preferencias políticas en octubre de 2003," 1073.

22. *La Prensa Gráfica*, "ARENA a pescar votos con el plan antimaras," 13 August 2003, 14.

23. José Miguel Cruz, "Las elecciones presidenciales desde el comportamiento de la opinión pública," *ECA* 665–666 (2004): 266.

24. GOES, *País Seguro: Plan de Gobierno 2004–2009* (San Salvador: GOES, 2004), 8.

25. See José Miguel Cruz and Marlon Carranza, "Pandillas y políticas públicas: El caso de El Salvador," in *Juventudes, Violencia y Exclusión: Desafíos para las Políticas Públicas*, ed. Javier Moro (Guatemala City: MagnaTerra Editores, 2006), 153.

26. MINGOB, *Construyendo juntos una política de prevención, atención y control de la violencia* (San Salvador: mimeo, 2004), 14–22.

27. *El Diario de Hoy*, "Se inicia la Súper Mano Dura," 31 August 2004, 2–3.

28. *La Prensa Gráfica*, "Libres primeros pandilleros del Supermano Dura," 3 September 2004, 12.

29. GOES, *País Seguro*, 40–41.

30. SJ, *Estudios de Base Jóvenes 2005: Informe de Resultados de la Encuesta Nacional de Juventud* (San Salvador: SJ, 2005).

31. SJ, *Plan Nacional de Juventud 2005–2015* (San Salvador: SJ, 2005).

32. Ibid., 3.

33. Ibid., 5.

34. Interviews with César Funes, youth secretary; Juan Carlos Barahona, youth welfare coordinator; Arthur Guth, Mano Amiga coordinator, Secretaría de la Juventud, San Salvador, 30 January 2006.

35. Interview with María Teresa de Mejía, legislation and public policy officer, UNICEF, San Salvador, 20 April 2006.

36. Sergio Arauz, "Secretaría de la Juventud se promociona a un costo inexplicable," *El Faro*, 26 May 2008.

37. Interviews with Anja Kramer, consultant for local economic development and employment, GTZ, San Salvador, 27 February 2006; Xochitl Marchelli, human rights instructor, ANSP, San Salvador, 4 May 2006, 19 June 2006.

38. Irving Spergel, *The Youth Gang Problem: A Community Approach* (New York: Oxford University Press, 1995), 292.

39. Klein and Maxson, *Street Gang Patterns and Policies*, 239–241.

40. Interview with Salvador Hernández, director, MOJE, Ilobasco, 11 July 2006.

41. Interview with Xochitl Marchelli, human rights instructor, ANSP, San Salvador, 4 May 2006, 19 June 2006.

42. Interview with Anja Kramer, consultant for local economic development and employment, GTZ, San Salvador, 27 February 2006.

43. Interview with Xochitl Marchelli, human rights instructor, ANSP, San Salvador, 4 May 2006, 19 June 2006.

44. Interview with Idalia Argueta, high-risk youth program coordinator, CRISPAZ, San Salvador, 9 May 2006.

45. Interview with Mauricio Figueroa, director, Fundación Quetzalcoatl, San Salvador, 25 May 2006.

46. Interview with Salvador Hernández, director, MOJE, Ilobasco, 11 July 2006.

47. Interview with Verónica Hill, youth program coordinator, Office of the Mayor of San Salvador, San Salvador, 14 June 2006.

48. Interviews with Verónica Hill, youth program coordinator, Office of the Mayor of San Salvador, San Salvador, 14 June 2006; Carlos Rivas, pastor general, Tabernáculo Bautista de Avivamiento, San Bartolo, Ilopango, 6 June 2006.

49. Interview with Tránsito Ruano, director, Centro de Formación y Capacitación de la Vicaría Divino Salvador, Archdiocese of San Salvador, San Salvador, 14 February 2006.

50. I requested evaluations of the Youth Secretariat through the Access to Public Information Law, but no evaluations were said to exist.

51. Popkin, *Peace Without Justice*, 192.

52. Amaya Cóbar, "Las políticas de seguridad en El Salvador 1992–2002," 222.

53. Interview with Armando Jiménez, executive director, CNSP, San Salvador, 5 July 2005.

54. Interview with Óscar Bonilla, president, CNSP, San Salvador, 31 March 2006.

55. Anonymous interview AI-008, 12 June 2006.

56. A list of communities marked for inclusion/exclusion was supplied by a CNSP staff member.

57. Anonymous interviews AI-005, 7 June 2006, and AI-008, 12 June 2006.

58. Anonymous interview AI-008, 12 June 2006.

59. CNSP and EU, *ProJóvenes de El Salvador. SLV/B7–3100/99/0133. Plan Operativo Anual* (San Salvador: mimeo, 2005), 2.

60. Ibid., 8.

61. EU, *Evaluación Final Proyecto ProJóvenes I* (San Salvador: Unión Europea, 2011).

62. Anonymous interview AI-005, 7 June 2006.

63. Interview with Óscar Bonilla, president, CNSP, San Salvador, 31 March 2006.

64. Anonymous interview AI-008, 12 June 2006.

65. Suchit Chávez, "14 voluntarios de provención de la violencia asesinados," *La Prensa Gráfica*, 15 February 2011, www.laprensagrafica.com/el-salvador/judicial/171915-14-voluntarios-de-prevencion-de-la-violencia-asesinados.html.

66. EU, *Evaluación Final Proyecto ProJóvenes II* (San Salvador: Unión Europea, 2014).

67. Telephone interview with Layla Parada, territorial supervisor, Social Prevention of Violence Program, CNSP, 6 December 2015.

68. Valeria Guzmán, "Nieta del presidente fue nombrada subdirectora del Injuve a pesar de no cumplir los requisitos," *El Faro*, 5 January 2015, www.elfaro.net/es/201501/noticias/16426/Nieta-del-presidente-fue-nombrada-subdirectora-del-Injuve-a-pesar-de-no-cumplir-los-requisitos.htm.

69. Ricardo Flores, "Fallece Óscar Bonilla, Ex Presidente CNSP," *La Prensa Gráfica*, 28 December 2010, www.laprensagrafica.com/el-salvador/politica/161253-fallece-oscar-bonilla-ex-presidente-cnsp.

70. Anonymous interview AI-013, 11 April 2006.

71. Telephone interview with Layla Parada, territorial supervisor, Social Prevention of Violence Program, CNSP, 6 December 2015.

72. Interview with Armando Echeverría, director of rehabilitation, CNSP, 25 January 2006.

73. Anonymous interview BI-001, 30 May 2006.

74. Interview with Óscar Bonilla, president, CNSP, San Salvador, 31 March 2006.

75. Interview with Lilian Vega, lecturer in economics, UCA, San Salvador, 2 May 2006.

76. Conversation with Gissele Moreno de Domínguez, coordinator, *granja-escuela*, Izalco, 17 February 2006.

77. Anonymous interview AI-012, 19 July 2005.

78. Anonymous interviews AI-004, 17 February 2006, and AI-013, 11 April 2006.

79. Anonymous interview AI-013, 7 April 2006.

80. Conversation with Omar Calix, supervisor, *granja-escuela*, Izalco, 13 June 2006.

81. Anonymous interview AI-013, 11 April 2006.

82. Interview with Armando Echeverría, director of rehabilitation, CNSP, 25 January 2006.

83. Interview with Armando Echeverría, director of rehabilitation, CNSP, 25 January 2006.

84. Telephone interview with Layla Parada, territorial supervisor, Social Prevention of Violence Program, CNSP, 6 December 2015.

85. Conversation with Armando Echeverría, director of rehabilitation, CNSP, 25 February 2006.

86. Anonymous interview AI-005, 7 June 2006.

87. *La Prensa Gráfica/Enfoques*, "Una ley revistida de muchas dudas y polémica," 24 August 2003, 6–8.

88. Aguilar and Miranda, "Entre la articulación y la competencia," 62.

89. Daniel Valencia, "El Salvador arrasa en informe sobre violencia," *El Faro*, 15 December 2008, archivo.elfaro.net/secciones/Noticias/20081215/noticias2_20081215.asp.

90. IUDOP, "Los salvadoreños evalúan la situación del país a finales de 2005 y opinan sobre las elecciones de 2006," *Boletín de prensa* Año 20, No. 3 (San Salvador: IUDOP, 2005), 4.

91. *El Diario de Hoy*, "Relanzarán Plan Súper Mano Dura," 21 December 2005, 12.

92. *La Prensa Gráfica*, "Remezón en área de seguridad pública," 20 December 2005, 2; *El Diario de Hoy*, "Inicia operaciones el grupo especial contra extorsión," 14 February 2006, 12.

93. Interview with Commissioner Óscar Chávez Valiente, secretary-general, PNC, San Salvador, 3 July 2006.

94. *La Prensa Gráfica*, "'Mano Dura' contra mareros," 24 July 2003, 2–3.

95. *El Diario de Hoy*, "Crean alianza contra las maras en C.A.," 5 April 2006, 2–3.

96. *El Diario de Hoy*, "Revive presunto vínculo Al Qaeda-MS," 15 February 2005, 12.

97. See David Whittaker, ed., *The Terrorism Reader*, 2nd ed., (London: Routledge, 2003), 5.

98. Telephone interview with Roberto Valencia, journalist, *El Faro*, 12 December 2015.

99. Interview with David LeValley, supervisory special agent, MS-13 National Gang Task Force, FBI, Washington, DC, 21 October 2005.

100. *La Prensa Gráfica*, "PNC compara pandillas con crimen organizado," 22 August 2003, 12.

101. Klein, *The American Street Gang*, 27.

102. Klein and Maxson, *Street Gang Patterns and Policies*, 186.

103. Aguilar, *Pandillas juveniles transnacionales*, 48.

104. Douglas Farah, "Organized Crime in El Salvador: Its Homegrown and Transnational Dimensions," in *Organized Crime in Central America: The Northern Triangle*, ed. Cynthia Arnson and Eric Olson (Washington, DC: Woodrow Wilson Center, 2011).

105. Thomas Bruneau, "The *Maras* and National Security in Central America," *Strategic Insights* IV (May 2005): 4.

106. Aguilar, *Pandillas juveniles transnacionales*, 29–30.

107. Héctor Silva, "El Viejo Santos y la revitalización de las clicas de Maryland," *Revista Factum*, 13 July 2015. revistafactum.com/el-viejo-santos-y-la -revitalizacion-de-las-clicas-de-maryland/.

108. For some of these initiatives, see Federico Brevé, "The *Maras*: A Menace to the Americas," *Military Review* (July–August 2007): 91–92.

109. The PNC and the FBI did not respond to my interview requests made in December 2015.

110. Peter Meyer and Clare Ribando Seelke, *Central America Regional Security Initiative: Background and Policy Issues for Congress*, CRS Report for Congress R41731, 6 May (Washington, DC: CRS, 2014).

111. Interview with Brian Duggan, director, Bureau for International Narcotics and Law Enforcement Affairs, US Embassy, San Salvador, 28 April 2006.

112. *El Mundo*, "El Salvador expone trabajo antipandillas," 3 April 2006.

113. *La Prensa Gráfica*, "Finaliza cumbre con impulso a centro CAT," 27 April 2007.

114. I requested information on the annual gang conference under the Access to Public Information Law, but the PNC claimed not to know anything about the event.

115. Samuel Logan, *This Is for the Mara Salvatrucha: Inside the MS-13, America's Most Violent Gang* (New York: Hyperion, 2009).

116. US Department of the Treasury, "Treasury Sanctions Latin American Criminal Organization," 10 November 2012, www.treasury.gov/press-center /press-releases/Pages/tg1733.aspx.

117. Interview with David LeValley, supervisory special agent, MS-13 National Gang Task Force, FBI, Washington, DC, 21 October 2005.

118. Tom Diaz, *No Boundaries: Transnational Latino Gangs and American Law Enforcement* (Ann Arbor: University of Michigan Press, 2009).

119. Ibid.

120. Celinda Franco, *The MS-13 and 18th Street Gangs: Emerging Transnational Gang Threats?* CRS Report for Congress RL34233, 30 January (Washington, DC: CRS, 2008), 8.

121. *La Prensa Gráfica*, "PNC compara pandillas con crimen organizado," 22 August 2003, 12.

122. Asamblea Legislativa, *Ley Contra el Crimen Organizado y Delitos de Realización Compleja*, Decreto No. 190 (*Diario Oficial*, 10 January 2007).

123. Interview with David LeValley, supervisory special agent, MS-13 National Gang Task Force, FBI, Washington, DC, 21 October 2005.

124. Interview with David LeValley, supervisory special agent, MS-13 National Gang Task Force, FBI, Washington, DC, 21 October 2005.

125. Klein and Maxson, *Street Gang Patterns and Policies*, 241.

126. Klein, *The American Street Gang*, 62.

127. Federal Law Enforcement Training Centers (FLETC), "ILEA San Salvador," www.fletc.gov.

128. Interview with Mauricio Cosme Merino, secretary-general, ANSP, Santa Tecla, 4 July 2006.

129. Wes Enzinna, "Another SOA? A Police Academy in El Salvador Worries Critics," *NACLA Report on the Americas* 41 (March–April 2008), www.nacla.org.

130. Carl Meacham, *The Mérida Initiative: "Guns, Drugs, and Friends,"* Report to the Senate Committee on Foreign Relations, 21 December 2007, www.gpo.gov/fdsys/pkg/CPRT-110SPRT39644/pdf/CPRT-110SPRT39644.pdf, 70.

131. Ibid., 52.

132. Interview with Xochitl Marchelli, human rights instructor, ANSP, San Salvador, 4 May 2006.

133. Meacham, *The Mérida Initiative*, 68.

134. Ibid., 54.

135. Kenneth Kaiser, *Statement before the House Committee on Foreign Affairs, Subcommittee on the Western Hemisphere*, 7 February 2008, www2.fbi.gov/congress/congress08/kaiser020708.htm.

136. *El Diario de Hoy*, "EE.UU. ayuda a investigar 17 homicidios y extorsiones," 2 November 2007, www.elsalvador.com.

137. Carlos Martínez and José Luis Sanz, "Te daban patadas en la cara, culatazos, te rociaban gas pimienta en el ano . . . ," *El Faro*, 8 October 2012, www.salanegra.elfaro.net/es/201210/entrevistas/9839/.

138. Klein, *The American Street Gang*, 191–192.

139. Kate Mather, "LAPD urges officers to be community guardians, not warriors on crime," *Los Angeles Times*, 21 August 2015, www.latimes.com/local/crime/la-me-warrior-guardians-20150821-story.html.

140. *El Diario de Hoy*, "Policías de EE.UU. se podrían integrar a Centro Antipandilla," 7 April 2008, www.elsalvador.com.

141. Geoff Thale, *Testimony before the House Committee on Foreign Affairs, Subcommittee on the Western Hemisphere (Hearing on "Central America and the Mérida Initiative")*, 8 May 2008, archives.republicans.foreignaffairs.house.gov/110/tha050808.htm.

142. Steven Boraz and Thomas Bruneau, "Are the *Maras* Overwhelming Governments in Central America?" *Military Review* (November–December 2006): 38.

143. International Human Rights Clinic, *No Place to Hide*, 46.

144. Ibid., 49–52.

145. Klein, *The American Street Gang*, 43–45.

146. Aguilar, *Pandillas juveniles transnacionales*, 3.

147. Interview with Guillermo García, president, AEIPES, San Salvador, 5 May 2006.

148. Hume, "*Mano Dura*: El Salvador responds to gangs," 739.

149. *La Prensa Gráfica*, "Gobierno niega existencia de grupos de exterminio de pandilleros," 19 August 2005.

150. *Diario Co-Latino*, "Aparece grupo de exterminio de pandilleros," 10 November 2005.

151. *Diario Co-Latino*, "'Sombra Negra' amenaza a extorsionistas y pandilleros," 1 September 2006.

152. *El Faro*, "Sicarios: ¿otra realidad de la violencia?" 18 July 2005.

Chapter 3

1. Ciaran McCullagh, *Media Power: A Sociological Introduction* (Basingstoke: Palgrave, 2002), 26.

2. David Croteau and William Hoynes, *Media/Society: Industries, Images, and Audiences*, 3rd ed. (London: Sage, 2003), 298.

3. Katherine Beckett and Theodore Sasson, *The Politics of Injustice: Crime and Punishment in America* (Thousand Oaks, CA: Pine Forge Press, 2000), 84.

4. Sallie Hughes, *Newsrooms in Conflict: Journalism and the Democratization of Mexico* (Pittsburgh, PA: University of Pittsburgh Press, 2006), 197.

5. Silvio Waisbord, *Watchdog Journalism in South America: News, Accountability, and Democracy* (New York: Columbia University Press, 2000), 5.

6. Carlos Chamorro, *El Poder de la Prensa* (Managua: mimeo, 2002), 18; Waisbord, *Watchdog Journalism*, 63.

7. Anne Germain Lefèvre, "Promoting Independent Media in El Salvador," in *Promoting Democracy in Postconflict Societies*, ed. Jeroen de Zeeuw and Krishna Kumar (Boulder, CO: Lynne Rienner, 2006), 240–241.

8. Ibid., 241.

9. Interview with Paolo Luers, journalist, *El Faro*, San Salvador, 27 May 2006.

10. Rick Rockwell and Noreene Janus, *Media Power in Central America* (Urbana and Chicago: University of Illinois Press, 2003), 137.

11. Interviews with Jaime López, director, Probidad, San Salvador, 19 June 2006; Nelson López, editor-in-chief, *Diario Co-Latino*, San Salvador, 28 April 2006.

12. Interview with Mauricio Funes, TV journalist, San Salvador, 20 June 2006.

13. Telephone interview with Alexander Renderos, journalist, San Salvador, 1 December 2015.

14. Delmy Peraza, "Derecho a la información y rendimiento de cuentas en Centroamérica," *ECA* 635 (2001): 817.

15. Jimmy Alvarado, "Así obstaculiza el gobierno el acceso a la información," *El Faro*, 19 October 2014, www.elfaro.net/es/201410/noticias/16050/Así-obstaculiza-el-gobierno-el-acceso-a-la-información.htm.

16. Lawrence Ladutke, *Freedom of Expression in El Salvador: The Struggle for Human Rights and Democracy* (London: McFarland & Co., 2004), 56.

17. Interview with Wilfredo Hernández, journalist, *El Diario de Hoy*, San Salvador, 16 June 2006.

18. On news routines, see Charlotte Ryan, *Prime Time Activism: Media Strategies for Grassroots Organizing* (Boston, MA: South End Press, 1991), 141–149.

19. Eoin Devereux, *Understanding the Media* (London: Sage, 2003), 7.

20. Croteau and Hoynes, *Media/Society*, 169.

21. Rockwell and Janus, *Media Power in Central America*, 200.

22. Ibid.

23. Interview with Antonio Herrera, president, APES, San Salvador, 1 July 2005.

24. Telephone interview with José Luis Sanz, director, *El Faro*, San Salvador, 4 December 2015.

25. Interview with Carlos Dada, director, *El Faro*, San Salvador, 24 May 2006.

26. Newspaper salaries range from about US $500–700/month to about US $2,000 for editors and directors. Salaries for television reporters start at US $250–300/month and can reach US $500–600/month. Radio journalists receive about US $500–650/month. Interview with Jaime Revelo, interview producer, Radio YSUCA, San Salvador, 1 December 2015.

27. Carlos Chamorro and Alberto Arene, *El turno de los medios* (Managua: mimeo, 2001), 12–13.

28. Chamorro, *El Poder de la Prensa*, 25.

29. Interview with Wilfredo Hernández, journalist, *El Diario de Hoy*, San Salvador, 16 June 2006.

30. Interview with Mauricio Funes, TV journalist, San Salvador, 20 June 2006.

31. Interview with José Luís Sanz, deputy director of information, *La Prensa Gráfica*, San Salvador, 27 May 2006.

32. Interview with Carlos Dada, director, *El Faro*, San Salvador, 24 May 2006.

33. Interview with Mauricio Funes, TV journalist, San Salvador, 20 June 2006.

34. Telephone interview with Serafin Valencia, president, APES, San Salvador, 7 December 2015.

35. Telephone interview with Roberto Valencia, journalist, *El Faro*, San Salvador, 12 December 2015.

36. Interview with Mauricio Funes, TV journalist, San Salvador, 20 June 2006.

37. On alternative media, see Waisbord, *Watchdog Journalism*, 27.

38. Interview with Mauricio Funes, TV journalist, San Salvador, 20 June 2006.

39. Interview with Carlos Dada, director, *El Faro*, San Salvador, 24 May 2006.

40. Interview with Nelson López, editor-in-chief, *Diario Co-Latino*, San Salvador, 28 April 2006.

41. World Bank, "Data on Internet users (per 100 people)," http://data.worldbank.org/indicator/IT.NET.USER.P2.

42. Interview with Héctor Vides, executive director, ARPAS, San Salvador, 14 July 2005.

43. Interview with Mauricio Funes, TV journalist, San Salvador, 20 June 2006.

44. Rockwell and Janus, *Media Power in Central America*, 44, 49.

45. Chamorro, *El Poder de la Prensa*, 23.

46. On *oficialista* or pro-government journalism, see Daniel Hallin, "Media, political power, and democratisation in Mexico," in *De-Westernizing Media Studies*, ed. James Curran and Myung-Jin Park (London: Routledge, 2000), 99.

47. Rockwell and Janus, *Media Power in Central America*, 45.

48. Guillermo Mejía and Raúl Gutiérrez, *Medios y democracia* (San Salvador: mimeo, 2005), 13.

49. Interview with Carlos Dada, director, *El Faro*, San Salvador, 24 May 2006.

50. Telephone interview with Alexander Renderos, journalist, San Salvador, 1 December 2015.

51. Waisbord, *Watchdog Journalism*, 5–6.

52. Croteau and Hoynes, *Media/Society*, 72.

53. Interview with Mauricio Funes, TV journalist, San Salvador, 20 June 2006.

54. Telephone interview with Serafin Valencia, president, APES, San Salvador, 7 December 2015.

55. Interview with Paolo Luers, journalist, *El Faro*, San Salvador, 27 May 2006.

56. Interview with Mauricio Funes, TV journalist, San Salvador, 20 June 2006.

57. Interview with Jaime López, director, Probidad, San Salvador, 19 June 2006.

58. Interview with Wilfredo Hernández, journalist, *El Diario de Hoy*, San Salvador, 16 June 2006.

59. The daily editions of each newspaper were scanned for items that referred to the gangs and gang control programs. Material included articles, editorials, opinion columns, features, photo essays, surveys, and paid advertisements. Photos were considered with the text as a single unit of analysis. Articles that referred to the gang problem elsewhere—notably in other Central American countries, Mexico, and the United States—were included because they aided in buttressing pro–Mano Dura coverage in El Salvador. A total of 2,874 items were chosen and then subjected to a close reading. Overall, I was interested in the ways in which linguistic devices, visual imagery, and reportorial practices portrayed gang members as destructive outsiders detached from the rest of society, a portrayal that would elicit public aversion to them and legitimize a fundamentally punitive state response.

60. Croteau and Hoynes, *Media/Society*, 126–129.

61. Nick Davies, *Flat Earth News: An Award-Winning Reporter Exposes Falsehood, Distortion and Propaganda in the Global Media* (London: Chatto & Windus, 2008), 114, 136.

62. Interview with José Luís Sanz, deputy director of information, *La Prensa Gráfica*, San Salvador, 27 May 2006.

63. *La Prensa Gráfica*, *Proyecto institucional "Todos contra la violencia"* (San Salvador: mimeo, 2006).

64. *La Prensa Gráfica, Manual para el Tratamiento Informativo de la Violencia* (San Salvador: mimeo, 2005).

65. John Tagg, *The Burden of Representation: Essays on Photographies and Histories* (Basingstoke: Palgrave Macmillan, 1988), 99.

66. Stanley Cohen, *Folk Devils and Moral Panics: The Creation of the Mods and Rockers* (Oxford: Martin Robertson: 1980 [1972]), 9.

67. Robert Reiner, "Media Made Criminality: The Representation of Crime in the Mass Media," in *The Oxford Handbook of Criminology*, ed. Mike Maguire, Rod Morgan, and Robert Reiner (Oxford: Oxford University Press, 2002), 404.

68. Gobernación emerged in 2001 when the Ministry of Public Security and Justice and the Ministry of the Interior were merged. In 2006, all security and justice attributions were placed with the newly created Ministry of Justice and Public Security.

69. Irene Vasilachis de Gialdino, "Representations of young people associated with crime in El Salvador's written press," *Critical Discourse Studies* 4 (2007): 4–5.

70. Klein and Maxson, *Street Gang Patterns and Policies*, 169.

71. Ibid., 165.

72. Tutela Legal, *La violencia homicida y otros patrones de grave afectación a los derechos humanos en El Salvador: Año 2006* (San Salvador: Tutela Legal, 2007), 36.

73. Klein, *The American Street Gang*, 29.

74. See Klein and Maxson, *Street Gang Patterns and Policies*, 71.

75. Martel, "Las maras salvadoreñas," 963.

76. Klein, *The American Street Gang*, 22.

77. Klein and Maxson, *Street Gang Patterns and Policies*, 81.

78. Tutela Legal, *La violencia homicida*, 32.

79. Nielan Barnes, *Transnational Youth Gangs in Central America, Mexico and the United States: Executive Summary* (Mexico City: ITAM, 2006), 8.

80. Klein and Maxson, *Street Gang Patterns and Policies*, 186.

81. UNODC, *Crime and Development in Central America: Caught in the Crossfire* (Vienna: UNODC, 2007), 63.

82. Klein and Maxson, *Street Gang Patterns and Policies*, 195.

83. *El Diario de Hoy*, "Homicidios: Víctimas tienen entre 15 y 39 años," 27 June 2005, http://archivo.elsalvador.com/noticias/2005/06/27/nacional/nac1 .asp.

84. UNODC, *Crime and Development in Central America*, 61.

85. Cohen, *Folk Devils and Moral Panics*, 10.

86. Matthew Bunson, *The Vampire Encyclopaedia* (London: Thames and Hudson, 1993), 262–264.

87. On episodic and thematic framing, see Shanto Iyengar, *Is Anyone Responsible? How Television Frames Political Issues* (Chicago: University of Chicago Press, 1991), 14.

88. Ibid., 16.

89. José Miguel Cruz, "Los factores asociados a las pandillas juveniles en Centroamérica," *ECA* 685–686 (2005): 1172–1174.

90. Ibid., 1165.

91. Ibid., 1162.
92. Ibid.; Smutt and Miranda, *El Fenómeno de las Pandillas en El Salvador*, 61–75.
93. José Miguel Cruz, Marlon Carranza, and María Santacruz, "El Salvador: Espacios públicos, confianza interpersonal y pandillas," in *Maras y pandillas en Centroamérica: Pandillas y capital social*, ed. ERIC, IDESO, IDIES, IUDOP (San Salvador: UCA Editores, 2004), 91–98.
94. On this type of "folk punishment," see Cohen, *Folk Devils and Moral Panics*, 95.
95. Telephone interview with Alexander Renderos, journalist, San Salvador, 1 December 2015.
96. Telephone interview with Héctor Silva, journalist, Washington, DC, 4 December 2015.
97. Interview with Paolo Luers, journalist, *El Faro*, San Salvador, 27 May 2006.
98. Jaap Van Ginneken, *Understanding Global News: A Critical Introduction* (London: Sage Publications, 1998), 200.
99. José Miguel Cruz and María Santacruz, *La victimización y la percepción de seguridad en El Salvador en 2004* (San Salvador: MINGOB and PNUD, 2005), 138.
100. Ibid., 147–155.
101. IUDOP, "Evaluación del país a finales de 2003 y perspectivas electorales para 2004. Encuesta de opinión pública," *Boletín de prensa* Año 18, No. 4 (San Salvador: IUDOP, 2003), 2.
102. IUDOP, "Los salvadoreños evalúan la situación del país a finales de 2005 y opinan sobre las elecciones de 2006," *Boletín de prensa* Año 20, No. 3 (San Salvador: IUDOP, 2005), 3–4; IUDOP, "Evaluación del país a finales del 2006 y perspectivas para 2007," *Boletín de prensa* Año 21, No. 3 (San Salvador: IUDOP, 2006), 3.
103. IUDOP, "Evaluación del país a finales de 2003," 2; IUDOP, "Evaluación de los salvadoreños sobre el gobierno de Francisco Flores y expectativas hacia el nuevo gobierno," *Boletín de prensa* Año 19, No. 2 (San Salvador: IUDOP, 2004), 3; IUDOP, "Los salvadoreños evalúan el primer año de gobierno de Antonio Saca," *Boletín de prensa* Año 20, No. 2 (San Salvador: IUDOP, 2005), 4.
104. IUDOP, "Los salvadoreños evalúan los cien días de gobierno de Antonio Saca," *Boletín de prensa* Año 19, No. 4 (San Salvador: IUDOP, 2004), 3; IUDOP, "Los salvadoreños evalúan el primer año de gobierno de Antonio Saca," 4.
105. IUDOP, "Evaluación del país a finales del 2006," 2–3.

Chapter 4

1. FESPAD, *Documento base de FESPAD* (San Salvador: mimeo, 1988).
2. Telephone interview with Francisco Díaz, founder of FESPAD, 3 December 2015.
3. Interview with María Silvia Guillén, executive director, FESPAD, San Salvador, 11 July 2006.

4. Interview with Nelson Flores, director, CEPES, FESPAD, San Salvador, 9 May 2006.

5. Interview with Ricardo Montoya, Juvenile Justice Program coordinator, CEPES, FESPAD, San Salvador, 8 July 2005.

6. In 2008, FESPAD's thematic and administrative centers were transformed into three thematic programs (citizen security and criminal justice; social, economic, cultural, and environmental rights; and transparency) and a series of administrative units in order to better implement the organization's mission.

7. Interview with Juan Carlos Sánchez, head, Project Planning Unit, FESPAD, San Salvador, 4 May 2006.

8. Interview with Abraham Ábrego, director, CECDH, FESPAD, San Salvador, 10 May 2006.

9. Interview with Juan Carlos Sánchez, head, Project Planning Unit, FESPAD, San Salvador, 4 May 2006.

10. Interview with María Silvia Guillén, executive director, FESPAD, San Salvador, 11 July 2006.

11. Interview with María Silvia Guillén, executive director, FESPAD, San Salvador, 11 July 2006.

12. Interview with Rina Aldana, director, CEDFI, FESPAD, San Salvador, 23 May 2006.

13. Interview with Juan Carlos Sánchez, head, Project Planning Unit, FESPAD, San Salvador, 4 May 2006.

14. *La Prensa Gráfica*, "Posición de FESPAD ante el Plan Mano Dura contra las maras," 30 July 2003 (paid ad).

15. Interview with Juan Carlos Sánchez, head, Project Planning Unit, FESPAD, San Salvador, 4 May 2006.

16. *El Diario de Hoy*, "Buses, neumonía, hiper garantismo y maras," 1 August 2003 (paid ad); "Hiper garantismo in defensa de las maras," 8 August 2003 (paid ad); "Sobre maras, FESPAD va del populismo a la politiquería calumniosa," 12 August 2003 (paid ad).

17. *El Diario de Hoy*, "Sobre maras, FESPAD va del populismo a la politiquería calumniosa."

18. Interview with María Silvia Guillén, executive director, FESPAD, San Salvador, 11 July 2006.

19. Interview with Ricardo Montoya, Juvenile Justice Program coordinator, CEPES, FESPAD, San Salvador, 8 July 2005.

20. *La Prensa Gráfica*, "Detenciones son 'ilegales', dicen jueces," 25 July 2003, 5.

21. *La Prensa Gráfica*, "Jueces niegan 'bloque' contra ley," 23 October 2003, 14.

22. Interview with Nelson Flores, director, CEPES, FESPAD, San Salvador, 9 May 2006.

23. On "shaming methodology," see Kenneth Roth, "Defending Economic, Social and Cultural Rights: Practical Issues Faced by an International Human Rights Organization," *Human Rights Quarterly* 26.1 (2004): 67.

24. Interview with Ricardo Montoya, Juvenile Justice Program coordinator, CEPES, FESPAD, San Salvador, 8 July 2005.

25. UNCRC, *Concluding Observations: El Salvador.*

26. See Keck and Sikkink, *Activists Beyond Borders*, 12–13.

27. Interview with Ricardo Montoya, Juvenile Justice Program coordinator, CEPES, FESPAD, San Salvador, 8 July 2005.

28. On "accountability politics," see Keck and Sikkink, *Activists Beyond Borders*, 24.

29. Interview with Ricardo Montoya, Juvenile Justice Program coordinator, CEPES, FESPAD, San Salvador, 8 July 2005.

30. On "created" and "invited" policy space, see Lisa VeneKlasen and Valerie Miller, *A New Weave of Power, People and Politics: The Action Guide for Advocacy and Citizen Participation* (Rugby: Practical Action Publishing, 2007), 208.

31. Interview with Ricardo Montoya, Juvenile Justice Program coordinator, CEPES, FESPAD, San Salvador, 8 July 2005.

32. Interview with Emilia Gallegos, Juvenile Justice Program assistant, CEPES, FESPAD, San Salvador, 9 June 2006.

33. David Morales, *Los Acuerdos de Paz, su agenda pendiente y los derechos humanos en El Salvador de hoy* (San Salvador: mimeo, 2007), 33.

34. René Hernández, "Justicia y seguridad ciudadana: Las reformas legales en El Salvador," in *Convivencia y seguridad: Un reto a la gobernabilidad*, ed. Jorge Sapoznikow, Juana Salazar, and Fernando Carrillo (Washington, DC: Inter-American Development Bank, 2000).

35. Communication with Nelson Flores, director, CEPES, FESPAD, San Salvador.

36. Communication with Ricardo Montoya, Juvenile Justice Program coordinator, CEPES, FESPAD, San Salvador.

37. Luke Dowdney, ed., *Neither War nor Peace: International Comparisons of Children and Youth in Organised Armed Violence* (Rio de Janeiro: Viva Rio, 2005).

38. Ibid., 11.

39. IUDOP and FESPAD, *Documento para la discusión de política pública municipal de prevención de la violencia de pandillas: municipio de Zacatecoluca* (San Salvador: mimeo, 2007), 6–8.

40. Telephone interview with Marlon Carranza, former IUDOP researcher, 30 November 2015.

41. Online communication with Medardo Alfaro, 30 November 2015.

42. IUDOP and FESPAD, *Documento para la discusión*, 6–11.

43. On these elements of gang control, see Klein and Maxson, *Street Gang Patterns and Policies*, 261.

44. Carlos Martínez, "La rebelión por la que sangra Zacatecoluca," *El Faro*, 3 November 2014, www.salanegra.elfaro.net/es/201411/cronicas/16173 /La-rebelión-por-la-que-sangra-Zacatecoluca.htm; Policía Nacional Civil, *Tasa anual de homicidios ocurridos en el municipio de Zacatecoluca (2006-2015)*, obtained through information request.

45. On advocacy planning phases, see VeneKlasen and Miller, *A New Weave of Power*, 83–85.

46. Ibid., 75.

47. Ibid., ch. 7.

48. Interview with Juan Carlos Sánchez, head, Project Planning Unit, FESPAD, San Salvador, 4 May 2006.

49. VeneKlasen and Miller, *A New Weave of Power*, 39.

50. Steven Lukes, *Power: A Radical View* (London: Macmillan Press, 1974).

51. Ryan, *Prime Time Activism*, 217–218.

52. On advocacy tactics and mechanisms of power, see VeneKlasen and Miller, *A New Weave of Power*, 50.

53. Ibid., 36.

54. Ibid., 52.

55. *La Prensa Gráfica*, "FMLN aboga por reos más peligrosos," 3 December 2005, 2–3.

56. *La Prensa Gráfica*, "El FMLN comete una alta traición a la patria," 3 December 2005, 2; *La Prensa Gráfica*, "Están en contubernio con las pandillas," 3 December 2005, 3; *La Prensa Gráfica*, "Buscan atribuir al FMLN un problema del Gobierno," 3 December 2005, 3.

57. *La Prensa Gráfica*, "Reconocidos reos convocaron a reunión," 3 December 2005, 4.

58. *La Prensa Gráfica*, "Gobernación cuestiona a ONG," 5 December 2005, 14.

59. Interview with Nelson Flores, director, CEPES, FESPAD, San Salvador, 9 May 2006.

60. Interview with Roberto Burgos, lawyer, IDHUCA, San Salvador, 15 February 2006.

61. *Diario Co-Latino*, "Abandonan catedral en silencio," 10 November 2005.

62. *La Prensa Gráfica*, "Toma catedral enfrenta a Gobierno y al FMLN," 9 November 2005.

63. *El Diario de Hoy*, "Alertan sobre tomas y protestas violentas," 11 November 2005, 8.

64. Interview with Roberto Burgos, lawyer, IDHUCA, San Salvador, 15 February 2006.

65. Interview with María Silvia Guillén, executive director, FESPAD, San Salvador, 11 July 2006.

66. Ryan, *Prime Time Activism*, 52.

67. Interview with Juan Carlos Sánchez, head, Project Planning Unit, FESPAD, San Salvador, 4 May 2006.

68. On "leverage politics," see Keck and Sikkink, *Activists Beyond Borders*, 23.

69. Interview with Abraham Ábrego, director, CECDH, FESPAD, San Salvador, 10 May 2006.

70. Interview with Juan Carlos Sánchez, head, Project Planning Unit, FESPAD, San Salvador, 4 May 2006.

71. Telephone interview with Abraham Ábrego, executive director, FESPAD, 7 December 2015.

72. Interview with Juan Carlos Sánchez, head, Project Planning Unit, FESPAD, San Salvador, 4 May 2006.

73. Interview with María Silvia Guillén, executive director, FESPAD, San Salvador, 11 July 2006.

74. Keck and Sikkink, *Activists Beyond Borders*, 16.

Chapter 5

1. The Grupo OPERA (*optimismo, paz, esperanza, renovación, y armonía*/optimism, peace, hope, renovation, and harmony) was formed in the Quezaltepeque prison between 1996 and 1997 to provide support to inmates of different prisons, including gang members. The NGO is managed by former MS member Dany Balmore, but is not accessible to researchers, and little public information exists about its work and impact.

2. The HU founding history, and Magdaleno's role in it, was reconstructed through a telephone interview with Magdaleno Rose-Ávila, founder, Homies Unidos, 20 March 2007.

3. Cruz and Portillo, *Solidaridad y violencia en las pandillas*, 155–162.

4. Ibid., 107–109.

5. Interview with Luis Romero, director, Homies Unidos, San Salvador, 22 July 2005.

6. Klein and Maxson, *Street Gang Patterns and Policies*, 234–235.

7. Klein, *The American Street Gang*, 148.

8. Irving Spergel, *Reducing Youth Gang Violence* (Plymouth: Altamira Press, 2007), 252.

9. Scott Decker and Janet Lauritsen, "Leaving the Gang," in *The Modern Gang Reader*, 3rd ed., ed. Arlen Egley, Cheryl Maxson, and Jody Miller (Los Angeles: Roxbury, 2006).

10. Scott Decker and Barrik van Winkle, *Life in the Gang: Family, Friends, and Violence* (Cambridge: Cambridge University Press, 1996), 272–273.

11. Decker and Lauritsen, "Leaving the Gang," 64–65.

12. Marlon Carranza, "Políticas juveniles y rehabilitación de mareros en El Salvador," in *Maras y pandillas en Centroamérica: Políticas juveniles y rehabilitación*, ed. ERIC, IDIES, IUDOP, NITLAPAN, DIRINPRO (Managua: UCA Publicaciones, 2004), 48.

13. *Raíces*, "Para mí la pandilla es como una religión," 16 May 2006.

14. Klein, *The American Street Gang*, 45.

15. Carranza, "Políticas juveniles y rehabilitación," 78.

16. Interview with Luis Romero, director, Homies Unidos, San Salvador, 3 July 2006.

17. Daniel Gilbert, Susan Fiske, and Gardner Lindzey, *The Handbook of Social Psychology*, 4th ed., vol. 2 (New York: Oxford University Press, 1998), 162.

18. Views expressed in interviews with Porfirio Chica, adviser, MINGOB, San Salvador, 31 May 2006; Sub-Commissioner Julio César Santana Vela, director, División Policía Técnica Científica, PNC, San Salvador, 27 January 2006.

19. The account of the NGO's formative years was reconstructed through telephone interviews with Magdaleno Rose-Ávila, founder, Homies Unidos, 20 March 2007; Julienne Gage, journalist and former HU volunteer, 20 March and 13 April 2007.

20. Telephone interview with Magdaleno Rose-Ávila, founder, Homies Unidos, 20 March 2007.

21. Telephone interview with Julienne Gage, journalist and former HU volunteer, 13 April 2007.

22. Telephone interview with Magdaleno Rose-Ávila, founder, Homies Unidos, 20 March 2007.

23. Telephone interview with Magdaleno Rose-Ávila, founder, Homies Unidos, 20 March 2007.

24. Telephone interview with Julienne Gage, journalist and former HU volunteer, 13 April 2007.

25. Telephone interview with Julienne Gage, journalist and former HU volunteer, 13 April 2007.

26. Telephone interview with Julienne Gage, journalist and former HU volunteer, 20 March 2007.

27. Telephone interview with Magdaleno Rose-Ávila, founder, Homies Unidos, 20 March 2007.

28. Telephone interview with Magdaleno Rose-Ávila, founder, Homies Unidos, 20 March 2007.

29. Robert Baron and Donn Byrne, *Social Psychology*, 10th ed. (Boston: Pearson, 2004), 160.

30. Gilbert, Fiske, and Lindzey, *The Handbook of Social Psychology*, 563.

31. Baron and Byrne, *Social Psychology*, 210.

32. Michael Hogg and Joel Cooper, eds., *The Sage Handbook of Social Psychology* (London: Sage Publications, 2003), 420.

33. Anonymous interview AI-013, 11 April 2006.

34. Communication with Heriberto Henríquez, director of rehabilitation, Homies Unidos, San Salvador; telephone interview with Magdaleno Rose-Ávila, founder, Homies Unidos, 20 March 2007.

35. Interview with Luis Romero, director, Homies Unidos, San Salvador, 22 July 2005.

36. Interview with Ryna Garay, executive director, FUNSALPRODESE, San Salvador, 24 May 2006.

37. Interview with Luis Romero, director, Homies Unidos, San Salvador, 3 July 2006.

38. Interview with Luis Romero, director, Homies Unidos, San Salvador, 3 July 2006.

39. Helen Schwartzman, *Ethnography in Organizations* (Newbury Park, CA: Sage, 1993), 43.

40. Interview with Porfirio Chica, adviser, MINGOB, San Salvador, 31 May 2006.

41. Interview with Luis Enrique Salazar, adjunct ombudsman for Rights of the Child, PDDH, San Salvador, 18 April 2006.

42. Keck and Sikkink, *Activists Beyond Borders*, 19.

43. Georg Gugelberger, "Introduction: Institutionalisation of Transgression," in *The Real Thing: Testimonial Discourse and Latin America*, ed. Georg Gugelberger (Durham, NC: Duke University Press, 1996), 9.

44. John Beverley, "The Margin at the Center," in *The Real Thing: Testimonial Discourse and Latin America*, ed. Georg Gugelberger (Durham, NC: Duke University Press, 1996), 27.

45. Kathleen Logan, "Personal Testimony: Latin American Women Telling Their Lives," *Latin American Research Review* 32 (1997): 200.

46. Beverley, "The Margin at the Center," 31.

47. For example, Rigoberta Menchú, *I, Rigoberta Menchú* (London: Verso, 1984).

48. For example, Luis Rodríguez, *Always Running: La Vida Loca: Gang Days in L.A.* (New York: Touchstone, 2005).

49. Klein and Maxson, *Street Gang Patterns and Policies*, 99.

50. Decker and van Winkle, *Life in the Gang*, 265; Joan Serra Hoffmann, *Youth Violence, Resilience, and Rehabilitation* (New York: LFB Scholarly Publishing, 2004), 133–134.

51. Interview with Luis Romero, director, Homies Unidos, San Salvador, 3 July 2006.

52. Interview with Luis Romero, director, Homies Unidos, San Salvador, 22 July 2005.

53. Roberto Valencia, "¿Quién mató a Christian Poveda?" *Revista Gatopardo*, December 2009, www.gatopardo.com/ReportajesGP.php?R=69.

54. Roberto Valencia, "Vivir en La Campanera," *El Faro*, 21 June 2010, www.elfaro.net/es/201006/especiales/1969/Vivir-en-La-Campanera.htm.

55. The reconstruction of the case is based on the following sources: an interview with Jorge Torres, lawyer, IDHUCA, San Salvador, 23 June 2006; IDHUCA case notes; the court file in the criminal case against José Heriberto Henríquez and Carlos Alberto Rivas Barahona at the Tribunal Quinto de Instrucción de San Salvador; Tribunal Quinto de Sentencia de San Salvador, *Sentencia en el proceso penal en contra de José Heriberto Henríquez y Carlos Alberto Rivas Barahona*, 300-3-2006, 13 February 2007.

56. Communication with staff at CRISPAZ, FESPAD, the Polígono, the CNSP, and a probation officer.

57. Homies Unidos did not have permission to enter the prisons.

58. *La Prensa Gráfica*, "Testigo vincula a directivo Homies Unidos a crimen," 15 August 2006.

59. Carlos Martínez and José Luis Sanz, "El Barrio roto," in *Crónicas negras desde una región que no cuenta*, ed. Sala Negra de *El Faro* (Mexico City: Aguilar, 2014).

60. *La Prensa Gráfica*, "Yo nunca estuve en ese lugar," 1 February 2007.

61. Communication with Luis Romero, director, Homies Unidos.

62. Telephone interview with Silvia Beltrán, former director, Homies Unidos-Los Angeles, 3 December 2015.

63. *La Prensa Gráfica*, "Pandilleros en rehabilitación denuncian acoso policial," 27 July 2006.

64. *La Opinión*, "Pandilleros se quejan de represión en El Salvador," 27 July 2006.

65. Communication with Christian Poveda.

66. *Diario Co-Latino*, "Policía cometió sacrilegio al realizar capturas en lugar santo," 19 July 2006.

67. International Human Rights Clinic, *No Place to Hide*, 51–52.

68. Communication with Luis Romero, director, Homies Unidos.

69. Efren Lemus, "Once condenas por el asesinato de Christian Poveda," *El Faro*, 9 March 2011, www.elfaro.net/es/201103/internacionales/3712/.

70. Roberto Valencia. "¿No será bueno fomentar el reencuentro de los pandilleros presos con sus familias?" *El Faro*, 15 July 2015, www.salanegra.elfaro

.net/es/201507/entrevistas/17177/"¿No-será-bueno-fomentar-el-reencuentro
-de-los-pandilleros-presos-con-sus-familias".htm.

71. *elPeriódico*, "'No somos monstruos.' Mareros en El Salvador denuncian
discriminación," 11 March 2007.

72. Communication with Luis Romero, director, Homies Unidos.

73. Interview with Porfirio Chica, adviser, MINGOB, San Salvador, 31 May
2006.

74. Interview with Luis Romero, director, Homies Unidos, San Salvador,
3 July 2006.

75. Communication with Christian Poveda, and Roberto Ramírez, probation officer, Juzgado Primero de Ejecución de Medidas al Menor, San Salvador.

Chapter 6

1. Morand Wirth, *Don Bosco and the Salesians* (New Rochelle, NY: Don
Bosco Publications, 1982), 16–17.

2. Giuseppe Ghiberti, *Don Bosco begegnen* (Augsburg: Sankt Ulrich Verlag,
2005), 109.

3. Wirth, *Don Bosco and the Salesians*, 297.

4. Ibid., 187–197.

5. Departamento de Organización del Espacio de la UCA, *Documentos del
Laboratorio del Habitat Popular: Comunidad "Las Iberias"* (San Salvador: mimeo,
2003), 6.

6. Interview with José Moratalla, director, PIDB, San Salvador, 22 June
2006.

7. Lorena Cuerno, *El Polígono Industrial Don Bosco: Una opción de vida para los
jóvenes en conflicto con la ley* (San Salvador: UNICEF, 2004), 21.

8. Interview with Miguel Azucena, president, Committee of Community
Leaders, PIDB, San Salvador, 30 May 2006.

9. Eduardo Contreras, *Diagnóstico: Capital Social y Tejido Social del Municipio
de San Salvador* (San Salvador: PNUD, 2010), 113–114.

10. Departamento de Organización del Espacio de la UCA, *Documentos del
Laboratorio del Habitat Popular*, 9.

11. Intercomunal Nor-Oriente and Fundación EDYTRA, *Diagnóstico de las
Comunidades Iberias y otras aledañas* (San Salvador: mimeo, 2006), 18.

12. Contreras, *Capital Social y Tejido Social*, 111.

13. Interview with Miguel Azucena, president, Committee of Community
Leaders, PIDB, San Salvador, 30 May 2006.

14. Interview with Roberto Valencia, journalist, *El Faro*, 12 December 2015.

15. Contreras, *Capital Social y Tejido Social*, 111.

16. Interview with Guadalupe Leiva, director, Fundación EDYTRA, PIDB,
San Salvador, 10 May 2006.

17. Interview with Karla Hananía de Varela, legislation and public policy
officer, UNICEF, San Salvador, 22 July 2005.

18. Interview with Jaime Martínez, director, UJJ, CSJ, San Salvador,
15 June 2006.

19. Interview with Raúl Ramírez, director of education, PIDB, San Salva-

dor, 26 May 2006. Data on juvenile offenders/gang members received in an interview with Aída Santos, judge, Juzgado Primero de Ejecución de Medidas al Menor, San Salvador, 8 May 2006.

20. Interview with Raúl Ramírez, director of education, PIDB, San Salvador, 29 May 2006.

21. *El Diario de Hoy*, "Piden oportunidad para los pandilleros," 15 November 2003, 32; IDB, "Reina Sofía de España participará en Foro de la Microempresa en El Salvador," 27 September 2007, www.iadb.org/es/noticias/comunicados-de -prensa/2007-09-27/reina-sofia-de-espana-participara-en-foro-de-la-micro empresa-en-el-salvador,4045.html.

22. *El Diario de Hoy*, "ARENA busca duplicar la obra del padre Pepe," 5 February 2004, 16; *El Mundo*, "Ávila: me gustaría debatir con los dirigentes del FMLN," 3 September 2008.

23. *Europapress*, "De la Vega visita al padre Pepe, soñador que transformó un basurero en centro de reinserción para maras," 11 August 2008, www .europapress.es/internacional/noticia-salvador-vega-visita-padre-pepe-sonador -transformo-basurero-centro-reinsercion-maras-20080811190743.html.

24. Interview with Raúl Ramírez, director of education, PIDB, San Salvador, 29 May 2006. In the Polígono, the term "technical staff" refers to the educators, psychologists, and administrative personnel, not to the workers employed in the cooperatives.

25. Interview with Guadalupe Leiva, director, Fundación EDYTRA, PIDB, San Salvador, 10 May 2006.

26. Interview with Raúl Ramírez, director of education, PIDB, San Salvador, 26 May 2006.

27. Interview with Guadalupe Leiva, director, Fundación EDYTRA, PIDB, San Salvador, 10 May 2006.

28. Interview with José Moratalla, director, PIDB, San Salvador, 22 June 2006.

29. Interview with Heriberto Herrera, director, Colegio Salesiano, Santa Tecla, 10 May 2006.

30. Ewell Roy, *Cooperatives: Development, Principles, and Management* (Danville, IL: Interstate Printers & Publishers, 1976), 6.

31. Interview with Guadalupe Leiva, director, Fundación EDYTRA, PIDB, San Salvador, 10 May 2006.

32. Communication with Raúl Ramírez, director of education, PIDB, San Salvador.

33. Interview with Víctor Rodríguez, director, Federative Council, PIDB, San Salvador, 31 May 2006.

34. Interview with José Moratalla, director, PIDB, San Salvador, 22 June 2006.

35. One Polígono worker stated that the low salaries made it difficult to maintain a family.

36. Carl Liedholm and Donald Mead, *Small Enterprises and Economic Development: The Dynamics of Micro and Small Enterprises* (London: Routledge, 1999).

37. Fundación EDYTRA, *Perfil del destinatario del Polígono Industrial Don Bosco* (San Salvador: mimeo, n.d.).

38. Communication with Raúl Ramírez, director of education, PIDB, San Salvador; interview with Aída Santos, judge, Juzgado Primero de Ejecución de Medidas al Menor, San Salvador, 8 May 2006.

39. Information obtained through personal interviews and consultation of PIDB internal files.

40. Interview with Guadalupe Leiva, director, Fundación EDYTRA, PIDB, San Salvador, 10 May 2006.

41. "Población de alumnos del Polígono Industrial Don Bosco, 1992–2007," provided by Raúl Ramírez, director of education, PIDB, San Salvador.

42. I interviewed a total of nine boarders, selected by NGO staff, from each target group. Although this procedure may have influenced the respondents' answers, their tight schedules and compulsory school attendance made it difficult to choose the interviewees independently.

43. Interview with Milton Vega, rehabilitation officer, CNSP, San Salvador, 11 April 2006.

44. Interview with Raúl Ramírez, director of education, PIDB, San Salvador, 26 May 2006.

45. Interview with Aída Santos, judge, Juzgado Primero de Ejecución de Medidas al Menor, San Salvador, 8 May 2006.

46. Interview with José Moratalla, director, PIDB, San Salvador, 22 June 2006.

47. Interview with Aída Santos, judge, Juzgado Primero de Ejecución de Medidas al Menor, San Salvador, 8 May 2006.

48. Interview with José Moratalla, director, PIDB, San Salvador, 29 June 2006.

49. The case histories of the two youths were reconstructed through personal interviews and consultation of PIDB-internal files, attendance at one of Pedro's quarterly court hearings, and a house call on Carlos with the designated probation officer.

50. Interview with Raúl Ramírez, director of education, PIDB, San Salvador, 26 May 2006.

51. Communication with Roberto Ramírez, probation officer, Juzgado Primero de Ejecución de Medidas al Menor, San Salvador.

52. John Braithwaite, *Crime, Shame and Reintegration* (Cambridge: Cambridge University Press, 1989), 73.

53. Interview with Raúl Ramírez, director of education, PIDB, San Salvador, 29 May 2006.

54. Interview with José Moratalla, director, PIDB, San Salvador, 29 June 2006.

55. Interview with José Moratalla, director, PIDB, San Salvador, 22 June 2006.

56. *El Diario de Hoy*, "Más restos en la Iberia," 19 November 2005, archivo .elsalvador.com/noticias/2005/11/19/nacional/nac16.asp.

57. Interview with Raúl Ramírez, director of education, PIDB, San Salvador, 29 May 2006.

58. The Mesa Interinstitucional para la Prevención y Atención de la Violencia y Delincuencia Juvenil.

59. Interview with María Teresa de Mejía, legislation and public policy officer, UNICEF, San Salvador, 3 February 2006.

60. Interview with Tránsito Ruano, director, Centro de Formación y Capacitación, Vicaría Divino Salvador, San Salvador, 14 February 2006.

61. Interviews with Raúl Ramírez, director of education, PIDB, San Salvador, 29 May 2006; Tránsito Ruano, director, Centro de Formación y Capacitación, Vicaría Divino Salvador, San Salvador, 14 February 2006.

Conclusion

1. See Claudio Fuentes, *Contesting the Iron First: Advocacy Networks and Police Violence in Democratic Argentina and Chile* (New York: Routledge, 2005).

2. For example, Robert Chaskin, ed., *Youth Gangs and Community Intervention: Research, Practice, and Evidence* (New York: Columbia University Press, 2010); Erika Gebo and Brenda Bond, eds., *Looking Beyond Suppression: Community Strategies to Reduce Gang Violence* (Lanham, MD: Lexington Books, 2014).

3. For example, Johnston, "An Ecuadorian Alternative"; Spergel, *The Youth Gang Problem*.

4. Klein and Maxson, *Street Gang Patterns and Policies*; Irving Spergel, *Reducing Youth Gang Violence: The Little Village Gang Project in Chicago* (Lanham, MD: Altamira Press, 2007).

Epilogue

1. MJSP, *Política Nacional de Justicia, Seguridad Pública y Convivencia* (San Salvador: MJSP, 2010).

2. Magdalena Flores, "PDDH tiene 158 expedientes contra militares," *ContraPunto*, 16 February 2011.

3. Sergio Arauz, "El día en que los militares volvieron a desaparecer personas," *El Faro*, 1 June 2015, www.elfaro.net/es/201505/noticias/17030/El-día-en-que-los-militares-volvieron-a-desaparecer-personas.htm.

4. Asamblea Legislativa, *Ley de Proscripción de Maras, Pandillas, Agrupaciones, Asociaciones y Organizaciones de Naturaleza Criminal*, Decreto No. 458 (*Diario Oficial*, 10 September 2010).

5. Corte Suprema de Justicia, *Sentencia de Inconstitucionalidad 4-2012*, 17 May 2013, www.jurisprudencia.gob.sv.

6. José Luis Sanz and Carlos Martínez, "'Aplicaremos el método de pacificación que se usa en las favelas de Río'," *El Faro*, 26 January 2012, www.salanegra.elfaro.net/es/201201/entrevistas/7374/.

7. José Luis Sanz, "Los andamios internacionales de la tregua," *El Faro*, 4 February 2013, www.salanegra.elfaro.net/es/201302/cronicas/10889/.

8. Roberto Valencia, "El promedio de Munguía Payés supera en 1.4 homicidios diarios al de Melgar," *El Faro*, 27 February 2012, www.elfaro.net/es/201202/noticias/7689/.

9. Óscar Martínez, Carlos Martínez, Sergio Arauz, and Efren Lemus, "Go-

bierno negoció con pandillas reducción de homicidios," *El Faro*, 14 March 2012, www.elfaro.net/es/201203/noticias/7985/.

10. Online communication with Paolo Luers, journalist and member of the Humanitarian Foundation, 19 October 2015.

11. Carlos Martínez, "El gobierno da la espalda a la tregua," *El Faro*, 9 December 2013, www.elfaro.net/es/201312/noticias/14157/.

12. Eva Saiz, "'No podemos exigir a las maras que renuncien a la extorsión, sin alternativas'," *El País*, 12 April 2013, http://internacional.elpais.com /internacional/2013/04/12/actualidad/1365778968_353156.html.

13. IUDOP, "Los salvadoreños y salvadoreños evalúan el cuarto año de gobierno de Mauricio Funes," *Boletín de prensa* Año 27, No. 1 (San Salvador: IUDOP, 2013).

14. Carlos Martínez and José Luis Sanz, "La nueva verdad sobre la tregua entre pandillas," *El Faro*, 11 September 2012, www.salanegra.elfaro.net/es /201209/cronicas/9612/.

15. Charles Katz and Luis Enrique Amaya, *The Gang Truce as a Form of Violence Intervention* (San Salvador: USAID, 2015).

16. Ashley Morse, Adam Isacson, and Maureen Meyer, *Tackling Urban Violence in Latin America: Reversing Exclusion through Smart Policing and Social Investment* (Washington, DC: Washington Office on Latin America, 2011), 6–9.

17. Fundación Salvadoreña para el Desarrollo Económico y Social (FUSADES), *Análisis crítico de los planes de gobierno del FMLN y ARENA* (San Salvador: FUSADES, 2014).

18. Sergio Arauz, "Por fin en la campana electoral un 'debate' sobre la tregua: Funes vs Arena," *El Faro*, 27 January 2014, www.elfaro.net/es/201401 /noticias/14548/Por-fin-en-la-campaña-electoral-un-debate-sobre-la-tregua -Funes-vs-Arena.htm.

19. Gabriel Labrador, "Quijano buscó un acuerdo con las pandillas tras perder la primera ronda," *El Faro*, 21 April 2014, www.elfaro.net/es/201404 /noticias/15264/.

20. CNSCC, *Plan El Salvador Seguro* (San Salvador: CNSCC, 2015).

21. Jimmy Alvarado, "El 0.12% de los morosos de Hacienda deben el 25% de la deuda tributaria," *El Faro*, 11 May 2015, www.elfaro.net/es/201505 /noticias/16942/El-012--de-los-morosos-de-Hacienda-deben-el-25--de-la -deuda-tributaria.htm.

22. Diana Escalante and Lilibeth Sánchez, "62 policías asesinados en lo que va de 2015," *El Diario de Hoy*, 18 December 2015, www.elsalvador.com/articulo /sucesos/policias-asesinados-que-2015-96541.

23. Suchit Chávez and Ezequiel Barrera, "Cinco muertes sin explicación," *La Prensa Gráfica*, 25 October 2015, www.laprensagrafica.com/2015/10/25 /cinco-muertes-sin-explicacion; Roberto Valencia, Óscar Martínez, and Daniel Valencia Caravantes, "La Policía masacró en la finca San Blas," *El Faro*, 22 July 2015, www.salanegra.elfaro.net/es/201507/cronicas/17205/La-Policía-masacró -en-la-finca-San-Blas.htm.

24. Telephone interview with Rosa Vargas, urban matters, youth and employment program expert, CORDAID, The Hague, 5 August 2015.

Bibliography

Acevedo, Carlos. "Los costos económicos de la violencia en El Salvador." In *Economía Política de la Seguridad Ciudadana*, edited by Fernando Carrión and Manuel Dammert. Quito: FLACSO, 2009.

Aguilar, Jeannette. *Pandillas juveniles transnacionales en Centroamérica, México y Estados Unidos: Diagnóstico de El Salvador.* San Salvador: IUDOP, 2006.

Aguilar, Jeannette, and Lissette Miranda. "Entre la articulación y la competencia: Las respuestas de la sociedad civil organizada a las pandillas en El Salvador." In *Maras y pandillas en Centroamérica: Las respuestas de la sociedad civil organizada*, edited by José Miguel Cruz. San Salvador: UCA Editores, 2006.

Ahmed, Shamima, and David Potter. *NGOs in International Politics.* Bloomfield, CT: Kumarian Press, 2006.

Albiac, Dolores. "Los ricos más ricos de El Salvador." *ECA* 612 (1999): 841–864.

Almeida, Paul. *Waves of Protest: Popular Struggle in El Salvador, 1925–2005.* Minneapolis: University of Minnesota Press, 2008.

Almog-Bar, Michal, and Hillel Schmid. "Advocacy Activities of Nonprofit Human Service Organizations: A Critical Review." *Nonprofit and Voluntary Sector Quarterly* 43.1 (2014): 11–35.

Amaya Cóbar, Edgardo. "Las políticas de seguridad en El Salvador 1992–2002." In *Seguridad y reforma policial en las Américas*, edited by Lucía Dammert and John Bailey. Mexico City: Siglo XXI Editores, 2005.

Americas Watch. *El Salvador's Decade of Terror: Human Rights Since the Assassination of Archbishop Romero.* New Haven, CT: Yale University Press, 1991.

Amnesty International. *El Salvador: "Death Squads"—A Government Strategy.* London: Amnesty International, 1988.

Anderson, Thomas. *Matanza*, 2nd ed. Willimantic, CT: Curbstone Press, 1992.

Arana, Ana. "How the Street Gangs took Central America." *Foreign Affairs* 84 (May-June 2005): 98–110.

Artiga, Álvaro, Carlos Dada, David Escobar, and Hugo Martínez. *La polarización política en El Salvador.* San Salvador: FUNDAUNGO, 2007.

Asamblea Legislativa. *Ley Anti Maras.* Decreto No. 158 (*Diario Oficial*, 10 October 2003).

———. *Ley para el Combate de las Actividades Delincuenciales de Grupos o Asociaciones Ilícitas Especiales.* Decreto No. 305 (*Diario Oficial*, 2 April 2004).

————. *Ley Contra el Crimen Organizado y Delitos de Realización Compleja*. Decreto No. 190 (*Diario Oficial*, 10 January 2007).

————. *Ley de Proscripción de Maras, Pandillas, Agrupaciones, Asociaciones y Organizaciones de Naturaleza Criminal*. Decreto No. 458, (*Diario Oficial*, 10 September 2010).

Atack, Iain. "Four Criteria of Development NGO Legitimacy." *World Development* 27 (1999): 855–864.

Azpuru, Dinorah, Ligia Blanco, Ricardo Córdova Macías, Nayelly Loya Marin, Carlos G. Ramos, and Adrián Zapata, eds. *Construyendo la democracia en sociedades posconflicto: Guatemala y El Salvador, un enfoque comparado*. Guatemala City: F&G Editores, 2007.

Baird, Adam. "Negotiating Pathways to Manhood: Rejecting Gangs and Violence in Medellín's Periphery." *Journal of Conflictology* 3.1 (2012): 30–41.

Barnes, Nielan. *Transnational Youth Gangs in Central America, Mexico and the United States: Executive Summary*. Mexico City: ITAM, 2006.

Baron, Robert, and Donn Byrne. *Social Psychology*, 10th ed. Boston, MA: Pearson, 2004.

Bartow, Joanna. "Essential Subversions: Reading Theory with Latin American Women's Testimonial Discourse." In *Woman as Witness: Essays on Testimonial Literature by Latin American Women*, edited by Linda Maier and Isabel Dulfano. New York: Peter Lang Publishing, 2004.

Beckett, Katherine, and Theodore Sasson. *The Politics of Injustice: Crime and Punishment in America*. Thousand Oaks, CA: Pine Forge Press, 2000.

Bernal, Victoria, and Inderpal Grewal, eds. *Theorizing NGOs: States, Feminisms, and Neoliberalism*. Durham and London: Duke University Press, 2014.

Beverley, John. "The Margin at the Center." In *The Real Thing: Testimonial Discourse and Latin America*, edited by Georg Gugelberger. Durham, NC: Duke University Press, 1996.

Binford, Leigh. *The El Mozote Massacre: Anthropology and Human Rights*. Tucson: University of Arizona Press, 1996.

Blanco, Sidney. "Apuntes sobre la Ley Antimaras." *ECA* 663–664 (2004): 125–137.

Blanco, Sidney, and Francisco Díaz. *Deficiencias policiales, fiscales o judiciales en la investigación y juzgamiento causantes de impunidad*. San Salvador: PNUD, 2007.

Boraz, Steven, and Thomas Bruneau. "Are the *Maras* Overwhelming Governments in Central America?" *Military Review* (November–December 2006): 36–40.

Bosch, Margarita. "NGOs and Development in Brazil: Roles and Responsibilities in a 'New World Order.'" In *NGOs, States and Donors: Too Close for Comfort?* edited by David Hulme and Michael Edwards. London: Macmillan, 1997.

Braithwaite, John. *Crime, Shame and Reintegration*. Cambridge: Cambridge University Press, 1989.

Brenneman, Robert. *Homies and Hermanos: God and Gangs in Central America*. New York: Oxford University Press, 2012.

Brevé, Federico. "The *Maras*: A Menace to the Americas." *Military Review* (July–August 2007): 88–95.

Brockett, Charles. *Land, Power, and Poverty: Agrarian Transformation and Political Conflict in Central America*. Boulder, CO: Westview Press, 1998.

———. *Political Movements and Violence in Central America*. New York: Cambridge University Press, 2005.

Bruneau, Thomas. "The *Maras* and National Security in Central America." *Strategic Insights* 4 (May 2005): 1–12.

Carranza, Marlon. "Políticas juveniles y rehabilitación de mareros en El Salvador." In *Maras y pandillas en Centroamérica: Políticas juveniles y rehabilitación*, edited by ERIC, IDIES, IUDOP, NITLAPAN, DIRINPRO. Managua: UCA Publicaciones, 2004.

———. "Del asistencialismo a la incidencia y el cabildeo: Las diversas respuestas de la sociedad civil organizada al fenómeno de las pandillas en Honduras." In *Maras y pandillas en Centroamérica: Las respuestas de la sociedad civil organizada*, edited by José Miguel Cruz. San Salvador: UCA Editores, 2006.

Casey, John. "Third Sector Participation in the Policy Process: A Framework for Comparative Analysis." *Policy & Politics* 32 (2004): 241–257.

Center for International Studies. *Engagement with Civil Society in Central America: Perspectives of Central American CSOs*. Dublin: Dublin City University, 2007.

Centro de Información, Documentación y Apoyo a la Investigación (CIDAI). "Los acuerdos de paz, diez años después." *ECA* 641–642 (2002): 209–234.

———. "Las elecciones municipales y legislativas del 16 de marzo de 2003." *ECA* 653–654 (2003): 171–196.

Chamorro, Carlos. *El Poder de la Prensa*. Managua: mimeo, 2002.

Chamorro, Carlos, and Alberto Arene. *El turno de los medios*. Managua: mimeo, 2001.

Chaskin, Robert, ed. *Youth Gangs and Community Intervention: Research, Practice, and Evidence*. New York: Columbia University Press, 2010.

Ching, Erik. "Patronage and Politics under General Maximiliano Hernández Martínez, 1931–1939." In *Landscapes of Struggle: Politics, Society, and Community in El Salvador*, edited by Aldo Lauria-Santiago and Leigh Binford. Pittsburg, PA: University of Pittsburgh Press, 2004.

Cohen, Stanley. *Folk Devils and Moral Panics: The Creation of the Mods and Rockers*. Oxford: Martin Robertson: 1980 [1972].

Consejo Nacional de Seguridad Ciudadana y Convivencia (CNSCC). *Plan El Salvador Seguro* (San Salvador: CNSCC, 2015).

Consejo Nacional de Seguridad Pública (CNSP) and European Union (EU). *ProJóvenes de El Salvador. SLV/B7–3100/99/0133. Plan Operativo Anual 2*. San Salvador: mimeo, 2005.

———. *Sistematización de la Experiencia de la Granja Escuela de Rehabilitación*. San Salvador: CNSP, 2006.

Consejo de Redacción. "Juicio político sobre las elecciones 2003." *ECA* 653–654 (2003): 151–170.

Contreras, Eduardo. *Diagnóstico: Capital Social y Tejido Social del Municipio de San Salvador*. San Salvador: PNUD, 2010.

Córdova Macías, Ricardo, Carlos G. Ramos, and Nayelly Loya Marín. "La contribución del proceso de paz a la construcción de la democracia en El Salvador (1992–2004)." In *Construyendo la democracia en sociedades posconflicto: Gua-*

temala y El Salvador, un enfoque comparado, edited by Dinorah Azpuru, Ligia Blanco, Ricardo Córdova Macías, Nayelly Loya Marín, Carlos G. Ramos, and Adrián Zapata. Guatemala City: F&G Editores, 2007.

Corte Suprema de Justicia. *Sentencia de Inconstitucionalidad 52–2003/56–2003/57–2003*. 1 April 2004. www.jurisprudencia.gob.sv.

———. Sentencia de Inconstitucionalidad *4–2012*. 17 May 2013. www.jurisprudencia.gob.sv.

Costa, Gino. *La Policía Nacional Civil de El Salvador (1990–1997)*. San Salvador: UCA Editores, 1999.

Covey, Herbert. *Street Gangs Throughout the World*. Springfield, IL: Charles C. Thomas, 2003.

Croteau, David, and William Hoynes. *Media/Society: Industries, Images, and Audiences*, 3rd ed. London: Sage, 2003.

Cruz, José Miguel. "Los factores posibilitadores y las expresiones de la violencia en los noventa." *ECA* 588 (1997): 977–992.

———. "Violencia, democracia y cultura política en América Latina." *ECA* 619–620 (2000): 511–525.

———. "Los acuerdos de paz, diez años después. Una mirada desde los ciudadanos." *ECA* 641–642 (2002): 235–251.

———. "Las elecciones presidenciales desde el comportamiento de la opinión pública." *ECA* 665–666 (2004): 247–267.

———. "Los factores asociados a las pandillas juveniles en Centroamérica." *ECA* 685–686 (2005): 1155–1182.

———. "Violencia, inseguridad ciudadana y las maniobras de las élites: La dinámica de la reforma policial en El Salvador." In *Seguridad y reforma policial en las Américas*, edited by Lucía Dammert and John Bailey. Mexico City: Siglo XXI Editores, 2005.

———. "El Salvador." In *La cara de la violencia urbana en América Central*, edited by Fundación Arias. San José: Fundación Arias, 2006.

———, ed. *Maras y pandillas en Centroamérica: Las respuestas de la sociedad civil organizada*. San Salvador: UCA Editores, 2006.

Cruz, José Miguel, and Marlon Carranza. "Pandillas y políticas públicas: El caso de El Salvador." In *Juventudes, Violencia y Exclusión: Desafíos para las Políticas Públicas*, edited by Javier Moro. Guatemala City: MagnaTerra Editores, 2006.

Cruz, José Miguel, Marlon Carranza, and María Santacruz Giralt. "*El Salvador: Espacios públicos, confianza interpersonal y pandillas.*" In *Maras y pandillas en Centroamérica: Pandillas y capital social*, edited by ERIC, IDESO, IDIES, IUDOP. San Salvador: UCA Editores, 2004.

Cruz, José Miguel, and Luís Armando González. "Magnitud de la violencia en El Salvador." *ECA* 588 (1997): 953–966.

Cruz, José Miguel, and Nelson Portillo. *Solidaridad y violencia en las pandillas del gran San Salvador: Más allá de la vida loca*. San Salvador: UCA Editores, 1998.

Cruz, José Miguel, and María Santacruz Giralt. *La victimización y la percepción de seguridad en El Salvador en 2004*. San Salvador: MINGOB and PNUD, 2005.

Cuerno, Lorena. *El Polígono Industrial Don Bosco: Una opción de vida para los jóvenes en conflicto con la ley*. San Salvador: UNICEF, 2004.

Curran, James, and Myung-Jin Park, eds. *De-Westernizing Media Studies.* London: Routledge, 2000.

Davies, Nick. *Flat Earth News: An Award-Winning Reporter Exposes Falsehood, Distortion and Propaganda in the Global Media.* London: Chatto & Windus, 2008.

Decker, Scott, and Janet Lauritsen. "Leaving the Gang." In *The Modern Gang Reader,* 3rd ed., edited by Arlen Egley, Cheryl Maxson, and Jody Miller. Los Angeles: Roxbury, 2006.

Decker, Scott, and Barrik van Winkle. *Life in the Gang: Family, Friends, and Violence.* Cambridge: Cambridge University Press, 1996.

Delaney, Tim. *American Street Gangs.* Upper Saddle River, NJ: Pearson, 2006.

Departamento de Organización del Espacio de la UCA. *Documentos del Laboratorio del Habitat Popular: Comunidad "Las Iberias."* San Salvador: mimeo, 2003.

Devereux, Eoin. *Understanding the Media.* London: Sage, 2003.

Diamond, Larry. *Developing Democracy: Toward Consolidation.* Baltimore, MD: John Hopkins University Press, 1999.

Diaz, Tom. *No Boundaries: Transnational Latino Gangs and American Law Enforcement.* Ann Arbor: University of Michigan Press, 2009.

Dirección General de Estadística y Censos (DIGESTYC). *Encuesta de Hogares y Propósitos Múltiples 2003.* San Salvador: Ministerio de Economía, 2004.

————. *Encuesta de Hogares y Propósitos Múltiples 2014.* San Salvador: Ministerio de Economía, 2015.

Doggett, Martha. *Death Foretold: The Jesuit Murders in El Salvador.* Washington, DC: Georgetown University Press, 1993.

Dowdney, Luke, ed. *Neither War nor Peace: International Comparisons of Children and Youth in Organised Armed Violence.* Rio de Janeiro: Viva Rio, 2005.

Dunkerley, James. *The Long War: Dictatorship and Revolution in El Salvador.* London: Junction Books, 1982.

————. *Power in the Isthmus: A Political History of Modern Central America,* 2nd ed. London: Verso, 1988.

Ebrahim, Alnoor. "Accountability in Practice: Mechanisms for NGOs." *World Development* 31 (2003): 813–829.

Edwards, Michael, and David Hulme, eds. *Making a Difference: NGOs and Development in a Changing World.* London: Earthscan, 1992.

————. "Too Close for Comfort? The Impact of Official Aid on Nongovernmental Organizations." *World Development* 24 (1996): 961–973.

————, eds. *Beyond the Magic Bullet: NGO Performance and Accountability in the Post–Cold War World.* West Hartford, CT: Kumarian Press, 1996.

————. "Introduction: NGO Performance and Accountability." In *Beyond the Magic Bullet: NGO Performance and Accountability in the Post–Cold War World,* edited by Michael Edwards and David Hulme. West Hartford, CT: Kumarian Press, 1996.

Egley, Arlen, Cheryl Maxson, and Jody Miller, eds. *The Modern Gang Reader,* 3rd ed. Los Angeles, CA: Roxbury, 2006.

Enzinna, Wes. "Another SOA? A Police Academy in El Salvador Worries Critics." *NACLA Report on the Americas* 41 (March–April 2008).

European Union (EU). *Evaluación Final Proyecto ProJóvenes I.* San Salvador: EU, 2011.

———. *Evaluación Final Proyecto ProJóvenes II.* San Salvador: EU, 2014.

Farah, Douglas. "Organized Crime in El Salvador: Its Homegrown and Transnational Dimensions." In *Organized Crime in Central America: The Northern Triangle*, edited by Cynthia Arnson and Eric Olson. Washington, DC: Woodrow Wilson Center, 2011.

Faux, Frédéric. *Les maras, gangs d'enfants.* Paris: Éditions Autrement Frontières, 2006.

Fernández, Jorge, and Víctor Ronquillo. *De los Maras a los Zetas: Los secretos del narcotráfico, de Colombia a Chicago.* Mexico City: Random House Mondadori, 2006.

Fisher, William. "Doing Good? The Politics and Antipolitics of NGO Practices." *Annual Review of Anthropology* 26 (1997): 439–464.

Fitzduff, Mari, and Cheyanne Church, eds. *NGOs at the Table.* Lanham, MD: Rowman and Littlefield, 2004.

Fowler, Alan. *Striking a Balance: A Guide to Enhancing the Effectiveness of Non-Governmental Organisations in International Development.* London: Earthscan, 1997.

Franco, Celinda. *The MS-13 and 18th Street Gangs: Emerging Transnational Gang Threats?* CRS Report for Congress RL34233. 30 January. Washington, DC: Congressional Research Service (CRS), 2008.

Fuentes, Claudio. *Contesting the Iron First: Advocacy Networks and Police Violence in Democratic Argentina and Chile.* New York: Routledge, 2005.

Fundación de Estudios para la Aplicación del Derecho (FESPAD). *Documento base de FESPAD.* San Salvador: mimeo, 1988.

———. *Estado de la Seguridad Pública y la Justicia Penal en El Salvador, Julio 2002–Diciembre 2003.* San Salvador: FESPAD Ediciones, 2004.

———. *Estado de la Seguridad Pública y la Justicia Penal en El Salvador, 2004.* San Salvador: FESPAD Ediciones, 2005.

———. *Estado de la Seguridad Pública y la Justicia Penal en El Salvador, Enero-Agosto 2005.* San Salvador: FESPAD Ediciones, 2005.

———. *Primer gobierno de izquierda: Una lectura de derechos humanos al Gobierno de Mauricio Funes (2009–2014).* San Salvador: FESPAD Ediciones, 2014.

Fundación Salvadoreña Educación y Trabajo. *Perfil del destinatario del Polígono Industrial Don Bosco* (San Salvador: mimeo, n.d.).

Fundación Salvadoreña para el Desarrollo Económico y Social (FUSADES). *Análisis crítico de los planes de gobierno del FMLN y ARENA* (San Salvador: FUSADES, 2014).

Garretón, Manuel Antonio. *Incomplete Democracy: Political Democratization in Chile and Latin America.* Chapel Hill: University of North Carolina Press, 2003.

Gebo, Erika, and Brenda Bond, eds. *Looking Beyond Suppression: Community Strategies to Reduce Gang Violence.* Lanham, MD: Lexington Books, 2014.

Ghiberti, Giuseppe. *Don Bosco begegnen.* Augsburg: Sankt Ulrich Verlag, 2005.

Gibelman, Margaret, and Sheldon Gelman. "Very Public Scandals: Nongovernmental Organizations in Trouble." *Nonprofit and Voluntary Sector Quarterly* 12 (2001): 49–66.

Gilbert, Daniel, Susan Fiske, and Gardner Lindzey. *The Handbook of Social Psychology*, 4th ed., vol. 2. New York: Oxford University Press, 1998.

Gobierno de El Salvador (GOES). *País Seguro: Plan de Gobierno 2004–2009*. San Salvador: GOES, 2004.

Gobierno de El Salvador (GOES) and Frente Farabundo Martí para la Liberación Nacional (FMLN). "Peace Agreement between the Government of El Salvador and the FMLN signed on 16 January 1992." Reprinted in *The United Nations and El Salvador 1990–1995*, United Nations Blue Book Series, vol. 4. New York: United Nations, 1995.

Gómez Hecht, Juan. "El crimen organizado en las cárceles: Las extorsiones desde los Centros Penales en El Salvador (2008–2009)." *Revista Policía y Seguridad Pública* 3.1 (2013): 131–171.

González, Luís Armando, and Roxana Martel. "Pobreza y sociedad civil: El caso de El Salvador." *ECA* 659 (2003): 881–904.

Goubaud, Emilio. "Mesas de mediación y negociación de conflictos con líderes juveniles: El caso de Villa Nueva." In *Juventudes, violencia y exclusión: Desafíos para las políticas públicas*, edited by Javier Moreno. Guatemala City: Magna Terra Editores, 2006.

Gourevitch, Peter, David Lake, and Janice Gross Stein, eds. *The Credibility of Transnational NGOs: When Virtue Is Not Enough*. New York: Cambridge University Press, 2012.

Gugelberger, Georg. "Introduction: Institutionalisation of Transgression." In *The Real Thing: Testimonial Discourse and Latin America*, edited by Georg Gugelberger. Durham, NC: Duke University Press, 1996.

Guzmán, Nataly. "Las elecciones presidenciales de 2004: Un estudio desde la prensa escrita." *ECA* 667 (2004): 419–438.

Hall MacLeod, Lisa. *Constructing Peace: Lessons from UN Peacebuilding Operations in El Salvador and Cambodia*. Oxford: Lexington Books, 2006.

Hallin, Daniel. "Media, Political Power, and Democratisation in Mexico." In *De-Westernizing Media Studies*, edited by James Curran and Myung-Jin Park. London: Routledge, 2000.

Hayner, Priscilla. *Unspeakable Truths: Transitional Justice and the Challenge of the Truth Commissions*. New York: Routledge, 2001.

Hernández, René. "Justicia y seguridad ciudadana: Las reformas legales en El Salvador." In *Convivencia y seguridad: Un reto a la gobernabilidad*, edited by Jorge Sapoznikow, Juana Salazar, and Fernando Carrillo. Washington, DC: Inter-American Development Bank, 2000.

Hilhorst, Dorothea. *The Real World of NGOs: Discourses, Diversity and Development*. London: Zed Books, 2003.

Hoffmann, Joan Serra. *Youth Violence, Resilience, and Rehabilitation*. New York: LFB Scholarly Publishing, 2004.

Hogg, Michael, and Joel Cooper, eds. *The Sage Handbook of Social Psychology*. London: Sage Publications, 2003.

Hopgood, Stephen. *Keepers of the Flame: Understanding Amnesty International*. Ithaca, NY: Cornell University Press, 2006.

Hughes, Sallie. *Newsrooms in Conflict: Journalism and the Democratization of Mexico*. Pittsburgh, PA: University of Pittsburgh Press, 2006.

Hulme, David, and Michael Edwards. "Conclusion: Too Close to the Powerful, Too Far from the Powerless?" In *NGOs, States and Donors: Too Close for Comfort*, edited by David Hulme and Michael Edwards. London: Macmillan, 1997.

———. "NGOs, States and Donors: An Overview." In *NGOs, States and Donors: Too Close for Comfort*, edited by David Hulme and Michael Edwards. London: Macmillan, 1997.

Hume, Mo. *Armed Violence and Poverty in El Salvador: A Mini Case Study for the Armed Violence and Poverty Initiative.* Bradford: University of Bradford, 2004. www.bradford.ac.uk/acad/cics/publications/AVPI/ poverty/AVPI_El _Salvador.pdf.

———. "Mano Dura: El Salvador Responds to Gangs." *Development in Practice* 17.6 (2007): 739–751.

Instituto de Derechos Humanos de la UCA (IDHUCA). "Policía Nacional Civil: ¿Depuración o apuro?" *ECA* 619–620 (2000): 603–609.

Instituto Universitario de Opinión Pública (IUDOP). "La delincuencia urbana: Encuesta exploratoria." *ECA* 534–535 (1993): 471–479.

———. "Evaluación del país a finales de 2003 y perspectivas electorales para 2004. Encuesta de opinión pública." *Boletín de prensa* Año 18, No. 4. San Salvador: IUDOP, 2003.

———. "Las preferencias políticas en octubre de 2003: La mano dura de ARENA." *ECA* 660 (2003): 1071–1078.

———. "Los salvadoreños frente a las elecciones presidenciales de 2004." *Boletín de prensa* Año 18, No. 3. San Salvador: IUDOP, 2003.

———. "Opinión pública a finales de 2003 y preferencias electorales: Encuesta de evaluación de fin de año." *ECA* 661–662 (2003): 1233–1241.

———. "Evaluación de los salvadoreños sobre el gobierno de Francisco Flores y expectativas hacia el nuevo gobierno." *Boletín de prensa* Año 19, No. 2. San Salvador: IUDOP, 2004.

———. "Los salvadoreños evalúan los cien días de gobierno de Antonio Saca." *Boletín de prensa* Año 19, No. 4. San Salvador: IUDOP, 2004.

———. "Los salvadoreños evalúan el primer año de gobierno de Antonio Saca." *Boletín de prensa* Año 20, No. 2. San Salvador: IUDOP, 2005.

———. "Los salvadoreños evalúan la situación del país a finales de 2005 y opinan sobre las elecciones de 2006." *Boletín de prensa* Año 20, No. 3. San Salvador: IUDOP, 2005.

———. "La transparencia en el Estado salvadoreño: La perspectiva de los empresarios." *Boletín de prensa* Año 20, No. 1. San Salvador: IUDOP, 2005.

———. "Evaluación del país a finales del 2006 y perspectivas para 2007." *Boletín de prensa* Año 21, No. 3. San Salvador: IUDOP, 2006.

———. *Evaluación Anual de la PNC, 2011.* San Salvador: UCA, 2012.

———. "Los salvadoreños y salvadoreñas evalúan el cuarto año de gobierno de Mauricio Funes." *Boletín de prensa* Año 27, No. 1. San Salvador: IUDOP, 2013.

———. *La situación de la seguridad y la justicia, 2009–2014.* San Salvador: IUDOP, 2014.

Instituto Universitario de Opinión Pública (IUDOP) and Fundación de Estudios para la Aplicación del Derecho (FESPAD). *Documento para la discusión de política pública municipal de prevención de la violencia de pandillas: municipio de Zacatecoluca.* San Salvador: mimeo, 2007.

Intercomunal Nor-Oriente and Fundación EDYTRA. *Diagnóstico de las Comunidades Iberias y otras aledañas.* San Salvador: mimeo, 2006.

International Human Rights Clinic. *No Place to Hide: Gang, State, and Clandestine Violence in El Salvador.* Cambridge, MA: Harvard Law School, 2007.

Iyengar, Shanto. *Is Anyone Responsible? How Television Frames Political Issues.* Chicago: University of Chicago Press, 1991.

Johnson, Mary. "National Policies and the Rise of Transnational Gangs." Migration Policy Institute, April 2006. www.migrationpolicy.org/article /national-policies-and-rise-transnational-gangs.

Johnston, Vanessa. "An Ecuadorian Alternative: Gang Reintegration." In *Small Arms Survey 2010,* edited by Small Arms Survey. Cambridge: Cambridge University Press, 2010.

Joint Group for the Investigation of Politically Motivated Illegal Armed Groups. *Report of the Joint Group for the Investigation of Politically Motivated Illegal Armed Groups in El Salvador.* UN Security Council (S/1994/989), 28 July 1994.

Juhn, Tricia. *Negotiating Peace in El Salvador: Civil-Military Relations and the Conspiracy to End the War.* Basingstoke: Macmillan Press, 1998.

Kaiser, Kenneth. *Statement before the House Committee on Foreign Affairs. Subcommittee on the Western Hemisphere, 7 February 2008.* www2.fbi.gov/congress /congress08/kaiser020708.htm.

Katz, Charles, and Luis Enrique Amaya. *The Gang Truce as a Form of Violence Intervention.* San Salvador: USAID, 2015.

Keck, Margaret, and Kathryn Sikkink. *Activists Beyond Borders: Advocacy Networks in International Politics.* Ithaca, NY: Cornell University Press, 1998.

Klein, Malcolm. *The American Street Gang: Its Nature, Prevalence, and Control.* New York: Oxford University Press, 1995.

Klein, Malcolm, and Cheryl Maxson. *Street Gang Patterns and Policies.* New York: Oxford University Press, 2006.

Koonings, Kees, and Dirk Kruijt. "Fractured Cities, Second-Class Citizenship and Urban Violence." In *Fractured Cities: Social Exclusion, Urban Violence and Contested Spaces in Latin America,* edited by Kees Koonings and Dirk Kruijt. London: Zed Books, 2007.

Kruijt, Dirk. *Guerrillas.* London and New York: Zed Books, 2008.

Ladutke, Lawrence. *Freedom of Expression in El Salvador: The Struggle for Human Rights and Democracy.* London: McFarland & Co., 2004.

Lafeber, Walter. *Inevitable Revolutions: The United States in Central America,* 2nd ed. New York: W. W. Norton, 1993.

Lang, Sabine. *NGOs, Civil Society, and the Public Sphere.* New York: Cambridge University Press, 2013.

La Prensa Gráfica. Manual para el Tratamiento Informativo de la Violencia. San Salvador: mimeo, 2005.

———. *Proyecto institucional "Todos contra la violencia."* San Salvador: mimeo, 2006.

Lara Klahr, Marco. *Hoy te toca la muerte: El imperio de las Maras visto desde dentro.* Mexico City: Editorial Planeta, 2006.

Las Dignas, FESPAD, and IDHUCA, eds. *El Salvador por dentro*. San Salvador: UCA, 2005.

Latin American Public Opinion Project (LAPOP). *The Political Culture of Democracy in the Americas, 2014*. Nashville, TN: Vanderbilt University, 2014.

Lawson, Chappell, and Sallie Hughes. "Latin America's Postauthoritarian Media." In *(Un)Civil Societies: Human Rights and Democratic Transitions in Eastern Europe and Latin America*, edited by Rachel May and Andrew Milton. Lanham, MD: Lexington Books, 2005.

Lefèvre, Anne Germain. "Promoting Independent Media in El Salvador." In *Promoting Democracy in Postconflict Societies*, edited by Jeroen de Zeeuw and Krishna Kumar. Boulder, CO: Lynne Rienner, 2006.

LeoGrande, William. *Our Own Backyard: The United States in Central America, 1977–1992*. Chapel Hill: University of North Carolina Press, 1998.

Leslie, Glaister. *Confronting the Don: The Political Economy of Gang Violence in Jamaica*. Geneva: Small Arms Survey, 2010.

Lewis, David, and Paul Opoku-Mensah. "Moving Forward Research Agendas on International NGOs: Theory, Agency and Context." *Journal of International Development* 18 (2006): 665–675.

Liedholm, Carl, and Donald Mead. *Small Enterprises and Economic Development: The Dynamics of Micro and Small Enterprises*. London: Routledge, 1999.

Lindo-Fuentes, Héctor, Erik Ching, and Rafael Lara-Martínez. *Remembering a Massacre in El Salvador: The Insurrection of 1932, Roque Dalton, and the Politics of Historical Memory*. Albuquerque: University of New Mexico Press, 2007.

Lister, Sarah. "The Consultation Practice of Northern NGOs: A Study of British Organizations in Guatemala." *Journal of International Development* 13 (2001): 1071–1082.

———. "NGO Legitimacy: Technical Issue or Social Construct?" *Critique of Anthropology* 23 (2003): 175–192.

Logan, Kathleen. "Personal Testimony: Latin American Women Telling Their Lives." *Latin American Research Review* 32 (1997): 199–211.

Logan, Samuel. *This Is for the Mara Salvatrucha: Inside the MS-13, America's Most Violent Gang*. New York: Hyperion, 2009.

Lukes, Steven. *Power: A Radical View*. London: Macmillan Press, 1974.

Lungo, Mario. *El Salvador in the Eighties: Counterinsurgency and Revolution*. Philadelphia: Temple University Press, 1996.

Maestría en Psicología Comunitaria de la UCA. *Diagnóstico Sobre la Caracterización de la Población Salvadoreña Retornada con Necesidades de Protección*. San Salvador: UCA, 2014.

Mahoney, James. *The Legacies of Liberalism*. Baltimore: John Hopkins University Press, 2001.

Martel, Roxana. "Las maras salvadoreñas: Nuevas formas de espanto y control social." *ECA* 696 (2006): 957–979.

Martens, Kerstin. "Mission Impossible? Defining Nongovernmental Organizations." *Voluntas: International Journal of Voluntary and Nonprofit Organizations* 13 (2002): 271–285.

Martínez, Carlos, and José Luis Sanz. "El Barrio roto." In *Crónicas negras desde una región que no cuenta*, edited by Sala Negra de El Faro. Mexico City: Aguilar, 2014.

Martínez, Juan José. *Ver, oír, callar: En las profundidades de una pandilla salvadoreña.* San Salvador: AURA Ediciones, 2013.

McCullagh, Ciaran. *Media Power.* Basingstoke: Palgrave, 2002.

Meacham, Carl. *The Mérida Initiative: "Guns, Drugs, and Friends."* Report to the Senate Committee on Foreign Relations, 21 December 2007. www.gpo.gov/fdsys/pkg/CPRT-110SPRT39644/pdf/CPRT-110SPRT39644.pdf.

Mejía, Guillermo, and Raúl Gutiérrez. *Medios y democracia.* San Salvador: mimeo, 2005.

Menchú, Rigoberta. *I, Rigoberta Menchú.* London: Verso, 1984.

Meyer, Peter, and Clare Ribando Seelke. *Central America Regional Security Initiative: Background and Policy Issues for Congress.* CRS Report for Congress R41731, 6 May. Washington, DC: Congressional Research Service (CRS), 2014.

Ministerio de Gobernación (MINGOB). *Construyendo juntos una política de prevención, atención y control de la violencia.* San Salvador: mimeo, 2004.

Ministerio de Justicia y Seguridad Pública (MJSP). *Política Nacional de Justicia, Seguridad Pública y Convivencia.* San Salvador: MJSP, 2010.

Montgomery, Tommie Sue. *Revolution in El Salvador: From Civil Strife to Civil Peace,* 2nd ed. Boulder, CO: Westview Press, 1995.

Moore, Joan. *Going Down to the Barrio: Homeboys and Homegirls in Change.* Philadelphia: Temple University Press, 1991.

Morales, David. *Los Acuerdos de Paz, su agenda pendiente y los derechos humanos en El Salvador de hoy.* San Salvador: mimeo, 2007.

Morse, Ashley, Adam Isacson, and Maureen Meyer. *Tackling Urban Violence in Latin America: Reversing Exclusion through Smart Policing and Social Investment.* Washington, DC: Washington Office on Latin America, 2011.

Murcia, Walter. *Las pandillas en El Salvador.* Santiago de Chile: CEPAL, 2015.

Neild, Rachel. "Sustaining Reform: Democratic Policing in Central America." *Citizen Security Monitor* 1.1. Washington, DC: Washington Office on Latin America, 2002.

Nelson, Paul, and Ellen Dorsey. *New Rights Advocacy: Changing Strategies of Development and Human Rights NGOs.* Washington, DC: Georgetown University Press, 2008.

Nieto, Clara. *Masters of War: Latin America and U.S. Aggression from the Cuban Revolution Through the Clinton Years.* New York: Seven Stories Press, 2003.

Paige, Jeffery M. *Coffee and Power: Revolution and the Rise of Democracy in Central America.* Cambridge, MA: Harvard University Press, 1997.

Paniagua, Carlos. "El bloque empresarial hegemónico salvadoreño." *ECA* 645–646 (2002): 609–693.

Parkman, Patricia. *Nonviolent Insurrection in El Salvador: The Fall of Maximiliano Hernández Martínez.* Tucson: University of Arizona Press, 1988.

Pearce, Jenny. *Promised Land: Peasant Rebellion in Chalatenango El Salvador.* London: Latin America Bureau, 1986.

———. "NGOs and Social Change: Agents or Facilitators?" *Development in Practice* 3 (1993): 222–227.

———. "Between Co-option and Irrelevance: Latin American NGOs in the 1990s." In *NGOs, States and Donors: Too Close for Comfort,* edited by David Hulme and Michael Edwards. London: Macmillan, 1997.

———. "From Civil War to 'Civil Society': Has the End of the Cold War Brought Peace to Central America?" *International Affairs* 74 (1998): 587–615.

Peraza, Delmy. "Derecho a la información y rendimiento de cuentas en Centro-américa." *ECA* 635 (2001): 815–833.

Petras, James. "Imperialism and NGOs in Latin America." *Monthly Review* 49 (1997): 10–27.

Pew Research Center. "Hispanics of Salvadoran Origin in the United States, 2013," 15 September 2015. www.pewhispanic.org/2015/09/15/hispanics-of-salvadoran-origin-in-the-united-states-2013/.

Popkin, Margaret. *Peace Without Justice: Obstacles to Building the Rule of Law in El Salvador.* University Park: Penn State University Press, 2000.

Procuraduría para la Defensa de los Derechos Humanos (PDDH). *Demanda de inconstitucionalidad contra la Ley Antimaras.* San Salvador: PDDH, 2003.

———. *Violaciones a los derechos humanos por responsabilidad de la Policía Nacional Civil de El Salvador.* San Salvador: PDDH, 2007.

Programa de las Naciones Unidas para el Desarrollo (PNUD). *Informe sobre Desarrollo Humano, El Salvador (IDHES) 2001.* San Salvador: PNUD, 2001.

———. *Informe sobre Desarrollo Humano, El Salvador (IDHES) 2003.* San Salvador: PNUD, 2003.

———. *¿Cuánto cuesta la violencia a El Salvador?* San Salvador: PNUD, 2005.

———. *Informe sobre Desarrollo Humano, El Salvador (IDHES) 2005.* San Salvador: PNUD, 2005.

———. *Informe sobre Desarrollo Humano, El Salvador (IDHES) 2013.* San Salvador: PNUD, 2013.

Ratcliffe, Jerry. *Intelligence-Led Policing.* Portland, OR: Willan Publishing, 2008.

Reiner, Robert. "Media Made Criminality: The Representation of Crime in the Mass Media." In *The Oxford Handbook of Criminology*, edited by Mike Maguire, Rod Morgan, and Robert Reiner. Oxford: Oxford University Press, 2002.

Risley, Amy. *Civil Society Organizations, Advocacy, and Policy Making in Latin American Democracies: Pathways to Participation.* New York: Palgrave Macmillan, 2015.

Roberts, Julian V., Loretta J. Stalans, David Indermaur, and Mike Hough. *Penal Populism and Public Opinion: Lessons from Five Countries.* Oxford: Oxford University Press, 2003.

Rocha, José Luís. "Violencia y políticas públicas hacia los jóvenes: Las pandillas en Nicaragua." In *Juventudes, violencia y exclusión: Desafíos para las políticas públicas*, edited by Javier Moro. Guatemala City: MagnaTerra Editores, 2006.

Rockwell, Rick, and Noreene Janus. "The Triumph of the Media Elite in Postwar Central America." In *Latin Politics, Global Media*, edited by Elizabeth Fox and Silvio Waisbord. Austin: University of Texas Press, 2002.

———. *Media Power in Central America.* Urbana and Chicago: University of Illinois Press, 2003.

Rodríguez, Luis. *Always Running: La Vida Loca: Gang Days in L.A.* New York: Touchstone, 2005.

Roth, Kenneth. "Defending Economic, Social and Cultural Rights: Practical Issues Faced by an International Human Rights Organization." *Human Rights Quarterly* 26.1 (2004): 63–73.

Roy, Ewell. *Cooperatives: Development, Principles, and Management.* Danville, IL: Interstate Printers & Publishers, 1976.

Rugendyke, Barbara, ed. *NGOs as Advocates for Development in a Globalising World.* London and New York: Routledge, 2007.

Ryan, Charlotte. *Prime Time Activism: Media Strategies for Grassroots Organizing.* Boston, MA: South End Press, 1991.

Santacruz, María, and José Miguel Cruz. "Las maras en El Salvador." In *Maras y pandillas en Centroamérica*, vol. 1, edited by ERIC, IDESO, IDIES, IUDOP. Managua: UCA Publicaciones, 2001.

Santacruz, María, and Elin Ranum. *"Seconds in the Air": Women Gang-Members and their Prisons.* San Salvador: IUDOP, 2010.

Santillán, Alfredo, and Soledad Varea. "Estrategias y políticas de inclusión (¿asimilación?) de pandillas en Ecuador: Dos modelos de ciudades, dos visiones sobre las potencialidades de los/as jóvenes pandilleros/as." *URVIO, Revista Latinoamericana de Seguridad Ciudadana* 4 (May 2008): 81–99.

Savenije, Wim. "La Mara Salvatrucha y el Barrio 18 St. Fenómenos sociales trasnacionales, respuestas represivas nacionales." *Foreign Affairs En Español* (April–June 2004).

Savenije, Wim, and Chris van der Borgh. "Youth Gangs, Social Exclusion and the Transformation of Violence in El Salvador." In *Armed Actors: Organized Violence and State Failure in Latin America*, edited by Kees Koonings and Dirk Kruijt. London: Zed Books, 2004.

———. "San Salvador: Violence and Resilience in Gangland—Coping with the Code of the Street." In *Violence and Resilience in Latin American Cities*, edited by Kees Koonings and Dirk Krujt. London: Zed Books, 2015.

Saxby, John. "Who Owns the Private Aid Agencies?" In *Compassion and Calculation: The Business of Private Foreign Aid*, edited by David Sogge, Kees Biekart, and John Saxby. London: Pluto Press, 1996.

Schlesinger, Philip, and Howard Tumber. *Reporting Crime: The Media Politics of Criminal Justice.* Oxford: Clarendon Press, 1994.

Secretaría de la Juventud (SJ). *Estudios de Base Jóvenes 2005: Informe de Resultados de la Encuesta Nacional de Juventud.* San Salvador: SJ, 2005.

———. *Plan Nacional de Juventud 2005–2015.* San Salvador: SJ, 2005.

———. *Plan Nacional de Juventud 2005–2015: Ejes de Acción.* San Salvador: SJ, 2005.

Secretaría Técnica y de Planificación de la Presidencia de la República (STPP) and Ministerio de Economía-Dirección General de Estadística y Censos (MINEC-DIGESTYC). *Medición Multidimensional de la Pobreza.* San Salvador: STPP and MINEC-DIGESTYC, 2015.

Segovia, Alexander. "Integración real y grupos centroamericanos de poder económico. Implicaciones para la democracia y el desarrollo regional." *ECA* 691–692 (2006): 517–582.

Silva, Héctor. *Infiltrados: Crónica de la corrupción en la PNC (1992-2013).* San Salvador: UCA Editores, 2014.

Simmons, P. J. "Learning to Live with NGOs." *Foreign Policy* 112 (1998): 82–96.

Sinnar, Shirin. "Mixed Blessing: The Growing Influence of NGOs." *Harvard International Review* 18 (1995–1996): 54–57.

Smutt, Marcela, and Lissette Miranda. *El Fenómeno de las Pandillas en El Salvador.* San Salvador: UNICEF and FLACSO, 1998.

Spence, Jack. *War and Peace in Central America: Comparing Transitions Toward Democracy and Social Equity in Guatemala, El Salvador, and Nicaragua.* Brookline, MA: Hemisphere Initiatives, 2004.

Spence, Jack, Mike Lanchin, and Geoff Thale. *From Elections to Earthquakes: Reform and Participation in Post-War El Salvador.* Cambridge, MA: Hemisphere Initiatives, 2001.

Spence, Jack, and George Vickers. *A Negotiated Revolution? A Two-Year Progress Report on the Salvadoran Peace Accords.* Cambridge, MA: Hemisphere Initiatives, 1994.

Spergel, Irving. *The Youth Gang Problem: A Community Approach.* New York: Oxford University Press, 1995.

———. *Reducing Youth Gang Violence: The Little Village Gang Project in Chicago.* Plymouth: Altamira Press, 2007.

Stanley, William. *Risking Failure: The Problems and Promise of the New Civilian Police in El Salvador.* Cambridge, MA: Hemisphere Initiatives, 1993.

———. *The Protection Racket State: Elite Politics, Military Extortion, and Civil War in El Salvador.* Philadelphia: Temple University Press, 1996.

———. *Protectors or Perpetrators? The Institutional Crisis of the Salvadoran Civilian Police.* Washington, DC: Washington Office on Latin America and Hemisphere Initiatives, 1996.

Tagg, John. *The Burden of Representation: Essays on Photographies and Histories.* Basingstoke: Palgrave Macmillan, 1988.

Thale, Geoff. *Testimony before the House Committee on Foreign Affairs, Subcommittee on the Western Hemisphere. Hearing on "Central America and the Mérida Initiative."* 8 May 2008. archives.republicans.foreignaffairs.house.gov/110/tha050808.htm.

Thornberry, Terence P., Marvin D. Krohn, Alan J. Lizotte, Carolyn A. Smith, and Kimberly Tobin. *Gangs and Delinquency in Developmental Perspective.* Cambridge: Cambridge University Press, 2003.

Truth Commission for El Salvador. *From Madness to Hope: The 12-Year War in El Salvador.* UN Security Council (S/25500), 15 March 1993.

Tutela Legal. *La violencia homicida y otros patrones de grave afectación a los derechos humanos en El Salvador: Año 2006.* San Salvador: Tutela Legal, 2007.

United Nations Committee on the Rights of the Child (UNCRC). *36th session. Consideration of reports submitted by states parties under Article 44 of the Convention. Concluding Observations: El Salvador.* CRC/C/15/Add.232, 30 June 2004.

United Nations Office on Drugs and Crime (UNODC). *Crime and Development in Central America: Caught in the Crossfire.* Vienna: UNODC, 2007.

Valdez, Al. "The Origins of Southern California Latino Gangs." In *Maras: Gang Violence and Security in Central America,* edited by Thomas Bruneau, Lucía Dammert, and Elizabeth Skinner. Austin: University of Texas Press, 2011.

Van Ginneken, Jaap. *Understanding Global News: A Critical Introduction.* London: Sage Publications, 1998.

Vasilachis de Gialdino, Irene. "Representations of young people associated with crime in El Salvador's written press." *Critical Discourse Studies* 4 (2007): 1–28.

VeneKlasen, Lisa, and Valerie Miller. *A New Weave of Power, People and Politics: The Action Guide for Advocacy and Citizen Participation.* Rugby: Practical Action Publishing, 2007.

Vigil, James Diego. *A Rainbow of Gangs: Street Cultures in the Mega-City.* Austin: University of Texas Press, 2002.

Waisbord, Silvio. *Watchdog Journalism in South America: News, Accountability, and Democracy.* New York: Columbia University Press, 2000.

Ward, T. W. *Gangsters Without Borders: An Ethnography of a Salvadoran Street Gang.* New York and Oxford: Oxford University Press, 2013.

Washington Office on Latin America (WOLA). *Youth Gangs in Central America.* Washington, DC: WOLA, 2006.

Whitfield, Teresa. *Paying the Price: Ignacio Ellacuria and the Murdered Jesuits of El Salvador.* Philadelphia: Temple University Press, 1995.

Whittaker, David, ed. *The Terrorism Reader,* 2nd ed. London: Routledge, 2003.

Wiarda, Howard. *The Soul of Latin America: The Cultural and Political Tradition.* New Haven and London: Yale University Press, 2001.

Williams, Philip, and Knut Walter. *Militarization and Demilitarization in El Salvador's Transition to Democracy.* Pittsburgh, PA: University of Pittsburgh Press, 1997.

Wirth, Morand. *Don Bosco and the Salesians.* New Rochelle, NY: Don Bosco Publications, 1982.

Wolf, Sonja. "Street Gangs of El Salvador." In *Maras: Gang Violence and Security in Central America,* edited by Thomas Bruneau, Lucía Dammert, and Elizabeth Skinner. Austin: University of Texas Press, 2011.

Wong, Wendy. *Internal Affairs: How the Structure of NGOs Transforms Human Rights.* Ithaca and London: Cornell University Press, 2012.

Wood, Elisabeth Jean. "An Insurgent Path to Democracy: Popular Mobilization, Economic Interests, and Regime Transition in South Africa and El Salvador." *Comparative Political Studies* 34 (2001): 862–888.

———. *Insurgent Collective Action and Civil War in El Salvador.* Cambridge: Cambridge University Press, 2003.

World Bank. *El Salvador: Estudio institucional y de gasto público en seguridad y justicia.* Washington, DC: World Bank, 2012.

Zhan, Xueyong, and Shui-Yan Tang. "Political Opportunities, Resource Constraints and Policy Advocacy of Environmental NGOs in China." *Public Administration* 91.2 (2013): 381–399.

Zilberg, Elana. "Fools Banished from the Kingdom: Remapping Geographies of Gang Violence Between the Americas (Los Angeles and San Salvador)." *American Quarterly* 56 (2004): 759–779.

Zinecker, Heidrun. *El Salvador nach dem Bürgerkrieg.* Frankfurt: Campus Verlag, 2004.

Index

www.ingramcontent.com/pod-product-compliance
Lightning Source LLC
Chambersburg PA
CBHW032344280326
41935CB00008B/441